MAO AND MARKETS

MAO AND MARKETS

THE COMMUNIST ROOTS OF

CHINESE ENTERPRISE

CHRISTOPHER MARQUIS

AND

KUNYUAN QIAO

Yale UNIVERSITY PRESS
New Haven and London

Yale University Press books may be purchased in quantity for educational, business, or promotional use. For information, please e-mail sales.press@yale.edu (U.S. office) or sales@yaleup.co.uk (U.K. office).

Set in Sabon by Westchester Publishing Services.

Printed in Great Britain at TJ Books.

Library of Congress Control Number: 2022942198

ISBN 978-0-300-26338-1 (hardcover: alk. paper)

A catalogue record for this book is available from the British Library.

10 9 8 7 6 5 4 3 2 1

For Alex and Ava and their generation as they navigate the complex relations between the world's most powerful countries.
—CHRIS

For my family as they are concerned with and hoping for better U.S.-China relations.
—KUNYUAN

Contents

Part III: The Effects of Mao's Mass Campaigns: The Great Leap Forward, the Cultural Revolution, and the Third Front

Part IV: The Effects of Mao's Socialist Institutions: Political and Economic Systems

MAO AND
MARKETS

Introduction

CHINA'S SPECTACULAR ECONOMIC GROWTH over the past four decades bears stark witness to the power of markets. Between 1978—when China began its economic reforms—and 2019, China's annual gross domestic product (GDP) growth rate averaged 9.45 percent, while its GDP per capita grew an astonishing sixtyfold.[1] Despite the COVID-19 pandemic and a trade war with the United States, China's GDP still grew by 2.3 percent in 2020, which made it the world's only major economy to experience growth that year, and this was even topped by 8.1 percent growth in 2021, the highest since 2011, and a trade surplus that hit a record high at US $687.5 billion.[2]

Thanks to these and other achievements, starting in 2017, the US National Security Strategy began referring to China as a primary strategic competitor.[3] Joe Biden echoed this point in his first foreign policy speech as president, highlighting an important pivot from Barack Obama's "engagement" strategy that many now consider to have been naïve and reflective of "wishful thinking" about China's ambitions.[4] As well, rather than following his other recent predecessors—including Donald Trump, George H. W. Bush, Bill Clinton, and George W. Bush—who forecast the demise of Chinese communism, Biden's foreign policy focuses on "durable coexistence" with China and its communist regime.[5] Yet, despite recognizing that China is the United States' biggest rival, and the "most serious long-term challenge to the international order,"[6] US policy has also been criticized for lacking coherence and an overarching strategy.[7]

Underlying this policy confusion, China's rise calls one of capitalism's most cherished beliefs about itself into question. Free markets are widely presumed to be more efficient than state-controlled economies and thus make the latter obsolete; moreover, they are thought to promote freedom in other spheres of life. Following traditional economic development theory, many people, including top China strategists in the White House, predicted that Chinese president Xi Jinping would push for economic reforms such as privatization of state-owned enterprises when his administration began in 2012.[8] Instead, he reversed what was seen as a liberalizing trend that started in the early 2000s and made a number of moves that harked back to the founder of the People's Republic of China, Chairman Mao Zedong, including a potential grant of lifelong tenure in the presidency for himself.[9]

In recent years Xi has urged all private companies to serve the state, extolling the patriotic entrepreneur Zhang Jian, who did so in the Qing dynasty; sent Chinese Communist Party (CCP) representatives to private firms; suspended the initial public offering of Ant Financial (the largest payment platform in China, owned by the Alibaba Group); made it increasingly hard for Chinese companies to list on US stock markets; and asked state entities to take stakes and board seats in important technology companies such as ByteDance (owner of TikTok), Sina Weibo (the most popular microblogging website), DiDi (the largest ride-hailing company), and others.[10] Today, many entrepreneurs are now concerned that they will be persecuted or their property will be confiscated. Some have even called for the "exit of private economy," offering to turn their businesses into state-owned enterprises in exchange for guarantees of protection.[11] Many private firms have received investments from the government or been taken over by it. For example, Anbang Insurance (worth more than $200 billion) and Hainan Airlines Group (worth more than $140 billion) were both transformed from private firms into state-owned enterprises.[12]

During the centenary celebration of the CCP on July 1, 2021, Xi doubled down on China's commitment to communism, commenting that "any attempt to separate . . . the CCP from the Chinese people will never succeed!" He also emphasized the importance of one-party rule and

Figure I.1 President Xi Jinping Leads Politburo Members in Renewing Their CCP Vows during the CCP Centenary Celebration
"China Crackdown," Associated Press, June 28, 2021. AP Photo/Ng Han Guan.

China's socialist institutions six times each.[13] In figure I.1, Xi leads senior political leaders in revisiting the CCP oath as part of the centenary celebrations.

Overall, Xi seems to have pulled China from decades of Western-style capitalist reform and embarked on a new path with heavy state intervention (for example, in 2021, the CCP-government issued more than a hundred regulations, including ones that targeted large private businesses), more equal distribution of wealth (for example, a policy called "common prosperity" that some see as "robbing the rich"), and stricter CCP control, all of which revisit the socialist version of the economy of his founding counterpart, Mao.[14]

Behind all these puzzling facts are questions about what kind of regime China is: a Marxist-Leninist state, a digital authoritarian country, a crony capitalist nation, or something else? It has gradually become clear that Americans do not have adequate knowledge of China and its system. Approaches to China seem to have followed established ideological principles, and in some ways reaction to China is like a Rorschach test: Americans' views reflect whatever picture they already have. This is reinforced by frequent negative portrayal of China and Chinese in American discourse—from the early, racist Fu Manchu comic books and movies to President Donald Trump's references to COVID-19 as the "China Virus" or "Kung Flu," which spurred anti-Asian hate crimes during the pandemic. Likewise, politicians from across the party aisle also vilify China. Bernie Sanders has claimed that America lost three million jobs due to its disastrous trade deal with China, and Marco Rubio said that the CCP is using power to infiltrate American politics and stealing trade secrets and technologies from the United States. Tom Cotton claimed that "America confronts a powerful totalitarian adversary [China] that seeks to dominate Eurasia and remake the world order," and in outlining the Biden Administration China policy, US secretary of state Antony Blinken said that "Beijing's vision would move us away from the universal values that have sustained so much of the world's progress over the past 75 years."[15] Overall, perspectives on China and even Chinese focus on knee-jerk condemnation of the country and its model, which is not helpful for fostering relations and counterproductive if America is to effectively deal with its greatest strategic and economic rival in the twenty-first century.[16]

Related to these hardened ideological stances, there has been too much wishful thinking about the CCP's future and overall an unrealistic imagination of life on the ground in China. Many people believe communism will collapse in China, as happened in the Soviet Union and other Eastern European countries three decades ago. These observers may have overestimated the liberalizing power of the marketplace and how much the United States and the West in general can affect China's domestic and foreign policies. As the foregoing examples suggest, Xi is committed to developing a model for China that is independent of the West.

Since the United States and China are the world's largest economies and most important national actors, we believe that *realistic* engagement is essential for both countries and for the world at large, especially given the recent concerns about decoupling (for example, in the technology and financial realms) and even discussion that we may be entering a new type of Cold War. In his China policy speech, Blinken recognized that "the United States and China have to deal with each other for the foreseeable future," and that "there is growing convergence about the need to approach relations with Beijing with more realism."[17] By realistic, we mean that the hard calculus of national interest should drive engagement. But to accomplish this, analysts and policymakers have to start with a more accurate and objective evaluation of China, rather than just relying on politics and empty hopes. To do so effectively, we are in dire need of more accurate knowledge of China's deeply seated ideology.

Many China commentators have focused on China's ideological flexibility in incorporating capitalist elements into its state-run economy since its opening in 1978 and are surprised when there are reversions as have occurred under Xi.[18] Our alternative view is that it is not a question of what has changed, but how it has and, even more importantly, what has remained the same. As we show in more detail, Mao, the powerful founder of the People's Republic of China, has left an enduring imprint on Chinese individuals, society, and institutions that even today strongly shapes China's economic and political activities. While there may be changes, or periods of flexibility, what is important to recognize is that they all take place within the constraints, or guardrails, originally established by Mao. They are the bedrock of Chinese governance—reflected in an oft-repeated phrase, "The CCP leads everything."

Overall, we suggest that the United States and the West need to understand the Maoist "playbook" to be able to deal with China more effectively. As even Xi has said repeatedly, "To understand China today, one must learn about the foundation of the CCP."

This in many ways may seem counterintuitive, as communism and capitalism are typically seen as diametrically opposed. However, as we show in this book, foundational economic policies and strategies in China can be traced back to Maoist principles. We aim to clarify the long-standing confusion about China and its contemporary economic model by tracing the deep communist roots of its enterprises and of the Chinese economy and state more generally. Our investigation of this understudied but critical topic has the potential to fundamentally change our understanding of private business in China, as well as how such a distinctive form of capitalism evolves, and even our understanding of recent shifts in governmental policy. This angle allows us to develop new insights for business practice, policy, and academic research, and provide a unique set of recommendations both for those who want to do business or invest in China and for policymakers. In the past, the United States paid a huge price for its inadequate knowledge and an automatic fear of communism, as exemplified by its involvement in the Korean and the Vietnam Wars. By approaching China's ideological system in a holistic way and from both the top down and bottom up, we provide a much clearer view of how it affects its economy and those who interact with it.

More generally, it is essential to rethink the connection between political and economic systems. Decades of interaction with China are based on the idea that economic liberalization predicts political democratization.[19] Accordingly, the United States supported China's entry into the World Trade Organization in 2001 under the assumption that as it became more prosperous and more integrated into the global economy, democracy would naturally follow. "By joining the WTO," President Clinton declared in 2000, "China is not simply agreeing to import more of our products, it is agreeing to import one of democracy's most cherished values: economic freedom. When individuals have the power . . . to realize their dreams, they will demand a greater say."[20] Germany has been criticized for similar assumptions about Russia, as its attempts to engage with the country economically—such as purchasing natural gas—left it vulnerable following the invasion of Ukraine.

This perspective went hand in hand with the idea that global communications technologies such as the internet were an inexorable force for freedom. In an even more evocative quote, Clinton famously said that controlling the internet was as hard as "nailing Jell-O to the wall," so it would provide a way for the Chinese populace to hear the voice of freedom from the bottom up, without the oversight of the CCP. Similarly, former US ambassador to China Jon Huntsman, in a 2011 presidential debate, anticipated that Chinese internet users would be allies of the West in "taking China down."[21] But today, China exerts strong control over the internet and has harnessed technology to more effectively monitor and supervise its population, as has been well demonstrated in the many COVID-19 lockdowns. Thus, such "wishful" projections of what happened in the West onto China have resulted in analysts frequently asking the wrong questions, such as how flexible the CCP is in implementing market reforms, and whether the CCP might change as dramatically as the Bolshevik party did in the former Soviet Union.[22]

As well, many have misunderstood the extent of the role that entrepreneurship and private business play in China, wrongly assuming that the economy is mainly state owned.[23] While there is significant state oversight and there have been some harsh crackdowns, particularly since 2020, private enterprises have increasingly been the engines of China's growth. According to recent statistics, 90 percent of the firms in China—twenty-five million in total—are privately owned, and they are run by more than fifteen million entrepreneurs. These firms account for more than 50 percent of China's tax revenue, 60 percent of its GDP, 70 percent of innovation, and 80 percent of urban employment.[24] Other than industries of strategic interest, which the Chinese government tightly controls, private entities can and sometimes are encouraged to invest broadly, and many have scaled into massive conglomerates. For example, Tencent was established in 1998 by Ma Huateng (also known as Pony Ma). In 2015 it became one of the most valuable firms in Asia, with a market value of $500 billion, and was ranked by the Boston Consulting Group as one of the most innovative firms in the world.[25] Alibaba was founded in 1999 by Ma Yun (also known as Jack Ma); since 2015, it has become the world's largest retailer and e-commerce company, generating $72 billion in revenue in 2020.

To understand these seemingly puzzling facts, build more general knowledge of capitalism and market development in China, and shed light on practical and policy implications, we need to not just rely on Western theories and assumptions but look historically at how communism and capitalism have combined into a distinctive system. Existing writings on China's economic transition have seldom examined its deep socialist ideology and how that leads to unique market phenomena. The result of this lacuna is an inaccurate and incomplete understanding in both China and the West. Throughout this book, we suggest that because of China's blend of communist political governance and capitalist markets, the traditional dichotomy of communism and capitalism does not apply.

To show the communist roots of the Chinese market and how Mao's key campaigns and institutions enduringly shape it, we will examine the key actors who sit at the nexus of the Chinese capitalist-communist hybrid today: business leaders and their private enterprises and the local politicians who manage economic growth. While a number of books have examined Mao's history and his influence on the CCP, these mainly focus on topics like communist ideology and revolutionary behavior, typically while Mao was in power. Furthermore, many analyses have also focused on how traditional Chinese culture—such as Confucian ideals—has a lasting influence on China.[26] Our contribution is to provide perspective for understanding the lasting and even penetrating influence of Mao's ideas on the business growth and entrepreneurship that has taken place since Deng Xiaoping's capitalist-oriented economic reforms.

To be clear, our goal is not to assess whether Mao and his influence on the CCP and China have been "good" or "bad" from a moral standpoint. Furthermore, we are not proposing that researchers and observers accept the current historical narrative articulated by the CCP in an effort to burnish the CCP centenary and legacy more generally. We have undertaken a deep and systematic study of Mao and Maoism, used contemporaneous accounts of his discourse and influence, and combined this investigation with a social scientific understanding of the effects of Mao and Maoism on individuals and the characteristics of China's systems and institutions.

Mao's legacy is profoundly mixed; the disastrous ideas and policies that led to the persecution and deaths of tens of millions cannot be forgotten or swept under the rug. But we think that the polarizing effects of his legacy have led to a blurred understanding of its influence. Many in the West emphasize Mao's murderous nature while underestimating his deep and lasting influence. In China, negative assessments of Mao are labeled "historical nihilism"—an idea invented by the CCP to describe criticism of such entities as the party, its leaders, national heroes, and others—and so banned; and many scholars and intellectuals have been persecuted for holding such "wrong" views of history.

The punchline of our book is that our decade-long research shows that Mao left an enduring imprint or legacy in the Chinese society, on both Chinese institutions and individuals. The CCP-government maintains these Maoist institutions and individuals hold beliefs deeply rooted in Maoism and pass them on to following generations. Therefore, Mao's influence on China will endure. We marshal diverse sources of data, from individual interviews to large-scale databases, to examine how and why Chinese entrepreneurs and politicians developed the deeply held values and cognitive frameworks that affect their economic decision-making and behavior, and how Chinese markets and politics reflect Maoist principles more generally. To paraphrase Karl Marx and Friedrich Engels's famous assertion in the *Communist Manifesto*, a specter is haunting China—the specter of Mao.[27]

BLENDING COMMUNISM AND CAPITALISM IN CHINA

Huawei's culture is the culture of the Chinese Communist Party, and to serve the people wholeheartedly means to be customer-centric and responsible to the society.

—Ren Zhengfei, founder and CEO of Huawei[28]

Ren Zhengfei, founder of the world-leading technology company Huawei, was born into a poor family in China's Guizhou Province in 1944, the eldest of seven children. Although both of his parents were employed as teachers at the time, the large family size forced them to borrow money almost every month to buy food, especially during the period from 1959 to 1961, when China experienced a great famine in which some thirty million starved to death. Ren said, "My biggest memory from youth to my adulthood has been hunger, and during the Great Famine, my biggest dream was to eat a steamed bun."[29] From kindergarten to high school, Ren had to wear clothes made by his mother, which he then handed down to his younger siblings. When he left for college, his mother collected bedsheets from a dumpster and washed them for Ren's use. According to Ren's own reflections in his famous memoir, *My Father and Mother,* these hardships made him and his siblings more mature and less selfish than others.[30] For example, he recalled that neither he nor any of his siblings ever hoarded food or ate more than their fair share—even during early childhood.

After high school Ren was admitted to what is now Chongqing University.[31] He obtained an engineering degree and got married. To prepare a marriage gift, Ren's younger siblings took on additional jobs building roads, at the not inconsiderable risk of being buried in landslides, and managed to send him 100 RMB (the equivalent of about $13) in cash.

Ren joined the army in 1974. While serving, he became obsessed with Mao's writings—*Quotations of Chairman Mao* and *Selected Works of Mao Zedong*—and won several awards for his excellence and proficiency in Maoism. He was proud of his achievement because during that time, being "red" (that is, loyal to Mao and proficient in his ideas) was more important than being expert in one's profession. Mao's ideology trumped everything, even military skills, and every solider was supposed to be knowledgeable about Maoism. Ren wanted to join the CCP, but the "questionable" background of his father, Ren Moxun—who had worked for a period as an accountant for the CCP's rival party, the Kuomintang—posed a problem. After Mao's death and Deng's early reforms, many of Ren Moxun's former students regained power and returned to important CCP-government positions. With their help, Ren joined the CCP in 1978.

Ren retired from the army in 1983. He and his wife, Meng Jun, were well positioned since his father-in-law, Meng Dongbo, was vice governor of Sichuan Province. This connection won him a management position in the China National Offshore Oil Corporation. However, Ren did not really understand business operations and his business lost 2 million RMB (around $541,000). As a result, he was dismissed from the firm and his wife divorced him. Worse still, Ren was indebted to the firm for hundreds of thousands of dollars.[32] To repay them, he established Huawei in 1987 with an initial capital of 21,000 RMB ($5,680) and leveraged his technical expertise—he had won numerous national awards for his excellence in telecommunications engineering.

Huawei's initial focus was on selling network switches; by 1993, Ren was rich, and Huawei had come to dominate the entire Chinese telecommunications market. Later, Chinese political leaders, including then-vice president Hu Jintao, brought Ren overseas to sell Chinese products, which helped Huawei expand internationally. Meanwhile, Ren spent millions of dollars per year on research and development and innovation.[33] Today, Huawei is one of the most innovative firms in the world. In 2021 it ranked fifth worldwide in patent holding, and it has the second-largest research and development outlay ($20 billion). It earned the equivalent of $140 billion in revenue in 2020 and $99.43 billion in 2021 despite sanctions initiated by former US president Trump.[34]

Ren and Huawei have been a source of consternation for Western lawmakers for decades and have faced many challenges in the United States and Europe, mostly due to national security concerns. Recently, the US government prohibited governmental entities to use any of Huawei's products or devices and banned US chip producers and other tech companies from supplying Huawei. As a result, many other firms, including Google, Intel, AMD, and Qualcomm, ceased doing business with Huawei.

While it is reasonable for countries to exclude foreign suppliers from certain industries of national importance, the characterization of Ren and his motivations is overly broad-brushed and is mistakenly focused on the question of whether his firm is formally state controlled. Current accounts have not tried to delve deeply into his ideology or management model, either.

It is important to look back to his early experiences in the CCP, and in particular the influence of Maoism on his thinking. While Huawei is private—neither owned nor controlled directly by the Chinese government—Ren is a dedicated communist and ingrains CCP values in Huawei, as the quote at the beginning of this section illustrates. For example, Ren has said, "I would still keep my word when joining the CCP as the Communist Manifesto is to serve all human beings . . . and Huawei was getting at this. . . . Our effort was effective and thus fulfilled the mission of the CCP." If the interests of the CCP ever conflicted with those of Huawei, Ren says, he would "choose the CCP whose interest is to serve the people and all human beings, and he could not betray the principles of serving all human beings."[35]

As we will show throughout this book, explicit state control—which is the typical focus of Western analysts—is incidental to the deep imprint that the CCP and Mao have left on Chinese citizens and institutions. As Ren reflects, "People of my generation exhibit a deep Maoist imprint because of the special period we lived through." Ren still reads Mao's writings frequently.[36] Joining the military and then the CCP were critical events for him to inculcate the values of hard work and devoting and even sacrificing himself for the interests of the people.[37] Through the strict indoctrination and socialization process that the CCP maintains for its new members (which we discuss in depth later), Ren swore to "be loyal to CCP, fight for communism for his whole life, sacrifice himself for the interest of people and the CCP, and never betray the CCP." On numerous occasions, Ren has affirmed that he has always kept his word.[38]

As Huawei grew, Ren instituted Maoist principles within the company. He often claimed, "Maoism is the guiding principle (and soul) of Huawei," and Huawei's "management philosophy and strategy are commercial applications of Maoism."[39] There are numerous examples of how Ren followed his spiritual mentor Mao. Surprising to many, Huawei is collectively owned by its employees, an imitation of Mao's socialist ideal, and has rotating co-CEOs, a reflection of Mao's strategy of swapping positions between different military leaders so that all of them would have a panoramic view (and it also ensures that none of those co-CEOs can threaten Ren's status, likely Mao's original intention as well). The CCP employs similar practices in the political realm.

In addition, independence and autonomy—key Maoist principles— are deeply rooted in Huawei's culture. Ren mandated that at least 10 percent of sales revenue be invested in research and development. He said, "Foreign firms are only after money in China. They would not teach Chinese technology and are not reliable, and we would never become independent by buying their technology directly."[40] Huawei responded to Trump's ban on US firms supplying Huawei by creating its own Harmony operating system to replace Android.

Ren and a number of Chinese entrepreneurs also apply Mao's military strategies to business competition, another area of focus in this book. For instance, the strategy of "surrounding cities from the countryside" is Mao's idea that revolutions should begin in rural areas to gain support from farmers and then, based on that strength, subsequently mobilize workers in urban areas.[41] Huawei faced tough competition from Alcatel, Lucent, and Nortel Networks in 1992. Ren countered by targeting market niches that were low income and difficult to access. His sales force went from village to village in those undeveloped regions, then gradually moved to big cities, provinces, and entire countries.[42]

So how should we think of Ren? How should we understand him and his management philosophy? The debate in the West over Huawei's ownership and control are somewhat of a red herring. Ren has made it very clear he is committed to the CCP, and his ideology and strategies are not uncommon among entrepreneurs in China.

Many Chinese entrepreneurs exhibit a similar commitment to the party and its principles. For example, Jack Ma—the founder and CEO of the Alibaba group—is another dedicated communist member. As such, he claimed that "Alibaba is ready to surrender Alipay [predecessor of Ant Financial, the payment-processing platform of Alibaba] to the CCP-government."[43] Ren and Ma are both *communist entrepreneurs*— that is, those who run private businesses or other enterprises but are also CCP members. Ren, Ma, and others not only pose challenges to the traditional economic and development theories but have even elicited persistent consternation among Western audiences concerned about China. How they internally reconcile the two conflicting ideologies is key to understanding this puzzle of China's market economy.

Since the CCP-government began encouraging and even promoting the private sector thirty years ago, many CCP members—a significant

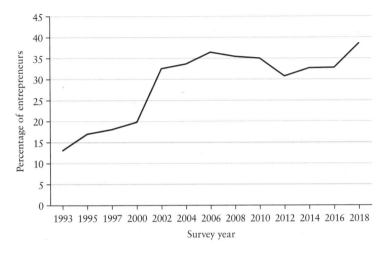

Figure I.2 Percentage of Entrepreneurs Who Are CCP Members
Data sources: Chinese Private Enterprise Survey and published papers and
reports. In recent years the survey team changed the sampling frame, so to
account for sampling differences and to ease facilitation, three-year averages are
used in the post-2001 period. Sources include Yang, Sainan, Wenping Ye, and
Xiaohua Su, "Does the Trust in Official Media Promote Private Enterprise
Investment in Innovation?," *Foreign Economics and Management* [in Chinese]
42, no. 5 (2020): 90–104; Chen, Guangjin, and Peng Lu, *Reports of Chinese
Private Enterprise Survey (1993–2016): From High-Speed Growth to High-
Quality Development* [in Chinese] (Beijing: Social Science Academic Press, 2019);
He, Xiaobin, "Report on Innovation, Transformation and Upgrading of Private
Enterprises—Based on the 13th Survey of Private Enterprises in China," *United
Front Studies* [in Chinese] 2019, no. 8 (2019): 34–47; and "An Analysis Report
on the Current Situation of Party Organization Construction in My Country's
Private Enterprises," http://www.acfic.org.cn/fgdt1/zjgd/201905/t20190523
_125262.html [retrieved on July 23, 2021].

number of whom had been government officials—started their own
businesses.

Based on a well-known national survey, we show that the share of
communist entrepreneurs in China has been growing (fig. I.2). In recent years an average of around 30–35 percent of all entrepreneurs
have been CCP members. The biggest jump came after 2001, when
then–Chinese president Jiang Zemin lifted the ban that prevented private entrepreneurs from joining the CCP in accordance with his Three
Represents Theory, which articulated that the CCP should represent
(1) the development trend of China's advanced productive forces (including

entrepreneurs), (2) the direction of China's advanced culture, and (3) the fundamental interests of the overwhelming majority of the Chinese people.

While many entrepreneurs at that time had been socialized into the CCP *before* founding their businesses, this policy change resulted in a new cohort of CCP members who became CCP members *after* their business success.[44] Our interviews with communist entrepreneurs (more details about these interviews appear later in the introduction and in the methodological appendix) suggest these two groups are able to effectively reconcile communist membership and a capitalist identity.[45] Although the second group is smaller than the first, over time more and more entrepreneurs who first achieved business success have become party members. In contrast, at the time, the estimated total population of communist entrepreneurs was over three million.[46]

These entrepreneurs frequently advocate for the benefits of CCP membership and communism for their firms, commonly establishing CCP branches (also referred to as cells) within their enterprises.[47] These club-like organizations have become increasingly common in private firms in China. A recent survey shows that the share of private firms with CCP branches increased from 27.4 percent in 2002 to 48.3 percent in 2018.[48] Importantly, this has since risen to over 92 percent of China's largest private firms and will likely soon be nearly universal, as it became mandatory in 2018 for domestically listed Chinese firms to have a party branch.[49]

Many Chinese entrepreneurs extol the benefits of these organizations. Cui Genliang, the founder of the Hengtong Group, which is China's largest power and fiber-optic cable manufacturer, was among the first in his province to establish a CCP branch in his firm to build ideological commitment. As he reflected, "Communism is a productive force."[50] Many Chinese entrepreneurs believe that market instruments (for example, salary and welfare benefits) alone are not enough to create cohesive cultures in their firms. CCP branches provide places for the socialization of new members and candidates, as well as morale-boosting events for existing members. At the same time, CCP branches are the fundamental way the CCP exerts control over private firms, so their existence has become an important area of dispute between the United States and China. Use of such organizations was rooted in Mao's revolutionary experience—battles fought by the CCP in the 1920s and 1930s convinced him to establish CCP branches in the army to secure the commitment of existing troops while transforming new recruits (many from "questionable" backgrounds) into communist soldiers and commissars (political workers). After the communist takeover in 1949, CCP branches were expanded to every aspect of Chinese society. For example, in state-owned enterprises, CCP branches are the governing bodies, and they make important decisions and indoctrinate communist beliefs in employees.

While interference by the CCP in private firms is a potentially serious issue, there is confusion about decision-making processes and information sharing within the CCP branch, and how lines of authority are divided between business managers and the CCP branch.[51] We believe such organizations should not be dismissed out of hand because of our own ideology; it is important to recognize that many communist entrepreneurs believe their activities are essential to their companies' social and economic development. More generally, we should try to understand their management model from within the Chinese system as opposed to from a Western perspective. That is why we use the more neutral translation of the Chinese term *zhibu* (支部) as "branch" as opposed to the ideologically tinged English word "cell." We will discuss the effects of these organizations on Chinese firms in more detail later.

Communist Entrepreneurs

The idea that entrepreneurs can fuse ideas from communism and capitalism bucks the conventional wisdom that communism and capitalism are diametrically opposed and incompatible. Marx and Engels's *Communist Manifesto* portrayed entrepreneurs and capitalists in general as class enemies. Many Western observers and academics therefore assume that the CCP could simply be forcing (or luring) entrepreneurs to join them so it can bend them to its will, or that the entrepreneurs use CCP membership as a way to gain personally. For instance, an entrepreneur could join the CCP or become involved in politics, such as by becoming a delegate to either the National People's Congress or the Chinese People's Political Consultative Conference (CPPCC), the two nominal legislative bodies in China, in order to have a way to informally deal with the poor property rights protections the government provides or to improve his or her bargaining position in negotiations with the government.[52] Long-standing academic research supports this idea. For example, a study showed that joining the CCP can help private entrepreneurs gain as much as a 10 percent profit premium over nonmembers.[53] The entrepreneur and CPPCC member Wang Xiang—founder and CEO of the Minsheng Group, one of the five hundred largest private enterprises in China—said as such explicitly: "Frankly speaking," he admitted, "the CPPCC role is 'protective' in nature. The CCP-government thinks of me as reliable and thus I can get big projects. This status makes me politically reliable and economically powerful, and thus others might not harass me."[54]

However, we believe that self-interest-based explanations are not complete, they overly rely on Western economic assumptions that people mainly follow their self-interest, and they reflect the idea that communism and capitalism are by definition oppositional. The alternative perspective we develop is that these actions stem at least in part from the entrepreneur's own deep-seated beliefs. There is growing evidence that for many, if not most, Chinese leaders, CCP membership trumps self-interest.[55] As noted, Ren claimed that the CCP's interest is above that of Huawei, putting his company in the crossfire of US-China trade tensions. Jack Ma of Alibaba said that he would surrender Alipay to the CCP if the latter wanted it, and Cui of Hengtong gave up his lucrative business to respond to the CCP's call by taking over a firm that was headed for bankruptcy.[56] Importantly, as noted, most communist entrepreneurs joined the CCP *before* rather than *after* they founded their firms, some before Deng's reform and opening up; so it is unlikely they foresaw the dramatic economic changes that would make CCP membership economically valuable.[57]

To better appreciate the paradoxical nature of China's economic and political governance, we need to appreciate how deeply the ideological influence of communism runs. From the Maoist perspective, the word "socialist" is at least as important as "market" when it comes to Deng's "socialist market economy" idea (within the so-called "socialism with Chinese characteristics").[58] When reading this English phrase, we tend to view "market economy" as the core idea and "socialist" as an adjective that modifies it. But in Chinese, words that come earlier are not necessarily of less importance. Perhaps a more appropriate translation would be "market economy within the Chinese socialist system," in which "market" is subordinate to "socialist system." Along these lines, Xi has increasingly emphasized the attribute "socialist" in his economic discussions. For example, on November 23, 2015, he said to the members of the CCP's Politburo, "We are developing a market economy under the major premise of the leadership of the CCP and the socialist system. We must never forget the attribute 'socialism.' The reason for saying that it is a socialist market economy is to uphold the superiority of our system and effectively prevent the drawbacks of the capitalist market economy."[59]

The general idea of the Maoist imprint that we develop is twofold. First, the personal values of Maoism were established early on in entrepreneurs' lives. Values formed in that life stage have a lasting influence on their behavior and cognition, as many studies have established. Influential research has shown that growing up during a depression can make individuals more risk averse, growing up in a recession can make them trust more in luck than merit, and entering a job market during an economic downturn can lead individuals to be more conservative in their business and financial decision-making.[60] Communist entrepreneurs tend to have more confidence in governmental communications than the private media, and they align their language with them. For example, when the CCP-government issued cautions about the penetration of foreign powers, communist entrepreneurs tended to stay away from them and depict them with words like "subversive." When the CCP-government began casting foreign cooperation in a more positive light, entrepreneurs shifted to using more friendly language to describe them.[61] Even if many communist entrepreneurs have accepted market-based, capitalist principles, they still exhibit the influence of Mao by responding to the party's call.

At a more macro level, we will also outline institutional elements that tie Chinese society to the Maoist path. These elements are likely to last well into the future. Research from many academic disciplines has shown how enduring the influence of important political figures—such as King Louis XIV, who established the centralized French state, and the United States' founding fathers (particularly Thomas Jefferson), who insisted on the separation of church and state, and local control of economic and other relations—can be.[62]

Likewise, Mao's initial ideas on governance left an imprint on the Chinese society and economy. As discussed earlier, the CCP still measures legitimacy in Maoist terms, even when undertaking dramatic reforms.[63] In that regard, Deng Xiaoping Theory emphasized four basic principles—sticking to the socialist road, the dictatorship of the proletariat, the leadership of the CCP, and Marxist–Mao Zedong Thought. Xi Jinping Thought on Socialism with Chinese Characteristics for a New Era also highlights socialism and communist governance, harking back to a Maoist emphasis on CCP leadership in all aspects of Chinese society.[64]

Contradictions and Chinese Governance

Communist entrepreneurs sit at the center of the paradoxical combination of communism and capitalism in China, and they provide a bridge between the CCP-government and the business world, helping to reduce whatever tensions may exist between "Mao and markets." Being a CCP member is as important to them as being an entrepreneur; some view their private enterprises as important tools to advance their commitment to the CCP.

The fact that communist entrepreneurs could combine Mao and markets might be surprising to Western audiences; however, it has roots in Eastern intellectual traditions that focus on the harmonization of conflicting forces. A simplistic but telling example is how the dualist concept of yin and yang shows that obviously opposite or contrary forces can be complementary, interconnected, and interdependent, and may even give rise to each other. This idea is less prevalent in Western thinking, which is based on the Greek (for example, Aristotelian) intellectual tradition that tends to avoid apparent contradictions and paradoxes. Many scholars before us have argued that such an intellectual tradition may reject duality in properties and suggested that a phenomenon can either be an affirmation or a negation but not both like yin and yang.

Thus, Eastern intellectual traditions are more comfortable with paradox and ambiguity than Western empiricism and take a more holistic view. Many studies in psychology and related disciplines have shown these differences. To cite one example of how deep and pervasive these differences are, scholars have found that when playing with their children, Western parents are more likely to focus on objects, pointing out their unique attributes and asking their children questions about them, and so aim to more clearly categorize them. In contrast, Asian parents tend to focus on social relations, using toys as tools to teach lessons about interpersonal relations consistent with a greater emphasis on wholeness and interdependence.[65]

Correspondingly, individuals in the West tend to understand ideas by isolating different aspects of them into identifiable categories—for example, treating the "state" and "market" as necessarily separate and dichotomous. Conversely, the CCP-government approach is to bind them together, with the CCP at the core of both state and market institutions. As Deng stated, "A little more plan or a little more market is not the fundamental difference between socialism and capitalism—the plan and the market are both economic tools."[66]

Contradiction is also an essential element in Marxism in general and Maoism in particular, which we discuss in more detail later. During Mao's period, society was understood solely in terms of class struggle—conflicts among different economic classes—as articulated by Marx and Engels. After the reforms in the 1970s, the CCP-government downplayed class struggle in order to embrace economic development, redefining the main contradiction as China's economic backwardness versus the people's increasing demands for a better life. The contradiction was officially described in 1981 as the "the ever-growing material and cultural needs of the people versus backward social production." In 2017 Xi elaborated it as the "contradiction between unbalanced and inadequate development and the people's ever-growing needs for a better life," adding the element of inequality as a problem that communism in China seeks to resolve.[67]

Adopting the idea of contradictions, we can better understand communist entrepreneurs, who themselves combine communist beliefs with a capitalist drive. They need internationalization strategies and foreign capital but are ardently nationalistic; they are relatively rich but many strive to lead a frugal life and contribute to their communities. It is hard to isolate these facts from one another.

According to the foundational social theorist Max Weber, historically China had a monarchical system that required dependent people to conform (centralization), and at the same time the government had to unify, control, and secure the obedience of different, geographically dispersed residential groups (decentralization). Since the Qin dynasty (221 BCE), legitimacy for the Chinese government has lain in its ability to conquer different provinces to achieve and maintain national unity. At the same time, the central government has had to honor local autonomy for economic development and the diverse social norms of its different regions.

Weber argued that a new social class emerged—*shidafu* (士大夫), the scholar-official class—to resolve this contradiction. These individuals were loyal to the emperor and the government and at the same time led their families and managed local communities, carefully balancing the centralizing and decentralizing forces.[68] For example, the family of Mu was in charge of the city of Lijiang in China's southwest Yunnan Province. This family was especially loyal to the emperor: most of its patriarchs—who were also chiefs of their jurisdictions—died in wars that helped the central government suppress armed rebellions and fight off invaders. They also wielded power to develop the local economy, and the central government did not intervene in these affairs. There were many other examples of shidafu, such as Zeng Guofan, one of the most famous chancellors in the Qing dynasty (1644 to 1912), who self-funded a militia to help the government suppress the rebellious Taiping Heavenly Kingdom. Even while he wielded enormous power of his own, he was steadfast in his loyalty to the emperor.

Seen through this lens, communist entrepreneurs play a similar role as the shidafu—they are dependent on the CCP-government but are also independent, entrepreneurial individuals. Both the shidafu and the communist entrepreneurs reconcile the contradictions of governance that have occurred over the millennia. Thanks to the shidafu, the central government could not only govern society and levy sufficient taxes and fees but also avoid becoming shorthanded.[69] In the recent period, the CCP-government has had to maintain control while allowing the private sector to flourish, driving the country's economic development. Communist entrepreneurs and their enterprises contribute to the Chinese economy while their communist beliefs ensure that the market forces remain under political control.[70] During our interviews with entrepreneurs in China, all of the CCP members and more than half of the noncommunist entrepreneurs said that they saw no conflict between following the CCP-government and their business interests.

Because of the central role they play in managing the contradictions in the political economic system, it is likely that communist entrepreneurs will only grow in importance for as long as the communist regime is in place. By joining the CCP, they will carry Maoism and later ideological innovations into the future.

Interestingly, the more communist entrepreneurs there are, the more support and less objection the CCP-government may face, because many potential threats from capitalism will have been absorbed into the CCP and communist machine. The CCP-government might even further encourage CCP members to become entrepreneurs and entrepreneurs to become CCP members.

HOW UNDERSTANDING THE LASTING INFLUENCE OF MAO HELPS CLEAR UP COMMON MYTHS ABOUT CHINA

Ray Dalio, the founder of Bridgewater, the world's largest hedge fund, claimed China was a riddle: "A communist country can be so capitalist that they have the second largest capital market in the world, produce billionaires, and simultaneously be Marxist." He claimed that "if you don't know how to answer that riddle, then you must not understand China."[71] While we are not fully sure Dalio himself has come to grips with the puzzle he identifies, we do agree that aiming to reconcile these seeming contradictions is essential for Western policymakers and businesspeople. However, prior work has been built on flawed assumptions such as that economic liberalization will inevitably lead to political democratization and that China can be understood through the Soviet example, as well as an overemphasis on the CCP's economic flexibility. Alternatively, we argue that understanding the lasting influence of Mao and Maoism (and therefore the bedrock principles of the CCP) is what is key to understanding the puzzle Dalio describes.

Myth 1: With Globalization and Economic Development, China Will Democratize

First is the teleological belief that all history is moving toward democratic governance as states modernize and economies develop, evocatively described by Francis Fukuyama's *The End of History and the Last Man*. The book was written against the backdrop of the Soviet collapse, predicting that liberal democracy will be the final form of government for all countries in the world.[72] Gordon Chang's *Coming Collapse of China* furthered this view, suggesting that the communist governance will soon be replaced in China. It is clear that these ideas run deep in the Western consciousness. Despite China's close to forty years of economic success and significant criticism of these ideas, there is still frequent discussion of how the CCP will fall soon because of the rapidly aging population, increasing debts, reversion of the trend of marketization, the deteriorating international environment, and, more recently, economic challenges resulting from stringent COVID-19 lockdowns.[73] With such a belief, observers fixate on signals of the CCP's potential decay and assess that Mao and his ideology are no longer relevant. Some writers have also suggested that as China's middle class rises and the country becomes more prosperous and globally integrated (for example, via the internet), the collapse of the CCP is inevitable.[74]

Others note that the legitimacy of the CCP's rule rests not on democracy but on (economic) performance and modernization.[75] Research has shown the longevity of such authoritarian regimes, particularly those that respond to people's needs through economic development.[76] For example, Singapore, Saudi Arabia, the United Arab Emirates, and other countries do not have democratic, multiparty elections. But given their economic performance, the regimes maintain stability. Accordingly, Samuel Huntington's so-called third wave of democratization in the 1970s and the Revolutions of 1989 occurred when severe economic problems led to civil unrest and the collapse of authoritarian and communist regimes throughout the Iberian Peninsula, Eastern Europe, and Russia.[77]

We believe that any kind of governance change in the near future is unlikely, based on China's current situation and historical precedent. For example, on average, political regimes (dynasties) in China typically last for around three hundred years before being replaced by another, while the CCP-government has only lasted for seventy years. Importantly, China has already been industrialized and the CCP-government has been quite responsive to the populace's material conditions through its economic development, its promotion of social fairness, and importantly, its silencing of critical voices and ruthless suppression of social protest.[78] While it is true that there is an aging population, a decelerating economic growth rate, growing debt, a demarketization trend, and an increasingly hostile international environment, Beijing seems to have adjusted its approach to at least initially address these challenges. For example, China no longer sees economic slowdown as a threat to its stability while it focuses on the quality of growth. Xi also claimed to abandon "GDP heroism" (where leaders focus on a growth-at-all-costs strategy) and that other social issues such as environmental protection are also important. At the same time, China increasingly focuses on high-tech industries and high-end manufacturing to blunt the impact of its shrinking workforce and believes that its debt issue is still controllable.[79] Also, there is evidence the CCP-government is pioneering a new techno-authoritarian model, using its digital capabilities to tighten social control and suppress political dissent, and aiming to do so without choking entrepreneurship and innovation.[80]

The error of prior generations of Western policymakers has started to sink in. Jake Sullivan, national security adviser to President Biden, has claimed, "I think one of the errors of previous approaches to policy towards China has been a view that through U.S. policy, we would bring about a fundamental transformation of the Chinese system. That is not the object of the Biden administration."[81]

Myth 2: China Can Be Understood through a Soviet Lens

Relatedly, Westerners tend to understand China based on the example of the former Soviet Union since both are ostensibly communist, a conceptual link between the experiences of these different countries and systems. But there are vast differences between the two countries in terms of economic and other institutions (which we will discuss in detail later)—for example, while local regions have a lot of autonomy in China, those in the Soviet Union did not. After the Soviet collapse in 1991, many predicted that China would follow, as it was in some ways much weaker than the superpower. This has clearly not happened. China's communist regime endured the 1997 Asian Financial Crisis and has grown ever since.

Indeed, China's developmental trajectory has been distinct from the general law of human society proposed by Marx and Engels, which was more closely followed by Vladimir Lenin and Joseph Stalin in the Soviet Union. Marx and Engels proposed a historical pattern that follows a linear path from prehistory to a slavery society, feudalism, capitalism, and finally communism.[82] But in China, the period of feudalism was short (Warring States period, 475–221 BCE). For most of its history, nobles did not have fiefs and China was a unified country with a centralized, absolute monarchy.[83] As we will describe in later chapters, Mao adapted Marxism-Leninism to fit the Chinese context, abandoning Lenin and Stalin's approach of mobilizing workers in city centers and instead devising a number of unique principles that fit the Chinese context, such as the famous strategy of "surrounding the city from the countryside."

The Soviet analogy is also well known to the Chinese, who have focused intensively on *not* being the next Soviet Union by adapting Marxism-Leninism for the Chinese context (that is, Maoism) and also cracking down on what the CCP terms "historical nihilism." Mao is retained as a saint rather than negated as Nikita Khrushchev did to Stalin. As Xi warned the top-level CCP leaders on January 5, 2013, "Why did the Soviet Union disintegrate? ... An important reason was that ... the Soviet Union completely denied its history, the history of the Communist Party, Lenin, and Stalin, and created historical nihilism and confusing thinking. ... The Party was scattered, and the Soviet Union, an enormous socialist country, disintegrated. This is a cautionary tale!"[84] Accordingly, as he put it in 2016, "Party, political, military, civil and academic, east, west, south, north and center, the Party leads everything," which was a famous 1962 quote from Mao and was written into the CCP Constitution in 2017.[85] In 2022, the CCP produced a documentary titled "Historical Nihilism and the Soviet Collapse." A well-known refrain expresses that the Soviet experience is constantly on the minds of CCP officials: "The Soviets won the October Revolution with only a few hundred thousand members; it defeated the Nazis with a few million; but when it had tens of millions of members, it suffered a tragic collapse."[86]

Myth 3: The Chinese (Communist) Government Is Flexible

While the CCP is certainly pragmatic, since China's opening many writers have overly focused on its flexibility. While we acknowledge that the CCP has indeed shifted policies in the economic realm, focusing on this change as fundamental and also expecting concomitant democratization of China misses the more fundamental Maoist roots of the CCP-government and China. Desmond Shum, author of *Red Roulette*, a 2021 memoir that reveals how he and his former wife, Whitney Duan, became rich through their political connections, expresses a similar sentiment, saying that he was fortunate to be active at a time when China was in poor economic shape and its government prioritized economic growth. But now that that objective has been achieved, the CCP has reverted to its Maoist foundations.

Over the past forty years, credit for China's rise is typically given to Deng's formulation of a "socialist economy with Chinese characteristics" that laid the conceptual groundwork for China's transition. But as we also examine, Mao and Maoism were the intellectual bedrock for Deng's theories, and the system still adheres to them. All of its adaptations have been made within that Maoist framework, and they even refer to Mao to gain legitimacy. Furthermore, Deng's statement "Let some people get rich first" is often quoted to justify market reform; the second half of his statement reflects its Maoist objective "for the purpose of achieving common prosperity faster."[87]

Thus, a theme that Xi continually sounds is, "Do not forget the original intention, keep the mission in mind."[88] By this, he means to stick to Maoist principles, such as seeking truth from facts (to test theory against reality) and the mass line (connect to the people), which we elaborate later.[89] During his centenary speech for the CCP on July 1, 2021, Xi reiterated that the CCP has been unswervingly steadfast, meaning that China's economic reforms have all been undertaken within the "guardrails" of communism and Maoism: "The CCP leads everything."[90]

The party is deeply embedded in all facets of China's political economy; people, capital, and ideology are all kept under increasingly tight control. When there are conflicts between markets and the state, it is the CCP that stands at the center as the ideological glue that holds these different institutions together.[91]

The CCP's heavy hand is something of a double-edged sword. Under Xi, the ideological climate has become more conservative. Mao and the CCP are frequently extolled, the communist ideology is highlighted as the paramount principle, and the Chinese media's anticapitalist and anti-Western rhetoric is increasingly fierce. The most recent version of *The Brief History of the CCP* cast Mao in a more positive tone than previous official histories and downplayed the effects of the Cultural Revolution.[92] During the centenary speech for the CCP, Xi quoted Mao's saying that "Only socialism can save China, only socialism can develop China," and stated, "At a fundamental level, the capability of our Party and the strength of socialism with Chinese characteristics is attributable to the fact that Marxism works."[93]

But these trends could create governance issues in the long run. As we discuss throughout this book, while Mao's ideas galvanized the population and his military strategies ultimately succeeded, he typically underemphasized economic performance and promoted ideological campaigns like the Great Leap Forward and the Cultural Revolution that led to economic disaster and widescale human tragedies. Economic problems have been at the root of the failures of other authoritarian regimes, and the Chinese leadership recognizes this. But, maintaining a COVID-zero policy and harsh lockdowns appears to be a recent-day example of placing ideological objectives over economic ones, as does the crackdown on many leading industries. Further, an overemphasis on ideology can lead to rigidity and fear and stifle innovation as lower-ranking officials avoid taking initiative, lest they be accused of ideological deviation, as such mistakes could be consequential to these officials' political careers or even personal safety.[94]

OVERVIEW OF THE BOOK

Our book provides a systematic understanding of the influence of Maoism on the Chinese economy and political system today.[95] Simply put, it is impossible to have accurate knowledge of Chinese business or markets without adequate knowledge of Maoism, which has been deeply imprinted on Chinese society and its institutions since the founding of the People's Republic. We concentrate on private enterprise, entrepreneurship, and market development, as these processes stand at the center of the contradictory forces of communism and capitalism in China and are an essential part of China's growth story over the past forty years.

We synthesize and build on the interdisciplinary literature that examines the lasting influence of the early life and career experiences of individuals in child development, economics, human ecology, neuroscience, psychology, sociology, and management. Our perspective is consistent with the "depression baby" hypothesis, which argues that individuals born in the Great Depression became more risk averse, but with China and Mao it is not just one cohort of individuals that was affected; the result was an entirely new economic model that forms the foundation for lasting economic and political governance.[96]

Types of Data and Evidence

The methodological appendix explains our approach in detail. But briefly, we combine qualitative and quantitative analyses to provide convincing and rigorous evidence for our ideas. On the qualitative side, our chapters are grounded in case studies of well-known entrepreneurs, based on secondary sources as well as original in-person and online interviews with thirty-two entrepreneurs and business leaders in Anhui, Chongqing, Guangdong, Heilongjiang, Hunan, Shanghai, Sichuan, and Zhejiang, where most of China's private enterprises are located.[97]

On the quantitative side, we drew on several sources to provide systematic evidence based on large samples. The Chinese Private Enterprise Survey has surveyed thousands of entrepreneurs from every province at a number of intervals since 1993. We drew on the Chinese Stock Market and Accounting Research Database for the annual reports of thousands of other entrepreneur-controlled firms that were publicly traded, and ran them through advanced, computerized analyses to capture language that prior research suggests can be seen as reflective of their thought processes. Also, we hand-coded data about politicians (for example, age, gender, position, date of enrollment in the CCP, and career history) from various websites to show how they shape private business and influence entrepreneurs.

We developed two databases to chart the impacts of Maoist principles in their own time. We obtained as many official newspapers as possible— for example, the entire run of the *People's Daily* between 1949 and 2010—since the CCP-government strictly controls such media as formal mechanisms of indoctrination. We also hired research assistants to search historical provincial dailies for various keywords. Together, they provided valuable insights into the ways Mao's ideas have endured, albeit waxing and waning at times, throughout the history of the People's Republic of China. To analyze entrepreneurship activities at the regional level, we used data from a survey of Chinese firms of different sizes, industries, and ages in every city in China, conducted by a research team at the National School of Development at Peking University.

Organization of the Book

In part I, which consists of chapters 1 and 2, we describe Chairman Mao Zedong, the communist regime he built, and his enduring influence on Chinese society. Then, in part II, we move on to important Maoist ideological principles (nationalism, frugality, a devotion focus, and his military ideas), consider their origins and meanings, and connect them to the business strategies of present-day entrepreneurs. Chapter 3 examines how nationalism affects firms' internationalization goals, and chapter 4 examines the business impacts of frugality. Chapter 5 considers how a devotion focus affects social contributions, and chapter 6 relates Mao's military strategies to contemporary entrepreneurs' business strategies and organization.

In part III, we delineate the three mass campaigns Mao initiated—the Great Leap Forward, the Cultural Revolution, and the Third Front Construction—his reasons for initiating them, and how they influence Chinese entrepreneurs today. Chapter 7 considers how the Great Leap Forward experience enduringly affects resource use, and chapter 8 explores how remembered experiences of the Cultural Revolution affect entrepreneurs' confidence in China's institutional environment. Chapter 9 considers the impacts of the Third Front Construction effort on regional entrepreneurship.

Part IV explores China's socialist institutions—economic and political systems—and specifically focuses on the unique politically centralized yet economically decentralized governance system and the influence of local Chinese politicians in the business landscape (chapter 10), as well as the state's control of private firms through ownership and party organizations (chapter 11). We conclude our book with five principles for doing business in China and five principles for understanding governance in China, followed by a general perspective on China's political and socioeconomic environment today and its likely future.

We believe that rather than expecting China's Maoist-communist roots to decay, politicians and business practitioners need to come to grips with the fact that they need to learn how to "coexist," "cooperate," "compete"—three frequent keywords from Blinken's China policy speech[98]—with communists for the long run. Thus, unraveling the dynamics that enable the coexistence of a vibrant market economy (capitalism) and Maoist principles (communism) is key to developing better economic and political relations with China.

This new understanding is particularly important and timely given Xi's revival of Maoist doctrines, launch of neo-Maoist movements, increasing insistence on the CCP's governance in private businesses and Chinese society, crackdowns on the media and civil society, and strong desire to subsidize state-owned enterprises and promote CCP-government forces in the economy.[99] Further, as numerous China observers have pointed out, by referring to himself with lofty titles that were previously only used by Mao (such as "helmsman" and "people's leader"), Xi is himself creating a cult of personality, even though Article 10 of the *Constitution of the Chinese Communist Party*, introduced in 1982, "forbids all forms of personality cult." Looking at these developments through a historical lens can help us understand where China is going in the future. As Winston Churchill said, "The longer you can look back, the farther you can look forward." We hope the business and governance principles we develop in this book will be helpful in this regard.

I   MAO ZEDONG, MAOIST PRINCIPLES, AND PRIVATE BUSINESS IN CHINA

Chairman Mao is the red sun that forever shines.
Long live/viva la [live ten thousand years] Chairman Mao.
                    —"Looking Back on the Cultural Revolution:
                        Mao Zedong as the Artificial Sun"

A CCP member should place the Party's interest above their own.

A CCP member must at any time respond to the Party's call.
                                        —Mao Zedong

Chairman Mao Is the "Red Sun in Our Heart"
"Chinese Propaganda Poster of Mao Zedong," Getty Images. Swim Ink 2, LLC/
CORBIS/Corbis Historical via Getty Images.

1 Maoism—Communism, Chinese-Style

Chairman Mao is the savior of the people.
> —"Looking Back on the Cultural Revolution:
> Mao Zedong as the Artificial Sun"

THERE ARE MANY BARRIERS to understanding Mao Zedong's influence on contemporary China. On the one hand, Mao's legacy is at the core of the legitimacy of the Chinese Communist Party (CCP), and so there has been strict censorship of criticism of Mao, and research and teaching on the economic and social catastrophes under his rule are generally prohibited. These trends have become heightened during Xi Jinping's rule.[1] On the other hand, some have speculated that the shadow of McCarthyism still obscures Americans' understanding of communism, and so academe has generally avoided systematic, unbiased examinations of its history and legacies.[2]

Yet at the same time, the deep influence of Mao is not a secret. As Xi has claimed a number of times, "To understand today's China, one must understand the CCP."[3] To Xi, Mao and Maoism are at the core of the CCP, which "must adhere to and make good use of the living soul of Mao Zedong Thought, build the Party well, and continue to advance the great cause of socialism with Chinese characteristics." He also claimed that for the CCP, "Mao Zedong Thought must not be lost; if lost, it will lose its foundation."[4] And in recent years, Xi and the CCP have been taking a tougher Maoist tone and an aggressive "Wolf Warrior" stance in foreign policy.[5] Their discourse emphasizes Maoist terms such as "struggle" (between different classes) and "contradiction" (tensions within a society that might produce constructive outcomes). During his centenary speech about the CCP, Xi declared, "The Chinese people will never allow any foreign forces to bully, oppress, or enslave us. Whoever wants to do this will surely have their heads broken and blood spilled in front of the great steel wall built by more than 1.4 billion Chinese people."[6]

In this chapter, we first describe Mao and provide an overview of his key ideas, which we argue are essential to understand China and the CCP and therefore China's business landscape and economic and political systems as well. Importantly, as the founder of the communist regime in China, Mao fundamentally shaped "Chinese-style" communism. Unlike the Soviet Union's satellite states in Eastern Europe such as Bulgaria and Romania, where the parties followed Joseph Stalin's and his successors' Marxist-Leninist prescriptions closely, Mao localized communism with his ideas and stipulated how it was practiced in China with uniquely Chinese characteristics.

Mao also stood at the center of a cult of personality to promulgate his ideas, which began when the communist troops were still weak and had to settle in the poor northwest province of Shaanxi. How could he have come to wield so much power, and how should we understand him as a person? Scholars have noted that Mao's "red sun" status was established through the bloody Yan'an Rectification Movement that purged many CCP leaders—including Xi's father, Xi Zhongxun, who had been a general and had the potential to threaten Mao's status.[7] Mao worship culminated during the Cultural Revolution (1966–76), when the Chinese people thought of Mao as infallible, addressing him as "ten thousand years" (a metaphor for emperor), "sun," and the "savior." Maoist thought attained a biblical status, which it retains to this day.

MAO'S ROAD TO POWER

Mao was born into a well-off peasant family in 1893. He was taught Chinese classics and read translations of Western authors such as Adam Smith, Montesquieu, Jean-Jacques Rousseau, Charles Darwin, and Aldous Huxley. He matriculated at First Normal University in Hunan at the age of twenty, with the aspiration of becoming a teacher. Instead, he became a communist. One of his professors was Yang Changji, who later moved to Peking University. Yang liked Mao (after his death, Mao would marry his daughter Yang Kaihui) and recommended him to Li

Dazhao, the director of the Peking University Library (and an important early leader of the CCP). Li offered Mao a position as librarian.

Around the same time, Cai Hesen, one of Mao's best friends, invited him to join the Diligent Work-Frugal Study Movement, which aimed to train young Chinese between sixteen and thirty as communists by sending them to work and study in France, and so experience a workers' movement firsthand.[8] Mao raised funds for the movement but did not participate in it. During his time in Beijing, he also audited many courses at Peking University, and through Yang Changji met many of the other future leaders of the CCP, including Chen Duxiu. Mao was one of the twelve attendees of the first national congress that marked the founding of the CCP on July 23, 1921, where Chen was elected as the top leader.[9]

The first period of CCP development (1921–34) is often called "the Communist International era," as the Soviet Union was the key sponsor and funder of CCP activities, which included armed antigovernment revolts in big cities. The top leaders of the CCP were seen as outlaws by the ruling Kuomintang (KMT) and many of them were arrested, tortured, and killed. By 1930, Mao had effectively become the CCP's leader, thanks in part to his successes in battle. But because the CCP received support from the Communist International, it had to follow instructions from Stalin and the Soviet Union.

To ensure control, Stalin arranged for Chinese students who had trained in the Soviet Union (known by the CCP as Bolsheviks) to lead the CCP. One of them, Wang Ming (original name Chen Shaoyu), effectively displaced Mao from the top position in June 1931.[10] In November, Wang went to Moscow to represent the CCP in the Communist International, temporarily handing his power over to Bo Gu (original name Qin Bangxian), another Bolshevik. Wary of Mao's influence, the Bolshevik faction forced Mao out of power in 1932, deriding him for his lack of international experience. Wang ridiculed Mao's ideas, saying that Marxism-Leninism cannot "emerge from the poor ravines," metaphorically referencing Mao's experientialist approach of practicing, testing, and developing communism in the vast poor countryside in China, which later became the most important building block of Maoism—"seeking truth from facts."[11]

Wang and his Bolsheviks were dogmatic disciples of Marxism-Leninism; as such, they failed to consider the drastic differences between the Soviet Union and China. The Russian Empire had set industrialization in motion before the October Revolution in 1917 and was at the time the fifth-largest industrialized country in the world. Thus, there were many factory workers, and the situation was consistent with Karl Marx's theory, which was developed in industrialized England and Germany and thus saw the factory as the locus of the revolution.

Mao's understanding of the Chinese situation and history and his tailoring of communism to it set the stage for a different kind of revolution. He surmised that peasant revolts had been the most successful drivers of regime change in China over the past two thousand years. China's hundreds of millions of peasants constituted the majority of the population. Mobilizing farmers made much more sense than mobilizing factory workers in an agrarian society like China's.

But Wang and his Bolsheviks did not listen, deriding Mao as a "hick" (literally "muddy-legs," a metaphor for ignorant peasants whose legs were dirty from working the fields). Though Mao's troops defeated the KMT in battle four times between October 1930 and March 1933, the Bolsheviks insisted that they attack cities instead. As a result, their army was very nearly annihilated.

Because of this fiasco, Mao advised the CCP to retreat; by the end of 1934, the remaining CCP troops had begun their famous Long March. In January 1935, they occupied the city of Zunyi, where the KMT had limited forces. Dissatisfied with the leadership of Wang and Bo, many Bolsheviks switched their allegiance to Mao. In Zunyi, the CCP Politburo ratified his military leadership and affirmed his strategy. This was a turning point for Mao, who then led the CCP troops to Yan'an, in Shaanxi Province. The Long March took more than a year, but the CCP survived. It began the second stage of its growth in 1935, under Mao's leadership.

Mao became the chairman of the Central Military Commission of the CCP in 1936 and thus the de facto leader of the CCP; his supreme leadership lasted until his death in 1976. However, he was not the de jure political leader of the CCP, as Zhang Wentian was elected as its temporary leader (between 1935 and 1945, the formal leadership position, general secretary of the CCP, was vacant). There has been a tradition in the CCP that the military leader wields the most power and assumes the de facto supreme leadership, reflecting Mao's famous dictum, "Political power comes from the barrel of the gun." For instance, Deng Xiaoping, the de facto supreme leader of China and the CCP after Mao, was not the de jure political leader. But he held the position of chairman of the Central Military Commission of the CCP and could depose the de jure leaders, such as Hu Yaobang and Zhao Ziyang. Since the Jiang Zemin administration (1989–2002), the top positions—general secretary of the CCP, Chinese president, and chairperson of the Central Military Commission of the CCP—have all been held by the same person.[12]

Unlike most other countries, where the military reports to the head of the state, in China it reports to the CCP. As Xi emphasized at an August 2020 "Military Political Work Conference," the "People's Liberation Army remains the Party's army and must maintain absolute loyalty to political masters."[13] Echoing Mao's famous saying, Xi also recently noted that "the Party commands the gun."[14]

Mao's position was still precarious when he became chairman of the Central Military Commission. First, the Communist International sponsored the CCP, and Moscow persistently interjected itself into its operations. Stalin and Mao had significant debates about whether the CCP should unite with the KMT, and whether the CCP or KMT should take over the administration of the territories in mainland China that the Japanese surrendered at the end of the Second Sino-Japanese War. Also, many CCP leaders, such as Zhou Enlai and Deng Xiaoping, were in the Diligent Work-Frugal Study Movement. This rival faction constrained Mao's power.

Furthermore, while political power may come from "the barrel of a gun," Mao in reality only controlled the First Front Army of the Chinese Workers' and Peasants' Red Army, which was only one of the four sets of troops under the CCP's leadership. In addition, nine out of ten of those troops had died or disappeared during the Long March. Mao's troops were outnumbered by the Red Army based in Shaanxi Province, which was led by Xi's father, Xi Zhongxun.

In February 1942, Mao initiated the Yan'an Rectification Movement, the first of many political campaigns he created, to force the Bolshevik faction—for example, Zhang Wentian and Yang Shangkun (later president of China)—out of power and solidify his own position. The movement focused on the localization of Marxism, added Maoism to the CCP's constitution, and eliminated Soviet control. Since overseas experience became a less important credential, it also undercut the power of the Diligent Work-Frugal Study Movement faction. Meanwhile, the other leaders at the time either died or eventually supported Mao. The military leaders Liu Zhidan and Xie Zichan both died on the battlefield, and Xi Zhongxun was arrested. Mao released him, and Xi became a strong supporter of Mao. Mao's status within the CCP was stabilized and he promoted his loyal supporters to the top of the hierarchy, such as later Chinese president Liu Shaoqi, an enthusiastic advocate of Maoism.[15]

AN ASPIRING PHILOSOPHER DEVELOPING UNIQUE COMMUNIST PRINCIPLES

Although many of his ideas were deeply rooted in Chinese culture and Confucianism—for example, the *Selected Works of Mao Zedong* cite the classic text the *Zuo Zhuan* more than forty times and the *Analects of Confucius, Mencius,* and other classics more than twenty times each—Mao developed his own ideas and ideology to shape the culture of the CCP and eventually all of China, leaving a long-standing mark on Chinese society and eventually cementing his unquestionable authority. Four important aspects of his life experience influenced the principles that now define Chinese communism.

First, Mao needed legitimacy for his leadership of the CCP. Many Western concepts, such as science, democracy, capitalism, and communism, were imported to China. Vladimir Lenin and Stalin closely adhered to Marxist orthodoxy such as "mobilizing industry workers to revolt in city centers" and also followed Marxist teachings on state ownership and a planned economy, nationalizing all businesses and making private enterprise illegal.[16] To gain legitimacy to govern, Mao needed to create his own authentic communist writings. He studied Marxism-Leninism and published several influential papers while in Yan'an.[17]

In particular, the publication of *On Practice* and *On Contradiction* in 1937 elevated Mao's position as a student of communism. Following Marxist dialectical materialism, *On Practice* argued that people must apply their knowledge to practice in reality to test its truthfulness, laying the foundation for his later dictum "seeking truth from facts." This idea also inspired Deng's slogan that "practice is the only standard for testing truth," which significantly shaped the reform and opening-up strategy. *On Contradiction* extended Marxist philosophy, suggesting that contradiction exists in all matters and is the basic property of nature, society, and human mentality. After the Korean War, when China and Mao won acclaim from countries in the Eastern Bloc, these two essays became required reading throughout the USSR. After receiving that recognition, Mao became increasingly focused on creating new theories and thoughts to amplify his influence in the global communist movement.

Second and relatedly, Mao needed to consolidate his power within the CCP. Since he deeply understood China and its history, he knew that a unified, absolute autocracy would be viable only if people accepted a common philosophy, culture, ideology, and religion.[18] Confucianism had served that purpose since 134 BCE, and the cornerstone Confucian ideal of loyalty to the monarch had been especially useful to China's leaders. Those leaders—initially called kings and then emperors starting with the Qin dynasty (221 BCE)—were also ideological leaders, analogous to the European concept of the divine right of kings, whereby the monarch's role extends to ideological and religious realms.[19]

By creating a similar hybrid of philosophy, culture, and ideology, Mao's words gained tremendous mobilizing power over time and strengthened his position; essentially no one in China could usurp him. Further, per Marx, communist beliefs can and should replace religion as the populace's guiding ideology.[20] Mao's writings, such as his little red book, *Quotations of Chairman Mao Zedong; Mao Zedong Thoughts;* and *Selected Works of Mao Zedong,* would thus become the official ideological teaching for Chinese society. By 1945, "Mao Zedong Thought" was written into the constitution of the CCP.

Third, when Mao was developing Mao Zedong Thought (Maoism), the CCP was not the ruling party of China. The KMT was, and it had greater military strength. However, Mao hoped to rule China, and he believed that by the 1940s, the ground would be fertile for his communist principles.

Over thousands of years, and even today, Chinese political philosophy has suggested that Chinese monarchs are bestowed with the Mandate of Heaven (that is, legitimacy to rule due to the peace and prosperity the ruler creates) and called "sons of heaven."[21] However, the Mandate of Heaven does not confer an unconditional right to rule. Retaining the mandate is contingent on the just and able performance of the rulers, and the people have the right of rebellion. Bad weather (for example, drought) or disasters (for example, floods) were signs of heaven's displeasure and even the mandate's withdrawal. If the calamities were catastrophic enough, the current emperor and his dynasty would become illegitimate and should be replaced.[22]

In Mao's time, there were ample signs that the KMT's Mandate of Heaven had been withdrawn. For instance, the KMT had destroyed the dike at Huayuankou, on the Yellow River in the Chinese city of Zhengzhou, in an attempt to halt the rapid advance of Japanese forces, and the resulting flood led to four million becoming homeless. Compared with many Chinese rulers in the past, who took the Mandate of Heaven seriously, Chiang Kai-shek was arguably lax in this regard. He was sluggish in providing disaster relief, resulting in tens of millions of refugees and a death toll of around one million. Chiang also was known for tolerating corruption and indulging his wife Soong Mei-ling's family, who were said to have embezzled $20 million in the 1930s and 1940s, when total fiscal revenue was less than $30 million per year.[23] Chiang also failed to implement effective policies to deal with income inequality and hyperinflation.

These factors together made Mao believe that he could obtain the Mandate of Heaven and legitimacy to rule. Mao met with Chiang for negotiations to form a united government in Chongqing from August 1945 to October 1945, when Mao's anti-colonialist and anti-imperialist ideas and the principles of the CCP were being widely disseminated, and he sensed that they were resonating.[24]

Fourth, it is important to recognize that Mao was extraordinarily ambitious—he wanted to become the supreme leader of China and also to be recognized as a great mind, someone who would be remembered eternally by the entire world. He wanted to be worshiped, like Marx, Lenin, and Stalin. His ambition was reflected in his poem "Patio Spring Snow," written just after the Long March in 1936. The poem includes the statement, "Qin Shi Huang and Emperor Wu of Han dynasty lacked literary grace. Emperor Taizong of Tang and Emperor Taizu of Song lacked a sense of poetry in their souls. Genghis Khan, Proud Son of Heaven, only knew how to shoot eagles with his bow and arrow. All are past and gone! For truly great men, look to our current age alone."[25] The emperors he denigrated were the most prominent in Chinese history. Qin Shi Huang, China's first emperor, unified the country; Emperor Wu vastly enlarged China's territory and military strength; and Taizong and Taizu founded dynasties in China's golden age. Genghis Khan conquered much of the world.[26] The poem is famous among the Chinese;

subjects 6 and 26 of our interviewed entrepreneurs cited it as their favorite of Mao's quotes.

The poem was published in newspapers in 1945, during the negotiations between the CCP and the KMT. Chiang jealously (but rightly) commented, "I think his poems have imperial thoughts, and he wants to go back to the old time and imitate first emperors of Tang and Song Dynasties. He wants to become a great monarch in China." Chiang tried to write a similar poem but failed to do so.[27]

MAOISM: AN OVERVIEW

Maoism, or communism Chinese-style, extends Marxism-Leninism to agricultural, preindustrial Chinese society in order to develop revolution and economic construction.

To understand what is unique about Maoism, we first summarize the key differences between capitalism and traditional communism (table 1.1).[28] Capitalist and communist ideologies differ substantially in terms of political institutions (systems of power, and press and communications); economic systems (ownership of property, basis of economy, claim of profit, and operation of economy); and social structures (class, wealth distribution, and priorities).

The most significant difference between communist and capitalist countries concerns their political systems. In communist countries, there is typically a party-state system—only one party is the legitimate ruler, such that party and state become a single entity. This is in sharp contrast with most capitalist countries, where different political parties keep each other in check and the government is a separate entity. Elections typically occur every few years (with the exception of authoritarian regimes, such as those in South Korea and Taiwan historically and Singapore today). Relatedly, while communism maintains state control of the media, under capitalism press and communications are typically privately owned and unconstrained.

Communism stipulates state ownership of the means of production and firms and government regulations and plans, whereas under capitalism there is private ownership, free enterprise, and less government regulation. Capitalism allows for greater differentiation of socioeconomic classes (for example, income inequality) and encourages merit-based wealth pursuit and individual freedom, whereas communism is

Table 1.1 Ideal-Typical Comparison between Capitalism and Communism

Ideology	Capitalism	Communism
Political institution		
System of power	Democratic and from the people	Monopolized by the ruling party
Press and communications	Mostly free and privately owned	Mostly state controlled
Economic system		
Ownership of property	Mostly private	Mostly by the state
Basis of the economy	Entrepreneurship and free enterprise	State-owned enterprise
Claim of profit	Individual	The entire nation
Operation of economy	Competitive market	Government regulated and planned
Social structure		
Class	Differentiated	Egalitarian and classless via struggles
Wealth distribution	Uneven and merit based	Equal and based on need
Focus on and priority of	Individual freedom	Community and society as a whole

Source: Based on authors' summary of facts and prior work, such as Qiao, Kunyuan, "Historical Political Ideology and Firm Innovation: Worldwide Evidence of R&D Investments (1982–2016)," *Academy of Management Proceedings* 2020, no. 1 (2020): 10089.

more egalitarian, with a more equal distribution of wealth, at least in principle.

In the next section, we briefly sketch the key elements of Maoism that we examine in more detail throughout the book, including Maoist ideological principles, Mao's mass campaigns, and the socialist institutions Mao created.

Maoist Ideological Principles

According to historical and contemporary CCP documents, Maoist communism turns on three major principles: nationalism, frugality, and the mass line.[29] Nationalism is the belief that the Chinese people should decide their futures on their own, rely on themselves, and downplay external aids. In the words of the CCP, "For a country's communist party to achieve victory in revolution and construction, it must be based on its own country's situation, its own reality, and its own revolutionary forces and people."[30] Mao claimed that "self-reliance should be our key approach" and "we Chinese people have the determination of realizing our splendid times with self-reliance."[31] He even praised KMT leader Chiang—his old opponent—for his nationalism, saying that Chiang "dared to defy the U.S. policy for 'two Chinas' in front of [John Foster] Dulles, proving that he is still a great nationalist."[32]

The second main ideological principle is frugality. Mao asserted, "We should be frugal to build factories, run stores, all state-owned and cooperative businesses, all other businesses, etc. and everything should be guided by the principle of frugality. Frugality is the fundamental principle of the socialist economy."[33] He also claimed that it was necessary because "China was a poor and economically underdeveloped country, and to make our country rich, we need to hold on to the frugal construction principles and shall never waste. It will take decades for China to become rich, but the principle of thrift should be held on to in the next few decades and even after we have achieved that goal. It is particularly necessary to promote frugality within a few decades, i.e., the several incoming five-year plans."[34] As we will discuss in more detail later, the principle of frugality has roots in traditional Chinese culture, and Mao borrowed it and highlighted it for his rule.

The third ideological principle is the "mass line," which leads to a focus on devotion for CCP members. The mass line maintains that "everything is for the [popular] masses, everything depends on the masses, and [the CCP's work and theory should come] from the masses, go and apply to the masses [for further development]." It is collectively reflected in Mao's "serve the people" proposition, which requires CCP members to sacrifice their own interests to those of society as a whole. All candidates, upon joining the CCP, swear to respond to the party's call and sacrifice their lives if necessary. This also originated in traditional Chinese culture, especially Confucianism (by Confucius, Mencius, and others), which emphasizes people-oriented thought that values the people, honors the people, cares for the people, and loves the people.[35]

Mao's military principles (or Mao Zedong Military Thought) are expounded in the *Collected Works on Military by Mao Zedong* and

Selected Works of Mao Zedong.[36] They have five major interrelated aspects: a pragmatic focus that follows the idea of seeking truth from facts; an emphasis on the CCP's leadership and ideology (for example, "political power comes from the barrel of a gun" and "serve the people"); the importance of mobilization; specific military strategies, such as surrounding cities from the countryside, never fighting a war unprepared, concentrating advantageous force to annihilate an enemy, and acknowledging the need for protracted war; and a theory of national defense that turns on modernization fueled by socialist construction. We will discuss later how these ideas of Mao were also influenced by traditional Chinese military thought, such as that of Sun Tzu.[37]

Socialist Construction with Mass Campaigns

The Maoist focus on socialist construction—including policy and approaches such as continuous revolution—led to three mass campaigns: the Great Leap Forward, which aimed to transform agrarian Chinese society into an industrialized one quickly after the socialist transformation of the Chinese economy; the Cultural Revolution, which tried to exterminate so-called unorthodox communist ideals (mainly Soviet revisionism and Western capitalism) and replace them with a focus on continuous revolution; and the Third Front Construction, which attempted to relocate China's industrial and military facilities to the hinterlands to protect them from the threats of Soviet invasion and US air raids.

Mao wanted to match the Soviet Union's success in industrialization. By 1956, China had finished its socialist transformation—that is, the private economy was nationalized, and the country's farms had been organized as collectives under the central control of the CCP-government. Mao thought that China should be able to quickly increase steel output and become fully industrialized, just as the Soviet Union had under Stalin in the 1920s and 1930s. Mao was particularly impressed by Nikita Khrushchev's speech during the fortieth anniversary of the October Revolution in 1957 on the Soviet Union's goal of surpassing the United States in fifteen years; Mao initiated the Great Leap Forward movement (1958–60) under the slogan of "catching up with and finally surpassing the United Kingdom and the United States."[38]

To accomplish this, agricultural labor was redirected to industry and many Chinese were ordered to melt down their metal cooking utensils in what came to be known as backyard furnaces, small-scale smelting operations distributed across the countryside that were designed to rapidly increase steel production. Since agricultural production was deprioritized, there was a sharp decline in crop yields. The result was the three-year Great Famine, in which upward of thirty million people died and millions more endured extreme hunger.[39]

Mao was directly responsible for the catastrophe and was forced by other leaders to self-criticize. With his authority diminished, he faced challenges from senior leaders such as Liu Shaoqi and Deng Xiaoping. Liu suggested Mao "retreat from the front line and de facto retire," and brought his wife on a speaking tour, which only supreme leaders had done in the past. Liu also prepared to publish his thoughts like Mao, another privilege that only the top leader of the CCP-government enjoys.[40] Mao implemented the Cultural Revolution (1966–76) to consolidate his power and counter the potential influence of Khrushchev's "capitalist reform," which he believed Liu and Deng wanted to bring to China.

While the stated purpose of the Cultural Revolution was to revivify the CCP, which Mao said had become overly bureaucratized, and mobilize the populace to engage in continuous revolution, the result was a decade of institutional upheaval and turmoil. The campaign demolished almost all CCP committees at the national and regional levels and replaced them with "revolutionary committees" (sometimes called "rebellious committees"). High-ranking officials and their subordinates who posed a threat to Mao were pushed out of power. Universities and colleges were shut down, and most employers in cities stopped hiring. The large population of idle young adults became a significant issue. So in 1967, Mao launched the send-down movement, in which tens of millions of urban youths were relocated to poor villages, where they starved alongside the peasants.[41] The intention of the movement was to help young people better understand the hardships farmers experience and to eliminate the differences between urban and rural areas and between mental and physical work. President Xi Jinping spent seven years in a rural area of Shaanxi Province as a "sent-down youth."

Around the same time, Mao initiated the Third Front Construction, which moved heavy—especially military-related—industries to the inner regions of China. Mao's agricultural collectivization had resulted in criticism from the Soviet Union. He thought that he was a better leader for the worldwide communist movement than Khrushchev, especially after China fought in the Korean War and helped the Soviet Union solve protest issues in Poland and Hungary.[42] Relations had been strained since 1956, in 1966 formal relations were severed, and in 1969 there were some military skirmishes.

While there had been some movement toward a rapprochement between China and the United States in the 1960s, China still viewed the United States as an enemy because of its support for Taiwan and escalation of the Vietnam War.[43] Remembering the damage Japan had done with its attacks on China's northeast industrial facilities and feeling threatened from all sides, Mao decided to move industry facilities to remote regions.[44] The strategy ("close to the mountains, dispersed, and hidden") was consistent with his experience of the Long March,[45] but its implementation was uneconomical and misallocated significant resources. The mountainous terrain raised construction costs and made the plants difficult to access.

Socialist Institutions

A key aspect of Chinese-style communism is its unique socialist institutions, which grew out of Mao's revolutionary experience. Their main features are their political centralization and economic decentralization.[46]

Political centralization means that power flows from the top down, with officials appointed by the supervising authorities rather than elected from the bottom up. China has CCP-governments at the national, provincial, prefectural (city), county, and township levels. National leaders appoint provincial leaders, who in turn appoint prefectural leaders, and so on. The system is consistent with Mao's belief that the CCP should lead everything and that a proletariat dictatorship under CCP control is the right approach for China's political institutions. The political centralization of China's socialist institutions is similar to what existed in the Soviet Union but contrasts sharply with most Western countries, where leaders are elected. In the United States, for example, state governors are elected by their own state and are not appointed by the president; though there are local and national offices with varying amounts of authority, the lines of control are not as hierarchical.

Yet scholars have also noted that Chinese regional leaders such as party secretaries and government heads (for example, governors and mayors who are vice-party secretaries in their provinces and cities) are responsible for appointing directors of the different bureaus in their jurisdiction to work with them, and that they are fully in charge of many of the economic and other affairs therein.[47] This diverges from the Soviet Union, in which ministers of different industries at the national level appointed directors of their corresponding industries at the republic level, who in turn appointed directors of the respective industries one level below. In China, the central authorities typically do not intervene in local leaders' economic decisions.

As noted, the system grew out of Mao's military experience. Military leaders pledged allegiance to him, but when many became regional CCP officials after the start of the communist regime, they maintained local autonomy, which follows from Mao's philosophy of seeking truth (that is, right and appropriate military strategy) from facts (that is, the frontline situation and the reality). Many popular and academic writings characterize this system as economically decentralized ("federalism") with Chinese characteristics.[48] Mao, in his famous essay "On Ten Major Relationships," also stated that "under the premise of consolidating the unified leadership of the central government, we should expand the power/discretion of the local government, giving the local government more independence, and let the local government do more."[49]

Both the economic and political structures of socialist institutions have remained basically unchanged, despite Deng's paradigmatic shift in economic policies and incentives for politicians. Before Deng's reform in 1978, China maintained a planned economy that local party secretaries implemented based on the national-level five-year plans, making plans for resource allocation in accordance with government mandates. Political leaders were judged by their allegiance and loyalty to Mao and Maoism. But after the economic reform in 1978, a market-based economy began to form, and local party secretaries issued policies to aid the market in the allocation of resources in certain industries. Political leaders have been increasingly judged by their economic performance, what Xi calls "GDP heroism."[50]

Mao and the CCP did not totally object to capitalism; recent studies reveal that the CCP-government began engaging in international trade well before 1949. The main issue was how to use capitalist forces without succumbing to them.[51] Today the CCP maintains state control of the private economy and firms via state investment, CCP branches, and the ideological work we discuss in this book. It exerts economic control by demanding voting rights to appoint directors (for example, for ByteDance, the parent firm of TikTok, and Sina Weibo, the Chinese counterpart of Twitter) and veto power (for example, with DiDi, the Chinese counterpart of Uber/Lyft). Meanwhile, a majority of companies now have CCP branches within their firms, which allows the CCP to exert political control.[52]

It is understandable that Mao's ideas would have been quite important during his lifetime, but their persistence—indeed, their increased importance—has surprised many Western observers. In the next chapter, we show how and why Maoist principles have become deeply embedded in Chinese society generally, and in private enterprise specifically.

2 Mao's Lasting Influence on China

Because of our special background, our generation is deeply imprinted by Chairman Mao Zedong.
            —Ren Zhengfei, founder and CEO of Huawei

Mao Zedong's way of thinking has a profound and lasting impact on our generation, and it also has many useful insights for my financial work.
            —Tang Shuangning, CEO of China Everbright Group
            (a Fortune Global 500 firm)

THAT MAO ZEDONG WOULD HAVE had a profound influence on China and the Chinese population during his time as a ruler goes without saying, but it is not fully obvious why his influence would endure, especially after Deng Xiaoping's Reform and Opening Up in 1978.

As noted, during the Mao administration (1949–76), Mao's ideas had near-biblical status—virtually every Chinese owned a copy of the little red book (*Quotations of Chairman Mao Zedong*) and could quote from it verbatim. People typically swore oaths based on their allegiance to Mao and his little red book, vowing, for example, "I promise to Chairman Mao I will tell the truth."

While many have discussed the period since Mao, and particularly the period of Hu Jintao and Wen Jiabao (2003–12), as one of greater liberalization and regard the revival of Maoism as surprising, we disagree. There are two interrelated reasons why many Chinese—including those engaged in private enterprise and market development—are still deeply influenced by Maoism. First, Mao inculcated a set of deep-seated personal values in individuals that not only includes the explicit indoctrination of Chinese Communist Party (CCP) members but also more general mechanisms that affected the population at large. Chinese education reinforces Maoist thinking, which resonates with many traditional values. Frugality, for example, is a traditional virtue and Confucian ideal.

Second, the CCP-government intentionally maintains Maoist principles and institutions for governance purposes. Although later leaders adapted Maoism to China's changed circumstances, official CCP ideology has always regarded it as its bedrock. For example, while Deng Xiaoping Theory focuses on economic development—that is, the modernization of agriculture, industry, national defense, and science and technology—and downplays the class struggle lest it become an obstacle for integrating the Chinese economy with the world, it still explicitly maintains these four principles: communism, dictatorship of the proletariat (the political system), leadership of the CCP, and Marxism-Leninism and Mao Zedong Thought.[1]

Mao's ideas are also used to legitimize subsequent leaders' articulated ideologies, such as Jiang Zemin's Three Represents Theory, which, as noted in the introduction, asks the CCP to "represent"—that is, incorporate—groups such as those in advanced production, including private entrepreneurs. This theory is clearly built on Mao's mandate that the CCP serve the people. As private enterprise was growing, it was essential to bring "worthy people from all sectors who are loyal to the motherland and to socialism" into the party.[2]

Similarly, people-oriented concepts—that is, "to take the interests of the people as the starting point and end point of all work and to continuously meet people's multifaceted needs and promote the overall development of people"—are at the center of Hu's Scientific Outlook on Development.[3] Hu's theory additionally focuses on two emerging issues in China: widening income inequality and environmental degradation.

Most notably and prominently, President Xi Jinping has reinvented aspects of Maoism for the present day, frequently citing Mao's teachings, such as the "Two Musts" (CCP members must be careful not to be arrogant or rash and must keep their hardworking spirit) and the "Six Nos" (CCP members should say no to celebrating birthdays luxuriously, gift-giving, formalism, bureaucracy, hedonism, and extravagance). In recent years, China's politics have drawn on a more radical flavor of communism.[4]

In this chapter, we examine how and why the influence of Mao enduringly permeates, on the one hand, the personally held values of many

Chinese and, on the other, China's socialist institutions as a reflection of Mao's legacy.

Will Maoism endure indefinitely? We will venture an answer at the end of this chapter.

IMPRINTING CHAIRMAN MAO ZEDONG'S IDEAS ON THE CHINESE PEOPLE

Communism might be the first thing most Westerners think of in regard to China; many believe that all Chinese are communists.[5] Such perceptions are partially true. As of 2022, the CCP has just over ninety-five million members, which is 6.6 percent of the total Chinese population.[6] These CCP members have undergone an intensive indoctrination process. As we discussed earlier, communist entrepreneurs—those at the nexus of the party and commerce—are an important example of how individuals can bear a Maoist imprint that influences their handling of business operations. But Mao had an enduring influence on Chinese society more generally; his words and ideas are tantamount to universal values in China. Most Chinese have absorbed Mao's teachings even if they have not joined the CCP.

Imprinting theory is a well-known social science concept. The Nobel laureate Konrad Lorenz coined the term after observing that when newly hatched geese are separated from their mother, they follow whomever they see and regard the creature as their "mother." The imprinting perspective has been applied to a number of social science fields, including child development, economics, entrepreneurship, human ecology, neuroscience, psychology, sociology, and business strategy, and a significant amount of evidence bears out that early experiences have a lasting influence on humans as well.[7]

Specifically, imprinting theory suggests that people are uniquely open to environmental stimuli in their "sensitive periods"—that is, such important life stages as early childhood (e.g., three to eight years old) and emerging adulthood (e.g., eighteen to twenty-five years old).[8] During these periods, individuals absorb prominent features of their external environments, including their institutional and ideological characteristics, that shape their cognition, values, and identity.

Research in child development and psychology provides evidence for the persistent influence of individuals' early childhood when they experience a growth spurt. Young children also experience more rapid cognitive development as they begin accumulating retrievable memories. Researchers have found that early childhood is a critical period for skill formation, hippocampal development for memory, linguistic acquisition, and musical training.[9] Likewise, developmental psychology and medical research suggests that environmental influences are especially powerful in early adulthood, when people look to peers, mentors, and their social contexts for behavioral cues to reduce anxiety attendant on the transition from late adolescence. As young people individuate from their parents, they explore and solidify their identities regarding work, romantic relationships, and world views; experience instability in relationships, residence, work, and education; and explore other life-altering possibilities.[10]

Closer to this book's concern with how early experiences influence later business activities, as noted in the introduction, finance scholars have shown that those who were born during or experienced the Great Depression as children became more risk averse when they grew up. Similarly, economists have proposed the "recession adult" hypothesis, suggesting that entering the labor market in a recession made individuals trust more in luck than effort, and support more government redistribution and left-wing parties.[11] In our recent research papers on Chinese business and political leaders, we find a persistent influence of communist indoctrination in their early lives—for example, during the Mao period, when the West was portrayed negatively. Those negative perceptions of (foreign) capitalism and their nationalist mindsets affect their actions in the international marketplace to this day.[12]

There is significant anecdotal evidence on these points as well. Numerous successful Chinese entrepreneurs openly attest to the deep influence Mao and his ideas had on their lives. Ren Zhengfei of Huawei said, "My mentor is Mao Zedong . . . and people of my generation exhibit a deep Maoist imprint."[13] Likewise, Zhang Ruimin (born in 1949)— the founder of Haier, one of the largest home appliance and consumer electronics companies in China and the world—deeply believes in Mao's ideological transformation and has applied it to Haier's mergers and acquisitions.[14] Jack Ma (born in 1964) of Alibaba also is known to have followed the example of Mao's Yan'an Rectification Movement when establishing his authority and Alibaba's culture, claiming, "Through these movements, we will transform employees' ideology to be consistent with our firm's value and expel all those who do not share the same values and sense of mission from our company."[15]

The entrepreneurs we interviewed also exhibited an admiration and deep appreciation of Mao, whether CCP members or not. Interview subjects 8, 18, and 31 are all CCP members, and they all praised Mao—for example, subjects 18 and 31 both volunteered, "I admire Chairman Mao very much." Many entrepreneurs who are not CCP members also spoke highly of Mao and cited his sayings. Subject 5 said, "I would not forget Chairman Mao's words for my whole life. . . . His words encourage us and motivate us when we encounter difficulties." Subject 9 said, "I believe Chairman Mao had great wisdom. . . . Many of his sayings are valuable for us, the next generation, to learn. I think it is still a treasure to give to us as young people, including the next generation. I think it is still a very good opportunity to learn from Chairman Mao's works." And subject 28 said that "Chairman Mao was a very great politician, thinker, and revolutionist."

To uncover the process of how such deep-seated beliefs are created, we first elaborate the indoctrination process that CCP members go through. CCP members are presumably more devout Maoists. But 93.4 percent of Chinese have not gone through this process.[16] So we also describe how Maoism is stamped on the Chinese population more broadly.

Indoctrination: The Process of Becoming a CCP Member

The CCP has strict procedures for indoctrinating new members, which have remained relatively consistent over time. Upon reaching adulthood, individuals can file an application to join the CCP with their local party branch. There is a prescreening process for candidates, which is akin to a background check. The CCP branch vets applicants' political attitudes and their behavior and performance at work or in class, and it may send a formal inquiry to a CCP branch near their parents' residence to ensure family loyalty to communism and the CCP.[17]

If their family background or something else that comes up in the screening process raises concerns—for example, if the applicant's parents were labeled as anti-revolutionists during the Cultural Revolution, they used to work for the Kuomintang (KMT), or they have ancestors who were capitalists or landlords—their application can be sidetracked. Xi's application was rejected around ten times because his father, Xi Zhongxun, was labeled as an anticommunist by Mao during the Cultural Revolution. He was not accepted into the CCP until his father was reviewed and cleared and had regained power.[18] Similarly, Ren could not join the CCP because his father worked for the KMT. Ren's background was cleared when former students of his father helped in his rehabilitation.

Short-listed candidates are assigned to CCP mentors, who are typically more-senior members. Then, candidates have to attend intensive socialization events. These include study sessions where they are taught about the CCP constitution and principles (which they are expected to memorize), learn about the CCP's latest policies, and engage in activities that help disadvantaged groups, such as the elderly. Speeches of senior CCP leaders—for example, General Secretary Xi and members of the standing committee of the CCP Politburo such as Premier Li Keqiang—are studied and candidates are asked to write reflections about them.

Candidates are also asked to watch documentaries that depict how the CCP grew from a handful of people to tens of millions, and that extol influential CCP role models such as Zhang Side, who was born in 1915 and joined the CCP in 1937. He worked as a guard for Mao in 1943 and later responded to Mao's call to engage in agricultural and industrial production in Shaanxi Province. He worked hard and was praised by coworkers. One day he and two coworkers were working in a charcoal kiln that suddenly collapsed. Zhang was able to save the two other workers before he was killed. Mao attended his funeral and wrote his famous "Serve the People" doctrine as his eulogy.

After each event, candidates talk to their CCP mentors and write reports about their impressions. Each quarter, candidates write more comprehensive reports about their experiences. After a certain period of time, typically one year, the CCP branch will hold a meeting to discuss the short-listed candidates and decide which ones will be accepted as probationary members.

Probationary members take an oath stating, "It is my will to join the Chinese Communist Party, uphold the Party's program, observe the provisions of the Party Constitution, fulfill a Party member's duties, carry out the Party's decisions, strictly observe Party discipline, guard Party secrets, be loyal to the Party, work hard, fight for communism throughout my life, be ready at all times to sacrifice my all for the Party and the people, and never betray the Party." However, they are still required to attend socialization events to solidify their communist ideals over the next year. After that, probationary CCP members apply to become full members. Typically, they are accepted. By the time they finish this process, they are well versed in the Maoist principles outlined in the last chapter, Deng Xiaoping Theory, Jiang's Three Represents Theory, Hu's Scientific Outlook on Development, and Xi Jinping Thought on Socialism with Chinese Characteristics for a New Era.[19]

Wholehearted support for and full dedication to the CCP and the government is key. Mao insisted that all candidates fully yield to CCP authority and see him as the central figure. Important sayings repeatedly communicated include "Only the CCP can save China, but the CCP would never thrive without Mao" and "Mao made the Chinese people stand up with dignity."[20]

Even when Mao committed significant errors, such as the Great Leap Forward, people found excuses and scapegoats—for example, saying it was not Mao's fault but his underlings', who made poor decisions and even deceived him. Under Deng's leadership, the CCP provided a very positive evaluation of Mao, claiming that Mao's overall contributions to Chinese society outweighed his errors. To this day, it is frequently said that Mao was 70 percent right and 30 percent wrong, although there is no official statement on this matter.[21] In the newest official history of the CCP, Xi praises Mao extravagantly.[22]

As a result of such intensive indoctrination, individuals form deep-seated, lifelong personal values that reflect a Maoist imprint.[23] This has particularly been the case in recent years, as Xi has asked CCP members to affirm their original intention and admission oath.[24] In a video that was widely circulated ahead of the CCP centenary, Xi and members of the standing committee of the Politburo of the CCP—the highest-ranked political leaders in China—renewed their oaths of allegiance.[25] A photo from this event is in the introduction (see fig. I.1).

Priority of the CCP-Government's Call

I am a "brick" of communism and ready to fit in wherever I am needed by the CCP-government.

—Cui Genliang, founder of the Hengtong Group[26]

Cui was born in 1958 in Zhejiang Province. He joined both the military and the CCP in 1978 and retired from the military in 1981. After that, he became the de facto owner of a chemical fiber factory. At the time, the CCP-government was privatizing many state-owned enterprises by turning them over to their former managers and local political leaders. The annual income of Cui's business was the equivalent of hundreds of thousands of dollars. Later, the party secretary of the local CCP branch asked Cui to take over a bankrupt silk garment factory. Many friends tried to persuade him to stay with the current business, which was financially healthy. Cui responded with a famous quote from Mao: "I am a 'brick' of communism and ready to fit in wherever I am needed by the CCP-government," adding, "Now that the CCP asks me to return, how can I not follow its call?" Cui turned the factory around, earning a profit of about $3 million. He was then asked to do the same for a factory that manufactured latex gloves and that was suffering huge losses. In 1994 he established what became the Hengtong Group, which is now a huge conglomerate, controlling seventy subsidiaries and three publicly traded firms specializing in fiber optics, power grids, new energy, and other industries.[27] Cui says, "The driving force that motivates me to keep moving forward at work is the identity of being a CCP member," and he set Mao's famous quote "Serve the people and devote to the society" as Hengtong's core business mission.

Most entrepreneurs are loyal to the CCP-government, whether they are CCP members or not. For example, subject 2 of our interviewed entrepreneurs claimed, "Although I am not a CCP member, I agree with many ideas of the CCP-government. I believe the external environment is good for the survival and development of enterprises, and the CCP-government's leadership has created a good business environment for entrepreneurs."

For those who had joined the CCP, their pride in membership was palpable. For example, subject 17 said, "I joined the Party when I was in college, and it was a very glorious thing at the time." Subject 5 claimed that the firm he founded helped him lead innovation as a CCP member; subjects 1 and 17 said they established their firms to be role models and vanguards for the people as CCP members; subjects 5, 11, and 18 said they used their enterprises to advance their ideal to "serve the people," a Maoist tagline. Subject 31 actually self-criticized in the interview and said he felt ashamed that he, as a CCP member, did not focus more on party activities in his firm.

It is worth noting that this sort of loyalty diverges strongly from the modern Western tradition. Most Enlightenment philosophers (for example, Thomas Hobbes, John Locke, and Adam Smith) and the founding fathers of the United States (for example, Thomas Jefferson, John Adams, James Madison, and Alexander Hamilton) tended to portray the government as a "necessary evil" or even a Leviathan.[28] Most Westerners are wary of government and seek to constrain it. Indeed, the US federal government was specifically designed to be small but increased its size and scope over time. This is in sharp contrast with China, where at least since Confucius, the government has usually been placed above and beyond the family as an object of loyalty. The Chinese translation of "country" or "nation" is a combination of "state" or "nation" (国) and "home" or "family" (家), with the former coming first.[29] Collectivism has been an ideal in China for millennia, so long as the ruling monarch or dynasty maintains the Mandate of Heaven.[30]

China's statism is buttressed by Confucianism, which emphasizes conformity and obedience to the central authority. For example, Confucius said, "The ancients who wished to preserve the fresh or clear character of the people of the world would first set about ordering their national life. Those who wished to order their national life would first set about regulating their family life. Those who wished to regulate their family life would first set about cultivating their personal life."[31] It is also reflected in the fact that businesspeople and merchants—however rich they are—have traditionally had low social status; to improve it, they pushed their children into government. This phenomenon persists today, even after the reform and opening up. As our own and other scholars' research shows, private entrepreneurs were discriminated against, especially in the early years of the economic transition.[32] Leaving a government job to start a business is called going *down* to the (business) sea (*xiahai*), reflecting a decline in social status. It is not hard to understand why entrepreneurs—particularly those who are also CCP members—are as obedient as they are. In China, financial capital (money) is always subservient to and controlled by political capital (state power). It is unlikely China will reverse that order anytime soon.

The Pervasiveness of Mao's Teachings in Modern China

As noted, the majority of Chinese are not CCP members, and an increasing number of private businesspeople came of age well after the Mao period. Yet these individuals are deeply influenced by Mao and Maoism as well.

Many of our interview subjects who are not CCP members turn to Mao's writings for inspiration and guidance. For example, subject 19 remarked, "Chairman Mao's teaching that 'solutions are always more than questions/difficulties' is what I usually use to encourage my employees." Subject 20 said, "Maoism is very inspiring for business owners as it stimulates a fighting spirit and is a spiritual power. How Chairman Mao stayed hopeful and later guided the CCP's victory is spectacular and useful for enterprising. . . . After you really understand Chairman Mao, you would find that current difficulties are only a small case and you will definitely overcome them."

This sort of influence is basically through cultural osmosis and is more subtle than the formal indoctrination of CCP members, but it is nonetheless deeply ingrained. According to recent surveys at Zhihu, a New York Stock Exchange–traded Chinese company that is similar to Quora or Reddit, Mao is ranked as one of the greatest and most influential people in the long history of China.[33] At the celebration of the CCP centenary on July 1, 2021, film star Jackie Chan said he had wanted to be a CCP member but unfortunately his moral failings left him unqualified. "I can see the greatness of the CCP," he said. "It will deliver what it says, and what it promises in less than 100 years, but only a few decades."[34] At the 2021 Tokyo Olympics, the gold-medal-winning cyclists Bao Shanju and Zhong Tianshi wore Mao badges on the podium (fig. 2.1).[35] To many Chinese, Mao is both a sacred symbol and a good-luck token.[36] On September 9, 2021, the forty-fifth anniversary of his death, many Chinese spontaneously commemorated the death of the "Great Helmsman." As one account put it, "They thought of Chairman Mao's great achievements, thought that without Chairman Mao, there would be no [ruling Chinese] Communist Party [CCP], and we wouldn't have the happy lives we have today."[37]

Other factors that ensure Mao's lasting influence include intergenerational transmission of Mao's ideas, the Chinese educational system, the overlap of Mao's ideas with many major tenets of traditional Chinese philosophy, the sustaining effect of media, and the promotion of red (communist-themed) tourism.

Young people absorb Mao's influence from their parents and other elders. Subject 5 of our interviewed subjects stated, "I will never forget Mao's words about self-reliance and hard work. . . . People of my par-

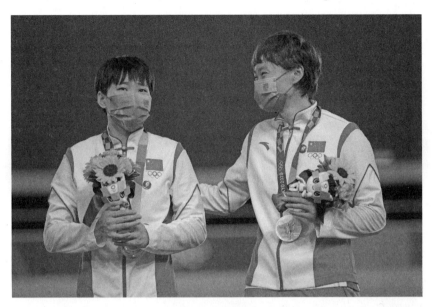

Figure 2.1 Chinese Athletes Wore Mao Badges When Receiving Their Gold Medals during the 2020 Tokyo Olympic Games: Bao Shanju (*left*) and Zhong Tianshi (*right*) "Tokyo Olympics Cycling," Associated Press, August 2, 2021. AP Photo/ Christophe Ena.

ents' generation passed on Chairman Mao's words to our generation, then we will pass them to my son's generation, who in turn will pass them on to our grandson's generation. This is a great legacy we have to pass on to future generations." Subject 9 suggested that "many of Mao's teachings are worthy of the next generation to learn." Likewise, subject 4 declared that "Chairman Mao left a deep influence on entrepreneurs like Lu Guanqiu, Zong Qinghou and their generation, so we are learning from Chairman Mao indirectly from them, regarding military strategic thinking, combat styles, and perseverance."

The Chinese educational system is explicitly committed to the intergenerational transmission of Mao's teachings, with the goal of nurturing "red successors" from early childhood. Starting in kindergarten, children are taught about the CCP's "splendid" history. To celebrate June 1, International Children's Day, kids typically pretend to be Red Army soldiers (fig. 2.2). Some play the role of landlords and other class

Figure 2.2 Communist Education during Elementary School
"China Beijing Red Army Schoolchildren," Associated Press, September 27, 2016.
Imaginechina (photographer: Liu Changlong) via AP Images.

enemies.[38] Political studies courses, in which children learn that many
CCP members martyred themselves in the revolution, are increasingly
important in primary schools. Students must get high scores for their
evaluation and entry into middle school.[39]

Between first and third grade (six to eight years old), pupils are encouraged to join the Red Pioneers to prepare for CCP membership. The
children are immersed in communist doctrine and wear red scarves to
show their commitment. When they enter middle school, they are required to take a course that is generally called "ideological and political studies," which emphasizes personal values and world views that are
consistent with communism and introduces communist institutions.
They are also strongly encouraged to join the Communist Youth League.
Adolescents receive further education about the CCP to strengthen their
communist beliefs.

Political courses are required in high school, which further elaborate on
Marxism, Maoism, China's communist institutions, and new theories by

later leaders. Students must pass exams on these subjects in order to graduate.[40] Similarly, college students must pass political courses to graduate; in many universities, these courses are heavily weighted and substantially affect students' grade point averages (GPAs). Doing poorly in them can undermine future educational and job prospects, since universities and companies typically review applicants' college GPAs. Scholars have found that these courses have a major impact on young people; students who used textbooks that were revised to extol the CCP even more fulsomely are more positive about communism and Maoism than those who used the older textbooks.[41] On September 1, 2021, China announced that there are now 147,000 "educational inspectors" who monitor schools at all levels. One important function of these jobs is to ensure that curriculums adhere to and cohere with communism, from Marxism-Leninism-Maoism to the latest Xi Jinping Thought.[42] Some inspectors found that elite universities are slacking off in their teaching of communist ideology, especially Xi Jinping Thought, and called for stepped-up enforcement.[43]

Almost all the entrepreneurs we interviewed, including many who were not CCP members, could quote Mao's most famous sayings from memory, such as "serve the people," "seeking truth from facts," "there is no right to speak without investigation," "self-reliance and hard work," "fighting the landlords and dividing their farmland," and "study hard, improve every day." For example, subject 28 reflected, "We have all studied Chairman Mao's poem 'Patio Spring Snow,' and Chairman Mao's statement of seeking truth from facts, there is no right to speak without investigation, and uniting everything that can be united. These famous sayings are really too many."

Mao enmeshed many of his thoughts and writings with traditional Chinese culture and was creative in using simple phrases to make his slogans accessible to the majority of Chinese. For example, the popular slogan "serving the people" echoed Confucius, who highlighted societal devotion as a core principle. Subject 14 of our interviewed entrepreneurs said that "Maoism is a continuation of and rooted in Chinese culture. . . . Chairman Mao's serving the people is actually a reinterpretation of our traditional culture in a modern way," and subject 17 suggested that "Chairman Mao really respected traditional culture, learned traditional culture, and then was particularly good at drawing strength from traditional culture."

While some of Mao's ideas clearly overlap with and reinforce traditional Chinese cultural ideas, he actively opposed certain elements at times. During the Cultural Revolution, he encouraged the Chinese people to destroy the Four Olds. These were Old Ideas (ideologies related to feudalism and capitalism), Old Culture (for example, the culture of the ancient period), Old Habits (ancestor worship), and Old Customs (related to entertainment, holidays, and marriage). Like Marx, who labeled religion the opium of the masses, Mao openly struggled against China's traditional religions, declaring that they were superstitions that should be discarded. In this way, Maoist communism became the dominant, indeed the only legitimate, national ideology for China, supplanting ancestor worship, feudalism, Buddhism, Taoism, and Confucianism. During his tenure, particularly in the Cultural Revolution, many temples and monasteries were damaged or even destroyed, and many monks and nuns were persecuted.

Starting in the 1920s, Mao pressed for the liberation of women, describing them as "the other half of the sky," challenging a subordinate status that had existed for thousands of years. He granted women more legal rights, mandated a quota in the CCP leadership, and established a specialized organization—the Women's Federation—within the CCP-government system to promote women's rights. In so doing, he gained the goodwill for himself and the CCP of half the population, although in reality there have been very few women in the upper ranks of the CCP-government or large companies—for example, no woman has served on the Standing Committee of the Politburo of the CCP.[44] Interestingly, the current US president, Joe Biden, used a similar quote, "Women hold up half the sky," when he nominated Kamala Harris as his running mate in August 2020.[45]

Since 2019, the CCP has been holding seminars on the topic of "not forgetting the original intention and keeping in mind the mission" to remind CCP members, including communist entrepreneurs, about the founding mission devised by Mao—to rejuvenate the Chinese nation (that is, make China great again). These activities aim to strengthen communist entrepreneurs' confidence in the CCP's leadership, highlighting the Maoist principles of "serving the people" and "seeking truth from the facts" (to test theory against reality rather than dogmatically sticking to Marxism-Leninism). Many communist entrepreneurs have taken active part in these events—for example, Cui Genliang, whom we discussed earlier, and many other leading entrepreneurs.[46]

Throughout its history, the CCP-government has actively used the media to promote communism in general and Maoism in particular. Almost all movies during Mao's period extolled Mao and the CCP; many described the CCP as the main force fighting the Japanese invasion during the Second World War and portrayed the "old society" before the communist regime as miserable. In the famous movie *Five Heroes of Langya Mountain,* a CCP military squad heroically fights off Japanese troops until just five men are left. When those heroes are cornered on the main peak of Langya Mountain, all five of them jump so as not to be captured. Likewise, another well-known movie, opera, and ballet, *The White-Haired Girl,* focuses on the brutal economic conditions endured by the common people under the KMT. The father of the protagonist Xi'er (the White-Haired Girl) is driven to his death because of the debts he owes a landlord. The landlord then rapes Xi'er, who takes refuge in a cave, where her hair turns white because of malnutrition. Once liberated by CCP troops and armed with Maoism, the people fight the landlord and redistribute his land.

Many recent films and television programs also pick up on these themes. *Beginning of the Great Revival* (literally "the great enterprise of the founding of the CCP"), which was released in 2011, describes the history of the CCP. *Mao Zedong* (2013) and *Teenage Mao Zedong* (2015) describe Mao's early life. *The Zunyi Conference* (2016) details how Mao's decisions saved the CCP, while *The Founding of an Army* (2017) describes how Mao established the CCP troops and later the People's Liberation Army and political institutions. The film *1921* (2021) is about the founding members of the CCP; particularly highlighted is Mao's role in establishing the *Xiangjiang Review,* one of the first CCP publications.[47] In addition to these new films, the CCP-government has been promoting television programs such as *Long March* (debuted in 2001) and *Jingang Mountain* (debuted in 2007), the latter of which describes how Mao led the CCP to establish the first military base.[48] Subject 28 of our interviewed entrepreneurs mentioned that she "often organizes party members to go to watch films" to strengthen "the fortress-like role of the CCP organization and members in business operations."

To celebrate the centenary of the CCP, the CCP-government required that all movie theaters play such "red" films.[49] In Shanghai, the CCP-government organized special screenings and discussions for elementary and middle school students.[50] The CCP-government in Anhui Province organized screenings of red-themed films on the campuses of colleges and universities.[51]

Since 2004, the CCP has promoted red tourism to strengthen revolutionary traditions, enhance patriotism, and otherwise promote and cultivate a unique national spirit. Visits to significant sites from the revolution also boost the economy of those regions, some of them remote. Around a quarter of Chinese tourists now visit CCP revolutionary areas, with total revenues exceeding $40 billion.[52] During the 2021 Chinese Labor Day, red tourist sites accommodated visits from millions of Chinese.[53] During the centenary celebration of the CCP, many local CCP-governments opened historical sites. The Shanghai government, for example, promoted visits to the meeting sites of the CCP's first, second, and fourth national congresses. Subject 20 of our interviewed entrepreneurs said, "Although I am not a CCP member, I did visit red tourist sites such as Jingang Mountain and Yan'an. . . . The spirit of Jingang Mountain should be enlightening to entrepreneurs and many people, as it concerns a fighting spirit and can give people spiritual power." She believed that "these are critical for enterprises, on teambuilding, on winning, and confidence."

THE PERSISTENCE OF MAO'S IMPRINT IN SOCIALIST INSTITUTIONS IN CHINA

Mao also implanted his values and ideas in China's communist institutions, which shape private enterprises, entrepreneurs, and businesses in their turn. Despite extensive economic reforms by Deng and succeeding leaders, the socialist institutions, per Mao's design, have been consistently maintained by the CCP-government as preconditions for any changes or potential liberalizations.

Political leaders—particularly the founders of regimes—shape institutions that last for decades or even centuries, and Mao was no exception.[54] As noted earlier, King Louis XIV imprinted France with a centralized state, which survived the French Revolution and the end of the absolute monarchy.[55] George Washington established the unwritten rule of a two-term limit for US presidents until it was broken by Franklin Delano Roosevelt (and written into the US Constitution as the Twenty-Second Amendment in 1951).[56] Vladimir Lenin imprinted the Soviet Union with one-party control by the Bolsheviks and the principle of democratic centralism.[57] Nasserism outlived Egypt's Gamal Abdel Nasser, who died in 1970, and led to the assassination of his successor,

Anwar Sadat, in 1981, in part because his efforts to negotiate peace with Israel ran against the grain of pan-Arabism.[58]

Mao's designs have been consistently maintained by the CCP-government, acting as a set of guardrails as it undertakes economic reforms.[59]

Maintaining the Maoist Center While Pursuing Economic Reforms

It is well known that after Mao's death, Deng implemented reform and opening-up policies that have guided the CCP-government in developing the country's economy since the late 1970s. What is less known is that this was part of a set of reforms that is summarized as one central focus and two fundamental points. The one central focus is shifting the core priority from the revolutionary class struggle that defined the revolutionary years and the Mao regime to economic construction and development. The first "fundamental point" that supports that central focus is the need to hold to four basic political principles—namely, maintaining socialist institutions, the dictatorship of the proletariat, communist governance (party), and Marxism-Leninism-Maoism (ideology). The second point is reform and opening up.

Thus, while on the surface, China's economic institutions may look similar to those of capitalist countries, what is unchanging and frequently overlooked are the facts that the four basic political principles are still in effect and that state ownership under CCP control is still widespread. The CCP remains at the center of all reforms. In fact, since the Hu Jintao administration (2003–12), and especially after the 2008 financial crisis, state ownership has been on the rise.

Thus, the CCP changed China's "means of production" in an incremental, stepwise fashion, without fundamentally altering its political identity. Some state-owned enterprises were privatized, and individuals were encouraged to pursue the profit motive within a market-oriented economy. Class struggle was downplayed, as it was seen as an obstacle to globalization.[60] Merit-based pay was not only allowed but emphasized. But the liberalization of the economy did not equal the liberalization of Chinese society, as reflected in Deng's comments during his famous 1992 Southern Tour: "Planned economy does not equal socialism and market economy does not equal capitalism. Socialism can have market mechanisms as well, and government planning and market are both economic means." Class struggle was not necessary for socialism, Deng said, claiming that "Marx said that the theory of class struggle is not his invention, the real invention is the theory of the dictatorship of the proletariat."[61] That is, the state apparatus and not the market is ultimately in control. Planning and markets can be seen as different tools in service of this more fundamental goal.

Comparisons between the Soviet Union and China

The Soviet Union adopted a completely different approach to reform under Mikhail Gorbachev, who tried to reform its political and economic systems simultaneously with perestroika (literally "restructuring") and glasnost (literally "openness" and "transparency"). Perestroika was initiated in 1987 to fundamentally transform the planned Soviet economy. In the words of state planners, the Soviet Union "needs to be built anew, not reformed."[62] Subsidies to state-owned firms were eliminated and the economy was opened to foreign competition, investment, and trade. Many could not adjust and went bankrupt. On January 1, 1990, Gorbachev adopted the 500 Day Program, which was designed to institute a full market economy by March 14, 1992. Ironically, the program was ended by the state collapse on December 26, 1991.

Simultaneously, the glasnost program allowed freedom of speech, and dissidents began to speak up about the crimes and failures of the Bolsheviks. Critiques of communism became popular within universities and in the media.[63]

The indelible lesson the CCP learned from the USSR's collapse was the overwhelming importance of having an overarching ideology and theory of governance to guide reform. As the "world's oldest living Bolshevik" in the Tony award–winning play *Angels in America, Part 2: Perestroika* put it: "How are we to proceed without Theory? What system of thought have these reformers to present to this mad swirling planetary disorganization, to the in-evident welter of fact, event, phenomenon, calamity? . . . Show me the words that will reorder the world, or else keep silent. If the snake sheds his skin before a new skin is ready, naked he will be in the world, prey to the forces of chaos. Without his skin he will be dismantled, lose coherence, and die."[64] While a work of fiction, the diagnosis of the USSR's situation under perestroika and glasnost is quite apt.

On March 14, 1990, Gorbachev revised the Soviet constitution. The statement in Article 6 that described the Bolsheviks as the "leading and guiding force of the Soviet society," "the vanguard of the working people in their struggle to strengthen and develop the socialist system and . . . the leading core of all organizations of the working people, both public and state," was deleted. Instead, the new constitution stipulated that "the Communist Party of the Soviet Union, other political parties as well as labor, youth and other public organizations and mass movements, through their representatives elected to the Councils of People's Deputies and in other forms participate in the policy-making of the Soviet state, in the management of state and public affairs."[65]

Deng and his successors understood the importance of using the CCP and Mao to provide the guiding theory to reform, so as to not suffer the problems that the Soviet Union faced. Extending this idea, more recently, some scholars have suggested that China's reforms were in fact a "grand strategy" for global dominance that uses Leninist one-party control to achieve its goal.[66] In contrast, the Soviet Union lacked such a focus for its goals. Gorbachev's approach to reform was so radical that he lost the confidence of other senior leaders, and in 1991 a number of more hardline leaders even attempted a coup d'état.

Overall, the CCP tightly maintained its overarching framework based on Mao's ideas and its own position as the only legitimate ruling party and focused on only revising the economic system in a gradual way, albeit with intense internal debate. Under Deng, reform was more gradual and focused on smaller-scale trial-and-error experiments, such that the CCP could roll back any policies that proved detrimental to the economy or threatened the CCP's rule.[67] For example, in May 1984, Deng and other Chinese leaders introduced a dual-price system for most products, in which there was a within-plan price determined by the government and an outside-plan price determined by supply and demand. The idea was to gradually transform the planned economy into a market-oriented one. However, people with connections to the pricing authorities were able to obtain commodities at the low, within-plan price and then sell them at market prices. To deal with the corruption, the CCP-government considered abolishing the system. However, the information was leaked, and Chinese residents rushed to purchase everything they could find at the lower prices, creating hyperinflation, so the CCP-government quickly backed off.

As opposed to the sweeping, nationwide reforms that Gorbachev undertook, China experimented with economic reforms in several cities, establishing the now well-known special economic zones in May 1980—

Shantou, Shenzhen, Xiamen, and Zhuhai. As the initial success strength-ened Chinese leaders' confidence, the reforms were gradually implemented in other regions. Also avoided were words like "private" that were anathema in Mao's time; the CCP introduced collective-owned enter-prises as an intermediate stage between state-owned and fully privatized enterprises.[68] Many essentially private firms, including Huawei, were initially registered as collective-owned firms. Private firms did not gain full legal status until 1992. Private ownership continued to be rare for some time after that.

China's incrementalism while retaining political continuity dramati-cally departed from the strategy of the Soviet Union, which had a tra-dition of radically negating the contributions of prior political leaders—a form of what the CCP labels "historical nihilism," which negates enti-ties such as the party, leaders, national heroes, and other aspects of CCP-approved history. Nikita Khrushchev's famous Secret Speech—"On the Cult of Personality and Its Consequences"—during the Twentieth Congress of the Communist Party of the Soviet Union in 1956 funda-mentally criticized Joseph Stalin, who had died three years earlier. Some scholars believe that this event sowed the seeds for Soviet collapse, as it shaped the values of Soviet leaders of Gorbachev's generation.[69] When Khrushchev was forced to step down in a coup led by Leonid Brezhnev, many of his reforms were reversed and Khrushchev was criticized.

The CCP leaders understood the potentially detrimental consequences of negating Mao. In the official assessment following his death, they maintained that Mao's contributions well exceeded his faults; his re-mains were embalmed and placed on display in Beijing for Chinese citizens to pay tribute to.[70] As subject 6 of our surveyed entrepreneurs put it, "It initially looked like our reform and opening up wanted to remove Maoism, only to have found that socialism could not survive without Maoism. Maoism is the soul of the CCP and the entire Chi-nese nation. The reform and opening up just reshaped Maoism."

The Rhetorical Strategy of the Economic Reform

Holding on to the fundamental principle of political control of the CCP, the Chinese government achieved economic reform through a care-ful rhetorical strategy that gradually legitimized the concepts of private ownership, entrepreneurship, and a market economy. There was intense internal debate about this; hardcore Maoists had to be brought along slowly as new elements were incorporated into the ideology in a way that was still consistent with it.[71] As Deng put it in his well-known saying on taking step-by-step reform, it was like "crossing the river [gradually] by feeling for stones [on the riverbed]."[72]

Specifically, "capitalism" (*ziben zhuyi*, 资本主义) and related words such as "market economy" (*shichang jingji*, 市场经济) were avoided at first. Zhao Ziyang, the CCP's secretary general, admitted that "we call it a commodity economy rather than a market economy to avoid pushback from conservative CCP members, but they are essentially the same."[73] The CCP also redefined entrepreneurs as diligent and conscious individuals who create wealth with their hard work and steadfast enterprises, whose business is to serve the people. As our prior research shows, in its statements and policies the government was careful to connect entrepreneurship to traditional Chinese culture, emphasizing the role of Confucian entrepreneurs: lofty and wealthy individuals who are benevolent, trustworthy, polite, wise, and faithful.[74] To this day, some entrepreneurial enterprises are still referred to as people-owned enterprises (*minying qiye*, 民营企业) rather than privately owned enterprises (*siying qiye*, 私营企业).[75] But in fact the CCP was creating a whole new way of operating the economy within a socialist framework. As Su Shaozi, a Marxist philosopher, put it in 1984, "There are no Marxist quotes for what we are doing now."[76]

Relatedly, the Chinese government tried to establish that entrepreneurs running Chinese private businesses are nothing like capitalists.[77] Before the early 2000s, the word "capitalist" was mostly used to refer to foreign investors, financiers, speculators, and arbitrageurs rather than domestic entrepreneurs. Those in the former set were portrayed as preying on the economy by maneuvering financial markets or exploiting cheap labor, while the latter were said to be productively developing the Chinese economy. In that spirit, subject 1 of our interviewed entrepreneurs noted that "not all capitalists are entrepreneurs. An entrepreneur has to be socially responsible and assume social duties." Similarly, subject 27 said, "So an entrepreneur or the real leader of an enterprise must be a person who can contribute to society . . . [such as to] make the country stable, make the environment safe, share worries for the country, solve the employment issue for the population, and solve the troubles of the family." Subject 31 stated, "I think entrepreneurs should not be called 'boss.' While the rival party KMT defeated by the CCP nurtured a lot of bosses and capitalists, entrepreneurs focus on the collective and the idea of entrepreneurs is close to the CCP."

WILL MAOISM ENDURE IN CHINA?

A natural question arising from our research is whether Maoism will endure as China's guiding ideology. Imprinting theory suggests that while imprints may be persistent, they need not be permanent.[78] But while the explicitly articulated focus on Maoism may wax and wane, it seems to us that the deep influence of Maoism at the center of Chinese politics and the country's economy will likely continue well into the future. The establishment of a guiding ideology, core institutions, and a permeating socialization mechanism, all of which reinforce each other, has ensured that Mao's grip on China is quite strong. In fact, it is growing in importance, as Xi is able to build on Mao's deep foundation to further secure his own position.

The CCP-government has strengthened its focus on Mao, increasingly incorporating Maoist rhetoric into its statements about domestic issues and foreign affairs.[79] Xi frequently cites Mao in his speeches and admonishes the CCP to learn from Mao Zedong Thought and Maoism.[80] During his centenary speech, Xi echoed Mao's use of words such as "exploitation," "imperialism," "struggle," and "oppression"; attacked the West for trying to separate the CCP from Chinese people; warned it not to bully China; and denigrated those who criticize China's institutions. He even quoted a sentence from one of Mao's most famous poems, that "there will be sacrifices because there is too much lofty ambition [of the CCP], and we [the CCP] dare to overturn the old world [referring to the Chinese society that was economically laggard and bullied by foreign powers] and change into a new look."[81]

Reinforcing the connection, Xi imitates Mao's gestures and visits places that commemorate him. During the centenary celebration, Xi wore a Chinese tunic suit—Mao's favorite style of dress for formal occasions (fig. 2.3).[82] His predecessors Jiang Zemin and Hu Jintao both wore Western suits with neckties at prior decennary celebrations. Like Mao, Xi delivered his speech in Tiananmen Square rather than in the Grand Hall of the People as his predecessors did. Like Mao, Xi has added his thoughts to the CCP constitution, allows others to call him

Figure 2.3 Xi Jinping Delivers the CCP Centenary Speech, Imitating Chairman Mao in Dress and Posture
"China-Beijing-CPC Centenary-Grand Gathering-Xi Jinping (CN)," Getty Images, July 1, 2021. Ju Peng/Xinhua News Agency via Getty Images.

"helmsman" (a term that was specifically used to refer to Mao), has promoted a cult of personality, and has removed presidential term limits from the constitution so that he—like Mao—can be a lifelong president. In addition, Xi has cracked down on freedom of speech and intensified state control of the economy and civil society.[83] In 2021 he revitalized Mao's "common prosperity" slogan and committed to narrowing income and consumption gaps.[84]

Additionally, as the Chinese economy has grown, the country's government and people are increasingly emulating Mao's assertiveness on the international stage.[85] During the Alaska summit in March 2021, China's top diplomat, Yang Jiechi, told his US counterpart that the United States did "not have the qualification . . . to speak to China from a position of strength."[86] This was celebrated online by Chinese commentators as an example of China "standing up" to imperialists. As tensions with the West increase, there has been a backlash against public intellectuals who espoused Western, liberal ideas such as democracy, rule of law, and civil society in the early 2000s. Such thinkers are now denigrated for "eating the CCP's meals, but smashing the CCP's pot."[87]

Relatedly, young people in China are increasingly blaming capitalism for China's emerging social problems, such as its widening wealth gap, unaffordable housing, dwindling job opportunities, and culture of overwork. Mao's analysis based on class has new relevance.[88] Young bloggers frequently reference the *Selected Works of Mao Zedong,* which are ranked highly on Douban, a Chinese social media service platform on books, film, and other media.[89] There is even a neo-Maoist movement that is implicitly supported by the CCP.[90] Interestingly, Maoism is also applied to issues in foreign countries; racial problems in the United States are frequently analyzed as class contradictions.[91]

With all these efforts—ideological imprinting of individuals, intergenerational transmission, pervasive education, institutional maintenance of the Maoist imprint, and movements and policies to revive Maoism, it is clear that Maoism will be with us for quite some time.

For all that, the West lacks an appreciation of Maoism's lasting strength. That lacuna is worrying. In Mao's words, borrowed from Sun Tzu, one should never fight an unprepared war. In part II, we elaborate on Mao's ideological and military principles and connect them to the business practices of Chinese entrepreneurs and private enterprises.

II MAO'S IDEOLOGICAL AND MILITARY PRINCIPLES AND PRIVATE ENTERPRISE

Our principle of development must be self-reliance.

Everything should follow the principle of frugality.

Members of the Chinese Communist party [CCP] should be ready to sacrifice themselves for the great cause.

A single spark can start a prairie fire.

—Mao Zedong

3 Nationalism and Internationalization

Many Chinese entrepreneurs have a strong sense of nationalism, which has impeded their internationalization.

—Sina Finance report, March 1, 2007

ZONG QINGHOU, founder of the Chinese beverage giant Wahaha, was born into a poor family in 1945. He dropped out of middle school because of poverty and later participated in the send-down movement, in which millions of mostly young Chinese were sent to rural areas.[1] Zong spent fifteen years on a desolate farm near the city of Zhoushan that was originally a labor camp known as the "Siberia of Zhoushan." The daily work on that farm was grueling, such as digging ditches and repairing dams or moving soil and rocks.[2] In his spare time, Zong read the *Selected Works of Mao Zedong* and other communist writings such as *How the Steel Was Tempered*, by Soviet writer Nikolai Ostrovsky, which was one of the most popular books in China at the time. While food was in short supply, he claimed that he absorbed unlimited nutrition from Mao's writings.

After Mao's death and the end of the send-down movement, Zong returned to his hometown and worked as a clerk in a state-owned food and grocery shop. The shop was almost bankrupt, so the government decided to privatize it. In 1987 Zong won the bid to take it over. To increase profitability, he realized that the shop needed to develop its own brand; health products for children seemed a likely prospect. Young children are frequently picky eaters, which worries their parents. Zong branded his nutritional beverage Wahaha—which literally means "children [*wa*, 娃] are laughing [*haha*, 哈哈, an onomatopoeia for laughter]."

By 1997, Wahaha had become one of the largest beverage producers in China, earning a profit of $300 million on revenues of $1.6 billion. Zong had made a point of raising money domestically. So, to further develop his business, he pushed for an initial public offering (IPO) in 1992. But the Chinese stock market was still in its infancy—it had only been established in December 1990—and given the CCP-government's gradualist approach, very few firms could be listed. So, the IPO failed.

Even then, Zong was wary of foreign investors. But after being persuaded by government leaders, he decided to form a partnership with the French conglomerate Danone, one of the largest food companies in the world. Zong chose Danone because, as he described it, the company was less condescending than other foreign brands, showed respect for its Chinese partners, and seldom interfered in their operations. Even so, he insisted that he be the chairman of the joint venture. Whenever he attended meetings in Paris, his French partners would raise the Chinese flag and play the Chinese national anthem. Zong would weep with pride.

But the honeymoon did not last long. Zong learned that Danone was not sharing important food technologies with Wahaha and that it had secretly invested in its competitor Robust (Wahaha had also made investments in rival firms without telling Danone). A conflict exploded between the two parties. On April 3, 2007, Zong accused Danone of entrapping Wahaha and trying to take it over, and of refusing to support the projects it was undertaking in response to the CCP-government's development program for Western China. Ye Honghan—CEO of Jianlibao, another gigantic soft-drink producer in China—praised Zong for his effort in protecting the Chinese brand and called for legislation against foreign monopolists.

When Danone pressured Wahaha to sell some of its ventures, Zong borrowed Mao Zedong's assertion that the Chinese people had "stood up." "China and the Chinese people have our dignity and are not subject to your threats and intimidation," he declared. Then he labeled Danone a foreign monopolist, claiming that it controlled five of the ten largest soft-drink producers in China. Zong also noted that Danone had sued another giant soft-drink producer, Bright Foods, in 2006, and so was able to increase its market share at a low price, portraying Danone as a predatory invader. Their nationalist feelings aroused, many internet users commented at the time that local Chinese brands were in a most dangerous time—echoing a line in the Chinese national anthem, "The Chinese nation is at its most dangerous time." After intervention by the French and Chinese presidents Nicolas Sarkozy and Hu Jintao, Wahaha and Danone sought a more peaceful solution to their disputes. Finally, Wahaha completely bought back Danone's shares.[3]

Many other Chinese entrepreneurs espouse a passionate nationalism in their business activities and resist foreign intervention. In his satire *Embracing Globalization but Don't Forget Our Nation*, Yin Mingshan, the founder of the multibillion-dollar motorcycle and automobile company the Lifan Group in Chongqing, urged Chinese entrepreneurs to be wary of so-called globalization. Yin held Mao's quote that "foreigners are unreliable, and we have to rely on ourselves" as his motto.[4] Chinese entrepreneurs do not benefit from globalization, he said, since they have to pay huge premiums for natural resources and technologies controlled by other countries. He also claimed that European countries, Japan, and the United States prohibit the export of technology to China and keep all but a very small portion of profits from international joint ventures for themselves. He concluded by calling for the preservation of national resources, the development of national technologies and brands, and the revitalization of national industry to carry forward China's national culture.[5] Yin said that he had declined many international cooperation opportunities, turning away the foreign investment banks that could have expedited the Lifan Group's IPO.[6] In 2019, when Yin and the Lifan Group were caught in a debt crisis, he was reluctant to ask foreign banks for help.[7]

Since the collapse of the Soviet Union in the early 1990s and the end of the Cold War, the world has become increasingly globalized, and most believe that China has been one of the biggest economic winners.[8] But many Chinese businesspeople—especially loyal disciples of Mao like Zong and Yin—object to internationalization, despite the fact that it serves their economic interests. Why do they resist it?

As Zong said and most Chinese believe, under Mao, China "stood up" as an independent nation instead of bowing to the West as it had following the Opium Wars.[9] Xi Jinping echoed Mao's rhetoric during the centenary speech of the CCP, saying, "The Chinese Communist Party and the Chinese people solemnly declare to the world with brave and tenacious struggle that the Chinese people have 'stood up' and the era of the Chinese nation being slaughtered and bullied is forever gone."[10]

Before the founding of the People's Republic of China in 1949, Mao said, the Chinese population was like a pan of loose sand. After, through his leadership, they became an organized populace. In this chapter, we describe Mao's experience and the political environments that shaped him and China, plotting trends in nationalist discourse since 1949 from *People's Daily* articles and other official newspapers published by regional governments in China.

Imbued with these ideas as they are, it is no wonder that some communist entrepreneurs are less likely to cooperate with foreign capitalists and, further, that others feel differently. For example, Alibaba's Jack Ma has actively pursued international collaborations. What accounts for these differences? Two factors are in play and sometimes in conflict—the nationalist mindset and the obligation to respond to the CCP-government's call. At the end of the chapter, we will discuss the escalating US-China trade tensions and potential decoupling of the two countries, as well as deglobalization processes more generally.

Throughout the chapter, we combine rich quantitative and qualitative data from various sources to illustrate our points. Details of the data and sampling processes are provided in the methodological appendix. We describe our statistical analyses in detail in our endnotes.

THE ORIGINS OF CHINESE NATIONALISM AS AN IDEOLOGICAL PRINCIPLE

A cornerstone ideological principle of Maoism is nationalism, which is further reflected in Mao's ideas about autonomy, independence, and self-reliance. Specifically, Mao stated that "for a country's communist party to achieve victory in revolution and construction, it must be based on its own country, its own reality, and its own revolutionary forces."[11] Mao further claimed that "self-reliance should be our key approach," and "we Chinese people have the determination of realizing our splendid times with self-reliance."[12] He even praised Kuomintang leader Chiang Kai-shek for his nationalism when Chiang refused Indian prime minister Jawaharlal Nehru's invitation to jointly attack the CCP in the Sino-Indian War in 1962. Chiang suspected that India would grab all the disputed territories between China and India, and like Mao, he thought that they were part of China and so should stay within China's jurisdiction.[13]

The political environment of Mao's early life shaped his nationalist focus. For most of human history, China had been one of the most powerful nations in the world; for eighteen centuries, both China's gross domestic product and its population were the largest in the world.[14] China was responsible for many important inventions, such as paper, printing, and gunpowder. During the Ming dynasty, China sent an extravagant fleet to travel to South and Southeast Asia, the Arabian Peninsula, and East Africa to show off its wealth and military strength. These treasure voyages occurred seven times between 1405 and 1433. They covered more than seventy thousand nautical miles, reflected advanced shipbuilding technology, and predated the European Age of Discovery by about seventy years.

For centuries, China had built and maintained an international system based on tribute—the name of China in Chinese is literally the "Central Kingdom"; weaker neighbors, essentially vassal states, such as Korea and Vietnam paid tribute, and the Chinese conferred legitimacy on their rulers and gave them generous gifts in return.

Emperor Kangxi (1654–1722) of the Qing dynasty (China's last imperial dynasty) was very interested in Western culture and was proficient in astronomy, mathematics, physics, and medicine. But at the same time, he dismissed Western knowledge as "magical" and "small tricks," fearing that if knowledge of Western science and technology became widespread in China, his rule would be undermined and possibly overturned. Instead, Chinese intellectuals continued their study of Confucian classics, as they had for over one thousand years. Thanks to the seclusion policy that China had followed since the fourteenth century, it was outpaced by the West and failed to experience the first Industrial Revolution.

But the 1839 Opium War and the "century of humiliation" that followed were a wake-up call that could not be ignored. Ignorant of the West, many Chinese complacently assumed they were superior. But the United Kingdom defeated China with a military that was a tenth the size of China's, suffering only sixty-nine casualties, while China lost more than four thousand soldiers. China was forced to sign treaties that ceded Hong Kong, opened "treaty ports" for bilateral trade, and paid war reparations to the United Kingdom.

After China gave up Hong Kong, the Portuguese demanded that it cede Macao, occupying it as a de facto colony in 1849 and formally obtaining control in 1887. China also ceded territories of around one million square

miles to Russia and lost Taiwan to Japan after being defeated in the First
Sino-Japanese War (1894–95). Mongolia also became an independent
country. During the Second World War, Japan occupied China's northeast
and established a puppet regime (the State of Manchuria) nominally led
by the former emperor of the Qing dynasty.

Mao's dream was that China would become a great country again
under his leadership, reviving its splendid history.[15] He further realized
that nationalism could be used to mobilize the popular masses, uniting
peasants in China's vast rural areas to rise up against the Kuomintang.
Indeed, the CCP was to some extent born in a nationalist environment:
May 4, 1919, saw a massive student protest against the government after
the loss of Qingdao to Japan in the Treaty of Versailles. Two years later,
the CCP was established by Chen Duxiu, the editor of the New Youth (La
Jeunesse).[16] Mao was deeply influenced by the magazine and systematically elaborated the importance of national struggle and nationalism in his
speeches and writings. The pronounced power differential between China
and the Western powers and the threat that China would be colonized or
broken up spurred his focus on autonomy and a spirit of independence.

Mao's nationalism fed his wariness of Soviet intervention and infil-
tration after the foundation of the communist regime. He visited Joseph
Stalin in 1949–50 to celebrate Stalin's birthday with other communist
leaders and solidify relations between the newly founded People's Re-
public of China and the USSR. The main points of contention between
Mao and Stalin were the Soviet military ports in China's Dalian and
Lushun, and the Soviet troops garrisoned along the railroad that tsarist
Russia had built in China (the Chinese Eastern Railway).

Mao insisted that these outposts violated China's sovereignty, while
Stalin wanted to maintain Soviet interests in China and refused to back
down, condescendingly refusing other meetings.[17] Unsatisfied with Stalin's response, Mao refused to leave Moscow. Western media reported
that Mao had been detained, and the UK government approached China
to potentially establish relations. At the same time, the United States indicated it would not prevent communist troops from occupying Taiwan. In public remarks, US secretary of state Dean Acheson reminded
the Chinese people that Russia had seized vast territories from China
and supported Mongolia's independence.[18] Angry at these reports and
fearing that China might ally with the West, Stalin finally agreed to
Mao's requests in order to establish the Sino-Soviet alliance.[19]

Nonetheless, Mao held a grudge against Stalin for his support of Mongolian independence and the East Turkestan independence movement in Xinjiang, among other things. Mao later criticized Nikita Khrushchev for his Secret Speech, which negated Stalin's contributions and exposed his crimes. But he applauded his critique of Stalin's mistakes in regard to China, remarking that Khrushchev "opened the lid [that covers many secrets] and made a mess."[20]

The Soviet Union's continuing encroachments on the CCP's autonomy and China's sovereignty fired up Mao's nationalism. In 1958 Mao sought to obtain technologies for nuclear weapons and nuclear submarines from the Soviet Union. In return, the Soviet Union proposed establishing a long-wave radio station on China's Hainan Island and, beyond that, building a united fleet under Soviet command.

Furthermore, the Soviet Union did not support Mao's Great Leap Forward. Khrushchev based his critique on the disasters in Ukraine and Kazakhstan during Stalin's tenure; agricultural collectivization had led to famine in those two Soviet republics, and between 1932 and 1933 millions of people in those regions were starved to death. Khrushchev had actually been working in Ukraine at the time and witnessed the tragedy.[21] And when it came to the United States, Mao was more of a hardline revolutionist, while Khrushchev sought détente. Because of these conflicts, the two largest communist countries split up, isolating China from both the Soviets and the West, reinforcing Mao's rhetoric about self-reliance.[22]

NATIONALISM, INDOCTRINATED

The importance of Chinese sovereignty was a mantra for CCP recruits. Many of Mao's statements on antiforeignism, self-reliance, and autonomy are still foundational in contemporary Chinese discourse. Mao's saying that "imperial countries and anti-revolutionists are all paper tigers" has even worked itself into the English language as an idiom. *Webster's* defines "paper tiger" as "one that is outwardly powerful or dangerous but inwardly weak or ineffectual."[23]

Mao's *Quotations* and *Selected Works* are filled with nationalist adages. For example, "We should concentrate on self-reliance . . . and we believe we can organize ourselves to win the battles against anti-revolutionaries in China and abroad," and "We Chinese people should have the determination to realize our splendid past and return to the prominent position in the world of nations all by ourselves." Although China needed foreign aid during his administration, Mao insisted, "We shall never rely on help from others, which is unreliable. . . . We must depend on our own effort."[24]

A popular political slogan was, "The liberation and independence of China require a spirit of self-reliance." As noted, almost all the communist entrepreneurs we interviewed mentioned the importance of independence, autonomy, or self-reliance. Maoism typically portrays capitalists as exploitative, mercenary, and ruthless and the West as an abyss of suffering and misery. Collaborating with them is seen as an intolerable betrayal of Maoism.

To show how nationalist rhetoric evolved in China, we draw on a database of official newspaper articles (described more in the methodological appendix) and track the use of nationalist keywords over time. Since the Chinese media is strictly controlled, official newspapers are the way the government communicates with the masses and so can be seen to reflect its mindset.[25] Mao often used them to disseminate his ideas and principles. For example, he systematically elaborated the principles of autonomy, independence, and self-reliance in speeches delivered on January 10 and August 13, 1945, which were subsequently published in the official newspaper *Liberation Daily* (Shanghai). In the first, Mao said, "We have to advocate self-reliance. We hope to have foreign aid, but cannot rely on it. We must rely on our own efforts and the creativity of all military and civilians." Doubling down in the next speech, he said, "Basing our policy on our own strength is called self-reliance. . . . We emphasize self-reliance, and we hope to have foreign aid but cannot rely on it."[26] In an interview with the US journalist Anna Louise Strong on August 6, 1946, Mao delivered his now famous dictum that "all reactionaries are paper tigers," elaborating that "on appearance, they are terrifying, but in reality they are not so powerful."[27]

Keywords are often tracked in social science research to capture the tenor of public discourse and opinion.[28] To assemble a complete list of terms related to nationalism, we followed established scientific method by reading existing studies and developing an initial list. We then asked three experts in this area to validate it. Our final list consisted of "independence and autonomy" (独立自主), "self-reliance" (自力更生), "imperialism" (帝国主义, which was often used to denigrate the Western powers),

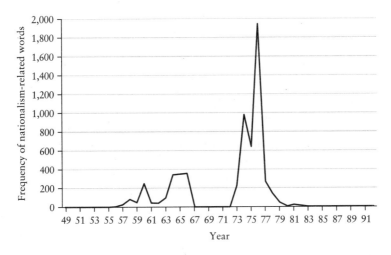

Figure 3.1 Frequency of Keywords Related to Nationalism in Official Newspaper Headlines (1949–1991)
Data sources: Official daily newspapers of each province's CCP committee. During the first phase of the Cultural Revolution (1966–72), many provincial dailies were sabotaged and some of them suspended publication. See Hu, Rennan, "Behind the Scenes of the Red Guard Newspaper," https://new.qq.com/omn /20201211/20201211A05BJW00.html [retrieved on August 27, 2021].

"revisionism" (修正主义, which was typically used to denigrate the Soviet Union and its satellite states), and "paper tiger" (纸老虎).[29]

We tracked the time trend of nationalism-related keywords (fig. 3.1). When we compared individual provinces we also found that, interestingly, Shanghai exhibits the most intense nationalist sentiment, perhaps because it was the birthplace of the CCP and the most international Chinese city. Many of Mao's ideas—such as the paper tiger metaphor— were first published in Shanghai's *Liberation Daily*. Between 1973 and 1976, when Mao died, nationalist rhetoric was heightened. Mao had been eager to export revolution to colonial countries, and many of his speeches and articles urged communists in Africa, Latin America, and the Middle East to fight for their independence. The small jump between 1957 and 1959 was driven by the strong rhetoric of self-reliance that accompanied the Great Leap Forward.

Following Mao's focus on ideas of independence and self-reliance, many provinces tended to report on how different firms followed this principle. For example, the *Beijing Daily* published a report under the headline "Relying on the Masses to Create a Path—Beijing Chemical Experimental Plant Is Developing Vigorously under the Guidance of the Policy of Independence and Self-Reliance" on October 8, 1974. Similarly, the *Fujian Daily* published an article titled "Longyan Radio Factory Adheres to the Policy of Independence and Self-Reliance and Manufactures Automatic Control High-Voltage Silicon Rectifier" on January 13, 1975.

Denigrations of imperialism, use of the paper tiger metaphor, and denouncements of revisionism increased between 1959 and 1966, thanks to Mao and Khrushchev's disagreements about agricultural collectivization and how to deal with the West. The *People's Daily* reported on "the privileged class of the Soviet Union and the Khrushchev revisionist clique" on July 14, 1964, calling Khrushchev a revisionist and traitor to communism. On August 18, 1966, the *People's Daily* wrote that "both the United States [imperialism] and Soviet Union [revisionism] are paper tigers, and Albanian comrades and African friends praise Chairman Mao's wise judgment on paper tigers."

Denouncements of revisionism were more frequent between 1973 and 1976, when Mao released Deng Xiaoping and allowed him to regain a leadership position, as Deng was often labeled as a "revisionist" who did not follow orthodox Maoism but wanted to develop the economy and imitate the West, as Khrushchev was said to do. Mao continued to worry that Deng would negate his legacy, and he pushed Deng out of power in 1976. In response, many government dailies piled on. A headline in the *Hebei Daily* on June 17, 1976, read, "The Employees of Hangu Petrochemical Plant Used the Victory of the Cultural Revolution to Severely Criticize the Revisionist 'Regulations' Concocted by Deng Xiaoping." The article went on to say that Deng wished to revive capitalism in the name of developing the Chinese economy and industries. On the same day, the *Liberation Daily* ran an article under the headline "Study Chairman Mao's Important Instructions and Deeply Criticize Deng Xiaoping's Revisionist Approach: Deng Xiaoping Is Not Allowed to Revive the Revisionist Developmental Approach of Sports."

Although it may seem there was a decline in the appearance of the keywords between 1967 and 1972, the nationalist mindset did not fade away. That was the most intense period of the Cultural Revolution, when antiforeign rhetoric and Chinese nationalism were at their peak.

Many official newspapers were taken over by factions rebelling against Mao's political enemies, as discussed in detail later. This resulted in many being forced to suspend publication.

Many popular nationalist slogans circulated extensively during the Cultural Revolution, including, "Bury capitalism and eradicate revisionism," "Throw out anything related to capitalism and fully embrace socialism," "Fight against capitalist powers, criticize capitalist scholars and bourgeoisie and reform education, art and anything that is incongruent with socialism," and "Promote that socialism is the most superior institution whereas capitalism is the root of all evil."[30] Textbooks from that period maintained that Western capitalism was rotten and exploitative.[31] In 1984 Deng recalled that everything Western was essentially prohibited during that period; those who did not criticize the West loudly enough were seen as slavish to foreigners and even accused of treason.[32]

Nationalist sentiment has been growing stronger over the past decade, propagated and reinforced by the CCP-government. As discussed earlier, many Chinese entrepreneurs, such as Wahaha's Zong, are still wary of foreign partners. As President Hu Jintao, who joined the CCP in 1964, put it in 2012, "We must recognize that international hostile forces are stepping up strategic attempts to Westernize China, and ideological and cultural fields are a focus for long-term infiltration."[33]

Another communist entrepreneur with strong nationalist feelings is Ren Zhengfei of Huawei. The name Huawei is actually an abbreviation of *zhonghua* (or simply *hua*, referring to China) *youwei* ("has promise/will prosper"). Despite the difficulty that Westerners have pronouncing and remembering the name, Ren refuses to anglicize it, saying, "We will not change the name of our brand and will teach foreigners how to pronounce it. We have to make sure they do not pronounce it like 'Hawaii.'"[34]

Following Mao's teaching that "independence, self-reliance, and frugality are our key to victory," Ren made them his own and his company's focus.[35] "Foreign firms are only after money in China," he has said. "They would not teach Chinese technology and are not reliable, and we would never become independent by buying their technology directly."[36] A 2019 *New York Times* report noted that Huawei's CCP culture was undermining its efforts to expand globally.[37] Soon after, Huawei was sanctioned by the US government. One of the main reasons was Ren's communist and nationalist rhetoric.[38]

Our firsthand interview data reveal the extent to which nationalism and self-reliance shape entrepreneurship in China. As noted, all of our interview subjects mentioned self-reliance, independence, or hard work. Five communist entrepreneurs volunteered that "the spirit of independence and autonomy is critical to our firm," and subject 14 specifically said, "Our independence is necessary to generate our own independent characteristics and models. . . . We should not rely on the relatively unstable foreign models." Similarly, subject 1 claimed, "I had doubts about going abroad, especially to European countries and the United States. There are more conflicts and troubles." Subject 26 also refused to internationalize her company, saying, "I think China now has a total of 9.6 million square kilometers, and its population accounts for one-sixth of the world's population. Such a large country and market is enough for me to develop." She also said, "After a few years in foreign countries, I think Chinese people are really hardworking. China is a hardworking nation. In addition to Chinese companies, entrepreneurs are very hardworking people, including myself."

Consistent with our ideas on the imprinting effect of CCP indoctrination, our paired t-test shows that communist entrepreneurs are more likely to use nationalism-related words in their official corporate statements (for example, annual reports or annual letters to their shareholders) than noncommunist ones (fig. 3.2). For example, Wang Xuehai, the CEO of Wuhan Humanwell Hi-tech Industry, a pharmaceutical firm on the Shanghai Stock Exchange, is a CCP member. His firm's annual report emphasizes "autonomy and independence" almost every year.[39]

Using the same approach, we content analyzed the interview transcripts of Chinese entrepreneurs, plotting the frequency of the words "independence," "autonomy," and "self-reliance" in the rhetoric of CCP members and nonmembers (fig. 3.3). We found that communist entrepreneurs use them almost twice as much as their noncommunist counterparts.

Our previously published research, which draws on the nationwide Chinese Private Enterprise Survey, also provides strong support for these claims. Entrepreneurs who went through the CCP socialization process were less likely to cooperate with foreign capitalists and investors than those who did not.[40]

Data from publicly traded Chinese firms that are controlled by entrepreneurs provide further evidence. We employed regression analysis to estimate the patterns in the data. Our findings were that, first, CCP membership is more positively related to entrepreneurs' nationalist mindset, which is reflected in their use of nationalism-related words in

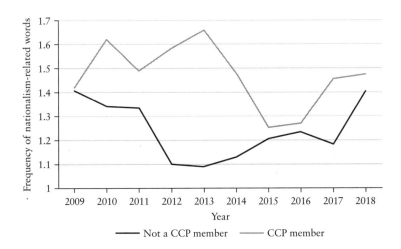

Figure 3.2 Frequency of Nationalism-Related Words in Annual Reports of Entrepreneur-Controlled Publicly Traded Firms
Data sources: Annual reports of firms listed on either the Shanghai Stock Exchange or the Shenzhen Stock Exchange. Calculated by the authors.

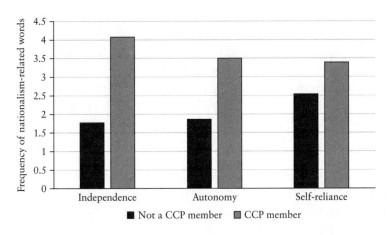

Figure 3.3 Frequency of Nationalism-Related Words by Surveyed Entrepreneurs
Data source: Authors' survey. Calculated by the authors.

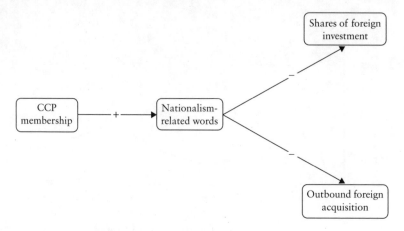

Figure 3.4 CCP Membership, Nationalism, and Internationalization
Data source: Chinese Stock Market and Accounting Research Database. Calculated by the authors.

annual reports. Second, entrepreneurs' sense of nationalism is negatively related to firms' internationalization efforts. Entrepreneurs who went through the CCP socialization process are less likely to accept foreign investment, explore foreign markets, or acquire a foreign firm because of their stereotyped and negative perceptions about the West and foreign capitalism in general (fig. 3.4).[41]

Thus, an implication of our prior work and the evidence presented here is that even if it is in entrepreneurs' economic interests to connect internationally, some still shun foreign business partners. Our own research and a follow-up study by finance scholars that replicates our results provide systematic evidence for this point.[42]

Interestingly, our interviews suggest that noncommunist entrepreneurs also tend to highlight independence, autonomy, and self-reliance. Subject 22 specifically said, "The development of the CCP-government under Chairman Mao and the related propagation indicated to us that we have to be self-reliant and independent. Only when we help ourselves can other people help us." As we elaborated earlier, Mao's "sacred" status, intergenerational transmission, and the resonances with traditional Chinese culture deeply ingrain his teachings. While those indoctrinated by Maoism and communism exhibit a stronger Maoist imprint, virtually all Chinese are influenced by Maoism to a certain degree.

NATIONALISM, DECAYED?

But if communist entrepreneurs share many beliefs, they do not all exhibit the same behaviors. Given the CCP-government's softening of its anti-foreign stance and its emphasis on foreign development after Mao's death, some communist entrepreneurs have accepted globalization, which we argue is at least in part an attempt to follow the government's call. Accordingly, as our prior research shows, communist entrepreneurs who have a bigger window into the CCP-government process have a better understanding of its evolving positions.[43]

Unlike Western democracies, China has limited ways for residents to participate in politics and governmental processes. One way to gain access to current government views is to participate in government-sponsored industry networks. Another is to become a delegate to one of China's two nominal legislative councils—the National People's Congress and the Chinese People's Political Consultative Conference. Delegates take part in law- and policymaking and so have fuller exposure to the new ideological guidance. Communist entrepreneurs who are members of the National People's Congress or Chinese People's Political Consultative Conference tend to be more open to globalization, since they are following the government's call. For example, Cui Genliang of the Hengtong Group, a delegate to the National People's Congress, stepped up his internationalization efforts in response to the Belt and Road Initiative.[44] In contrast, subject 11 of our interviewed entrepreneurs, who is also a CCP member, but not a member of either council, expressed his concerns regarding internationalization, saying, "There is high risk of internationalization regarding the CCP-government's policy and attitude, and I am not fully clear about that."

After 2001, when China joined the World Trade Organization, the government implemented a new national developmental strategy: Go Global.[45] Following this, some communist entrepreneurs moderated their isolationism. Jack Ma claimed that he stepped up Alibaba's internationalization efforts as a direct response to the Go Global campaign.[46] A research report about private entrepreneurs in Jiangsu Province indicated that the government's efforts in promoting foreign direct investment helped reshape entrepreneurs' perceptions of the capitalist world, while a survey by a research team of the CCP Jiangsu Committee's United Front Department indicated that the government's encouragement of

Figure 3.5 Nationalist Movements in China Invoking Mao
"China Anti-Japan Protests Continue," Associated Press, September 20, 2012.
The *Yomiuri Shimbun* (photographer: Kentaro Aoyama) via AP Images.

foreign direct investment helped alleviate entrepreneurs' political concerns.[47] Regarding international cooperation, subject 30 of our interviewed entrepreneurs said, "I must follow the national strategy and will
not go against the national strategy."

NATIONALISM, REVIVED?

As we have discussed, nationalist feelings could be revived if the
CCP-government promotes them, and recently it has done just that.
For example, figure 3.5 shows anti-Japanese demonstrators holding
Mao's portrait. This is natural. Many writers have argued that when a
country is doing well, its nationalism and national pride are likely to
be accentuated.[48] Given their economic accomplishments of the last four
decades, the Chinese people are rightfully proud of their country and
its government. A similar rise of nationalist feeling occurred in the United
Kingdom after the Industrial Revolution and in Germany after its uni-

fication in the mid-nineteenth century. After the United States developed quickly following the Civil War, it began to assert itself overseas. The popular rhetoric is that Mao laid the foundation for China's current prosperity through his focus on industrialization and economic development, as well as his refusal to bow to the West.[49]

On November 29, 2012—two weeks after he became the supreme leader of China—Xi proposed the concept of the "Chinese Dream," his overarching plan to restore China to a central place in the world order, an idea that originated with Mao.[50] The phrase has become an iconic slogan of the Xi administration, and Xi's Belt and Road Initiative and Made in China 2025 Initiative are both inspired by it.[51] Nationalist propaganda serves two purposes—it keeps the Chinese people motivated, and it warns the West that it must learn to coexist with the CCP-government's economic model. As Xi declared in his centenary speech, "The Chinese Communist Party and the Chinese people will march forward with their heads up on the path they have chosen, and firmly hold the destiny of China's development and progress in their own hands!"[52]

This is in stark contrast to the early stages of China's reform and opening up, when it downplayed Maoist rhetoric. Deng, describing the approach at the time, said that China must "hide its strength and bide its time," asking the CCP-government to focus on economic development in a low-profile fashion. Today, in the face of criticism for human rights abuses, lack of democracy, and other violations of what are seen as "universal values" in the West, Xi has unapologetically revived the more assertive Maoist vocabulary, arguing that "Marxism-Leninism-Maoism has been marginalized, hollowed, and symbolically labelled in some fields."[53]

The revival of nationalism has taken many forms. First, there has been a backlash against Chinese university professors, media figures, lawyers, and other public intellectuals who advocate Western standards in areas such as human rights, constitutional democracy, and voting. Until the 2010s, members of this group were key opinion leaders on China's online platforms such as its Twitter-like platform Weibo, and they cumulatively attracted hundreds of millions of supporters.

Starting in 2010, the Chinese government began recruiting writers to support the CCP-government in the media and especially on online platforms like Weibo. A 2017 study estimated that the CCP-government employs between five hundred thousand and two million internet trolls.[54]

Known as the "fifty-cent party," they are paid half a Chinese yuan (around seven US cents) for every post that they delete that is critical of the CCP-government and every positive post they add. Reports indicate that each year they make billions of fake posts. Another twenty million "internet volunteers" do the same thing for free, according to a 2021 interview.[55] The backlash against those critical of the CCP-government intensified after the election of Donald Trump; some prominent figures were stigmatized and even persecuted.[56] The journalist Qiu Zimin, for example, was arrested and sentenced to eight months in prison for the crime of impugning the reputation and honor of the heroes and martyrs who died in the 2020–21 China-India skirmishes.[57] And in September 2021, a "Rumor Refutation Platform" was introduced to collect tips and reports of content that "smears Party history" and "slanders and discredits CCP leaders." A person found to have spread such rumors might face up to fifteen years in prison according to Chinese law.[58]

The backlash has been felt by celebrities too. In August 2021, netizens noted that a rising actor, Zhang Zhelan, was smiling when he visited Yasukuni Shrine in Tokyo, where the ashes of Japanese war dead are interred. Japanese war crimes are a sensitive topic; the Japanese were responsible for the deaths of millions of civilian Chinese in the last century. Zhang was blacklisted and his acting career effectively ended.[59] Similarly, the CCP-government has been increasingly stringent about the one-China rule, which makes it illegal to refer to Taiwan as a separate country. Taiwanese actors who violate it are blacklisted and their movies and television shows banned or recast. Formerly, Taiwanese actors could be active in mainland China so long as they did not support Taiwan's independence; now they have to support reunification.[60]

There are numerous examples of ways that resurgent nationalism has affected Chinese businesses and entrepreneurs. A number of Chinese brands have emerged that cater to nationalist sentiment, such as NIO, a Chinese electric car maker that aims to be the Tesla of China, and Heytea, a Chinese tea drink chain that aspires to be Starbucks. Ubras is a Chinese lingerie maker that aims to emulate Victoria's Secret, and Li Ning is a homegrown sports brand that aims to replace Nike and Adidas.[61] On its website, NIO says, "We have never thought that domestic brands can make cars comparable to those of BBA and Tesla, but NIO has done it, even better in some aspects, and it is getting better and better. We are truly proud that our own national brand can achieve this level!"[62]

Since 2017, the Chinese government has promoted a "national champions" policy, especially in technology. A number of new high-tech companies have emerged, such as the video surveillance company Hikvision, the voice-recognition software company iFlytek, the image-recognition software company Megvii, and the vision- and speech-recognition firm Yitu Technology. All of them have been sanctioned by the US government for alleged violations of human rights through the surveillance systems they provide, which strengthen the CCP's "high-tech dictatorship."[63] Undeterred, the CCP-government has promised them up to $150 billion in subsidies by 2030 to help them compete in the global artificial intelligence market.[64] At the same time, they are exporting their surveillance technologies to other authoritarian regimes, such as Ecuador's.[65]

On the other side of the coin, Chinese residents have boycotted products from countries that were targets of nationalist sentiment—a phenomenon that has been called consumer or market nationalism.[66] For example, in 2012, Japanese products were boycotted and Japanese-owned factories sabotaged because of the dispute over the Diaoyu Islands.[67] More recently, in 2018, Dolce & Gabbana was boycotted when one of its advertisements and a comment from its cofounder Stefano Gabbana were seen as disrespectful.[68] Foreign brands such as H&M and Nike were also attacked after issuing statements criticizing China's treatment of the Uighurs in Xinjiang. Chinese officials claimed that they did not explicitly encourage any of these nationalist actions; even if that is the case, they still reflect the nationalist sentiment that the CCP-government has encouraged.[69]

On July 21, 2020, Xi articulated five points of hope to entrepreneurs. The first is about patriotism. "Enterprise marketing knows no borders," he said, "but entrepreneurs have their motherland. Excellent entrepreneurs must have a high sense of mission and a strong sense of responsibility for the country and the nation, and closely combine the development of their enterprises with the prosperity of the country, the prosperity of the nation and the happiness of the people, and take the initiative to bear the responsibility and share the worries for the country. . . . [Examples range] from Zhang Jian in the late Qing dynasty to Lu Zuofu and Chen Jiageng during the war, and then to Rong Yiren and Wang Guangying after the founding of the PRC."[70] During his November 2020 trip to Jiangsu Province, Xi doubled down on these points while praising Zhang

Jian, a Chinese industrialist and educator in the late nineteenth and early twentieth centuries.

ByteDance was accused of falling short of that patriotic ideal. When Trump announced a US ban on its main product, TikTok, ByteDance founder Zhang Yiming prepared to sell its US subsidiary to an American company, which was rumored to be Microsoft or Oracle.[71] But Zhang faced nationalist headwinds, as the CCP-government and many Chinese demanded that the company stand up against Trump's bullying. Before the rumored deal could close, the CCP-government quickly issued the "Catalogue of China's Banned and Restricted Export Technologies" to scuttle the sale.[72] Similarly, the CCP-government cracked down on the Chinese ride-hailing giant DiDi, which went against governmental guidance when it went public in the United States on July 1, 2021, accusing it of delivering sensitive data to the US Securities and Exchange Commission that threatened Chinese national security.[73] The CCP-government then reportedly sought to buy a controlling interest in the company.[74]

At the broader level, Xi also proposed the domestic-international "dual" circulation strategy on May 14, 2020, which aims to reorient the Chinese economy by prioritizing domestic consumption ("internal circulation") and lessening China's existing international trade and investment ("external circulation"). The action was similar to Mao's moves between 1949 and 1952 to reduce connections to foreign capitalism.[75] Xi has pressed the strategy in response to the current economic downturn, pressures from the United States, and the COVID-19 pandemic.[76]

The intensification of US-China trade tensions following the election of Trump also reflects this new spirit of "China first."[77] Rather than seeking a truce with the United States, the CCP-government intensified the nationalist fervor, claiming that "no force can stop the Chinese people from achieving their dreams."[78] Liu He, vice prime minister and China's chief representative at US-China trade talks, said that "China is not afraid, nor is the Chinese nation!"[79] CCP media claimed that the United States was launching a large-scale trade war. "Re-learning Mao Zedong's thoughts and methods of dealing with external pressures can add to calmness, allay any fear of bullying, and firm [up] confidence and strong motivation to resist external pressures," one government statement counseled.[80] At the same time, internet users called Trump a paper tiger, insisting that he was not as strong as he looked and that the

US economy heavily depends on Chinese companies (and Chinese subsidiaries of American companies) for electronic products, chemical raw material, and a host of daily necessities. They also revived Mao's determination to "unite all forces that can be united" against the United States, proposing alliances with European countries, Japan, and others to alleviate the damages from the trade war.[81] "Wolf Warrior" diplomats in China adopted a defiant tone on issues related to Hong Kong, Xinjiang, and others. For example, the Chinese state media openly encouraged hostility toward Western journalists for their reporting of the flood in Henan Province in July 2021.[82]

In the international realm, the rise of nationalism is manifested in China's controversial Belt and Road Initiative. The initiative promotes the outward internationalization of Chinese firms, invoking the Chinese economy's historical connections to East, Central, and Southeast Asia; the Indian subcontinent; the Arabian Peninsula; Egypt; Mediterranean countries; and so on. Infrastructure investment, specifically railways and highways, real estate, power grids, and iron and steel, are the current foci of the Belt and Road Initiative. One aim is to transfer domestic overcapacity in production abroad and facilitate economic cooperation. While China claims to be peacefully inserting itself into the international order, it has been establishing China-centric institutions such as the Asian Infrastructure Investment Bank and the New Development Bank, the latter of which is focused on Brazil, Russia, India, China, and South Africa. China has also pushed for the Regional Comprehensive Economic Partnership between China, Japan, South Korea, Australia, New Zealand, and the ten Association of Southeast Asian Nations countries to counter the influence of the Trans-Pacific Partnership, which did not involve China.[83]

The ebb and flow of nationalist ideas in China stems from a Maoist imprint that fundamentally shapes Chinese business and entrepreneurship. But their recent spike can also be seen as part of a worldwide trend toward isolationism and disengagement in reaction to the many middle-class jobs that were lost to off-shoring and immigration. Populist leaders and parties rose to power in Austria, Brazil, Denmark, Germany, Hungary, India, Italy, Sweden, and of course the United States.[84] The United Kingdom voted for Brexit and left the European Union, while

Trump revived the isolationist slogan of the 1930s, "America first," and launched trade wars against many countries.[85]

How will multinational firms navigate the increasingly hostile business environment in China? While it is indeed challenging to operate in the Chinese market, there are many strategies that firms can use to be successful there. Notable successful examples include KFC, Volkswagen, Tesla, and Microsoft.[86] We discuss these strategies in more detail later, but in brief, most have adopted a localization strategy, which not only allows them to more quickly adapt to the Chinese market but makes it less likely that they will clash with its unique culture and institutions.[87] After Nike suffered a backlash due to its statements about forced labor in Xinjiang, its CEO, John Donahoe, publicly said that "Nike is a brand that is of China and for China." While that did not endear Nike to the human rights community, it smoothed over its relationship with China.[88]

4 Frugality and Cost Reduction

My shoes only cost me around 80 Yuan/RMB [$12] and I have been wearing them for two years. My shirts are all under 30 Yuan/RMB [$4.20].
—Li Shufu, founder of the Geely Group, a large Chinese automaker (owner of Volvo and the largest shareholder of Daimler)

THE CHINESE AUTO MAGNATE Li Shufu is known as the Chinese Henry Ford. Li was born in 1963 in Taizhou, Zhejiang Province, and like Ford, he was the son of a farmer. Li was known to be an avid follower of Mao Zedong, especially when it came to frugality. He claimed that he could accumulate scraps and discarded materials and turn them into gold and silver. Following success in the refrigerator business, he invested in automobiles and named his company Geely, a word whose sound is similar to the Chinese word for "lucky."

Geely's success was based on cost reductions and low prices, values that he carried over to his life; he drives an ordinary car made by Geely and eats his meals with his employees in large dining halls. When he visited his Beijing subsidiary, he wore clothes that were so old and worn that he was stopped by a security guard who mistook him for a poor migrant worker.[1] Geely acquired Volvo in 2010 and now earns more than $30 billion in annual revenues. To show his appreciation and admiration for Mao's influence, Li has invested in Mao's hometown in Hunan province.[2]

Wahaha's Zong Qinghou also attributes his thriftiness to Mao: "I learned from Chairman Mao and kept frugality as my habit."[3] He claims to live on less than $6,000 per year, emphasizing cost control as the "key element in operations" that allows Wahaha to "provide cheap but high-quality products."[4] Huawei's Ren Zhengfei is well known to take taxis rather than the company limousine, while Liu Yonghao—founder, CEO, and chairman of the conglomerate New Hope Group—pays less than one dollar for his haircuts. Niu Gensheng, founder of Mengniu—one of the ten largest dairy firms in the world—usually wears a necktie that cost him less than three dollars. All of these spectacularly wealthy businessmen attribute their success to their frugality, which they have made a cornerstone of their management styles.[5]

Mao and the Chinese Communist Party (CCP) asked the Chinese to endure years of hardship as China industrialized. The principle stuck, as also shown by our interviews. Subject 1 mentioned that "we should put frugality first. . . . Profits come from our cost savings in the manufacturing process." Subject 14 said, "Saving and being thrifty is a must. . . . How to increase revenue and reduce expenditure in an enterprise must be considered. . . . We save as much as possible when we manage the business." Even some noncommunist entrepreneurs maintain a frugality focus. Subject 4 said, "I read many books by Chairman Mao and successful entrepreneurs such as Lu Guanqiu and Zong Qinghou. I learned from Chairman Mao directly and also indirectly from these entrepreneurs. . . . Saving and resource conservation for sustainability of businesses, for corporate planning, and vision . . . and frugality is crucial for survival and innovation." Subject 24 claimed that "cost saving is a must. . . . Every penny earned by an enterprise is from very, very hard work." She then went on to say that "doing business really means saving every penny." Such sentiments were echoed by subjects 5, 9, 20, 31, and 32.

In this chapter, we first discuss why Mao emphasized frugality in his ideology. Then we describe how the Chinese entrepreneurs who came of age during the Mao period maintain this frugal mindset and why they are likely to pass it on to future generations.

FRUGALITY AS A MAOIST IDEOLOGICAL PRINCIPLE

Mao persistently advocated thrift as a basic principle and the correct approach to developing the Chinese economy. Specifically, he asserted, "We should be frugal to build factories, run stores, all state-owned and cooperative businesses, all other businesses, etc. and everything should be guided by the principle of frugality. Frugality is the fundamental principle of the socialist economy."[6] In 1955, he claimed that frugality was necessary because "China is a poor and economically underdeveloped country, and to make our country rich, we need to hold on to the frugal construction principles and shall never waste. It will take decades for China to become rich, but the principle of thrift should be maintained even after we have achieved that goal. It is particularly necessary to promote frugality within a few decades, i.e., the incoming several five-year plans."[7]

Mao was not the first to propose frugality as an important principle; he borrowed from Confucian traditions that had prevailed for more than two thousand years. Saving is a deep cultural virtue in China, and extravagance and waste are seen as immoral. Many writers in ancient China warned monarchs about this issue. For example, Mozi, a student of Confucius, said that "as the king, as long as you can be frugal like ordinary people, have clothes to wear and enough to eat, you could surely govern the country well and make it prosperous." Mao was a great admirer of Mozi.[8]

Mao also paid attention to the fact that the first emperor of China, Qin Shi Huang, known for his lavish funerary compound outside current-day Xi'an, with its thousands of terracotta warriors, and his extravagant palace that was later burned down by a rebellious general, squandered his legacy with his spending. Despite his strong military and extremely tight control (citizens were required to surrender any sharp metal pieces to authorities, lest they revolt and use them as weapons), his dynasty was replaced by the Han dynasty within fifteen years.[9]

In contrast, Emperor Wen of the Han dynasty was so thrifty that he and all his family members and servants wore cheap clothes like ordinary people, and he prohibited excessive governmental spending. Before his death, he ordered his son, the future emperor Jing, to ensure that there was no metal among his funeral goods, but only cheap pottery. This went against the social norm that children should spend almost half of the family wealth on funerary goods to show their filial devotion. Grave robbers never defiled Emperor Wen's tomb, because they knew it held nothing valuable.[10] Thanks to his careful management, China enjoyed a great boom that lasted for almost a century—and his dynasty endured for three centuries after that.[11] Mao aspired to surpass him and other famous emperors.[12]

Although he was born into a landowning family, Mao was known to have worn the same pair of pajamas for twenty years; he had them patched scores of times.[13] China was a poor country, and while the CCP was supported by the Communist International, it could not afford lavish spending. Its frugal lifestyle was consistent with that of its recruits, the great majority of whom were poor farmers. The rival Kuomintang, in contrast, was known to be both corrupt and extravagant.

After the victory in the Second Sino-Japanese War, Chiang Kai-shek's in-laws, who had spent significant time abroad, converted to Christianity, which they considered more advanced than Chinese culture that lacked formal religions.[14] Even during the hardest times, when Soong Mei-ling undertook a speaking tour in the United States to ask for aid, she was shamelessly ostentatious. When she visited the White House, her luggage included dozens of suitcases filled with Chanel handbags, shoes with large pearl decorations, and sumptuous clothes. US first lady Eleanor Roosevelt was shocked, and many of Chiang's high officials were resentful.[15]

In contrast, CCP leaders led an "ascetic" life in Xi'an, Shaanxi Province. All of the CCP-occupied regions—most of them in rural areas—were poor. For instance, Mao, Zhou Enlai, Zhu De (the main military commander under Mao), and Xi's father, Xi Zhongxun, famously did not discard clothes, quilts, or blankets that were worn out but, as Mao did with his famous pajamas, patched and repatched them. Mao set the rule that "corruption and squandering money are both crimes."[16]

After the CCP became the ruling party, Mao worried about China's lagging economic development. "China is a poor country," he declared. "To make us rich, we need decades of hard work, and one of the most important guiding principles to build China is the promotion of frugality." Simply put, "frugality is a fundamental principle for everything under socialism." Mao was astonished by the Soviet Union's industrial capacity during his visit in 1949–50 and was eager to build up China's. "We need to tighten up our belt [and so cannot eat too much but save these resources] for industrial construction," he declared. This was even more important after the Sino-Soviet split, when the Soviet Union canceled its aid to China.[17]

Many who research the CCP argue that Mao's promotion of frugality as a national development strategy was what laid the foundation for China's industrialization.[18] Jiang Zemin (top leader from 1989 to 2002) echoed Mao in claiming that frugality was one of the core values of socialism.[19] His successor Hu Jintao's Eight Honors and Eight Shames and Three Types of Awareness emphasized the importance of frugality, and more recently, during the COVID-19 emergency, Xi called on the

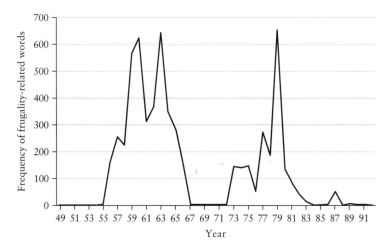

Figure 4.1 Frequency of Keywords Related to Frugality in Official Newspaper Headlines (1949–1991)
Data sources: Official daily newspapers of each province's CCP committee. From 1967 to 1972 many provincial dailies suspended operations. Calculated by the authors.

Chinese to stop wasting food.[20] As a result, competitive binge-eating videos, which were very popular on Chinese social media, were banned.[21]

We first show the general propaganda pattern surrounding frugality based on content analysis of Chinese newspapers, specifically the frequency of three keywords: "frugality" (节约), "waste" (浪费), and "diligent and thrifty" (勤俭).

We determined the time trend of these keyword frequencies (fig. 4.1). Between 1955 and 1961, frugality was heightened, reflecting Mao's push to industrialize China quickly. Looking across provinces, we also found that frugality ideas were promoted the most in Shanghai, as with nationalism in the last chapter, probably because of Shanghai's special status as birthplace of the CCP, its geographical location as an international frontier, and Mao's preference for Shanghai's *Liberation Daily* as a vehicle for his ideas. Before the founding of the communist regime, Shanghai had been the most capitalist city in China. The CCP-government might have pressed its ideas especially vigorously there in order to negate capitalism's influence.

In the May 4, 1955, issue of the *Hebei Daily*, Mao declared, "Work hard and frugally to build factories, run shops, all state-owned and cooperative businesses, and all other businesses, and everything should follow the principle of frugality. This is the basic principle of the socialist economy. China is a big country, but it is still very poor. It will take decades for China to become rich, and the principle of hard work and frugality will also be implemented in the next few decades, but in particular, it is necessary to promote hard work and frugality, and pay special attention to saving." On February 27, 1957, in an essay entitled "On the Correct Handling of Contradictions among the People," he wrote, "It is a great contradiction for all cadres and all people to always think of our country as a big socialist country, but also a poor country with economic backwardness. To make our country prosperous and strong, it will take decades of frugal accumulation, including the implementation of the policy of hard work and thrift in economic construction." The essay was extended and republished in the *People's Daily* on June 19 of the same year. These were finally included in *Selected Works of Mao Zedong*.

Many provincial dailies propagated Mao's frugality principles. The *Gansu Daily* mandated frugality in agriculture ("Extensively, Deeply and Healthily Carry Out the Campaign of Increasing Production and Saving," dated January 4, 1957); the *Jilin Daily* promoted frugality via the example of a local agricultural collective ("Respond to the Party's Call for Increased Production and Saving, Continue to Carry Out the Advanced Producer Movement," dated February 28, 1957); and the *Hebei Daily* noted the frugality of a steelmaking firm ("How Did the Tangshan Steel Plant's Party Organization Strengthen the Leadership of the Production Increase and Saving Movement?," dated November 20, 1957).

Another wave of frugality discourse came just after the Cultural Revolution in 1977. Mao had died, but his principle endured in articles in the *Hubei Daily* (dated June 16, 1977) and the *Hunan Daily* and *Jiangxi Daily* (both dated November 23, 1977), which emphasized frugality with examples from the agricultural sector, and the *Ningxia Daily* (dated September 28, 1977) and *Jilin Daily* (dated November 14, 1977), which promoted frugality in manufacturing, among many other examples. When Deng Xiaoping regained a top leadership position, he followed Mao's frugality ideology, calling for Chinese to save every penny for the economic reform that would turn China into an industrialized, export-oriented country. "If we do not promote hard work, diligence and thrift," Deng wrote in March 1979, "our goal [of doubling GDP] cannot be achieved."[22] He repeated the sentiment frequently.

THE FRUGAL MINDSET OF ENTREPRENEURS: AN IMPORTANT FACTOR FOR SUCCESS

Given Mao's importance in shaping the ideological principles of Chinese society, many individuals' behavioral patterns and cognitive frames come to reflect his ideals. To deal with an environment with poor resources—as most Chinese entrepreneurs had to as they were growing up—it was necessary to husband them. For many, such habits and values persisted the rest of their life, even after becoming rich. As Ren Zhengfei put it, "Chairman Mao taught us to be frugal and it is critical for us at Huawei."[23]

Many other entrepreneurs spontaneously articulated the relationship between Maoist frugality and their own focus on cost reduction. For instance, Chen Kaixuan, the founder of Liby, one of the largest laundry supply firms in China, says that Mao's teachings about frugality are an important weapon for business success.[24] Recalling his meeting with Mao when he was young, Liu Yonghao, the founder, CEO, and chairman of the New Hope Group, who is known for being frugal and often asks his employees to cut costs, says that he will always imitate Mao's frugal lifestyle.[25] Xi reminisced that in his early adulthood, he and his friends had to "save everything edible and otherwise would live in constant hunger."[26]

In our examination of the different databases on Chinese entrepreneurs and their business operations, we also found significant evidence of a focus on frugality among Chinese entrepreneurs, particularly those who have gone through CCP socialization. First, we investigate the frugality focus in the annual reports of publicly traded, privately controlled (as opposed to state-owned) firms. As we did in our study of nationalism, we coded the frequency of three keywords, "frugality," "waste," and "diligence and thriftiness," with content-analytical techniques. We found that communist entrepreneurs emphasized frugality more than noncommunist entrepreneurs, which is also supported by our statistical analyses (fig. 4.2).

For example, Li Xiulin, founder and CEO of Jilin Aodong, a pharmaceutical company traded on the Shenzhen Stock Exchange, is a CCP

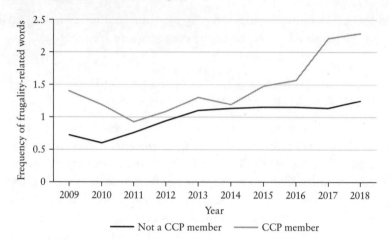

Figure 4.2 Frequency of Frugality-Related Words in Annual Reports of Entrepreneur-Controlled Publicly Traded Firms
Data sources: Annual reports of firms listed on either the Shanghai Stock Exchange or the Shenzhen Stock Exchange. Calculated by the authors.

member. Formerly a factory manager and party secretary of the predecessor firm to Jilin Aodong, he took control of the company during the CCP-government privatization campaign. Li adopted numerous approaches to save costs, such as using innovative production techniques involving the separation of heat from different sources, which cuts production time by thirty minutes and saves tens of thousands of dollars. To further reduce costs, Li flattened his management team so that subsidiary managers report directly to him, eliminating a layer of management.

Our interview data provide further support for the view that entrepreneurs who came of age during the Maoist era are imprinted with frugality, and that those who went through the CCP indoctrination process are even more so. We found that CCP members have a stronger focus on thrift, a difference that is statistically significant (fig. 4.3). Subject 31 highlighted, "I think cost saving is very important. . . . In the internal operation and management of the enterprise, we put more emphasis on saving. I think saving in our work and management is a cost concept that every employee and cadre needs to have. If a company is extravagant, then it will definitely not be able to survive. So, I think this is one of the fundamentals of the survival of a company. Therefore, sav-

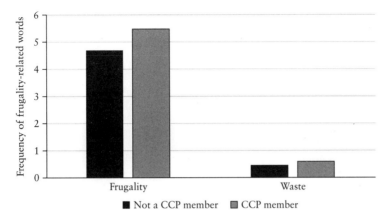

Figure 4.3 Frequency of Frugality-Related Words by Surveyed Entrepreneurs
Data source: Authors' survey. Calculated by the authors.

ing money and developing a good habit is an important early guarantee for the development of the enterprise."

Noncommunist entrepreneurs also maintain a focus on frugality, which underlines the pervasiveness of Mao's and the CCP's influence. At least half of the noncommunist entrepreneurs we interviewed emphasized frugality as a top priority in their firms. Subjects 7 and 9 both admire Mao and said that "being frugal and saving are to minimize costs and maximize profits." Subject 20 said, "Being frugal and saving is of course a traditional virtue and our generation has deeply held such kind of values because of growing up in Chairman Mao's period. There is certainly no reason to waste." Similarly, subject 32 believed, "Increasing income and reducing expenditure are absolute top priorities in any company. On the one hand, you have to build up your business volume, and at the same time, you have to control costs internally."

Our prior research using the Chinese Private Enterprise Survey also shows that entrepreneurs who lived through the Mao period practiced frugality at a heightened rate, spending less on average on operational costs.[27] We show the descriptive patterns in figure 4.4. Compared with their noncommunist counterparts, communist entrepreneurs control operating costs (as the share of revenue) more effectively.

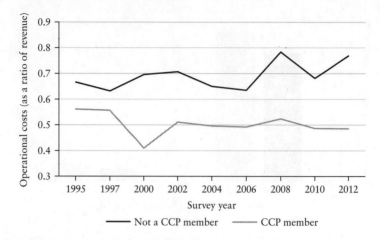

Figure 4.4 Operational Costs of Firms Controlled by Communist and Non-communist Entrepreneurs
Data source: Chinese Private Enterprise Survey. Calculated by the authors.

Frugality and Firm Performance

Frugality is an important attribute for any for-profit business. As myriads of commentators and a large body of academic research suggest, many startups fail due to overspending. Lean times promote sobriety in business management.[28] When Ren was negotiating one of his first big orders in Serbia, he rented just one hotel room for his team, which numbered ten people.[29]

We also use data from publicly traded Chinese firms to provide further and more systematic evidence on the link from CCP membership to frugality rhetoric and frugal practices (a low level of costs), and then to firm performance (fig. 4.5). Using regression analysis, we found that, first, firms with founders or CEOs with CCP membership have a stronger culture of frugality than those controlled by noncommunist entrepreneurs, as shown by their more frequent use of frugality-related words. Second, these communist entrepreneurs tend to reduce costs more than their noncommunist counterparts. Third, their firms enjoy better performance.[30]

The findings are consistent with published studies that show CCP membership brings economic benefits.[31] However, prior accounts emphasize the economic benefits that flow from greater networking op-

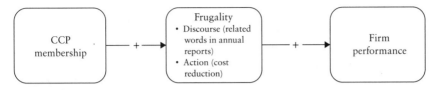

Figure 4.5 Frugality Focus, Cost Reduction, and Firm Performance
Data source: Chinese Stock Market and Accounting Research Database. Calculated by the authors.

portunities with government officials, such as low-interest loans, tax rebates, and other benefits. We argue that we also need to attend to the nonpecuniary aspects of CCP membership that affect financial performance, such as frugality, which our analysis and prior research jointly show may contribute to economic success through cost-reduction strategies.[32] We believe that this "nonrational" perspective can complement the existing ones, contributing to a more holistic understanding of the influence of communism on entrepreneurship.

Frugality is emphasized in top business schools in China, but it is important to recognize that it is not a uniquely Chinese characteristic.[33] In fact, there is a long stream of thought on how frugality may benefit firm performance. In his seminal book *The Protestant Ethic and the Spirit of Capitalism,* Max Weber argued that the Protestant focus on saving rather than consuming underlies the spirit of capitalism.[34] Economic historians and development economists such as Nobel laureate Sir William Arthur Lewis also believe that frugality is an important attribute for entrepreneurs and credit it for the emergence of the Industrial Revolution in Great Britain, where the savings rate was high enough to facilitate large-scale manufacturing.[35]

Many entrepreneurs in the West are also well known for their frugality. A historical example is the cotton-spinning firm McConnel and Kennedy, established in 1795. The two founders, James McConnel and John Kennedy, saved money and lived austerely. Within five years, the firm's capital increased twelve times, and in another decade it had become the largest and most technologically advanced cotton enterprise in the United Kingdom.[36] In 1828 John Kennedy told a journalist that "[entrepreneurs] have to see their enterprises as their lives and form a habit of frugality. Only these people have the ability to lead their firms through various crises. . . . Many industrialists in Manchester are like this."[37] Many successful present-day entrepreneurs also exhibit frugality. For example, during the time he was building Amazon, Jeff Bezos was known for driving an old Honda Accord.[38] Warren Buffet spends little money on his house and meals and pays just $18 for his haircuts, and Ingvar Kamprad (the founder of IKEA) drove an old Volvo and bought clothes at a local flea market.[39]

Frugality over Generations?

Given the fact that the average age of entrepreneurs has decreased over time in China—as of 2021 it was only twenty-nine years old—will Mao's frugality teaching affect future generations of entrepreneurs?[40] There have been many cases where second-generation entrepreneurs turn out to be spendthrifts. Wang Sicong, son of the real estate magnate Wang Jianlin, previously one of the richest men in China, and Yin Xidi, son of the Lifan Industrial Corporation's Yin Mingshan, are notorious for their ostentatious spending. Wang is now on a blacklist of defaulters kept by the Chinese government and as a result cannot travel by air, receive loans from banks, open a credit card, or assume high-level jobs in corporations such as owner, director, or advisory board member.[41] An old Chinese saying suggests that wealth cannot last over three generations. Chinese entrepreneurs often express their concerns about this issue and wonder how generous they should be with their children.[42]

But many Chinese entrepreneurs hope to create enduring "business dynasties" for their families, and they thus still fervently encourage their children to obtain socioemotional wealth through forced austerities. When asked, "Will you and your daughter be different when doing business or starting a business?" Zong Qinghou said, "Like me, she is also thrifty and frugal."[43]

Westerners looking to do business in China should keep in mind that frugal entrepreneurs are likely better business partners. While at first glance they and their firms might look "shabby," one should look past their outward appearances and into the details of their operations. Before it imploded, costing investors billions of dollars, oFo was one of China's two most popular bike-sharing companies; many attribute its failure to its focus on lavish benefits. If a firm uses its resources efficiently and keeps costs down, then it is a good signal for business cooperation.[44]

A frugal mindset also goes along with resiliency, the ability to weather hard times, and a general attitude of prudence and modesty.[45] Rather than expanding aggressively, the Fotile Group maintained a steadfast strategy; it is now the best-known high-end brand in China's cooking and appliance industry.[46] But entrepreneurs can become complacent after their initial successes and lose a sense of prudence and the need for risk control.[47] The Hurun Report's Rich List, published since 1999, tracks and ranks the richest people in China. A number of top-ranked businesspeople on this list have endured bankruptcies or imprisonment. For example, Li Hejun, founder of the gigantic Hanergy Holding Group, which sells solar and photovoltaic-related products, topped the list in 2015 but expanded too boldly and quickly. Hanergy's debt was more than twice its profits and in some years was even higher than its revenue. The group went bankrupt in 2020.[48] Similarly, Wang Jianlin, founder of the Wanda Group, one of China's largest business conglomerates, became the richest person in China in 2016 but was soon found to owe more than $60 billion. He has been on the brink of bankruptcy ever since.[49]

Frugality is both a useful signal and a cherished virtue, especially in the Chinese context. Communist entrepreneurs are particularly good at embracing it, although noncommunist entrepreneurs who admire Mao also keep it as a good habit. Though market-oriented capitalism has only existed for about four decades in China, it was planted on fertile ground.

5 Devotion and Social Contribution

I am a CCP member and so have a responsibility to contribute to the society.

—Wang Jinduo, founder of Shuntian Electrode, the world's largest
manufacturer of silicon electrodes

WANG JINDUO WAS BORN IN 1957, and after graduating from college, he worked at a chemical fertilizer factory. He then became a government official in the Bureau of Economy and Trade. In 1987 he was assigned to manage the economically distressed Great Wall Electrode Factory. Before Wang came, the firm had suffered a loss of more than $200,000 (around $8 million in current US dollars), and 98 percent of its assets were loaned.

Wang responded to the call of the Chinese Communist Party (CCP) and led his team to listen to their customers' needs. According to Wang, they were just following Chairman Mao Zedong's teaching to stay close to the popular masses and serve them. As a result, they decided to develop large-scale graphite electrodes, heating elements for the electric arc furnaces that melt scrap to produce new steel. After learning that the total investment would exceed US$1.4 million and take more than two years to complete, Wang sought advice from all directions to develop a unique Chinese technology. In less than six months, they had succeeded. Wang attributed his success to the strength of the popular masses.[1]

In 2000, when Wang learned that some pupils had to go to school in another village miles away because the local school was so run-down, he donated $100,000 for new buildings. The CCP constitution asks all

CCP members to pay regular membership fees, and in emergencies and other urgent situations, they are encouraged to contribute to special funds. After the massive 2008 Sichuan earthquake, 45.5 million CCP members donated around US$1.37 billion for relief, an average of $30 per person. Wang donated $50,000. He also helped lift more than six hundred families out of poverty, responding to the CCP-government's mandate to exterminate poverty by 2020.[2] As he put it, it is the responsibility of CCP members to help society. He recalled that as an entrepreneur, he "benefited from the Party and nation, and should be charged to give back."[3]

There are many other examples of communist entrepreneurs' social responsibility. As mentioned in previous chapters, both Jack Ma of Alibaba and Ren Zhengfei of Huawei have spoken of their obligations to serve the people.[4] More recently, this trend has been reinforced by the CCP-government's renewed emphasis on "common prosperity," which is a political slogan and campaign focused on all members of society achieving prosperity (as opposed to the prior development path, whereby some could "get rich first"). The idea was proposed by Mao and revitalized by Xi Jinping, who has committed to narrowing income and consumption gaps.[5] Many private firms and communist entrepreneurs responded to this recent focus, which stipulated that their efforts should be in service of the people. For example, the Chinese technology giant Tencent—the developer of the social app WeChat and employer of thousands of CCP members—announced that it was donating $7.7 billion (50 billion yuan/RMB) for a "sustainable social values" program in response to the common prosperity initiative to reduce poverty and income inequality. The new funds will help rural revitalization, increase income for the poor, improve the medical system, and balance the development of education programs.[6]

In this chapter, we discuss why China's communist entrepreneurs are more focused on contributing to society than noncommunist entrepreneurs. We first elaborate Mao's teachings for CCP members in this regard—for example, a focus on devotion, the mandatory response to the CCP-government's call, the collectivist emphasis, and a prioritization of the interests of the CCP-government. Unlike many press accounts and academic studies that explain philanthropy and other forms of corporate social responsibility from instrumental and strategic perspectives, we conclude that it also reflects deeply held values.

DEVOTION: ORIGIN AND MAO'S TEACHINGS

The devotion focus corresponds to another fundamental aspect of Maoism—the "mass line." This principle maintains that everything is for the (popular) masses, everything depends on the masses, and the CCP's work and theory should come from the masses. It is collectively reflected in Mao's proposition that CCP members should place the interests of the CCP and society above their own. CCP candidates take an oath that they would be ready to sacrifice their lives for these principles.

The CCP emerged in 1921, when China was divided and dispirited. Over the previous decades, Sun Yat-sen and his Kuomintang had mobilized dozens of uprisings against the Qing dynasty but failed for lack of a strong military.[7] Then Sun allied with Yuan Shikai, who was a high-ranking chancellor and general in the Qing dynasty. Yuan forced the last emperor to abdicate on February 12, 1912. Afterward, Sun and Yuan split and formed two rival governments—the official Beiyang government and the nationalist government led by Sun and the Kuomintang.

It was difficult for the weak and emerging CCP to recruit members, given that there were already two important political forces in China at the time. To bolster its "brand," Mao designed a lofty set of principles for CCP members that would make them feel as if they were contributing to Chinese society. In addition to the nationalism focus discussed earlier, Mao emphasized social devotion and China's storied past.

Mao claimed that "CCP members are a collection of excellent people . . . [who] are willing to sacrifice themselves." According to the CCP's constitution, the party and the people's interests are paramount—in Mao's own words, the "basis of any action of CCP members is the interest of the CCP."[8] Many communist entrepreneurs actively practice this mantra. We mentioned Cui Genliang, the founder and CEO of the Hengtong Group, as an example of a communist entrepreneur who believes that he is a revolutionary "brick."[9] One of our interviewed entrepreneurs who is a CCP member, subject 31, said, "As entrepreneurs, we must lead for everyone, and follow the requirements of our Party, so that our people can become rich and have more happiness. This is an important manifestation of the devotion and social responsibility of my company."

Mao consistently denigrated individualism and emphasized collectivism, which is deeply rooted in Chinese culture. After the collapse of the Qing dynasty, former generals, ministers, and chancellors fought for control of China's regions. Many provinces announced independence, and China was on the verge of being split into a dozen sovereign states.[10] Mao and the CCP had to unite these different regions, and so a collectivist ideal was a necessary tactic. In his article "Anti-individualism/liberalism," Mao pointed out that "the life of the CCP is collectivistic . . . CCP members should care about the Party, the masses, and others more than themselves, that is what defines a qualified CCP member."[11] Recently, a group of communist entrepreneurs held a conference to affirm their original CCP oaths and mission. In their statements, many emphasized collectivism as one of their fundamental principles.[12] As we mentioned earlier, the devotion focus is also consistent with Confucianism, especially the "spirit of shidafu," the class of scholar-officials, gentlemen, bureaucrats, or literati who shouldered the responsibility of the nation, maintaining a high level of morality and ethics.[13]

THE DEVOTION FOCUS IN CCP COMMUNICATIONS

Again, we provide empirical evidence with a content analysis of CCP-government rhetoric from official newspapers to show general trends of the devotion focus. Keywords concerning the devotion focus include "mass line" (群众路线) and the famous phrase "serving the people" (为人民服务). We show the time trend of these keyword frequencies (fig. 5.1). From 1955 to 1959, discussion of the mass line was heightened, as Mao was about to finish the socialist transformation of the economy, particularly the collectivization of agriculture. Collectivization meant the expropriation of land from farmers, and thus the CCP-government had to follow its mass line as a guiding principle; otherwise, farmers might collectively resist, as happened in the Soviet Union. For example, on July 31, 1955, Mao claimed, "Farmers have unlimited creativity, and the CCP-government should trust them. They can organize themselves, march to all places and departments where they can exert their power, march to the depth and breadth of production, and create an increasing number of welfare undertakings for themselves through collectivization."[14] Many provincial dailies followed up on Mao's rhetoric. For example, on October 29, 1955, the *Gansu Daily*

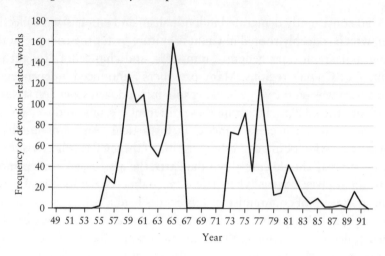

Figure 5.1 Frequency of Keywords Related to Devotion in Official Newspaper Headlines (1949–1991)
Data sources: Official daily newspapers of each province's CCP committee. From 1967 to 1972 many provincial dailies suspended operations. Calculated by the authors.

published an article titled "The Experience of the Mass Line in the Co-operative Movement." The *Qinghai Daily* published a report entitled "The Work Methods of the Mass Line Must Be Carried Out in the Reform of Agricultural Technology" on June 29, 1956.

The emphasis on the mass line culminated during the Great Leap Forward campaign from 1958 to 1960, when the level of collectivization was elevated: farmers would eat together at established communal dining halls and all their harvests would be shared within their communities. Different provincial dailies frequently issued mass line–related statements to ingratiate themselves with Mao.[15] For example, the *Shanxi Daily* claimed that "the Great Leap Forward enriched the Party's mass line" on January 8, 1959. A follow-up report was published on February 15 in the same year, saying, "The mass line is invincible. The Satellite Commune summed up the great victory of the mass line in the Great Leap Forward. All members enhanced their knowledge, enriched their experience, and became more energetic and incentivized." At almost the same time (January 13, 1959), the Shanghai *Liberation Daily* stated, "The electrolytic copper workshop of the Shanghai Smelter Factory has done a good job in one year of the Great Leap Forward, and has achieved

high levels of experience: taking the mass line, anti-conservative thinking, 'intensively farming' the experimental field, and popularizing good
experience."

The other important rhetorical phrase was "serve the people." For example, in his famous February 27, 1957, essay, *On the Correct Handling
of Contradictions among the People*, Mao stated that "state organs must
rely on the people, and the staff of state organs must serve the people."[16]
The statement has become an official motto for the CCP. The *Qinghai
Daily* applied the principle to the wholesale industry ("Establish the
Idea of Thoroughly Serving the People, Dulan Civil Trade Company
Organizes Its Employees to Criticize the Capitalist Management Style,"
dated January 10, 1965); the *Beijing Daily* applied it to the manufacturing industry ("Putting the Idea of Serving the People to Work, the
Boiler Section of the Mechanical Repair Power Plant of Beijing Paper-
making Plant Has Not Only Supplied Enough Steam, but Also Saved
Coal," dated August 19, 1965); and the *Tianjin Daily* applied it to the
service industry ("Learn from Customers to Better Serve the People,"
dated October 13, 1965).

Deng Xiaoping's economic reform in the late 1970s borrowed the devotion focus to give it credibility from a Maoist perspective. Many
provincial dailies cast "serve the people" as a principle for businesses
to better serve customers. For example, on March 23, 1977, the *Hebei
Daily* reported that Qinhuangdao commercial front workers "served the
people wholeheartedly." On July 10, 1977, the *Beijing Daily* introduced
the model workers of the Beijing Municipal Finance and Trade Department to show how customer service improvements serve the people glo-
riously. Likewise, on October 5, 1977, the *Liaoning Daily* profiled the
experienced salesperson Wang Zhanlan as a role model for serving the
people wholeheartedly.

FROM A DEVOTION FOCUS TO SOCIAL
CONTRIBUTIONS

A notable example of the application of Maoist ideology and rhetoric
in business is Chinese business leaders' joint engagement in philanthropic efforts, which we call collective philanthropy.[17] Specifically,
based on our interviews and survey data of Chinese entrepreneurs over
the years, we discovered that Chinese entrepreneurs tend to mobilize

their collective economic, political, and social capital to address social needs that better China. In 2015, for example, Jack Ma organized a group of like-minded entrepreneurs, even his long-term rival Pony Ma (founder of Tencent), to establish the Paradise International Foundation, which aims to foster environmental sustainability in China. While such a model is rooted in China's Confucian tradition (shidafu and the resulting tradition of group philanthropy) and the important role of social relationships in Chinese culture (*guanxi,* or a system of social connections and influential relationships that facilitates business and other dealings), Mao's principles also play a role.[18] Many high-profile members of this initiative are CCP members, such as Liu Chuanzhi (founder of Lenovo), Li Dongsheng (founder of TCL, one of the largest electronics companies in China), and Lei Jun (founder of Xiaomi, another one of the largest electronics companies in China).[19]

Many communist entrepreneurs see social contribution as one of their missions. Xu Jingxin, the founder and CEO of Jianhua Building Materials, a $2 billion conglomerate, donated $15 million to COVID-19 relief, saying, "I am a CCP member and shall be the first to sacrifice for society."[20] Similarly, Wei Yongxiang, founder, chairman, and party secretary of Henan Tiejun Culture Media, responded to the CCP's call to fight against COVID-19 by mobilizing CCP members in his firm to volunteer to help in Wuhan. Before the team departed, Wei wrote his will, in which he stated, "When the CCP-government is in need, we CCP members should stand in the forefront and ready to sacrifice for the CCP and the nation."[21]

Subject 6 of our interviewed entrepreneurs is a CCP member. He said that "for us CCP members, social responsibility is the most important task, especially during the COVID-19 pandemic." Similarly, subject 31 stated, "I think social responsibility is more important, because our soul and our team building is based on social responsibility, which enhances the cohesion of our strong team and results in a stronger and larger company . . . just like the CCP."

The CCP-government has been faced with a number of challenges in recent years, including environmental issues, health care, poverty, unequal regional development, unemployment, and educational inequality. Before the massive privatization wave that started in the early 2000s, Chinese firms were not only companies but parts of the socialist bureaucracy. As such, they had units such as hospitals, kindergartens, and other social components to support their employees. Privatization shed them, leaving large gaps in social services.[22] In Western countries, nongovernmental organizations would typically fill in these gaps. But the Chinese government has been wary about such entities, seeing them as rival power structures that could be used by the West to infiltrate Chinese society and subvert the government.[23] Instead, it calls on communist entrepreneurs to fill these social service gaps.

Cui of the Hengtong Group, for example, has donated millions of dollars to the Guangcai ("glory" in English) project for poverty reduction, a program the CCP-government actively called on entrepreneurs to contribute to.[24] Cui said, "I have always been responsive to the CCP-government's call and like the slogan of Guangcai suggests, I would declare war against poverty."[25] Zhou Haijiang, chairman and CEO of the $7 billion conglomerate Hongdou Group, also donated millions of dollars, saying, "My grandfather, my father, and I are all CCP members and we are proud of it. . . . Devotion to society is a key principle for us and our firm."[26]

Collectivism demands that the masses and the CCP come first; for example, if the interest of the CCP should ever conflict with Huawei, Ren would "choose the CCP, whose interest is to serve the people and all human beings."[27] Likewise, Wahaha's Zong Qinghou says that he would buy houses for his employees and local residents to improve their well-being.[28]

We offer further evidence of entrepreneurs' devotion focus from two different sources. First, we show it in annual reports of publicly traded, entrepreneur-controlled firms by analyzing the frequency of three devotion-related keywords: "devotion," "mass line," and "serve the people." Communist entrepreneurs focus more on devotion than their noncommunist entrepreneurs, as reflected in their use of these keywords (fig. 5.2). For example, Huang Hongyun, CEO of Jinke Stock, a real estate firm listed on the Shenzhen Stock Exchange, is a CCP member. "Focusing on devoting to residents for better living quality and urbanization" is Jinke Stock's mission statement.[29] Huang also claimed to "win the battle against poverty and contribute power of the private firm," donating hundreds of millions of dollars to philanthropy.[30]

Based on our interviews, we compared the frequencies of entrepreneurs' use of devotion-related words. CCP members use "mass line," "serving the people," and "devotion" more frequently than non-CCP members (fig. 5.3). This was also borne out by statistical tests on our

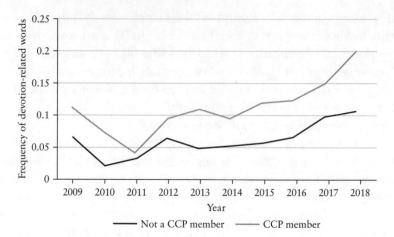

Figure 5.2 Frequency of Devotion-Related Words in Annual Reports of
Entrepreneur-Controlled Publicly Traded Firms
Data sources: Annual reports of firms listed on either the Shanghai Stock
Exchange or the Shenzhen Stock Exchange. Calculated by the authors.

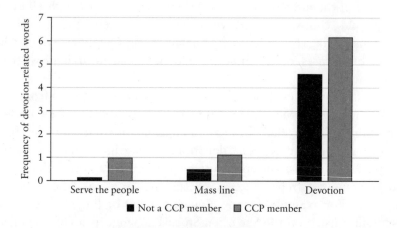

Figure 5.3 Frequency of Devotion-Related Words Used by Surveyed Entrepreneurs
Data source: Authors' survey. Calculated by the authors.

sample of Chinese public companies described earlier. They also donate
more of their revenues. Results from the Chinese Private Enterprise Survey provide further evidence of this.[31] All of this is consistent with our
prior research and a finance study that replicates our work in that paper.[32] Figure 5.4 visually depicts this relationship.

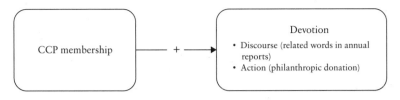

Figure 5.4 Entrepreneurs' Communist Membership and Donations
Data sources: Chinese Private Enterprise Survey and Chinese Stock Market and Accounting Research Database. Calculated by the authors.

At the same time, our interviews showed that noncommunist entrepreneurs also acknowledged devotion to a considerable extent. As shown repeatedly in previous chapters, Mao's influence has penetrated Chinese society deeply and broadly. Around 35 percent of the noncommunist entrepreneurs highlighted devotion during their interviews, frequently connecting the idea to Mao. For example, subject 9 said that "devotion is critical for venturing and being an entrepreneur. . . . After we make money, we shall give it back to the society." Subject 15 said that "current business training often talks about learning Chairman Mao's management philosophy and it is very beneficial . . . and social responsibility is the top priority of my firm." Her firm has donated around $2 million for disaster response, support for the elderly, poverty reduction, education, and support for veterans of the Second Sino-Japanese War. Likewise, subject 20 said, "I think now we should study Maoism seriously, which provides spiritual power for our business, . . . and devotion is critical, for example, charitable donations."

We also compared donations by communist versus noncommunist entrepreneurs. Examining data for both publicly traded firms that are entrepreneur controlled and private firms that are included in the Chinese Private Enterprise Survey using statistical tests and regression analysis, we found that while all entrepreneurs focus on donations to some extent, communist entrepreneurs donate more (as a percentage of revenue) than their noncommunist counterparts.

This trend has been reinforced recently by the CCP-government's renewed emphasis on common prosperity, which articulates that all members of society should achieve prosperity. Mao proposed the idea on December 6, 1953, saying that "gradually achieving the socialist transformation of agriculture is realizing co-operation, eliminating an economic system based on peasants and landlords so that all rural people can get rich together." Deng reformulated the idea, suggesting that while the CCP-government allowed some to become rich first, the final goal is to achieve common prosperity by asking the rich to help the poor to become rich.[33] More recently, on August 17, 2021, Xi proposed staged goals for common prosperity, with income and consumption gaps narrowing in stages between 2025, 2035, and 2050. Part of his speech was published in the most authoritative theory journal of the CCP, *Qiushi* (Seeking truth).[34] It has also been noted that in 2022 Xi and the CCP-government have backed off from this focus to stabilize growth in the run-up to the 20th Party Congress where Xi's potential third term will be decided.[35] But given the deep resonance of this idea in Chinese culture and Mao's teachings, and clear need for China to address income inequality, we believe this idea will endure in the future.

Numerous communist entrepreneurs answered this call; while our perspective suggests that at least part of their rationale is a result of their long-standing ideology, we also should not ignore potentially coercive processes as well. For example, Zhou Haijiang and his Hongdou Group, mentioned earlier, have articulated a mission to "serve the country with industry, achieve common prosperity, win-win for all parties, and benefit the society." Following the government's call, the company invested in the western Chinese province of Xinjiang to reduce poverty. As its business model, Hongdou Group committed to a "three-in-one" structure: "modern enterprise system + CCP/Party building + social responsibility." Zhou also has said that "private enterprises and entrepreneurs are part of China's reform and opening-up policy who are 'allowed' to get rich first. So they have the responsibility and obligation to drive and help the poor to become rich." Similarly, communist entrepreneurs such as Zong Qinghou and Hu Yuling—the latter the founder and CEO of Hongda Thermal Power, which has a registered capital of $10 million—both claimed that "common prosperity is the responsibility of entrepreneurs."[36]

The Maoist emphasis on the devotion focus underlines our argument that Chinese entrepreneurs are not a "bourgeoisie" that will undermine the communist government.[37] They have been co-opted into the statist system, just as influential political science research on "red capitalists" suggests.[38]

There have been myriad writings about corporate philanthropy and other forms of corporate social responsibility in China, many focused on firms' strategic intentions. As noted, there is evidence that corporate social responsibility improves the performance of firms.[39] But while these studies provide important insights into Chinese business, social contribution is not solely driven by economic and instrumental incentives. Some entrepreneurs and firm leaders embrace it as a tool to fulfill their social identities, such as CCP membership, or respond to Mao's call. Our interview subject 24 claimed that as an entrepreneur, "you must first have the spirit of dedication and sacrifice, and then you must take responsibility, have a sense of responsibility, and have a sense of mission." Subject 28 said, "Not just me, entrepreneurs like us, including your previous interviews, may have a devotion focus. If you do not have a devotion focus, you should not be an entrepreneur, you cannot be an entrepreneur." Subject 30 said, "Because the ultimate mission of an enterprise must be to serve the people and contribute to society, social responsibility must be the most important." While Maoism provides a powerful incentive for corporate social responsibility, China is not unique in this regard. There are many examples in other cultures of entrepreneurs who are driven to improve social welfare, enhance sustainability, or create positive impacts on workers, customers, suppliers, community, and the environment.[40]

The focus on social contribution has implications for doing business in China more generally. For example, AstraZeneca, a multinational pharmaceutical and biopharmaceutical company headquartered in the United Kingdom, has a corporate rule that foreign subsidiaries should not donate to local governments. But donations for disaster relief in China are typically made through the Ministry of Civil Affairs—a government organ—and its subordinate organization the Red Cross Society of China. After the 2008 Sichuan earthquake, AstraZeneca's Chinese subsidiary suffered severe backlash from Chinese residents for being stingy. Its CEO explained the situation to headquarters and, after a long delay, obtained approval to donate. But AstraZeneca's reputation had sustained significant damage.[41]

Multinational firms enter into an implicit contract with the Chinese people when they operate in China. Local residents not only require economic contributions to promote growth and employment but also social ones. When the donations of foreign firms like Coca-Cola, Gucci, Nokia, and Samsung fell short of those of local firms, such as the drink brand Wang Laoji, they, like AstraZeneca, experienced a significant backlash.[42] Multinationals should strive to match the commitments of local firms, especially those whose leaders have a devotion focus. Otherwise, they will pay an even larger cost in reputational damage.

6 Mao's Military Thought and Business Strategy and Management

With scant money I cannot start from large cities. I would have to replicate Chairman Mao's success with the surrounding cities from the countryside strategy.
—Shi Yuzhu, founder and CEO of the Giant Group, a large conglomerate that earned US$5 billion in 2020

SHI YUZHU, BORN IN 1962, is an enthusiast of Mao Zedong and applies his military strategies to the Giant Group, the business he founded, which he hopes will become a Chinese version of the giant technology firm IBM. The main strategy he used for its growth was "surrounding cities from the countryside," which he learned from the Maoist idea that revolution in China should start in the countryside, where one can build on initial, small-scale successes to grow over time and eventually conquer the larger and more populated areas. Shi started out selling a melatonin hormone supplement, which he branded as Brain Platinum and which he claimed would be a great gift for children to give their parents to help them sleep. He sent his sales force to rural villages and marketed it one household at a time. Based on his initial success, Shi expanded to big cities and finally to the whole country. Within three years, Brain Platinum was China's top-selling health product; it has remained a symbol of filial devotion for almost two decades.[1] As noted earlier, Ren Zhengfei also claimed to have surrounded cities from the countryside in driving the growth of Huawei.[2]

Mao's military strategies are as applicable to the Chinese business environment as they are because the national economic developmental strategy of the Chinese Communist Party (CCP) is a continuation of Maoism. To feed industrialization, Mao suppressed the prices of agricultural products and elevated those of industrial ones. This harmed farmers, whose income was kept low, incentivizing them to migrate to cities to make a better living—and, tragically, at times resulting in catastrophic food shortages.

To ensure that people remained in their rural areas, Mao implemented the Hukou household registration system, in which Chinese citizens were compelled to reside in the locations where they were born. The policy remains in place to this day, even though hundreds of millions of Chinese have sought jobs in urban environments, making them ineligible to receive health care, get married, or send their children to public schools. But more than five hundred million Chinese are still rural, and they provide opportunities for entrepreneurs to gain footholds in markets where there is limited competition and they can build their strength.

Huawei, Pinduoduo, and Wahaha all started out in the low-end, rural markets that were ignored by established players like Bell, Alcatel-Lucent, Coca-Cola, and Pepsi. More recently, Pinduoduo, founded in 2015, became one of the largest e-commerce and technology platforms in China. To avoid head-to-head competition with established giants such as Alibaba and JD.com, Pinduoduo started out by focusing on underserved populations in rural areas and gradually moved to small cities, large cities, and the entire country.

The principles of military thinkers like Carl von Clausewitz and Sun Tzu are frequently taught at leading business schools, and Mao was a close reader of both.[3] Similarly, Mao's battlefield-tested military strategies and principles have been widely adopted by Chinese entrepreneurs. Lei Jun, a cofounder of Kingsoft (a large Chinese software company), Joyo.com (an online shopping platform that was acquired by Amazon to become Amazon China), and most recently the cellphone powerhouse Xiaomi (one of the largest electronics companies in China), is a loyal fan of Mao's Military Thought. Kingsoft's original business model was based on Mao's idea of guerilla warfare and being flexible. As Lei reflected, the founding and growth of Xiaomi followed a similar guerilla mindset: the company did not have a formal structure until 2018 and relied heavily on low prices to occupy underserved rural markets.[4]

Briefly, Mao Zedong Military Thought, as captured in *Collected Works on the Military by Mao Zedong* and *Selected Works of Mao Zedong*, includes five major interrelated aspects:[5]

1. Its methodology strictly follows the ideas of seeking truth from facts and adapting theories to objective realities. This includes collecting and analyzing information about the adversary's political environment, economic power, military strength, and geographical factors, as well as a focus on learning from one's successes and failures. Mao also emphasized the importance of having a panoramic view and not losing sight of the objective, while also taking care to maintain soldiers' fighting spirit, courage, and morale.

2. The theory of the people's military emphasizes the absolute leadership of the CCP ("political power comes from the barrel of a gun"), a people-centric focus (closely connected to Mao's philosophy of serving the people), ideological and political work, and modernization. To maintain the CCP's strict control, CCP branches should be built at the company level, with CCP members acting as vanguards and role models. The theory also answers the important question of whose interest the CCP and its military fight and stand for, which is the Chinese people.

3. It emphasizes the importance of mobilization, based on Mao's statement, "Revolutionary war is a war of the masses. War can only be waged by mobilizing the masses, and war can only be waged by relying on the masses."[6] CCP troops come from the people and should go to the people to serve them. At times, CCP officials attributed China's campaign against COVID-19 as a "people's war."[7]

4. It emphasizes specific strategic doctrines, including "Surround cities from the countryside," "Never fight an unprepared war," "Concentrate advantageous force to annihilate the enemy," "Engage in protracted war," and others. As we will show in this chapter, all of these strategies are frequently used by Chinese entrepreneurs.

5. It provides an overall theory of national defense that focuses on modernization fueled by socialist construction while emphasizing the importance of military science, industries, and education, which are fundamental to China's battle readiness. It also highlights the principles of independence, autonomy, self-reliance, and hard work.[8]

In this chapter, we describe how Mao Zedong Military Thought is used as business strategies, and the related principles of organizing an army also provide principles of business organization for Chinese entrepreneurs and business leaders.

APPLICATION OF MILITARY STRATEGIES TO BUSINESS COMPETITION

We elaborate the origins, meaning, application, and general implications of the five concepts that are core to Maoist military strategy: never fight an unprepared war, a single spark can start a prairie fire, surround cities from the countryside, concentrate advantageous force to annihilate an enemy, and engage in protracted war.

Never Fight an Unprepared War

A foundational Maoist military strategy is "Never fight an unprepared war," which corresponds to Sun Tzu's "Know yourself and know your enemy, then you will never fail in the war." Mao first stated this as a military principle in 1947, and Chinese entrepreneurs tend to apply it by carrying out thorough market research and on-the-ground field surveys.[9] Shi Yuzhu claimed that he devoted 70 percent of his energy to understanding consumers, talking at length to the rural seniors who initially purchased his melatonin product Brain Platinum. His conclusions were that people who grow up in poverty develop thrifty habits that do not change when their conditions improve, to the point that they would be reluctant to splurge on a health product for themselves. But if their children bought it for them, they would be willing to accept it as a gift. Based on these insights, Shi targeted the children of the elderly, leveraging traditional filial piety.[10]

The video game *Zhengtu* (Journey to war; a multiplayer online game) is another iconic product that Shi sells. To increase its popularity, Shi talked to six hundred players online and met their requests for improvements. For example, players must fight monsters in order to move to the next level, which can be physically draining because they must concentrate intensively and keep their hands moving for as long as seven or eight hours straight. One player in Ningbo, a large city near Shanghai, actually died in an internet café because of the stress. Shi abolished this norm, allowing players to press a button so that the computer will automatically fight. Players can pause, grab a cup of coffee, and watch. The game can continue in an automatic mode, even when the computer is turned off. This change dramatically increased the game's popularity.[11]

Similarly, Zhu Dekun, founder and CEO of the washing-machine maker Little Swan, sought to understand potential consumers by analyzing newspapers, television, and other media. From the data he collected from large cities such as Beijing and Wuhan, he figured out that there is significant market potential, as many residents need washing machines but cannot afford the high prices charged by established brands such as Haier, Sanyo, LG, and Siemens. Zhu deployed his sales forces and promoted his lower-cost products. Little Swan then became popular in these cities and later expanded nationwide.[12] Subject 9 of our interviewed entrepreneurs also claimed, "Firsthand surveys are critical preparation for market entry. Today as leaders, we often have to go down to the grassroots level to understand what is happening on the front line. Otherwise, we will not know how to manage the business. Chairman Mao conducted solid field work in China's rural areas and understood what people really wanted and thus came up with clever fighting strategies. I think Chairman Mao's strategy is very well placed in China. . . . I feel that we should learn from his strategy and strategic positioning." Likewise, subject 28 claimed, "When reporting your work, you need to investigate and understand the situation." She told us that Mao's adage "There is no right to speak without investigation" was her mantra. This also echoes Benjamin Franklin's saying "By failing to prepare, you are preparing to fail."

A Single Spark Can Start a Prairie Fire

Mao's military dictum "A single spark can start a prairie fire" comes from an exchange he had with Lin Biao, a high-ranking military official of the CCP and later vice president. Temporary setbacks should not diminish their confidence, Mao said; what they needed to do was to accumulate enough small wins that they would add up to a triumph. Many Chinese entrepreneurs take this saying as their motto.[13] When Yin Shengxi took over Beijing Dawancha (literally "big bowl tea"), a tea company, he opened a tea stand that sold tea at 0.2 cents per bowl, confident that he could accumulate small wins into a big success. Similarly for Shi Yuzhu. Despite being deeply indebted, the team had faith in Shi and their products and believed that the situation would eventually be turned around. Their small victories in lower-income regions—the spark—later became a nationwide success, which Shi credits to this Maoist strategy.[14] Subject 18 of our interviewed entrepreneurs said, "Although our initial business is not big, as long as our mission is clear and the product positioning is accurate, we have reason to believe that we will succeed step by step. Overall, as Mao suggested, a 'single spark can start a prairie fire.' One needs to be confident and optimistic in their organization's success— despite temporary setbacks—and should accumulate small wins into a later big success."

Surround Cities from the Countryside

An adaptation of orthodox Marxism-Leninism to the Chinese context, surrounding cities from the countryside was one of the guiding principles of the CCP. As noted earlier, orthodox Marxism-Leninism focused on mobilizing workers in factories to seize political power. Earlier leaders of the CCP followed this teaching and suffered significant defeats. Mao mandated that the CCP should not dogmatically implement communism that was developed and practiced in industrialized nations. Since China's was an agrarian economy, the CCP should mobilize farmers rather than workers.[15]

A recent business example of the principle can be found in China's bike-sharing industry. Hellobike began in lower-income villages and cities to evade competition from Mobike and oFo, the two industry giants at the time. After it established its brand, it quickly expanded to larger cities. As of 2021, Hellobike is the largest bike-sharing company in China and plans to go public in the United States.[16] Two entrepreneurs we interviewed also acknowledged that surrounding cities from the countryside is an important strategy. Subject 5 said, "I used Chairman Mao's surrounding cities from the countryside well. I could not beat industry giants such as Suning and Gome and thus have to go to the countryside. At first my 500 chain stores were all in different villages, and step by step, I sieged cities from villages." Subject 16 said, "Our company is strictly following the surrounding cities from the countryside strategy. We started in villages around Chongqing, next moved to Chongqing, and then to Beijing." In general, this strategy implies that firms should find an untapped (usually rural) market niche to survive and build resources, which can then be used later to enter more competitive markets such as in larger cities.

Consistent with Mao's lifelong ambition to unite the developing world in Africa, Asia, and Latin America, the CCP-government is gaining global influence by focusing on relatively underdeveloped regions in which its established competitors (for example, the United States) have less of a presence. Some writers have speculated that China aims to establish its hegemony in these developing countries and gradually expand to more industrialized economies. The Belt and Road Initiative and the proposal of Community of Common Destiny—a foreign policy framework focused on promoting global governance that was inserted into the Chinese constitution in 2018—are specific approaches to this end.[17]

Concentrate Forces to Annihilate the Enemy

During the Chinese Civil War (1945–49), the CCP forces were outnumbered by the Kuomintang. On September 16, 1946, Mao ordered the CCP to concentrate its forces—that is, to focus significant attention on one specific battle with the deadliest possible effect—instead of dispersing its troops across a larger front.[18]

Many Chinese entrepreneurs follow a business version of this strategy.[19] Shi of Brain Platinum said, "I think Mao was right in concentrating resources on one specific spot. I would not move to another city before being 100 percent sure that I had fully occupied the city I was focusing on."[20] Chapter 23 of the Basic Law of Huawei says that Huawei should maintain the principle of concentrating its resources on specific areas of potential growth and allocate more resources than its competitors to those areas.[21]

This strategy remains salient not just because of Mao's ideology but because of the way he designed China's economy: the state-owned sector is core and the private one supplementary. Private firms face a David and Goliath situation at all times, and such a strategy is essential in that situation.

Engage in Protracted War

Mao proposed the idea of "protracted war" in May 1938 to dismiss two extreme views that suggested China would either gain victory over Japan or fall to it quickly. The overly optimistic view was called "quick-win theory," which supposed that other countries would help China militarily while the communist party in Japan overthrew the emperor. The overly pessimistic view was called "subjugation theory."

This presumed that Japanese troops would secure major victories and occupy vast territories in China in as short a time as three months, as some Japanese politicians and officers claimed. Some Chinese believed that industrialized Japan was unstoppable and would do to China what the United Kingdom had done to India. Mao argued that both views were ungrounded. On the one hand, aid from other countries and a communist revolution in Japan might not happen soon enough; China could not expect to beat Japan quickly given its limited military strength. On the other hand, China had a larger population than Japan, its people were being mobilized by the CCP, and it was not totally isolated internationally. Thus far, its military failures were because of the Kuomintang's poor leadership, not China's intrinsic weakness or Japan's intrinsic strength.[22] China could prevail in a protracted war.

Shi applied this thinking to Brain Platinum, noting that a "brand needs time to build and many firms constantly change their brand building process. However, it is not right."[23] Li Dongsheng, founder of TCL, the world's third-largest television manufacturer, often told his employees that "the only way to succeed eventually is to design a strategy for a protracted war."[24] In a meeting on August 3, 2005, he told his managers that "internationalization will be a protracted war, requiring three stages—'turning around, stalemate, and growing,'" acknowledging that it would take at least ten years to establish the brand worldwide. In the meantime, he said, TCL should make small technological and commercial breakthroughs in a guerilla warfare fashion. As those victories accumulated, its chances of becoming an international giant would improve.[25] Similarly, Lei Jun—founder and CEO of Xiaomi—reflected that the founding and growth of the company followed the idea of protracted war. He told staff members, "For Xiaomi's mobile phone business, we must lose the illusion of quick victory, tolerate the slightest misjudgment of the situation, and we must not let go of competition for a minute and a second, and we must fight a 'protracted war.'"[26]

Subject 30 of our interviewed entrepreneurs said, "In my process of starting a business, I was particularly depressed at a certain stage and encountered too much resistance. At that time, I read Mao's 'On the Protracted War' over and over again. It can really be said that I have gained confidence and obtained new thoughts each time I read it, because there are two [Chinese] words in it that are very important, that is, persistence [the two words are 坚持, *jian chi* in Chinese]. Persistence is important in many of our lives." Existing research has also shown that persistence and confidence are critical for business success.[27]

The protracted war strategy is often used in combination with surrounding cities from the countryside and concentrating advantageous force to annihilate the enemy.[28] Mao's speeches and statements often focused on grit, stamina, and the virtues of hard work. Many Chinese entrepreneurs have adopted phrases from them, such as, "The future is bright, but the road is tortuous and full of difficulties," and "Make up your mind, don't be afraid of sacrifice, overcome all difficulties, and strive for victory," as their mottos. For example, subject 3 said, "I deeply agree with many of Chairman Mao's *Quotations,* such as the revolutionary tradition of hard work. I was doing the same and actually these two words are vividly reflected in myself." Subject 15 said that "Chairman Mao's saying that 'there is nothing difficult in the world if people are determined to achieve it' means perseverance and we should never give up quickly."

The doctrine of protracted war is often applied by Chinese businesspeople and even the government in negotiations.[29] For example, when the United States and China normalized their relations in the late 1970s, a tactic adopted by the Chinese side was to prolong the negotiations, which led their American counterparts to become impatient and eager to make a deal. As a result, the US side paid insufficient attention to the Chinese translation of "The U.S. government acknowledges the Chinese position that there is but one China and Taiwan is part of China." "Acknowledges" was used to refer to knowledge and understanding (*renshi dao* [认识到] in Chinese), but the Chinese side translated "acknowledges" as *cheng ren* (承认), which means "recognizes and assents," a much stronger term.[30]

Along these lines, after this agreement was signed, MIT political scientist and sinologist Lucian Pye remarked, "In contrast to American practices, the Chinese do not treat the signing of a contract as signaling a completed agreement; rather, they conceive of the relationship in longer and more continuous terms, and they will not hesitate to suggest modifications immediately on the heels of an agreement."[31] The Chinese government also used this protracted approach in the more recent US-China trade talks, but the US negotiators had learned their lesson and reportedly secured more benefits.[32]

ORGANIZATIONAL PRINCIPLES BASED ON MAO'S THEORY OF THE PEOPLE'S MILITARY

Another important element of Mao Zedong Military Thought is the Theory of the People's Military, or how to organize the CCP military. Entrepreneurs apply it to team- and morale-building.[33]

Team-Building: Socialization and Attrition

Both media reports and our studies show that Chinese entrepreneurs apply Mao's Theory of the People's Military to organize their ventures, particularly in the area of team-building.[34] Jack Ma has said he imitated what Mao did in Yan'an—nurturing core employees and firing or essentially "purging" those whose values did not fit with Alibaba. He specifically said that Mao's "Anti-Japanese Military and Political University is about team management and cadre management." To this end, Ma established two training schools—"A Hundred Years' Plan" for employees and "A Hundred Years' Ali" for managers—which he says turned the initially guerrilla Alibaba team into a regular military, with well-developed skills and a shared core of values.

"An enterprise depends on capturing opportunities to succeed," Ma says, "and instilling values is the most difficult task." To do this, he follows the approach Mao used in the Yan'an Rectification. In 2001, he told his employees, "If you think we are crazy, please leave." He then fired those who would not follow him, claiming, "Through these movements, we will transform employees' ideology to be consistent with our firm's value and expel all those who do not share the same values and sense of mission as our company." Like Mao, Ma believes that "the values and culture we advocate should not stay on as only slogans, but should be implemented in actions."[35]

Ma is not an outlier in this respect. Subject 18 of our interviewed entrepreneurs said, "I admire Chairman Mao very much, and his thinking is a driving force of our company and applicable to our company regardless of the stage of development." Subject 30 stated that it is important to "use the spirit of the CCP and that of CCP members to lead the team."

Motivating Employees by Example

Many entrepreneurs adhere to the principle that CCP members are "vanguards" in their enterprises and thus serve as role models for other employees. For example, Ren Zhengfei claimed that "excellent people of my time would all join the CCP." Subject 17 of our interviewed entrepreneurs specifically mentioned that "it was a big honor to join the CCP." Cui Genliang of Hengtong said, "At the critical moment, it is the CCP members who take the lead and stick to their posts to ensure the smooth progress of research and development."[36] Subject 28 of our interviewed entrepreneurs also claimed that it is critical to "let these CCP members play a vanguard role. We also need to select outstanding CCP members and incorporate them into the construction of corporate culture . . . so that they can guide the work." Subject 31 echoed, "I think that enterprises with Chinese characteristics should have CCP member culture. Let our employees truly feel the advanced nature of our CCP's leadership and CCP members, which can lead the growth and development of our employees. Therefore, the combination of corporate culture and CCP culture can facilitate a good cultural construction within the enterprise. I think this is very important." Li Shijiang, founder of the publicly traded firm Do-Fluoride Chemicals, which in recent years has earned over $4 billion in revenue, said that "CCP members' vanguard role is critical for me in restructuring and developing the enterprise." He claimed that "only the CCP armed with Marxist-Maoist scientific theories can keep our firms on a path of healthy development."[37] Subject 27 of our interviewed entrepreneurs also believed that "for our own enterprise, it must be very helpful if we can really study Mao Zedong Thought more, and Maoism, especially its emphasis of CCP members' vanguard role, must be very helpful to the development and construction of the enterprise."

Consumer Orientation

Mao's Theory of the People's Military also clarifies for whom the CCP's troops are fighting. This is an application of "serving the people" and "mass line," emphasizing that the only purpose of the people's military is to stand closely with the Chinese people and serve them wholeheartedly.

Mao said that "without a people's military, then we will have nothing of the people."[38] As noted earlier, this principle informs entrepreneurs' consumer-oriented focus, especially since Deng Xiaoping's economic reform.

Our interviewed entrepreneurs acknowledge this principle. Subject 26 noted, "Chairman Mao said 'serving the people.' In fact, we as businesspeople are essentially serving our customers as a way of serving the people. . . . Just like when we are a company, I also serve companies, employees, society, and customers. Everything is everyone's business, and your pride is my pride. In this way, the self-arrogance and the tendency of being supercilious in our hearts will disappear, and there will be a sense of awe. This is why the company has been established for so many years, and I have received help from so many people, because I have a mentality of serving others, and others will help me." Similarly, subject 23 said that "Mao's idea of connecting to popular masses is very useful in our company. Issues regarding marketing, e-commerce, and production in our company are basically handled by the employees themselves. I listen to everyone."

Several entrepreneurs we interviewed reinterpreted Mao's quotes, assigning new meanings to them in the context of employer-employee relations. For example, subject 7 repurposed the phrase "fighting the landlord and dividing land," which originally referred to Mao's eradication of the exploitative land rent system, for the context of profit sharing. "We have overcome many difficulties to establish this platform and the market," he said. "After the platform has been built, we then share our results to everyone and also create values together. After that, we will share some of the benefits here, and then let our employees live a better life."

Mao Zedong Military Thought led to a David-versus-Goliath-type victory over the Kuomintang, an opponent with much greater resources. Although Mao was less inspired when it came to economic construction, and his ignorance of the basic laws of economics often led to catastrophic consequences, his optimism and grit in the military realm continue to inspire the Chinese decades after his death.

Many Chinese businesspeople, especially those who came of age around the time of the reform and opening up in 1978, did not receive formal business educations and so relied on Mao when devising their business strategies. But even those who attended business schools in the United States, like Huang Zheng of Pinduoduo, who obtained a master's degree from the University of Wisconsin–Madison, frequently cite Mao. Given the current revival of Maoism in China and the CCP-government's heavy hand in the business sector, it is likely that will continue to be the case for some time.

Mao's Theory of the People's Military also informs many Chinese entrepreneurs' team-building efforts and their consumer-centric orientation. Many of our interviewed entrepreneurs said that Mao's principles and ideas inspire them as people and entrepreneurs and lend them strength in the face of discouragement. Subject 21, for example, said, "Quotes by Chairman Mao created a mindset of independence in people like us since childhood, and so I dare to continue to explore new things and enterprise, even if many people disagreed with me."

In part III, we discuss three important campaigns that Mao initiated—the Great Leap Forward, the Cultural Revolution, and the Third Front Construction—and explore how they have influenced both entrepreneurship and Chinese society at large.

III THE EFFECTS OF MAO'S MASS CAMPAIGNS: THE GREAT LEAP FORWARD, THE CULTURAL REVOLUTION, AND THE THIRD FRONT

After agricultural co-operation, we have the conditions and it is necessary to make a great leap forward on the production front.

The Cultural Revolution leads to chaos of the whole nation and then order of the whole nation, and should occur every seven to eight years.

The imperialist U.S. will not wait for us to complete the Third Front Construction [which will provide China with military potential].
—Mao Zedong

Mass Parade in the Mao Era
"Chinese National Day Parade," Getty Images, January 1, 1960. Bettmann via
Getty Images.

7 The Great Leap Forward and Resource Use

Because of resource scarcity during the Great Famine ... I learned to manufacture treasure from existing scraps.
—Lu Guanqiu, founder and CEO of Wanxiang Group, the largest automotive components manufacturer in China

LU GUANQIU WAS BORN into a poor peasant family in 1944. He dropped out of middle school during the Great Leap Forward (1958–60) and tried to find a job as a laborer. He became a blacksmith but lost this job during the Great Famine. Lu returned to his hometown and worked as a farmer. In 1969 the Chinese Communist Party (CCP) government allowed each township government—then called people's communes (they were organized like agricultural collectives)—to own one agricultural machinery factory. Lu successfully won the bid with borrowed funds of 4,000 yuan/RMB (around US$1,600 then, or US$50,000 today).

He struggled to find raw materials for the factory, but as he put it later, his famine experience helped him.* It is ironic, considering that tens of millions of Chinese died during the Great Leap Forward, but

* Chairman Mao Zedong launched the Great Leap Forward campaign with the goal of transforming agrarian Chinese society into an industrialized one in a short period of time. Yet his unrealistic expectations, lack of knowledge of economic development, and overoptimistic attitude resulted in one of the most serious human tragedies in the twentieth century—a famine in which tens of millions of Chinese starved to death. We in no way discount what an incredible tragedy the famine was or suggest that some unexpected benefits to those who survived could to any extent make up for the millions of lives lost or somehow mitigate Mao's culpability. In this chapter, we want to systematically examine the oft-expressed idea that experiences during the Great Leap Forward famine led to a generation of Chinese entrepreneurs who use resources efficiently, as they were forced to do so during that time.

many entrepreneurs and leaders similarly credit their subsequent successes to the lessons they learned from scarcity they experienced at this time. As Lu recounted in an interview, "During the three years of the great famine, I became swollen from eating tree bark and grass roots . . . but such experience made me creative in finding edible things and to work to feed myself. For example, I started with repairing bicycles and steel wire carts in rural areas."[1]

"Innovation is not to invent out of thin air," he continued. "It is impossible to innovate without reality. What we have is the basis for making anything new."[2] Lu thought creatively and repurposed resources designed for one environment into another. He went to Hangzhou to collect scrapped tractor parts and tools and learned to transform them into farm machines. There were many similarities between agricultural machines and automotive components, and the latter were in high demand. So Lu repositioned his firm to produce universal joints (万向节, wanxiang jie), an important automotive component that is commonly used in drive shafts, and renamed his company Wanxiang. To sell them, Lu went to Jiaonan County, Shandong Province, for the National Auto Parts Ordering Fair in 1980. Since his firm was a farmer-owned, township-village enterprise, organizers did not allow him to enter the exhibition. Lu put up a stall outside the exhibition hall and took orders. In 1983 he bought shares in the factory, using fruit-tree seedlings as collateral to obtain a loan of 20,000 yuan/RMB (around US$160,000 today); after that, 50 percent of the company was owned by Lu and 50 percent was owned by the township government. In 1988 Lu paid another 15 million yuan/RMB (around US$45 million today) to the government and gained full control of the firm. By 1999, his universal joints had garnered more than 65 percent of the total market share in China.

After signing export contracts with two US firms, Lu actively leveraged those connections to further grow the firm. For example, he asked his US partners to help arrange tours of US firms for his employees. Eventually Wanxiang established subsidiaries in the United Kingdom, Germany, and Canada. Lu appeared on the cover of *Newsweek* in 1991—the second Chinese citizen after Deng Xiaoping to be so featured.[3] At home he was profiled in the *People's Daily* and on China National Radio and met with senior leaders such as Deng, Jiang Zemin, and Xi Zhongxun and visited the United States with Hu Jintao and Xi Jinping.[4] While Wanxiang initially was a supplier of the Zeller Corporation—at the time the largest holder of universal joint–related patents and a major dealer of automotive components—twenty years later, Wanxiang acquired Zeller. Wanxiang now controls four publicly traded firms in China and earns $8 billion in annual revenues.

Lu's innovations are an exemplar of "exaptation," the ability to use features or capabilities developed for one environment or purpose in another. "Eating tree bark and grass roots," he said, "made me aware that the biggest problem is how to utilize resources efficiently."[5] Scholars have studied how many fortunes have been built on exaptation. For example, the CD-ROM was developed to record and replay sound without physical contact between parts, but since it stored large quantities of data, it could be adapted by the computer industry to store all kinds of data. The magnetron was invented for radar applications during the Second World War, but it later was found to heat food and thus became a core component of microwave ovens.[6] Our prior work has shown that the capabilities that US banks acquired when they began opening intrastate branches were adapted to allow them to acquire out-of-state banks once interstate branching became legal.[7] Many studies have found that exaptation benefits entrepreneurs and that successful entrepreneurs like Lu employ it to transform their enterprises across different industries—for example, moving from one industry (agricultural machines) to another (automotive components)—and shift them from domestic markets to global markets.[8]

There are many other such examples—for instance, Cao Dewang, chairman of the Fuyao Group.[9] Cao was born in 1946 and forced to drop out of school in 1960 because of the famine. He helped his father sell pipe tobacco but could not continue because the Cultural Revolution, which started in 1966, prohibited such businesses. Cao then switched to selling fruit. Cao recalled that he had to get up at three o'clock every morning and carry three hundred pounds of fruit to a market that was dozens of miles away from home. In the summer he had to stay out in the extreme heat and could not return home until late at night. Through such hard experiences, Cao saved about $19,000, which he used in 1976 to acquire a state-owned glass factory that had experienced seven years of significant losses. After achieving profitability, Cao repurposed the facilities to become an auto glass maker. In time, he sought and received international investments, which he used to expand into Hong Kong and the United States.

With more than ten thousand workers around the world, Fuyao Glass is valued at about $10 billion today, including its US subsidiary in Ohio that was featured in the Academy Award–winning documentary *American Factory*. As Cao reflected, "The Great Leap Forward famine made me stronger" and "gave me creativity so that I can think outside the box and solve problems in a different way."[10]

Consistent with the stories of Lu and Cao, our statistical analysis of a database of Chinese entrepreneurs found that surviving the Great Leap Forward and the resulting famine provided some Chinese entrepreneurs with a mindset that enabled them to achieve future success by utilizing their resources more efficiently.[11] Another example is Wang Shi, founder of China Vanke, at one time the country's biggest property developer. Wang's firm used to sell appliances, scientific instruments, garments, watches, and soft drinks, and he was able to transform the resources gained into success in the real estate market. In his words, "I need to leverage whatever resource I have for my businesses, and it is critical to use resources efficiently."[12]

As noted earlier, entrepreneurs make this connection themselves, describing how they boiled belts and other leather belongings to feed their families and otherwise recycled, repurposed, and adapted and exapted items. Frugality became second nature to them. By repeatedly repurposing and saving, individuals tended to develop a frugal mindset and an ability to repurpose something designed to serve one purpose for new ends. We in no way intend to put a gloss on this tragic period of Chinese history, but simply to understand from a social science perspective how it changed some of the individuals who lived through it and, more broadly, how it affects entrepreneurship in China to this day.

THE GREAT LEAP FORWARD MOVEMENT AND THE GREAT FAMINE (1958–61)

By 1956, China had finished its domestic socialist transformation and its industrial output grew by 31 and 10 percentage points in 1955 and 1956, respectively. Mao Zedong believed that China's initial success corresponded to Vladimir Lenin's statement that socialism is superior to capitalism, and he hoped to quickly industrialize the agrarian Chinese economy. "Can we avoid the detours that the Soviet Union has gone through, and move faster than the Soviet Union, and with higher quality?" he asked. "We should strive for this possibility."[13] Some senior leaders, such as Zhou Enlai (the prime minister) and Liu Shaoqi (the vice president), were more cautious about the Chinese economy and understood that the fast growth rate was more a result of reconstruction after the Second World War. But Mao disparaged their opinions and suppressed others' opposing views. After that, few dared to correct him.

Mao held a grudge against Joseph Stalin, who had intervened in the CCP, and he hoped to gain equal status with the USSR. But he did not have enough confidence to confront Stalin directly.[14] With Nikita Khrushchev, it was a different story.

In Moscow in 1957, during his commemoration of the fortieth anniversary of the October Revolution, Khrushchev asserted that the Soviet Union could surpass the United States in agricultural and industrial production in fifteen years. After the Korean War and the 1956 crises in Poland and Hungary, Mao gained a sense of superiority over Khrushchev. While he initiated the Great Leap Forward under the slogan of "catching up with and surpassing the United Kingdom and the United States,"[15] more recent studies suggest his real aim was to supplant Khrushchev and the Soviet Union as the leader of the global communist movement.[16]

On November 13, 1957, the *People's Daily* published an article entitled "Initiate All Our People to Discuss the Forty Outlines [1956–67 National Agricultural Development Program] and Set Off a New Upsurge in Agricultural Production." "After the agricultural cooperation," the article said, "we have the conditions and need to make a great leap forward on the production front." The article claimed—quite incorrectly, as it turned out—that China's agricultural yields would increase dramatically and that sales of that surplus would subsidize China's rapid industrialization. So began the Great Leap Forward.

KEY ASPECTS OF THE GREAT LEAP FORWARD AND THE GREAT FAMINE

There were two major aspects of the Great Leap Forward: agricultural production and steel manufacturing. First, Mao mandated further agricultural collectivization, combining agricultural collectives and township governments and renaming them people's communes. Before the Great Leap Forward, farmers voluntarily joined agricultural collectives and still owned the means of production—farmland, poultry, and livestock. The people's commune system forced them to hand over their land and livestock as well as all their personal belongings, including pots and pans and tables and chairs. All farmers would eat in communal dining halls. Meals were free and compensation was uniform within the commune based on average yield. This institutional design was meant to motivate farmers by eliminating inequality and ensuring that no one would go hungry. But many farmers slaughtered their poultry and livestock in order not to have to share them with others. Meanwhile, the distribution system dampened farmers' incentives and encouraged free riding, while the communal dining halls encouraged them to eat more than they needed. All of these factors caused a sharp decline in crop yields.[17]

Because officials who disagreed with Mao were punished, most overreported agricultural yields. Liu had tried to talk to Mao about the unrealistic goals at first but was criticized. Later, he ingratiated himself with Mao, proposing the antiscientific and senseless slogan, "How bold the people are, how productive is the land." Many people's communes overreported their rice yields by a hundred times, claiming they produced 33.456 tons (30,351 kilograms) of rice per acre. However, this was impossible; by 2020 the world-record yield for hybrid rice was only 10.342 tons (9,382 kilograms) per acre.[18]

As would be expected, the official dailies published more than two thousand articles promoting the Great Leap Forward in different industries in China; the *People's Daily*, controlled by the central government, published one article every three days over the three-year period. One published on August 27, 1958, featured Liu's slogan in its headline: "How Bold the People Are, How Much Yield We Have (Situation of the Great Leap Forward of Agricultural Production in Shouzhang County, Shandong Province)." This slogan became an iconic phrase in the movement that went against scientific assessments.

As elaborated earlier, a main approach of the Great Leap Forward was agricultural collectivization as people's communes. We tracked mentions of the term "people's commune" in different provincial dailies (fig. 7.1).

Scholars have found that officials' overreporting of agricultural yields correlated with the likelihood of their being promoted.[19] Such trends are quite apparent from the frequency of the term "agricultural production per mu" (亩产; mu is the Chinese agricultural area unit, about 17 percent of an acre) in Chinese newspapers at the time (fig. 7.2). Also

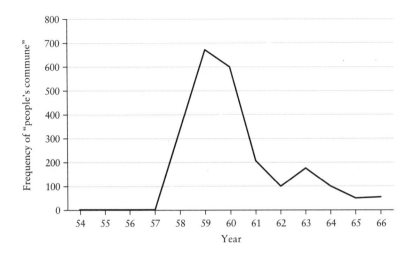

Figure 7.1 Frequency of the Keyword "People's Commune" in Official Newspaper Headlines (1954–1966)
Data sources: Official daily newspapers of each province's CCP committee. Calculated by the authors.

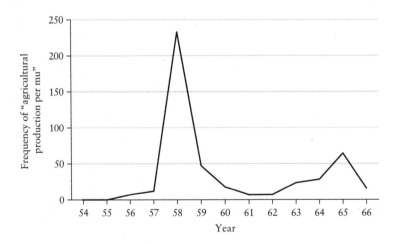

Figure 7.2 Frequency of the Keyword "Agricultural Production per mu" in Official Newspaper Headlines (1954–1966)
Data sources: Official daily newspapers of each province's CCP committee. Calculated by the authors.

commonly used was the term "signaling satellites." Mao perceived the Soviet Union's launch of Sputnik as proof of the superiority of communism. In this context, "satellite" is metaphorically used to suggest agricultural yields would skyrocket.

And they did, at least in local officials' false reports. On June 8, 1958, the *People's Daily* reported that Suiping County in Henan Province had obtained an average wheat yield of 1,007.5 kilograms per mu, a number that increased to 1,178.5 kilograms per mu on June 9 in Guchen County in Hubei, and 1,197.0 kilograms per mu on June 11 in another Hebei county. As other counties competed to report the greatest yield, the number rose to 4,292.7 kilograms per mu. Reported rice yields were driven to delusional heights by the competition as well: the number started at a substantial but realistic 1,637.5 kilograms per mu in a county in Fujian but rose to 30,215.8 kilograms in a county in Guangdong.

Mao was initially skeptical, but he allowed himself to be convinced by his sycophantic advisers. The renowned scientist Qian Xuesen (also known as Hsue-Shen Tsien), a mathematical physicist who had taught at MIT and CalTech and worked on the Manhattan Project, curried favor with Mao by saying that the reported yields were theoretically possible.[20] The most exaggerated report, from Xushui County in Hebei Province, claimed that its rice yield was 661.4 tons (0.6 million kilograms) per mu—a figure that was about ten thousand times greater than possible. But by late 1959, Mao could no longer deny the truth. On January 14, 1961, at the Ninth Plenary Session of the Eighth Conference of the Chinese Communist Party, the end of the Great Leap Forward was announced. Mao was publicly criticized by Liu, and he also self-criticized, accepting much of the blame for the catastrophe.

The second major part of the Great Leap Forward was steel manufacturing. Mao believed that since collectivization would dramatically increase agricultural production, rural labor could be transferred to manufacturing. Steel output would have to be dramatically increased. Mao and the CCP put forward the wildly unrealistic goal of doubling it within a year. Steel production became China's top priority, and around ninety million people, or two-fifths of its labor force, were deployed. Millions of backyard furnaces were fired up and many people melted down their cooking utensils to help meet the goal (fig. 7.3). Many people donated their iron products—such as handles and cooking utensils—to increase steel output.

Figure 7.3 Backyard Furnaces during the Great Leap Forward
"Great Leap Forward, the Kuhsien Steel Mill in Changchi City Added about 220 Small Local-Type Furnaces in Seven Days, Increasing the Daily Steel Output from a Meager 90 Tons to 2,150 Tons—Surpassing the Daily Output of the Taiyuan Iron and Steel Plate," Getty Images, January 2, 2013. Sovfoto/Universal Images Group via Getty Images.

However, these furnaces could not produce steel but only less refined pig iron, which was mostly useless for industrial applications. Worse still, because labor was transferred to produce steel, there was a shortage of farmworkers; about 10 percent of crops could not be harvested. The estimated daily per-capita availability of food (1,500 calories) dropped well below the average requirement (2,100 calories); death rates spiked to 2.5 percent, 3.7 percent, and 2.5 percent of the population in 1959, 1960, and 1961, respectively, compared with 1.1 percent for the years 1956 through 1958 (fig. 7.4).[21] Crop yields dropped by more than 25 percent, cotton yields by 35 percent, oil crops by more than 50 percent, and pork production by 56 percent. Tens of millions of Chinese died of hunger. Moreover, it is estimated that 140,000 to 200,000 refugees fled from mainland China to Hong Kong illegally because of the famine.

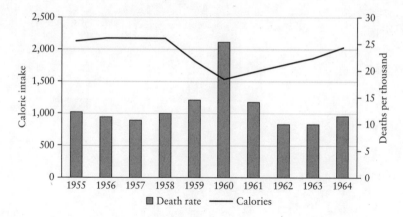

Figure 7.4 Death Rate and Average Caloric Intake of Chinese during the Great Leap Forward
Data source: Ashton, Basi, Kenneth Hill, Alan Piazza, and Robin Zeitz, "Famine in China, 1958–61," *Population and Development Review* 10, no. 4 (1984): 615, 617.

For many years, the Chinese official media euphemistically referred to the period as the "three years of natural disasters," glossing over the manmade issues stemming from Mao's prioritization of agricultural collectivization and backyard furnaces. But as even Vice President Liu admitted, "thirty percent of the problem was driven by natural disasters and seventy percent of the problem was human made."[22] The official media finally began referring to the period as the "three years of hardship" after June 27, 1981, when the Sixth Plenary Session of the Eleventh Central Committee of the Chinese Communist Party summarized the lessons of the previous thirty years of communist governance and provided an overall evaluation of Mao.[23] Even so, the institutional form of people's communes was maintained.

But eventually, grassroots pressure led the communes to a de facto breakdown. In one famous case, on November 24, 1978, due to the difficulty of maintaining their livelihoods, eighteen farmers in Xiaogang Village in Fengyang County of Anhui Province signed a "Life and Death Certificate" and distributed the land in their village so that individual farmers were responsible for their own plots. They promised each other that if any of the group were prosecuted and found guilty, the others would take care of their families. A year later, twelve of the eighteen households each produced more than five thousand kilograms of grain, their output of oil surpassed the total of the twenty years since the start of collectivization in 1957, and the collective income of the members increased by six times over the previous year. Xiaogang sold grain and oil to the country for the first time since the collectivization, exceeding its quota for grain by six times and for oil by eighty times. Deng took notice and decided to abolish the people's commune system.

FROM FAMINE EXPERIENCE TO BUSINESS SUCCESS

Accounts from entrepreneurs and our analysis suggest that the famine experience, tragic though it was, inculcated two important qualities in entrepreneurs: greater frugality and efficiency in the use of existing resources and a penchant for repurposing seemingly useless resources.

Frugality and Cost Reduction

Faced with such overwhelming resource scarcity, people were forced to capture as much value as they could from what they had. Further coloring individuals' experiences during this period was the ideology underlying the Great Leap Forward. These included "working hard and saving" and "building socialism quickly and economically," built on the foundational Maoist principle of frugality.[24]

Both the actual scarcity and the constant propaganda likely resulted in the same kind of imprinting process we discussed in earlier chapters. As established in social science research in the United States, people who live through hardship are less likely to overestimate their ability to obtain resources as compared with those who experienced resource-rich environments, who are more likely to misattribute the ease of obtaining resources to their own abilities.[25] Further, and as noted earlier, research suggests that surviving hardships such as the Great Depression can make individuals more psychologically resilient and healthy.[26] Subject 17 of our interviewed entrepreneurs suggested that such experiences made two uncles of hers—who later became entrepreneurs—stronger in both their abilities and their psychology. Subject 32 also said that frugality and cost saving were his firm's top priorities, explaining, "I have been poor and I am afraid of being poor, so I dare not do high-risk things but save every penny."

Many Chinese entrepreneurs have articulated the relationship between their early experiences with privation and their intense focus on cost reduction today. Chen Ruifeng began working at the age of ten, babysitting and selling tofu. Eventually she became a "barefoot doctor" (a minimally trained rural health care provider). When she was fifty-two, she established her firm, Putian Fuxin Mopei Computer Numerical Control Company. The firm earns millions of dollars in revenues, but Chen maintains a frugal lifestyle, taking a bus to meetings of the National People's Congress and admonishing her children and grandchildren to, in her words, "not waste time on dressing up, eating and playing, you must be ambitious and work on your career with your feet on the ground."[27] Likewise, Xu Jiayin, founder, CEO, and chairman of the real estate group Guangzhou Evergrande and for a time the richest man in China, commonly reflected, "I still remember Chairman Mao's words on frugality and thus kept a thrift style when I was starting Evergrande."[28] Xu claimed that he "had bitter memories of starvation during his early childhood" and "would not tolerate wasting a single bottle of mineral water."[29] While Xu's frugality may have been critical for his success, his later overspending created problems for his firm. In late 2021, Evergrande was found to owe investors more than $300 billion (2 percent of the Chinese gross domestic product and twice as much as the company's total assets), and many believe it will go bankrupt.[30]

We also provide more systematic evidence based on our data from the nationwide survey of Chinese entrepreneurs. We calculated that firms run by entrepreneurs who experienced the Great Leap Forward famine in their early lives (zero to fourteen years of age) save 13.9 percent (50.5 percent versus 64.5 percent, or 21.6 percent in relative terms) more in costs for their firms than those who did not have such experiences, and they charge their firms 10 percent less (15.5 percent versus 25.5 percent, or 39.2 percent in relative terms) in personal costs (fig. 7.5). This contributes to a 13 percent increase in performance.[31]

Similarly, we reexamined our findings with CEOs of publicly traded firms in China. On average, CEOs who experienced the Great Leap Forward famine in their early lives save 55.1 percent more revenue from the total costs of the firms they are managing than those who did not have such experiences. This translates into a 1.5 percent greater return on assets.

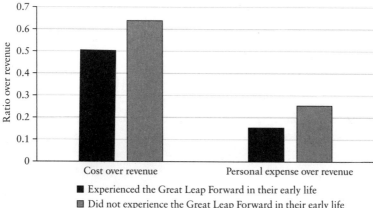

Figure 7.5 Costs, Personal Expenses, and Entrepreneurs' Great Leap Forward Experience
Data source: Chinese Private Enterprise Survey. Calculated by the authors. Costs and personal expenses are divided by total revenues.

Repurposing Resources

Another effect of the Great Leap Forward famine is that it forced some future entrepreneurs to think outside the box and repurpose the limited resources they had. This ability is particularly important for new ventures, as they are often underfunded in their early stages. Compared with cost reduction, repurposing is a more indirect method of utilizing resources efficiently, as it involves reallocating resources that had been intended for a different purpose to a more productive end. For many, repurposing was a matter of desperation (for example, boiling and eating leather belts).[32]

But in the cases of Lu Guanqiu of the Wanxiang Group and Cao Dewang of Fuyao, it was transformative. Many of our interviewed entrepreneurs who experienced the Great Leap Forward also expressed this. Around 30 percent of them described repurposing or exapting their firms' existing capabilities for new uses. For example, subject 26 invested money in etiquette training for her employees so they could better serve her customers. Later, she repurposed that capability by providing etiquette training to other firms and individuals. Similarly, subject 27 invested a great deal of time and money into establishing a data analysis department for his company. Later, he repurposed that capability when he extended his firm's business into consulting. Likewise, subject 30 spent a lot of resources to train his employees to learn product and operational design for his agricultural business. This later became the basis of his brand management department.

Many entrepreneurs who experienced the Great Leap Forward repurposed foreign investment into global expansion (and vice versa). As elaborated earlier, the CCP-government has had a two-step macroeconomic development strategy since the reform: first attracting foreign capital and then letting domestic firms go global to compete in the international market. Foreign investment and international expansion involve similar capabilities in a firm, and they fall under similar administrative auspices in terms of the CCP-government's policy and regulative regimes. As such, the skills and connections developed in one arena can be repurposed for use in the other. For example, venture capital from developed countries often brings opportunities for new market entry, and entrepreneurs might reconfigure their resources and organizational processes to support international expansion. Entrepreneurs who experienced the Great Leap Forward famine tend to be more adept at redeploying resources to leverage opportunities, gain access to finances and lower-cost capital, and solicit trust and reduce uncertainty within potential host markets.

Thus, Cao leveraged his connections to foreign investors to obtain sufficient funds for international expansion, and Lu sent his employees to learn from foreign investors. Receiving foreign funding from venture capitalists can also help establish reputations, as firms from emerging markets such as China's often lack credibility. Wang Dianjie, who was born in 1956, is the founding CEO of the multinational garment company Xianglong. He has suggested that his early experiences with hardship helped him turn foreign investment in his firm into a reputational advantage.[33]

We show evidence based on the nationwide survey of Chinese entrepreneurs as well (fig. 7.6). Entrepreneurs who experienced the Great Leap Forward famine in their early lives were 4.4 percent (9.4 percent versus 5.0 percent, or 89.4 percent in relative terms) more likely to leverage foreign venture capital into international expansion than those who did not experience the famine (i.e., the likelihood of investing abroad

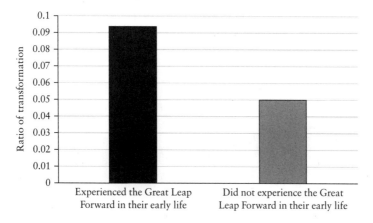

Figure 7.6 Transformation of Inward Foreign Investment into Outward Foreign Investment and Entrepreneurs' Great Leap Forward Experience
Data source: Chinese Private Enterprise Survey. Calculated by the authors.

when they have received inward foreign investment). The statistical analyses in a research paper we recently published also bear this out.[34] Our analysis of the database of publicly traded firms that are controlled by entrepreneurs yielded similar results.

IMPLICATIONS OF RESOURCE USE DRIVEN BY THE GREAT LEAP FORWARD

While repurposing means allocating existing resources that had been intended for one end to another purpose ex post, reducing costs means allocating existing resources that have not yet been expended to more meaningful purposes ex ante. Hence, repurposing and reducing costs represent, respectively, indirect and direct ways of utilizing existing resources more efficiently.

Entrepreneurs' experiences affect how they evaluate, identify, select, and act on different opportunities and navigate different processes, influencing their likelihood of success. Entrepreneurs with famine experience are likely more cautious but also more creative. They tend to carry out thoughtful and practical strategies and commit fewer major errors. Given the high failure rate of new ventures—95 percent in China—and the possibility that entrepreneurs may suffer from cognitive biases and an overreliance on heuristics that could prove disastrously wrong, such a prudent and steadfast mindset can be seen as a distinct competitive advantage.[35] For example, Liu Yonghao, founder of the agricultural products company New Hope Group, recalled that the Great Famine experience made him cautious and prudent and thus is responsible for his success.[36] Chen Kaixuan, the founder of the leading cleaning products company Liby, suggested that his success was partially due to his cost-cutting strategies, which were a result of his famine experience.[37]

As terrible a human tragedy as the Great Leap Forward and the subsequent famine were, some of their survivors drew benefits from their hardships. Indeed, while the negative effects of such crises are significant, research—including our own prior academic papers—has discerned potential silver linings. For instance, a recent finance article shows that early-life exposure to natural disasters—earthquakes, volcanic eruptions, tsunamis, hurricanes, floods, and fires—can make CEOs more entrepreneurial and resilient. The rationale is that having lived through disaster, they are better able to navigate risk and more confident in their ability to do so. In addition to detailed statistical analyses, the article's authors cite a number of compelling anecdotal examples, such as Apple's Steve Jobs and Tim Cook, who both witnessed numerous deaths due to natural disasters and as a result, they claim, became greater risk-takers and more adventurous.[38] Another paper shows via statistical analysis what many Chinese entrepreneurs who lived through the famine intuit: that the rate of entrepreneurship in the counties that were the hardest hit during the famine is the highest.[39]

More recently, the world was struck by the COVID-19 pandemic, the impacts of which will likely be felt for years. History has witnessed many such crises and disasters, and the lessons they teach us are grim. The media frequently compares COVID-19 with the 1918 influenza pandemic, which infected more than five hundred million people and killed seventeen million to fifty million globally.[40] Social scientists have found that survivors experienced lifelong consequences that might be associated with the 1918 pandemic, including reduced educational attainment, increased rates of physical disability, and lower incomes and socioeconomic status. They also found that people who were exposed to influenza in utero were more likely to suffer from poorer health and have a higher mortality rate.[41] There is abundant evidence for other long-lasting negative effects from severe economic downturns, such as reduced educational attainment and weaker work ethic.[42]

We in no way mean to discount the severity of the Great Famine or dismiss its tragic toll. Tens of millions of Chinese people starved to death; hundreds of millions have suffered from long-term negative consequences such as shortened height and life expectancy, as well as more frequent mental disorders.[43] The Great Leap Forward is responsible for subsequent disasters as well. The catastrophic dam failures in Henan Province during Typhoon Nina in 1975 killed tens of thousands—possibly as many as 250,000. The dams were hastily planned and constructed during the initiative; many used low-quality materials because of the focus on steel production. Deforestation, driven by the push to industrialize, exacerbated the flooding.[44]

However, we suggest that the lasting effects of such disasters and crises on human populations are complex. As we have seen, many entrepreneurs credit their success to their early hardships, which they believe made them more prudent and creative in using limited resources. As subject 1 of our interviewed entrepreneurs put it, "In fact, [the Great Leap Forward] may show that China or the Communist Party may have taken some detours, but I think it is the same with doing business: just like if we take a train and flight, the highway does not have a straight line to reach the destination. As long as the general direction is right, there must be some twists and turns in this process." Subject 27 said, "Through different experiences, we develop different approaches or different actions. These actions are for living better and more safely, and we can better survive with a sense of crisis." In line with our discussion, others have pointed out that some of the most creative and successful companies of the last decade were founded during the 2008 financial crisis.[45] Recent studies suggest that COVID-19 has enhanced solidarity among people and increased support for world leaders, which could have potentially positive implications for entrepreneurship.[46] Productivity increases because of these factors might offset and even override some of the pandemic's long-term negative effects. As the German philosopher Friedrich Nietzsche said, "What does not kill you makes you stronger."

8 The Cultural Revolution and Institutional Confidence

Many Chinese entrepreneurs experienced the Cultural Revolution . . . and thus are unconfident about the Chinese institutional system and less likely to abide by the law. They are aware that their wealth might be gone overnight.
—Huang Nubo, owner of the $2.3 billion
Beijing Zhongkun Investment Group

HUANG NUBO WAS BORN IN 1956. In 1960, his father, Huang Junfu, was accused of being a counterrevolutionary. Unable to bear the stigma, he committed suicide. During the Cultural Revolution (1966–76), five types of "enemies of the people" were singled out for persecution— landlords, rich farmers, counterrevolutionaries, bad influencers, and capitalist sympathizers (called rightists in China). People were assigned to those categories based on their class backgrounds and family origins, so their children, like Huang, were labeled future anticommunists. Huang frequently engaged in fistfights to maintain his dignity. To lose his stigma, he denounced his father and joined the Red Guard—the paramilitary youth organization that aimed to guard its "Red God" Mao Zedong and further the revolution. He attended many "struggle sessions," where class enemies were publicly tortured and humiliated, and once used his "iron fists" to punch a former landlord, who died soon after.

All of this imbued him with a deep cynicism about the Chinese system. For "people who lived through the Cultural Revolution," Huang later wrote, "there is no use trying to figure out who is a human and who is a ghoul. . . . The Cultural Revolution taught my generation that you must act like a wolf in order to survive."[1] When the Cultural

Revolution was over and universities reopened, Huang was the first student from his province to be admitted to Peking University. After graduating, he rose through the ranks in the party. In 1995 he became an entrepreneur and launched the Beijing Zhongkun Investment Group.

Evidence suggests that entrepreneurs who came of age during the Cultural Revolution tend to be less law abiding, since the decade-long political campaign sabotaged laws and regulations and encouraged contempt for Chinese institutions. According to the Annual Report of Entrepreneurs' Corruption Crimes, the majority of present-day corruption cases were committed by people alive during the Cultural Revolution.[2] Some reports explicitly attribute those offenders' crimes to the "original sin" of the Cultural Revolution.[3]

Since 2015, the Chinese government has passed regulations targeting people who ignore court orders to pay their debts, labeling them "defaulters" and the "shameless" and banning them from plane travel, applying for loans and credit cards, and promotions. Huang, like many of his generation, has been on the defaulters list ten times and has had to sell a significant portion of his property.[4]

Many Chinese entrepreneurs sought to leave the country after they became rich, either because they feared for their personal and financial security or because they had committed crimes and wanted to escape punishment. As his business grew, Huang kept a lookout for opportunities to escape.[5] At one point, he offered to pay $160 million for a lease on land in Iceland that he proposed to develop into a tourist site (Iceland rejected his offer).[6] At the time, Huang expressed his fears that the Cultural Revolution would recur, saying that the "harm" it had brought to "his heart" could never be undone.[7] The real estate developer Chen Tianyong, who also lived through the Cultural Revolution, escaped to Malta, declaring that he had lost his faith in China under the Chinese Communist Party (CCP) government.[8] Hundreds of other Chinese entrepreneurs have fled from China over the past decade, fearing that President Xi Jinping will start a new Cultural Revolution.[9]

In this chapter, we explore the lasting effects of the Cultural Revolution, one of the most critical periods in China since the communist takeover in 1949. Entrepreneurs who lived through this epoch are more likely to bribe and commit other crimes, to default on their debts, and to expatriate. The damage it did to China's institutional credibility is almost incalculable.

THE CULTURAL REVOLUTION

While historians continue to debate his explicit intentions, most agree that Mao implemented the Cultural Revolution to solidify his authority as the undisputed intellectual and spiritual leader of both China and world communism.[10] That authority had waned since Mao's disastrous Great Leap Forward initiative and the subsequent famine. Because of the backlash, he had "retreated to the second line," delegating his power as leader of the government to President Liu Shaoqi, and allowed Mao Zedong Thought to be dropped from the CCP's constitution. But Mao remained chairman of the Central Committee of the CCP, and since the CCP is above the government, he was still the supreme leader.[11]

In the meantime, Liu wielded enormous power; like Mao, he focused on publishing his own "Theory" and took on a speaking tour to promote a cult of personality of his own.[12] To make things worse, the foreign media called Liu's wife the "first lady" of China, which made Mao's wife Jiang Qing furious.[13] Mao became concerned that Liu was trying to usurp his position and feared that he would be negated or even demonized after his death, as had happened to Joseph Stalin. Such revisionism, Mao believed, was tantamount to practicing capitalism, and he saw the reforms Liu and Deng Xiaoping were undertaking—for example, dividing the land to reverse the people's communes he had established—as tantamount to betrayal. While quarreling with Liu in May 1962, he shouted, "If the Three Red Flags [General Guideline of Socialist Construction, the Great Leap Forward, and the People's Commune] are gone and the land is also divided, how can we maintain socialism and the CCP's rule? I cannot imagine what might happen after my death!"[14]

More broadly, Mao suspected that the whole party system had turned against him. He started his counterattack in September 1962, criticizing Liu for being too pessimistic and only focusing on the dark side of socialist construction. Then he led the Politburo to demote those who challenged him but were of a lower political rank than Liu and Deng, such as Peng Dehuai (the chief commander of Chinese troops in the Korean War and then vice prime minister and minister of defense) and Xi Zhongxun (Xi Jinping's father).

To further consolidate his power, Mao put forward the theory of continuing revolution under the dictatorship of the proletariat, the conceptual foundation of the Cultural Revolution. The theory proposed a cultural revolution to exterminate the five forces opposing China's socialist development—landlords, rich peasants, anti-revolutionists and reactionaries (the Kuomintang in Taiwan), bad influencers, and foreign powers (revisionists such as the Soviet Union, its satellite states, and senior leaders such as Liu and Deng and those belonging to the capitalist camp). In this way, Chinese society could achieve a purer socialism, with Mao's influence at the center.

Mao invented the term "capitalist order"—powerful people or groups who demonstrated a marked tendency to pull the Chinese revolution in a capitalist direction—to tarnish Liu, Deng, and the other rival leaders who threatened his leadership. Mao implied that Liu was the Chinese version of Nikita Khrushchev. Senior leaders who wished to get promoted, such as Lin Biao, eagerly promoted Mao's cult of personality. Lin eventually replaced Liu as vice chairman of the CCP's Central Military Commission and became Mao's officially recognized successor.

Once that groundwork was laid, Mao officially launched the Cultural Revolution on May 16, 1966, with his "Notice to the Central Committee of the CCP" (also known as the "516 Notice"). "The Decision of the Central Committee of the Chinese Communist Party on the Great Proletarian Cultural Revolution" was officially published on August 8, 1966, in the *People's Daily*.

How the Cultural Revolution Unfolded

The main focus of the Cultural Revolution was the overthrow of the existing institutional system.[15] It had three main thrusts: replacement of the CCP's committees and governments with revolutionary committees loyal to Mao and displacement of the CCP's rules on cadre appointments; the persecution, torture, and killing of class enemies, led by Red Guards and "rebellious factions"; and establishment of the send-down movement, in which young people were relocated to poor villages to gain a better understanding of rural life and the hardships farmers experience. University entrance exams were suspended and universities were closed for the next eleven years.

CCP committees and government organs at the national and regional levels were replaced with "revolutionary committees" under Mao's supervision. Liu and Deng were called "commanders of the capitalist order," heavily criticized, and ultimately removed from power. As Deng sarcastically put it later, "Chairman Mao bombarded the headquarters of capitalist order led by Comrade Liu Shaoqi and me."[16] At the national level, the Central Cultural Revolution Group displaced the CCP Politburo and became the de facto highest decision-making entity in China. At the local level, Chen Pixian—the party secretary of the CCP Shanghai committee—was replaced by two members of the Gang of Four (a group of high-ranking officials loyal to Mao, consisting of his wife Jiang Qing, Wang Hongwen, Zhang Chunqiao, and Yao Wenyuan). One of them was Wang, who rose from a low-ranking cadre to become Mao's successor and vice chairman of the CCP by rebelling against Chen and the CCP Shanghai committee after Lin's mysterious death.[17]

The Cultural Revolution sabotaged the existing political system, allowing those who were loyal to Mao to quickly rise to power without going through the official, bureaucratic procedure of cadre appointments, in which individuals would gradually rise from the level of township through the county, prefectural or city, provincial, and finally national levels. It typically takes as long as thirty years for an official to rise through all five levels. Presidents Hu and Xi took twenty-seven and twenty-eight years, respectively, to rise from township-level officers to vice president and de facto president-to-be. For Wang, it took just seven years. There are many other examples of Mao loyalists' rapid rises. Despite being semiliterate, Chen Yonggui rose from a party secretary of the model village Dazhai to a national-level leader in 1973, and then vice prime minister in 1975. Two female model workers whom Mao liked, Wu Guixian and Li Suwen, rose from below the township level (without a political rank) to national-level leaders within seven years.

There were massive persecutions, killings, and violence throughout the period, affecting millions of Chinese who had been labeled as capitalists (former CCP committee leaders, intellectuals, clergypersons, and so on) and feudalists (landlords, rich peasants, monks, and so on). As class enemies, they were denounced and forced to apologize publicly in "class struggle sessions" and their property was confiscated. Some were housed in camps and forced to do manual labor on farms to atone for their anticommunist deviancy. Torture was common, and there were many suicides. Liu, Peng, and He Long, a marshal of the Chinese army, all died when they were refused medical treatment after being tortured by Red Guards. According to the December 20, 1980, *Beijing Daily,* be-

Figure 8.1 Mobilized Female Red Guards
"Performance during Cultural Revolution," Getty Images, March 4, 1974.
Bettmann via Getty Images.

tween August and September 1966, 1,772 people were killed by Red
Guards in Beijing, including many teachers and principals, 33,695
households suffered confiscation, and 85,196 families were forced to
leave their homes. More than 100,000 people died of persecution in
Guangxi Province.

Mao encouraged the violence, admonishing a Red Guard leader
named Song Binbin that she should change her name from Binbin
(meaning "polite, refined, and courteous") to Yaowu (to be violent and
militant). On August 5, 1966, Song led a group of Red Guards into the
High School for Female Students Attached to Beijing Normal University (now the Experimental High School Attached to Beijing Normal
University), and they beat the principal, Bian Zhongyun, to death, the
first recorded killing of the Cultural Revolution (see photo of female
Red Guards performing their loyalty to Mao in fig. 8.1). Violence

between factions loyal to Mao was common as well, with weapons that ran the gamut from sticks and bricks to rifles, grenades, and even tanks that were stolen from arsenals. Chongqing, Luzhou in Sichuan Province, and Xuzhou in Jiangsu Province essentially entered a period of civil war, and nationwide, there were more than seven million casualties and 237,000 deaths before Mao realized that the situation had gotten out of control and issued a notice on July 3, 1968, to end such violence.[18]

Tens of millions of youths were affected by the Cultural Revolution. Countless adolescents joined the Red Guards when they entered middle or high school, eager to follow Mao by denouncing their teachers, denigrating knowledge, and torturing anyone they thought of as anti-Mao, counterrevolutionary, capitalist, or feudalist. These youths were the executive forces for confiscation and class struggle sessions, and their violence was justified by Mao's saying that revolution is innocent and rebellion is reasonable.[19] Since universities were shut down, professors were sent to the countryside or factories to do manual labor. Jobs in cities became scarce because the national priority was "continued revolution," not economic construction, and most employers stopped hiring. To deal with the masses of idle students, Mao initiated the send-down movement in 1967, relocating tens of millions of youths living in urban areas to poor villages, where they joined peasants living in poverty and starvation so they could better understand the hardships farmers experience and apply their knowledge to farming, eliminating the differences between urban and rural areas and between mental and physical work. One of the millions of young adults who were sent to the country was Xi Jinping, whose father had fallen out of favor with Mao again. The sudden influx of youths created problems in many villages, which lacked adequate food for their own needs. Fistfights and even armed fighting were common.

The huge urban-rural differential and the poor organization of work in rural areas resulted in chaos. Many of these urban children could not live through hardship. For example, Xi ran away, but he was later persuaded to return by his uncle; ultimately, he stayed in the country for seven years. When his father was rehabilitated, Xi became a Worker-Peasant-Soldier student at Tsinghua University.[20] But he was an exception; only those whose parents were high-ranking officials or who performed very well in the send-down movement could return from the countryside.

There were numerous incidents of sexual assault and rape. Between September 1973 and December 1974 in Shanghai, 90 percent of criminal cases related to the send-down movement involved sexual violence. One clerk of the send-down movement office was found to have raped three female sent-down youths and assaulted sixteen others. Army officers in Heilongjiang, Inner Mongolia, and Yunnan raped many female sent-down youths. When they were finally allowed to return to cities, there were a limited number of city residence permits; bribery to obtain them was common. Many officials solicited sexual favors from young women who were desperate to return to college, or they demanded that the women marry them.[21]

In addition to the sabotage of the institutional system, the massive and violent struggles, and the send-down movement, the chaos and violence were reflected at the top of the leadership hierarchy of the CCP. After Mao had grabbed power back from Liu and Deng by 1969, he appointed Lin as his official successor. In 1971 Lin, who was already in poor health, was said to have died in a plane crash. Mao then nurtured Wang as his potential successor, whose incompetence and luxurious lifestyle were widely critiqued.[22] In April 1976, five months before his death, Mao removed Wang from the succession and appointed Hua Guofeng in his place.

The institutional upheaval undermined both the authority and credibility of the CCP. As Huang Nubo put it, "Many Chinese entrepreneurs maintained a Cultural Revolution mindset and were less confident of China's rule of law."[23]

The End of the Cultural Revolution

On September 9, 1976, Mao passed away. His final messages to his designated successor, Hua, were, "Do not be hasty and work steadily," "Follow the established guidelines," and "I am assured if you are working on things," which were widely interpreted as expressions of confidence and became the source of Hua's power.[24] However, the Gang of Four argued that "working on things" is not the same as "taking charge," and that "Follow the established guidelines" in fact meant that they should be in power. Mao himself had admitted that he was not in his right mind, they said, given his advanced age and deteriorating health. On September 16, the Gang of Four asked many important newspapers, including the *People's Daily* and Shanghai's *Liberation Daily,* to publicize their interpretation of "Follow the established guidelines." Between September 17 and October 4, more than 280 of the printed tributes to Mao did just that.

Hua invited the Gang of Four to attend a meeting and arrested them when they arrived. On October 7, the Politburo of the CCP formally appointed him president of the CCP and the CCP's Central Military Commission. Hua announced the end of the "first" Cultural Revolution but suggested that the class struggle was not over.

To further buttress his legitimacy as Mao's successor, Hua then published his famous "Two Whatevers," in which he vowed to resolutely uphold "whatever" policy decisions Mao had made and unswervingly follow "whatever" instructions he had given. Deng then published a rejoinder, "Practice Is the Only Standard for Testing Truth," which most CCP members endorsed. Hua was forced to self-criticize, and Deng pushed him out of power in 1978. Deng also initiated the Sino-Vietnamese War, which solidified his power and status within the CCP. As the de facto leader of China, he then ended the Cultural Revolution. The new period, reform and opening up, began under his leadership, and the central focus changed from class struggle to economic development.

THE LASTING EFFECTS OF THE CULTURAL REVOLUTION ON PRIVATE ENTERPRISE

The experiences of the Cultural Revolution fundamentally shape private enterprise in China through their enduring effects on entrepreneurs' values and beliefs.[25] Entrepreneurs who lived through it are more cynical than their younger peers and have less confidence in the rule of law; as we have seen, they are less likely to abide by contracts and more likely to commit crimes such as bribery, default on their debts, and flee the country.

Due to the poor corruption control in China, there have been many high-profile prosecutions for bribery in recent years.[26] One case that attracted significant media attention in 2004 involved Tang Wanxin's Delong Group, the largest private firm in China to go bankrupt that year. Tang was born in 1964; his father died after he was persecuted in the Cultural Revolution. As a result, Tang said he lost his belief in doing the right thing and flouted the law as he built his company.[27] Finally, in

2004, Tang was prosecuted for bribery, insider trading, and illegal fund-raising. He was sentenced to eight years in prison and his firm had to pay a fine of $700 million, which bankrupted it.[28] Another prominent case was that of Mou Qizhong, a high-profile businessman and writer. Born in 1941, Mou was a Red Guard and communist and wrote an essay, "Where China Should Be Going," to promote radical revolution. Nonetheless, he fell afoul of the authorities and was sentenced to death for his writings. Although he ultimately only spent four years in prison and was released in 1979, he had lost all faith in China's institutions. The first business he started exploited the price differences in China's dual-track economic reform, in which commodities were priced low within the plan but one needed government connections to get them. By bribing officials, Mou was able to become rich by buying commodities at the low inside price and reselling them for a profit.[29] He kept his freewheeling ways and in 2002 was found guilty of foreign exchange fraud, for which he received a life sentence.[30] He was paroled in 2016.

Yang Bin, who founded the gigantic conglomerate Shenyang Ouyang, was born in 1960 and was orphaned when both parents died after being tortured. In 1997 Yang shopped his business ideas on greenhouses and high-tech agriculture around and secured a contract with the Shenyang government. Yang deceived investors by overstating his business's wealth and cheated banks on loans of billions of dollars. When his firm went public, he was ranked second on the Hurun Richest People list. But it was all flimflam. Soon after, it was exposed that the business experiences Yang claimed to have were fake and his businesses did not involve high-tech agriculture. He was arrested for the crimes of falsely reporting capital registration, the illegal possession of agricultural land, contract fraud, and bribery.[31]

We used data on all Chinese publicly traded companies (not state-owned enterprises) to examine how CEOs' Cultural Revolution experiences (that is, during their primary to senior high school stages, ages six to eighteen) affected their tendency (i.e., likelihood) to become involved in financial misconduct (for example, financial fraud, intentional misrepresentation, insider trading, and stock price manipulation). On average, CEOs with Cultural Revolution experiences are 2.7 percent (5.7 percent versus 3.0 percent, or 90 percent in relative terms) more likely to be involved in financial misconduct than those without them (fig. 8.2). The statistical effect is substantial.

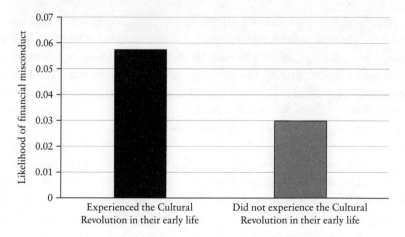

Figure 8.2 Likelihood of CEOs' Involvement in Financial Misconduct
Data source: Chinese Stock Market and Accounting Research Database. Calculated by the authors.

To better understand some of these crimes, we also examined the richest entrepreneurs and businesspeople based on the Hurun Richest People list. The Hurun list was established in 1999 and included the fifty richest people initially. The list kept growing, and in 2020, 2,041 people were ranked on it.[32] In addition, in 2009, 2011, 2014, and 2015 Hurun published its Special Report of China's Richest People to highlight wealthy people who committed crimes. Around 1.1 percent of the people on Hurun's list were convicted of crimes and thus included in those special reports.[33]

Of the criminal entrepreneurs on Hurun's list, 97 percent experienced the Cultural Revolution (table 8.1), while 88 percent of the total list experienced it. This suggests that entrepreneurs who experienced the Cultural Revolution are more likely to commit crimes than entrepreneurs who did not. The two major types of crimes committed were bribery and fraud.[34]

Another probability we examined is the likelihood of conducting financial fraud. China is in the process of establishing a formal credit system. Unlike developed countries such as the United States, where a number of companies use a systematic process to collect data for credit ratings, in China the system is more fragmented and incomplete, with many financial companies involved, the best-known of which is Ant

Table 8.1 Summary of Richest Chinese Businesspeople Who
Were or Are Jailed

Name of entrepreneur	Birth year	Firm	Crime
Cai Dabiao	1971	Kungfu Foods	Embezzlement
Feng Yongming	1953	Guangming Furniture	Bribery
Gu Weijun	1959	Greencool Holdings (refrigerants)	Fraud
Guan Guoliang	1960	New China Life Insurance	Embezzlement and bribery
He Xuekui	1969	Hekou Flowers	Fraud
He Yan	1961	Guoteng Electronics	Embezzlement
Hua Bangsong	1965	Huisheng Engineering Group	Bribery
Huang Guangyu	1969	Gome Electrical Appliances	Bribery and insider trading
Huang Hongsheng	1956	Skyworth (televisions)	Fraud
Jia Tinliang	1956	Datuhe (Shanxi) Coking & Chemicals	Bribery
Lan Shili	1960	East Star Airlines	Fraud and tax evasion
Li Songjian	1963	Shanghai Electric	Embezzlement and bribery
Liang Yaohui	1967	Aoweisi Hotel	Fraud and bribery
Liu Genshan	1958	Maosheng Machinery Manufacturing	Embezzlement and bribery
Liu Han	1965	Hanlong Group (conglomerate)	Bribery and murder
Liu Jun	1966	Taiyue Real Estate	Bribery
Luo Zhongfu	1951	Fuhai Fuyingshi New Material	Occupying agricultural land and deforestation
Mou Qizhong	1941	Nande Conglomerate	Fraud
Tang Wanxin	1964	Delong Group (conglomerate)	Fraud, bribery, and stock manipulation
Wang Fusheng	1951	Beijing Fuhua Construction and Development	Tax evasion
Wu Zhijian	1960	Zhenghua Conglomerate	Fraud and bribery

(*Continued*)

Table 8.1 (*Continued*)

Name of entrepreneur	Birth year	Firm	Crime
Xu Ming	1971	Shide Group (conglomerate)	Bribery
Xu Shuqing	1958	Guangxi Wuzhou Zhongheng (conglomerate)	Bribery
Xu Xiang	1977	Zexi Investment	Stock manipulation
Yan Liyan	1962	Shanghai Dade Investment	Embezzlement and fraud
Yang Bin	1960	Shenyang Ouya Group (conglomerate)	Fraud and bribery
Yu Guoxiang	1970	Xinhengde Real Estate	Embezzlement and bribery
Zhang Keqiang	1960	Huamei International Investment	Bribery
Zhang Liangbin and Zhang Bin (brothers)	1963 and 1970	Sichuan Lixin Investment Group	Fraud and bribery
Zhang Rongkun	1973	Fuxi Investment and Consulting	Embezzlement and bribery
Zhang Wenzhong	1962	Wumart (retail company)	Embezzlement, fraud, and bribery
Zhou Weibin	1963	Jinguan Coating Materials	Fraud and tax evasion
Zhou Xiaodi	1955	Zhou's Real Estate	Theft and fraud
Zhou Yiming	1974	Minlun Conglomerate	Embezzlement and fraud
Zhou Zhengyi	1961	Shanghai Real Estate Group	Embezzlement and fraud
Zhu Xingliang	1959	Suzhou Gold Mantis Construction	Bribery

Data sources: Authors' compilation of information from "Hurun's Special Report on China's Richest People Is Released, 49 People Have Changed in 10 Years," http://news.cctv.com/law /20090829/101118.shtml [retrieved on December 22, 2021]; Zhang, Yi, "In the 12 Years since the Hurun Rich List Was Released, a Total of 24 People Have Been Sacked, and the Average 40-Year-Old Has Problems," https://finance.ifeng.com/money/special/hurun2010/20110119 /3234275.shtml [retrieved on December 22, 2021]; and Han, Jiahui, ed., "China's Richest 'Special' Report: 18 'Rich' in Prison (Table)," http://www.xinhuanet.com//politics/2015-12/17/c _128538545.htm [retrieved on December 22, 2021].

Financial, the payment-processing subsidiary of Alibaba. Starting in 2013, the Chinese Supreme People's Court has been building the afore-mentioned defaulters' list of people colloquially known as "the shame-less." The court cooperates with airlines and railway companies to bar these defaulters from purchasing tickets, based on ID card information and their passports. Anecdotal and other evidence suggests that entre-preneurs with Cultural Revolution experiences are more likely to be-come "shameless." In Huang Nubo's words, "I used to be a Red Guard and have no ethical bottom line."[35]

Corrupt entrepreneurs frequently tie their lack of ethics to their Cul-tural Revolution experiences. Xiao Wenge, born in 1967 and named after the Cultural Revolution (wenhua da geming in Pinyin, abbreviated as wenge), witnessed the turmoil of the Cultural Revolution during his early childhood. He established Yinji Media in 1993, which was worth $7 billion by 2019. When Xiao engaged in insider trading and cashed out billions of dollars, he said that having lived through the Cultural Revolution, he did not feel guilty about his corrupt practices.[36] Xiao is also one of the shameless. Jia Yueting, founder of Leshi Internet Informa-tion & Technology, which was worth $20 billion at its peak but was later delisted for owing tens of billions of dollars, was also shaped by the Cultural Revolution.[37] As Song Yongyi of California State University at Los Angeles put it, the "Cultural Revolution turned people into beasts, and some people cannibalized others."[38] This is quite consistent with Huang's reflection that the "Cultural Revolution made us demons."[39]

More than a quarter of China's entrepreneurs have left the country since they became rich, and reports suggest that almost half of those remaining are thinking about doing so.[40] Again, this trend is more pro-nounced for entrepreneurs who experienced the Cultural Revolution. In an interview, Liu Chuanzhi, founder of the world-leading multina-tional technology company Lenovo, said that many of his cohort who experienced the Cultural Revolution had escaped China.[41] A significant wave of flights occurred in 2012, especially in the city of Chongqing, where the city's then–party secretary Bo Xilai initiated his campaign of Singing the Red, imitating many practices of the Cultural Revolution and singling out entrepreneurs for harassment.[42] More recently, some entre-preneurs worried about the precarious status of private firms and pro-posed a new idea called "Exit the Private Economy," in which they would exchange their property in return for guarantees of personal

Table 8.2 Summary of Richest Chinese Businesspeople Who Later Disappeared

Name	Birth year	Current status	Reason
Chen Jinyi	1961	Missing (escaped)	Owed millions of US dollars
Guo Wengui	1970	In the United States	To avoid bribery and fraud charges
Li Yan	1963	Missing (escaped)	Owed billions of US dollars
Liu Yingxia	1972	Missing (in the United States)	To avoid fraud charges
Song Ruhua	1962	Missing (in the United States)	To avoid embezzlement charges
Sun Liyong and Fang Xiaojian (couple)	1971 and 1973	In the United States	Owed tens of millions of US dollars
Xu Zonglin	1959	In Canada	To avoid fraud charges

Data sources: Authors' compilation of information from "Hurun's Special Report on China's Richest People Is Released, 49 People Have Changed in 10 Years," http://news.cctv.com/law /20090829/101118.shtml [retrieved on December 22, 2021]; Zhang, Yi, "In the 12 Years since the Hurun Rich List Was Released, a Total of 24 People Have Been Sacked, and the Average 40-Year-Old Has Problems," https://finance.ifeng.com/money/special/hurun2010/20110119 /3234275.shtml [retrieved on December 22, 2021]; and Han, Jiahui, ed., "China's Richest 'Special' Report: 18 'Rich' in Prison (Table)," http://www.xinhuanet.com//politics/2015-12/17/c _128538545.htm [retrieved on December 22, 2021].

safety.[43] Many entrepreneurs make sure that their children have passports from the United States, Canada, or Australia. For example, Huawei founder Ren Zhengfei's daughter, Yao Anna (Annabel Yao), is reportedly a US citizen.[44]

In June 2004, Tang Wanxin suffered a psychological blow as numerous creditors of the Delong Group demanded repayment. On July 18, 2004, while attempting to board an international flight in Beijing, Tang, who had been under twenty-four-hour surveillance, was arrested. Later he was found guilty of fraud, bribery, and stock manipulation and sentenced to eight years in prison.[45] We have identified other entrepreneurs who appeared on the Hurun list but escaped China successfully (table 8.2). All of them lived through the Cultural Revolution.

A NEW CULTURAL REVOLUTION?

It is all the more important that we understand the effects of the Cultural Revolution because reports suggest that a new one may be brewing in China today. As discussed in previous chapters, Xi Jinping is reviving Maoist ideas and imitating Mao in a number of significant—and ominous—ways. The state-controlled media has begun referring to Xi as the "great helmsman" and "people's leader," honorifics that were previously reserved for Mao. Much as Mao did in his final decades, Xi is creating a cult of personality around himself that ensures that his mistakes will be systematically ignored or, as in Mao's day, attributed to the people who carried out his policies, such as Liu, Deng, Lin, and the Gang of Four. Even the official verdict on the Cultural Revolution and Mao, issued on June 27, 1981, did not specifically lay the blame at his feet. The document, "Resolutions on Several Historical Issues of the Party since the Founding of the People's Republic of China," merely stated that the "ten-year 'Cultural Revolution' was a period of civil turmoil that was wrongly launched by the leaders and used by counter-revolutionary groups to bring serious disasters to the party, the country, and the people of all ethnic groups."[46]

To further solidify his power, Xi has prosecuted many rival leaders who could pose challenges to his rule—for example, Zhou Yongkang, who was a member of the standing committee of the CCP's Politburo and so one of the top seven leaders of China. In the past, the CCP norm was that standing committee members should not be charged with crimes, but Xi saw to it that Zhou was tried for accepting bribes, abusing power, and disclosing state secrets, and Zhou was sentenced to life imprisonment and had his property confiscated as a result.

Xi has undertaken a massive anti-corruption movement that is unprecedented in the CCP. So far, some two million government officials have been prosecuted.[47] To find a precedent in Chinese history, you would have to go back eight centuries to the reign of Zhu Yuanzhang, the first emperor of the Ming dynasty (1368–1644), who prosecuted around 150,000 officials.[48]

Xi's anti-corruption campaign can be seen as a part of his power struggle with former president Jiang Zemin, which intensified after Xi took office. CCP governance norms are such that prior supreme leaders hold significant power after stepping down, and Jiang had acted as a shadow ruler since he was succeeded in late 2002. But Xi could not become an absolute leader under such a setup. Because Zhou was a key member of Jiang's faction, Xi took him down.[49] Anecdotal evidence suggests that the anti-corruption campaign has focused especially on members of the Jiang faction, who are prominent in Shanghai and Jiangsu Province, where Jiang first established his power base, and Jilin and Liaoning Provinces, where Jiang's trusted aide Wang Min built his faction. Like Zhou, many of Jiang's allies—and Xi's targets—work in the petroleum industry and in the public security bureau, procurator-ate, and court that Zhou formerly controlled.[50] Xi has also established new groups to carry out his governance, which resembles the Central Cultural Revolution Group, which has taken over some of the areas that used to fall under the auspices of Premier Li Keqiang's State Council. Xi also relies heavily on Vice Prime Minister Liu He, who was his schoolmate in middle school.

After the Cultural Revolution, Deng and the CCP-government ac-knowledged some of the issues created by the permanent employment of cadres—a problem that the Soviet Union had failed to grapple with effec-tively. Many long-standing political officials were too old to work but re-mained in their roles—or, like Konstantin Chernenko in the USSR, rose to supreme leadership but became fatally ill. Deng abolished the permanent employment of political officials in China and asked other senior leaders to retire when he did. These retired officials then formed the Central Advi-sory Commission to help the new generation of officials. In return, an unwritten norm for the CCP system was that national leaders could rec-ommend one of their children to become a political official at the provin-cial level. Deng's son Deng Pufang was appointed chairman of China's Disabled Persons' Federation, a provincial-level position, and later was promoted to vice chairman of the Chinese People's Political Consultative Conference, a national position. Xi Zhongxun's son Xi Jinping was ap-pointed governor of Fujian and Zhejiang Provinces and later became pres-ident and general secretary of the CCP. Jiang's son Jiang Mianheng was appointed president of Shanghai Tech University (a provincial-level posi-tion), and Hu Jintao's son Hu Haifeng is currently a party secretary of the city of Lishui (prefectural level). Xi, however, seems interested in reversing this rule and going back to Mao's precedent of no term limits.

Relatedly, since Deng the custom has been for the leader to serve no more than two five-year terms, and for the prior leader to designate the successor in advance (known as designation across generations). Thus, Deng appointed Hu to succeed Jiang, and then Jiang appointed Xi to succeed Hu. But Xi appears to have suspended this tradition. Most observers believe that he will seek a third term; and he may intend to remain president for life. If he does, that will increase the likelihood of a power struggle after his death, as occurred with Mao—and as often occurs in one-party countries. Khrushchev gained power after arresting the Stalin loyalist Lavrentiy Beria (executed in 1953), who had wielded enormous power as the head of the secret police (the People's Commissariat for Internal Affairs, the supervising authority of the KGB) but was hated by other senior Soviet leaders for his brutality.

Under Xi, the ideological climate in China has become increasingly conservative and radical in a way consistent with Mao and Maoism. Communist rule over the private economy and the CCP's power are paramount.[51] Even when honoring heroes of the fight against COVID-19, Xi used the rhetoric of class struggle. In one recent speech, he used the word "struggle" thirty-one times, summoning Mao with such phrases as "the spirit of struggle," "dare to fight and be good at fighting," and "adjust the struggling strategy in time according to changes in the situation."[52] In his speech celebrating the centenary of the CCP, he used the word "revolution" seventeen times and "struggle" eight times, explicitly invoking Mao's famous "We [the CCP] dare to overturn the old world and change into a new look."[53]

More ominously, Xi has been working to soften the CCP's already equivocal condemnation of Mao and the Cultural Revolution. The new official brief history of the CCP says that "although the first 27 years (1949 to 1976) were full of setbacks, the CCP-government made great achievement and we should not negate these first 30 years." In previous editions, a whole chapter was devoted to the Cultural Revolution, but in the new version it is covered in two pages.[54] Mao is generally seen in a more positive light, and fully a quarter of the book is devoted to Xi's own contribution, a chapter-length explication of the ideological foundations of Xi Jinping Thought on Socialism with Chinese Characteristics for a New Era.

In addition to all this, pressure is being brought to bear on the private sector, particularly the technology and cultural industries. Examples include the suspension of Ant Financial's initial public offering, the levy of a $25 billion fine on Alibaba for monopoly, and an investigation of DiDi for its suspected delivery of Chinese consumer data to US regulators when it had an initial public offering on the New York Stock Exchange. Entrepreneurs and celebrities are being accused of being foreign agents or otherwise contaminating Chinese culture. The famous actress Zhao Wei was attacked for wearing a dress with a rising sun design, which was said to whitewash the Japanese invasion; she was accused of hiring a Taiwan separatist and a Japanese militarist to work on a movie, and, as earlier noted, her costar Zhang Zhelan was widely condemned for smiling when he visited the Yasukuni Shrine in Japan. All of their works were taken out of circulation as a result. A retired editor, Li Guangman, wrote an essay describing the emerging "new wave of Cultural Revolution," which aims to shift China from a capital-centered orientation to a people-centered one and build the foundation for a purified socialism and the restoration of the CCP's original mission.[55] Indeed, in a speech delivered at the opening ceremony of the Eleventh National Congress of the Federation of Literature and Art and the Tenth National Congress of the Chinese Writers Association on December 14, 2021, Xi quoted Mao's talks at the Yan'an Forum on Literature and Art, which mandated that literature, art, and all entertainments should adhere to CCP principles and serve the CCP.[56]

Though the Cultural Revolution ended decades ago, its influence has not died. The CCP-government's propaganda sustains its influence. For example, the village of Dazhai in Shanxi Province became famous when Mao said "agriculture should learn from Dazhai." Today, the village is a red tourist site. Zhao Mingxing, the owner of Dazhai's Chinese Dream Red-Theme Museum, attests to his nostalgia for the period. "My grandfather and my father were steeped in Mao Zedong Thought, and I was influenced by it as well," he says. "Honestly, I think it has positive aspects. At that time, locals in Dazhai really didn't lock their doors at night. It was very safe. When the persimmon and walnut trees by the roadside ripened, no one picked the fruit for themselves. In the past, our lives were bitter, but everyone was on the same level and people were spiritually satisfied. Today, the gap between the rich and poor is widening. The rich are getting richer, and people without money find it more difficult to live."[57]

One of our interviewed entrepreneurs, subject 26, also spoke positively about the legacy of the Cultural Revolution, particularly the send-down movement. She said, "The people who participated in the send-down movement devoted significant effort to the construction of China. I really want to thank that generation very much. If there is no dedication from the next generation, the speed of China's development will not be so fast. Participants in the send-down movement implanted culture in the mountains of the countryside, and now the Belt and Road Initiative, precise and targeted poverty alleviation, and others are its continuation, with just the name changed. The CCP is still doing some real things. Our hometown, Tongjiang, is a well-known poverty-stricken county in China, and one of the targeted counties for precise and targeted poverty alleviation."

The legacy of the Cultural Revolution is complex and inescapable. What lessons should Westerners, and especially Western businesspeople, draw from it? We need to understand that some of the entrepreneurs who experienced its chaos are extremely cynical about the law. Thus, it is necessary to do careful background checks of potential customers, clients, suppliers, and partners. The Chinese government now provides free access to multiple websites where one can check whether a business or an individual entrepreneur is a defaulter.[58] Additionally, while we do not suggest that all people who experienced the Cultural Revolution are unreliable, it is important to understand how far-reaching its effects have been.

Foreign businesses must tread carefully in China's increasingly nationalistic and authoritarian environment. While it is important not to compromise the missions and values of one's firm, a spirit of compromise and patience is called for.[59] China's increasingly radical political climate is troubling and may discourage Western investors. As understandable as that is, we do believe that some of China's most confrontational rhetoric is meant for domestic consumption—in the face of slowing economic growth and widening income inequality, the CCP is looking to divert the blame from itself and onto a new set of foreign and counterrevolutionary adversaries. Of course, exiting the Chinese market is always an option, but that should be a last resort.

9 The Third Front Construction and Private Entrepreneurship

The skills and social capital I gained from Third Front Construction firms facilitated my startup.
—Wang Danfu, founder of Xiaogan Yiteng Optoelectronics Technology

ALTHOUGH LESS WELL KNOWN than the Great Leap Forward and the Cultural Revolution, Mao Zedong's Third Front Construction was no less consequential. The campaign relocated critical national defense industries to interior regions in anticipation of an invasion—by the Soviet Union, after the Sino-Soviet split, or the United States, as the Vietnam War escalated. For example, China's First Automobile Manufacturing Plant was in Changchun in northwestern Jilin Province, which is near the border with the Soviet Union. So the Second Automobile Manufacturing Plant was built in the more centrally located (and much more defendable) Shiyan in Hubei Province. The program remained confidential until the late 1980s.[1]

Wang Danfu was born in 1985 and entered the Beijing Institute of Technology in 2003. After graduating in 2007, he joined Plant 238, which is now Huazhong Optoelectronics Technology, in the city of Xiaogan in China's central Hubei Province. The plant and the whole city were part of Mao's Third Front Construction campaign. Wang gained work skills and experience as a technician, as well as important social connections. Both later helped him when he launched his own enterprise, Xiaogan Yiteng Optoelectronics Technology. Like Wang, many other technicians began their own ventures after working for Third Front firms in Xiaogan—enough to form a dense cluster of industries there. For example, there are now thirty-three defense firms in Xiaogan's High-Tech Industrial Development Zone, all of them founded by former technicians.[2]

In this chapter, we examine how the Third Front helped create a foundation for private entrepreneurship and market development in China. First, it scattered many military and industrial firms across the country, which were later taken private. Second, it distributed human capital much more widely. But it had negative consequences as well. Because the underlying logic of the initiative was to locate facilities in places that were difficult to access, many quickly became obsolete and were deserted. China's rust belt—that is, a region that has experienced industrial decline, population loss, and urban decay—is an unanticipated legacy of the Third Front Construction.

THE THIRD FRONT CONSTRUCTION

The "Third Front" is a geo-military concept introduced by Mao that is focused on the large-scale construction of national defense, science and technology, power and transportation infrastructure, and other industries for the purpose of preparing for future wars and famines.

Mao said in May 1964, "Our first front is coastal regions, second front is the line that cuts from Baotou to Lanzhou, and southwest is the third front. . . . In the period of the atomic bomb, we need a strategic rear for retreat, and we should be prepared to go into mountains [to become guerilla]. We need a place like this."[3] The military thought a war of massive scale might break out, given tensions with both the Soviet Union and the United States, and worried that China's most important industries were concentrated in what would likely be the initial battlefronts. The fourteen large cities in those areas held around 60 percent of China's manufacturing industries, 50 percent of its chemical industries, and 52 percent of its national defense industries. China's population centers and most of its railway hubs and ports were in eastern coastal areas and vulnerable to attacks from air and water. By establishing a relatively complete industrial system in the southwest and northwest regions (including western Hunan, western Henan, and western Hubei), China would gain some of the redundancy it needed to survive.

The northeast had been China's industrial center since the 1930s, when the Japanese occupied and tried to industrialize the region. Although

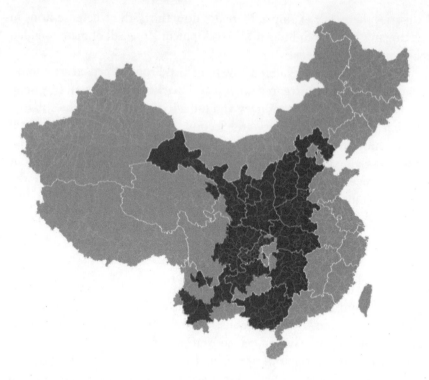

Figure 9.1 Cities Involved in the Third Front Construction (in dark shade)
Data source: Authors' coding of different cities involved in the Third Front
Construction.

Soviet troops looted many of those facilities, after the founding of the
People's Republic of China, the USSR had built 156 major industrial
projects on the Chinese side of the border. After the Sino-Soviet split,
Mao was rightly concerned that they might try to take them back.

China's coastal regions, another area of significant industry, were vulnerable to US bombers. After the Gulf of Tonkin incident on August 2,
1964, during the Vietnam War, the Seventh Fleet was deployed around
China's Hainan Island. To China's east lay Taiwan, from which the Kuomintang could launch an attack.

Eastern Gansu, northwest Guangxi, Guizhou, Henan, Hunan,
Ningxia, Qinghai, Shaanxi, south Shanxi, Sichuan (including Chongqing), Yunnan, and parts of Hebei provided China with a strategic rear-
guard (fig. 9.1). All of those regions had been less touched during the

Second Sino-Japanese War (1937–45), when almost half of China's territory had been occupied by Japanese troops. By moving facilities into that Third Front and building new ones there, Mao and the Chinese Communist Party (CCP) could leverage the strategic advantages of remote and mountainous regions, just as they had in their battles against the Kuomintang—and as the Vietcong were doing in South Vietnam. As Mao put it, "We must pay attention to the study of guerrilla warfare in South Vietnam. There are only a few million people, not as big as ours, but Vietnamese guerrilla warfare is as good as ours."[4]

The campaign was mostly carried out in secret; the choice of location for the facilities followed the principle of being "close to the mountains, dispersed, and hidden." Because of the remoteness and steep slopes, many projects fell years behind schedule. To maintain secrecy, the plants were not identified by location but rather numbered, and all workers shared the same mailbox. For example, the common address of all staff working for Plant 3614 was the four-digit number 3614, which is where letters would be sent and received from. Letters between plant workers and their families were subject to scrutiny and frequently censored to protect confidential information. There were also strict rules within the plants; a worker might need different sets of papers to gain access to, say, the computer department, the weapons research laboratory, or the personnel department.[5]

The articulated foci for the Third Front Construction were to "choose the best people and best horses for the Third Front" and "get ready for war and famine for the people." Thus, many engineers, intellectuals, and scientists were transferred to these hinterland facilities. Former president Hu Jintao was stationed at the Liujiaxia Hydropower Station in China's northwest Gansu Province for two years. The person who was in charge of the Third Front Construction in the northwest area, Song Ping, appreciated his work and promoted him a number of times. Song was also partially responsible for Hu's selection as president through his recommendation to Deng Xiaoping.[6]

Important universities, such as Peking University and Tsinghua University, established branches in Hanzhong, a city in China's northwest Shaanxi Province (Project 653), and Mianyang, in China's southwest Sichuan Province (Project 651), respectively. But most of the investment went into new manufacturing plants, especially for heavy industries like steel, weaponry and related equipment, and infrastructure development.

Factories that made cannons, tanks, artillery shells, and other materiel were established in China's north Shanxi Province. Panzhihua Steel Base in Sichuan Province later became a national firm.

Because the locations were chosen for noneconomic reasons, construction could be exceedingly costly. The 012 Airplane Factory/Base in Hanzhong had twenty-eight production units, spanning two districts and seven counties. One unit was spread across seven villages. This made coordination particularly difficult.[7] Investment in these projects accounted for as much as one-half of China's spending in 1971; the overall cost was $25 billion, more than a third of China's spending over the fifteen years of the program.[8]

Following the US-China rapprochement, the military purpose of these projects waned. Given their unprofitability—many accounts have stated that these investments were "too soon and too much"—the Chinese government gradually wound the initiative down.[9] After the reform and opening up in 1978, the government followed a "shut down, cease, merge, transform, and move" strategy to deal with the plants, especially those in mountainous areas or those established in caves where mobility between facilities was limited. Hundreds of thousands of workers lost their jobs, typically in plants. The result was a Chinese rust belt.[10] For example, Plants 5433 (a factory for tank shell assembly) and 5443 (a factory for tank shell stamping machines) in Yuncheng, Shanxi Province, were both shut down because travel between the facilities was so costly.[11] Other plants were privatized, laying the foundation for private entrepreneurship in those regions. For example, Shaanxi Auto Gear General Works became privatized as Shaanxi Fast Auto Drive Company and the manager Li Dakai became the new owner.

Some military firms entered the civilian market. Jialing Motors, one of the largest motor makers in China, used to make tanks, and the Changhong Group, one of the biggest television makers in China, used to manufacture wireless and electronic devices. Some firms moved from their obscure locations to cities.

As with the Great Leap Forward and the Cultural Revolution, the Third Front Construction project's influence was far reaching. Many firms, including private ones, are direct legacies of this mass campaign, and those once-remote regions continue to benefit from the influx of specialized labor, technical skill, and know-how. On the other hand, it also left a negative legacy of industrial and urban abandonment and decay.

ENTERPRISE AFTER THE THIRD FRONT CONSTRUCTION

A large proportion of Third Front Construction plants and facilities were taken over by their old managers as China privatized firms from the 1980s to the early 2000s, so that it did not have to continue directly funding them, but they would continue employing individuals. Chengdu Tianxing Instrument and Meter, for example, was begun in 1974 as Plant 5004, a manufacturer of military equipment.[12] Its current owner, Yang Gao, acquired it from the government in the 1990s and transitioned it into an automotive parts maker. As the management and many employees reflected, "The fine industrial foundation based on the Third Front Construction facilitated Tianxing's transition and fit with the market economy."[13] On April 22, 1997, it became one of the first companies in Sichuan Province to go public, and its market value is now more than $2 billion.

Similarly, the previously mentioned Shaanxi Auto Gear General Works was founded in 1968 in a valley of the Qin Mountains in Shaanxi Province. The firm could not adjust to the market environment after the reform and opening up and was on the brink of bankruptcy by 1996, forcing it to suspend employees' pay. Li Dakai became its chief manager, initiated a series of market-oriented reforms, and took it private. To enhance productivity and efficiency, he laid off some low-level managers (cadres), his wife among them. Eventually the company became the largest automotive transmission producer in the world, with annual revenues in excess of $10 billion.[14]

Both cases show that the existing talents and social relations among workers were key to successful transformation—in those firms and, thanks to technological diffusion and knowledge spillovers, in other firms in the region.[15] Lifan Motors, for example, was founded in 1992 by Yin Mingshan, who modeled the firm after Jialing Motors—a famous state-owned firm that was transformed from Jialing Machine Works, which produced cannons during the Third Front Construction period. Lifan has been one of the largest and most successful motor producers in China for two decades.[16]

According to research on entrepreneurship, human capital, financial capital, and social capital are three critical antecedents. The former technicians who took so many Third Front companies private possessed all these characteristics. As Wang Danfu put it, "Working for Third Front Construction firms provided me with precious experience and skills for a high-tech start-up, as there has always been an apprentice model where senior employees tend to coach junior ones."[17] More importantly, each plant in the Third Front Construction initiative was a relatively isolated and independent community where almost everyone knew each other. This helped build networks and social capital, which made it possible for entrepreneurs to bootstrap—that is, obtain resources from relatives, friends, and others to fund their ventures.[18] Wang's initial capital came from his colleagues and was obtained without any formal contracts or IOUs.

Cities involved in the Third Front Construction have enjoyed high entrepreneurship rates because they are seeded with physical and human capital. Mianyang and Bazhong are neighboring cities in Sichuan Province. While the former is near a mountain, the other is built on a plain and thus did not qualify for the guiding principle of "easy to hide and close to mountains." Mianyang is now a high-tech city with numerous start-ups, while Bazhong has a low entrepreneurship rate and a less vigorous economy.[19] Similarly, Jingmen, in Hubei Province, is one of the most innovative and entrepreneurial cities in China.[20] In contrast, nearby Suizhou, which did not participate in the Third Front, has a much lower entrepreneurship rate due to its lack of infrastructure. Traditional economic theory would predict that all of these places would suffer from slow economic development due to their geographical disadvantages.[21] But in these and other cases, the traditional model was turned upside down.

We obtained data from a research team at the National School of Development at Peking University to examine more systematically how cities' Third Front involvement affects their entrepreneurship. The team surveyed Chinese firms of different sizes, industries, and ages in every city in China and created a database that includes the number of new firms; the extent of foreign, venture capital, and private equity investment; and patent and trademark registrations, providing an overall index of entrepreneurship and innovation that is adjusted for city size (population and area).[22]

Many cities involved in the Third Front Construction have rates of entrepreneurship that are comparable to the most developed east coast cities (fig. 9.2). On average, based on the scale, cities involved in the

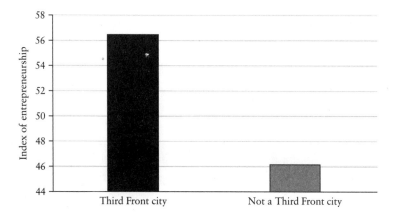

Figure 9.2 Entrepreneurship Index of Cities Categorized by the Third Front Construction
Data sources: Authors' hand-collection of whether a city is in the Third Front and the Enterprise Survey for Innovation and Entrepreneurship in China by Peking University. Calculated by the authors.

Third Front Construction are 22.4 percent $(= 56.4 / 46.1 - 1)$ more active in entrepreneurship activities than cities that were not involved in this campaign.

The industrial foundation left by the Third Front Construction clearly provided resources for Deyang and Shiyan to transform and adapt to the new economic era. Shiyan was built from scratch—before Mao's initiative, there was no such city in Hubei Province. To establish the Second Automobile Manufacturing Plant, the CCP-government moved more than thirty design organizations and thirty professional factories from major industrial provinces along the coast and the Yangtze River to Shiyan. Eventually, more than one hundred thousand people were relocated. From the 1980s to the mid-1990s, many small firms founded by former employees of China's Second Automobile Manufacturing Plant (now called Dongfeng Motor Corporation) emerged to produce automotive components and other related products. With further help from the city government, which worked to attract foreign investment and help small and medium-size enterprises with financing, land, and tax rebates, Shiyan became one of the most innovative cities in China and a model of industrial transformation.[23]

DEALING WITH CHINA'S RUST BELT

The Third Front campaign also came at a significant cost. For one, significant resources were invested in operations that turned out to be too costly to sustain.[24] More importantly, a lot of the Third Front regions now make up China's rust belt. This includes Chongqing (originally part of Sichuan Province but an independent provincial-level municipality since 1998), Deyang, Mianyang, and Panzhihua in Sichuan; Guiyang, Liupanshui, and Zunyi in Guizhou Province; Shiyan, Xiaogan, and Yichang in Hubei Province; Lanzhou, Jiayuguan, and Tianshui in Gansu Province; Baoji, Hanzhong, and Xi'an in Shaanxi Province; and others.

While Shiyan and Hefei, in Anhui Province, were successfully transformed into centers of high-tech and financial business services, Panzhihua, in Sichuan Province, a major city for steel production during the Third Front Construction, has suffered from a population outflow and many of its plants have been shut down and deserted. Some were transformed into industry relics in a bid to attract tourists. Panzhihua's government is making other efforts to attract people, such as providing subsidies to those who settle there and give birth to second and third children.[25] Similarly, the CCP leaders of Hanzhong, in Shaanxi Province, are trying to upgrade and transform their heavy industries.[26]

Besides entrepreneurship activities, what other approaches might help these cities revive? Some cities in the United States, Western Europe, and Japan have made comebacks—for example, Cleveland and Pittsburgh.[27] Historically and globally, there are two fundamental models for industrial transformation: industrial deepening, which is focused on enhancing capabilities fostered by prior industries, and industrial widening models, which place significant focus on wholly new industries.

In an example of the former, California began its development in earnest in the nineteenth century when it built railroads, deepening its industry base. After the Second World War, when the United States faced the problem of excess industrial capacity, Silicon Valley became the main engine for the Third Industrial Revolution. Similarly, Pittsburgh focused on high-tech, education, tourism, and other service industries after its steel industry became unsustainable. Its robotics industry is particularly strong worldwide and was built on its engineering expertise at well-known higher education institutions, such as Carnegie Mellon University and the University of Pittsburgh. Detroit has embarked on a similar path and has been developing artificial intelligence since its auto industry declined.

This is the road that Hefei has taken. Like Silicon Valley, which is home to Stanford University, Hefei is home to one of the best technological universities in China—the University of Science and Technology of China. Thanks to its ample supply of human capital, Hefei has developed capabilities in high-tech, alternative energy, and semiconductor industries. In 2008 the Hefei government spent 80 percent of its fiscal revenues—$3.5 billion—to take over BOE Technology (or Jingdongfang), synthesizing its existing industrial capacities to manufacture military semiconductor products for telecommunications and displays. BOE Technology is now one of the leading manufacturers of semiconductor display products worldwide.[28] In 2020 the Hefei government invested in NIO, a multinational automobile manufacturer specializing in the design and development of electric vehicles, in order to integrate it with its existing Third Front firm Hefei Changan Automobile. NIO is now one of the most successful electric vehicle manufacturers in China.[29] Likewise, Mianyang managed to revive its manufacturing industry via high-end equipment manufacturing and new materials, transforming its legacy manufacturing economy into one that is greener, higher tech, and more service oriented.[30]

In contrast, Nevada went the route of looking at entirely new industries. It was known for its silver mines and turned to tourism and services after they were depleted. When it legalized gambling, it became a hub for both domestic and international tourism. Likewise, Chicago abandoned many of its traditional heavy industries in the 1950s and concentrated on food, printing, and metal processing while building an international air hub and an international fiber optical communication center. It developed strengths in service industries and later in telecommunications and information technology.

Some Third Front rust belt cities, such as Liupanshui (Guizhou Province) and Shizuishan (Sichuan Province), are promoting tourism and agriculture. The Modern Agricultural Industrial Park of Shuicheng County, Liupanshui, is one of the most important of its kind in China.[31] Liupanshui has also made investments in six other growing industrial sectors: new materials, new energy and chemical industries, tourism equipment manufacturing, textiles, the Internet of Things, and modern logistics.

Unlike the handful of existing studies and accounts of the Third Front Construction, which argue that its investments were mostly wasted, we argue that the industrial foundation it laid in the Chinese hinterlands has enabled a significant amount of private enterprise, mostly through the privatization of existing plants by former employees. At the same time, we recognize that the initiative also created a vast rust belt once it was abandoned.

What are some of the implications of the Third Front Construction for doing business in China? First, most current foreign investors concentrate on coastal regions like Beijing, Shanghai, and southeast China (for example, Guangdong Province), which are arguably overdeveloped and have begun experiencing some population outflows.[32] As we have shown in this chapter, foreign businesspeople and investors should seriously consider opportunities in former Third Front cities, such as Xi'an in Shaanxi Province. The CCP-government's latest grand policy for developing the western regions, *Guiding Opinions of the Central Committee of the Chinese Communist Party and the State Council on Promoting the Development of the West in the New Era and Forming a New Pattern* (*Guiding Opinion* for short), highlights Xi'an's advantages in electronic information, high-end equipment, aerospace, energy and chemical engineering, and advanced materials. The government aims to provide support for solving key bottlenecks in national strategic areas and industrial development, especially aircraft manufacturing. This may represent enormous opportunities for Western air companies, such as Boeing and Airbus, which can enter into business partnerships with potential suppliers in Xi'an.

The *Guiding Opinion* also suggests that because of their industrial foundations and special geographical locations, Chengdu, Chongqing, and Xi'an are likely to become international gateway hubs and metropolitan cities like Beijing and Shanghai.[33] Chengdu recently won the opportunity to build the National Artificial Intelligence Innovation Application Pilot Zone; international artificial intelligence and other high-tech firms might consider partnering with some of its firms. The cities of Chengdu,

Chongqing, and Xi'an are increasingly forming a technology delta such as exists in the Yangtze Delta (Shanghai, Jiangsu, and Zhejiang Provinces) and Pearl River Delta (Guangzhou, Shenzhen, and Zhuhai).[34]

In addition to these core cities, high-tech firms might find partnership and business opportunities in Mianyang, while firms focusing on eco-tourism might look to Liupanshui and Shizuishan. Automobile manufacturers can find a rich ecosystem of suppliers and talent, not to mention tax and financing benefits, in the city of Shiyan, as we described earlier. The city has well-functioning facilities, a strong supply chain for the industry, and a government that is eager to attract investment. Many of the Third Front Construction cities are also involved in the Belt and Road Initiative, which can provide additional opportunities for foreign firms.

IV THE EFFECTS OF MAO'S SOCIALIST INSTITUTIONS: POLITICAL AND ECONOMIC SYSTEMS

Top-down party control is our fundamental institution.

After liberation, China copied the Soviet experience in industrial management and planning management, resulting in dogmatism. Therefore, it was necessary to break the influence of the Soviet Union and carry forward our original spirit . . . implement the principle of unified leadership and hierarchical management, and reform the management system of planning, industry, infrastructure, materials, finance, prices, and commerce. The core of the reform is to delegate management power to local governments to achieve decentralization.

State ownership, socialism, and the Communist Party are an interdependent and inseparable whole. Without state ownership, there would be no socialism, and the Communist Party would lose its value of existence.

Any [military] company with a CCP branch has high morale and bravery in combat, and the chief officer can also receive effective democratic supervision.

—Mao Zedong

10 The Political System and Private Enterprises in China

We should delegate power from central to local. . . . Political centralization and economic decentralization should coexist.

—Mao Zedong

WHEN ONE THINKS OF CHINA, communism is likely the first thing that comes to mind—along with a few big questions. How does the Chinese Communist Party (CCP) maintain its institutional control? Could China transition into a democracy, as its geographical and cultural neighbors Japan and South Korea did in the twentieth century?

In this chapter, we look at how the Chinese political system works, especially at the local level, and how that affects private businesses. Mao Zedong dictated that while politically China should be centralized and the party should exercise strict top-down control, local governments should be more autonomous when it comes to economic policymaking. As a result, government officials at different levels have pursued very different growth strategies, particularly the extent to which they follow Maoism.[1]

The provincial-level city of Chongqing and Guangdong Province provide a well-known contrast of how local leaders' ideologies can make a big difference when it comes to economic development.[2] Chongqing—one of four provincial-level cities under the direct administration of the central government—experienced political turmoil in 2012 after the arrest of its party secretary Bo Xilai. Bo was an avowed Maoist. In Chongqing, his governance model emphasized Maoist ideas through "singing red songs" (i.e., those that extol Mao Zedong). Commercial content was banned from the media and replaced with revolutionary songs, and there was a crackdown on organized crime, including the persecution of entrepreneurs and businesspeople and confiscation of their property, among them Li Jun of the Chongqing Junfeng Property Limited Company. Many entrepreneurs left Chongqing as a result, and others were frightened to do business there. Chongqing grew, but mainly as a result of state investment.

Bo's childhood friend Wang Shi, founder of Vanke, at one time the largest real estate enterprise in China, put it best. "During the period of singing the red and fighting the evil [organized crime and corruption], a large number of Chongqing entrepreneurs in manufacturing and service industries were forcibly imprisoned and their property was confiscated," he said. "Even the lawyer who defended them was wrongly sentenced to imprisonment." Those actions, he continued, not only "violated the principles of the rule of law" but "have had a negative impact on entrepreneurs. They've given me the cold sweats."[3]

Wang Yang preceded Bo as Chongqing's party secretary and later became party secretary of Guangdong Province, the vibrant manufacturing center in southern China. Wang was a leader of liberal reform within the CCP and a leading advocate of the free market economy; he even extolled the advantages of American individualism.[4] When he was mayor of the city of Tongling in Anhui Province in 1991, he had written in the *Tongling Daily* that China's economic reforms should be continued, even after the 1989 Tiananmen Square Massacre. Wang's Guangdong Model thus focused on depoliticizing the economy and society and promoting business and economic activities. Thanks to his achievements in Guangdong Province, Wang gained a seat on the Politburo Standing Committee.[5]

This chapter provides historical perspective on Mao's ideas about communist governance and how they are implemented at the local level. Unlike Europe, which has been divided into different countries for all of its recorded history, China has maintained a strong centralized government since it was unified by Qin Shi Huang in 221 BCE. Before then, it experienced a short feudalist period and perennial wars just as Europe and other parts of the world did (in the Warring States period, 475–221 BCE). Qin Shi Huang realized the enfeoffment system that distributes land to male heirs to establish their own kingdoms was problematic, so thereafter, Chinese nobles had honorary titles but did not control land.[6] Political centralization persisted for most of the next two millennia with rare and short interruptions, such as the Northern and Southern dynasties (420–589 CE), the Five Dynasties and Ten Kingdoms period (907–79 CE), and more recently, the confrontations between the Beiyang government in the north and the Kuomintang government in the south (1925–28). Confucianism, which urges sincere allegiance to the monarch, became a spiritual and political norm. The authoritarian regime adopted by the CCP can thus be seen as a continuation of the long Chinese tradition of absolute monarchy with a centralized political structure. It is likely that if the Kuomintang had stayed in power, it would have instituted a similarly authoritarian regime. That is in fact what it did when it moved to Taiwan, where democratization did not begin until 1987.

But this brief comparison of Chongqing and Guangdong suggests, within this centralized system, there are large regional variations in the ways that businesses and governments interact, and economic decentralization amplifies the importance of lower-level politicians. Local politicians' ideas and ideologies and their zeal for political promotion influence their policies.

Local leaders—like Bo and Wang—compete against one another for political promotion, frequently based on economic performance, and they are granted considerable discretion over the handling of economic affairs within their jurisdictions, so long as they are fully obedient to their supervising authority. As a result, localities such as provinces and cities have become the nexus of China's economic growth, and their top leaders are portrayed as essentially chairpersons and CEOs of their governed locales. In the words of a longtime observer of China's car industry, "Think of it [the city of Shanghai] as Shanghai Inc., with the mayor as the chairman and CEO."[7] But as we elaborated in earlier chapters, politicians, like all people, are influenced by their early experiences. So, politicians with a strong Maoist imprint that is antagonistic to Western capitalism are thus less likely to build connections with entrepreneurs or implement policies that are conducive to the growth of the private economy.

Because so many Western commentators wrongly portray China and the CCP as akin to the Soviet Union, we specifically compare the two systems. China's more decentralized system was able to accommodate Deng Xiaoping's gradual introduction of reforms, whereas the USSR and the other countries in the Eastern Bloc used shock therapy to change their systems all at once, with very different consequences.[8] In our recommendations that flow from this chapter, we advise foreign firms to consider local politicians' backgrounds when making location decisions—and to leverage the competition among local governments.

THE SOCIALIST SYSTEM IN POST-1949 CHINA

The Western archetype for communist countries is the former Soviet Union, which many writers and readers wrongly presume followed the same governance model as China.[9] While the Chinese political system—especially its top-down power structure—resembles the Soviet Union's in some ways, it differs regarding local autonomy, which has very important implications for economic reform.

Political Centralization

Top-down control is a basic characteristic of a Leninist party with a strong centralized hierarchy that dictates the political process.[10] In China, the central or national-level authority selects provincial-level party leaders (party secretaries and CCP committee members). Then those provincial-level leaders select prefectural-level party leaders. Continuing in this fashion, leaders are determined down to the lowest, township level.

CCP-government leaders at the provincial level decide who to appoint as city- or prefectural-level political leaders (fig. 10.1). This group in turn forms that level's CCP standing committee, including the party secretary (the top-ranked official), the government leader (for example, the city mayor, the second most senior official, who is at the rank of vice party secretary), and other vice party secretaries. In this way, the political leadership of geographic entities follows a politically centralized logic, which contrasts with the structure of most Western countries, where national-, provincial- or state-, and local-level officials are elected from the bottom up by voters in their respective jurisdictions, and there are no superordinate-subordinate relationships between different levels of government. For example, US president Joe Biden recommended that New York State governor Andrew Cuomo resign following the revelation of his sexual abuse scandal rather than removing him from office, which he did not have the authority to do.[11] In contrast, Jiang Chaoliang, the

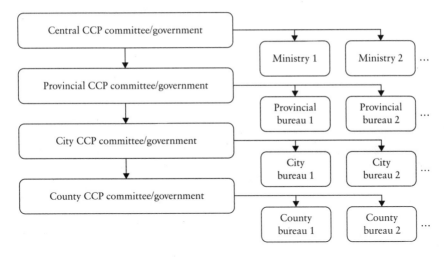

Figure 10.1 The Top-Down Structure of Political Power in China
Data source: Based on authors' research and prior work, including Qian, Yingyi, and Chenggang Xu, "The M-Form Hierarchy and China's Economic Reform," *European Economic Review* 37, no. 2 (1993): 541–48; and Xu, Chenggang, "The Fundamental Institutions of China's Reforms and Development," *Journal of Economic Literature* 49, no. 4 (2011): 1076–151. Figure drawn by the authors.

party secretary of Hubei Province, was removed from office by higher authorities within three weeks after he failed to contain the COVID-19 pandemic in Hubei's capital city, Wuhan.[12]

Economic Decentralization

To understand how a geographic entity like a province or city manages the economy within its jurisdiction, it is important to understand in more detail how political appointment proceeds in China. As noted, political leaders are appointed by the level above them. They then appoint the directors of the different bureaus or agencies within their jurisdictions. Among other responsibilities, such as city management, the economy, environmental protection, science and technology, and transportation, these directors have responsibility for the different industries within the locale, as well as its overall economic development. In other words, the management of the economy follows a *decentralized* logic.[13] While this structure existed before China's opening, following 1978,

Figure 10.2 The Soviet Form of Governance
Data sources: Based on authors' research and prior work, including Qian, Yingyi, and Chenggang Xu, "The M-Form Hierarchy and China's Economic Reform," *European Economic Review* 37, no. 2 (1993): 541–48; and Xu, Chenggang, "The Fundamental Institutions of China's Reforms and Development," *Journal of Economic Literature* 49, no. 4 (2011): 1076–151. Figure drawn by the authors.

different locales competed with each other in a "GDP [gross domestic product] tournament" that rapidly advanced China economically.

Comparing the Political and Economic Structures of China with the Soviet Union's

All communist countries have been politically centralized. But in contrast with China, the Soviet Union was economically centralized as well. There was top-down, vertical control of the different industries (fig. 10.2). For example, the governing body of the manufacturing industry at the central level determined personnel and production plans at the republic level, which controlled them in turn at the oblast level, and so on down. Lower-level communist (Bolshevik) committees were only in charge of party issues and agriculture. Using the analogue of corporate structures, if we compared the Soviet Union to a firm, then each Soviet industry—for example, manufacturing, finance, telecommunications, and military—would be a department and headquarters (the central government) would allocate resources among them. This form is called a unitary form.

China, in contrast, maintains a multidivisional form, where each regional government is a subsidiary with its own set of industries. The central government only maintains vertical political control. Regional governments are horizontally responsible for all the industries within their jurisdictions. Regional committees make plans for their industries and political leaders appoint various directors to manage them. For example, Wang Yang upgraded Guangdong's manufacturing, focusing on high-end manufacturing in Dongguan and Foshan, and worked to connect Guangzhou's service industries to Hong Kong's financial industry. In contrast, Bo Xilai promoted state investments in infrastructure in Chongqing.

Even as small a region as a village might control a portfolio of industries.[14] The well-known example of Huaxi Village in Jiangsu Province illustrates this. Huaxi's village-level CCP-government leader, Wu Renbao, has pressed for the development of different industries since 1978, including metal hardware, plastic bags, and pesticide applicators. In 1993 Huaxi Village was incorporated as the Huaxi Village Group, which controlled more than sixty firms in such industries as wholesale agriculture, environmental protection, finance, logistics, ocean shipping, real estate, steel, tourism, and warehousing, and it went public in 1999.[15]

Consistent with our imprinting argument, China's governance system was shaped by Mao's early revolutionary experience, as well as the broad sweep of Chinese history. When Mao took control of the CCP in 1935, it had four major armies, and he only controlled one of them. Hence, Mao had to honor a certain degree of autonomy among the other military leaders. Further, as Mao Zedong Military Thought teaches, strategies should be determined by frontline circumstances (that is, realities), so military commanders need discretion. While the Yan'an Rectification Movement established Mao's absolute political authority, military leaders at the battlefront had significant discretion in their operations. In contrast, in the Soviet Union, Vladimir Lenin and Joseph Stalin controlled all Bolshevik troops and Stalin purged many high-ranking officials, including the founder of the Soviet Red Army, Leon Trotsky, to further centralize his power.

After the founding of the People's Republic of China, many military leaders retired and assumed civil positions, while the command structures of their armies were converted to regional and provincial political bureaus that kept their economic and operational autonomy and political loyalty and conformity. This decentralized structure was further expanded in 1958, when a large number of rights regarding enterprise management, plan management, project approval, labor management power, and taxation were devolved to local jurisdictions. A second wave of decentralization began in 1970 for two purposes: to make localities self-sufficient and provide more incentives for higher growth.[16]

For all of China's authoritarian traditions, it has a long history of economic decentralization, because emperors did not appoint officials below the county level. Towns and villages self-managed their socioeconomic affairs.[17] Local officials commonly used such phrases as, "The mountains are high, and the emperor is far away," and "The upper body has its policies but we have our countermeasures," to describe their independence. Scholars have shown that for many local officials, the immediate reaction to new regulations from above was how to get around them.[18] In addition, for thousands of years, within China's border regions there have been different ethnic groups, and the national government typically delegated more autonomy to those border regions, such as those in the northwest, northeast, and southwest.

Russia's history of centralization is also of long standing. In the eighteenth century, Czar Peter the Great concentrated resources to industrialize Russia and centralize power. To recover from the First World War and the Russian Civil War, Lenin and Stalin did the same by adopting a centralized economic system. They nationalized all industries and concentrated on developing region-based industry clusters—for example, heavy industry in Ukraine (aviation, tank making, shipbuilding), mining in Kazakhstan, and petroleum in Azerbaijan. Furthermore, the Russian Empire started from small principalities (for example, the Grand Duchy of Moscow), and its population in those formative stages was mostly Russian. The empire did not expand to other East Slavic, Caucasian, and Asian countries until the mid-eighteenth century. Rather than honoring different ethnic groups' traditions, the empire forced non-Russian people—such as those in Kazakhstan, Kyrgyzstan, and Uzbekistan—to abandon their languages and traditions and become Russianized and Islam, their religion, was effectively banned in central Asia in the 1920s.[19]

Implications of the Two Different Types of Political Organization for Economic Transitions

Like China, Russia and the socialist republics it controlled tried to liberalize their economies in the 1980s and 1990s, but they were largely unsuccessful and suffered from negative economic effects and in some cases the collapse of their entire economy. The strategy followed was a whole-scale reform, collectively known as shock therapy that was intended to transition the planned economy in these countries into a free market one through the sudden release of price, currency, and tariff controls and regulations; the immediate elimination of state subsidies to state-owned firms; and even privatization of these firms. However, such a sudden transformation led to chaos. Because of this, many people believed that because the Iron Curtain had fallen, the "Bamboo Curtain" would be next—that China's economic liberalization efforts would infect and ultimately undermine its political system. The Tiananmen Square protests in 1989 suggested that that was the case. But China's economic transition turned out to be much smoother and, so far, more successful than the USSR's. And as we have argued in these pages, much of Mao's legacy remains intact.

Consistent with existing scholarly work, we suggest that one reason for this difference is the unique multidivisional form of China's socialist institutions described earlier.[20] As Xi Zhongxun (father of Xi Jinping) told Deng Xiaoping in 1979, "In a country as big as China, each province has its own characteristics, and should be developed according to the characteristics of the province."[21]

Under the Soviet model, each industry was managed separately, so different regions and republics tended to become highly specialized. Incrementalism was impossible, as changes in one republic and its flagship industries would affect the other republics and their industries via interconnected supply chains. Thus, incremental and region-wide reform of this sort was much more logistically difficult and would lead to significant industrial gaps in many regions. As the economist Grigory Yavlinsky put it at the time, the Soviet Union "needs to be built anew, not reformed."[22] And so he proposed the 500 Days Program, a shock therapy regime that aimed to change it from top to bottom in less than two years, which ultimately led to the collapse of the USSR.[23]

Under China's decentralized economic institutional arrangement, an incremental, region-by-region, market-oriented reform was more feasible. As Deng asserted, "We should reform incrementally from one region . . . and then spread to the whole country."[24] Deng first introduced capitalist practices, such as establishing free-trade zones, allowing private firms to engage in manufacturing for exportation, and introducing market mechanisms to determine workers' wages, in Guangdong Province while keeping the other provinces under a planned economy. If the experiment failed, the CCP-government could roll it back. If it succeeded, it could be gradually applied to other provinces.

As recent research has shown, the Chinese leaders did initially consider a shock therapy–like approach.[25] As described in earlier chapters, the initial plan was to quickly deregulate prices in 1988. Yet word got out before the official announcement, and there was a rush to stockpile goods, which created bank runs and hyperinflation.[26] This failed policy and the Tiananmen Square Massacre in 1989, which resulted in the purging of many of the leaders who had promoted faster liberalization, such as Zhao Ziyang, solidified the CCP-government leaders' determination that reforms be implemented gradually.[27]

LOCAL POLITICIANS AND MARKET DEVELOPMENT

Given the high level of economic discretion in China, local government officials play a critical role in development. Research across a number of social science disciplines has shown how local government officials' competition drives economic growth by attracting businesses to their jurisdictions, typically via tax and other financial incentives. A typical method is to sell land to enterprises and collect fiscal revenues to develop infrastructure.[28] Local governments are made up of "political men," who care about their political rank and promotion and seek to advance them via demonstrations of their "GDP growth heroism."[29] Many politicians wine and dine potential investors and business owners. Shen Changyou, CCP party secretary of the city of Dongying in Shandong Province, visited one potential investor several times to win a contract; some politicians have written guidance for other leaders on how to attract firms and promote growth.[30] The political leaders of the city of Sanmenxia, in Henan Province, supported the development of the East Hope Group by granting it the right to purchase bauxite, an essential raw material for producing aluminum, which had previously been monopolized by the state-owned giant Chinalco. Today the East Hope Group is China's largest aluminum producer.[31] Scholars have provided abundant evidence that politicians who outcompete their peers in developing their regions' GDPs are more likely to climb the political ladder. Poor performers might be punished for their lackluster performance.[32]

Of course, not all politicians are the same. Specifically, while there are strong incentives for politicians to be probusiness, their life histories also shape their attitudes.[33] The imprinting we described earlier should apply to politicians just as much as it does to entrepreneurs, and our statistical research bears this out. Politicians with a strong Maoist imprint—those who joined the party before the 1978 economic reform—were more antagonistic to business.[34] Specifically, politicians who joined the CCP in the Maoist era (before 1978) were less likely to make connections with entrepreneurs—for example, by inviting them to one of the two nominal legislative councils in China. As with entrepreneurs, these cognitive frameworks may trump their self-interest. Even though the promotion of economic growth is beneficial for their careers, some politicians—specifically those with a deeper Maoist imprint—are resistant. For example, Bo Xilai's use of "red" songs to motivate the populace and his policies (e.g., using state banks to invest and finance small- and medium-size firms and developing cheap government-funded housing for low-income farmers) reflect a deep Maoist imprint. His operations were harmful to the Chongqing economy and many entrepreneurs fled from Chongqing, and he ended up being sentenced to life in prison.

Wang Yang's imprinting was different. Early on, he was a teacher at the May Seventh Cadre School in Suxian, Jiangsu Province. Mao established the May Seventh Cadre Schools as labor camps that combined hard agricultural work with the study of his writings in order to "reeducate" cadres and intellectuals. Wang became disillusioned with Maoism and the Cultural Revolution after seeing how poorly the interned people were treated. In 1979 he was sent to the CCP's Central Party School to learn the most updated communist theories of political economy. This experience firmed up his belief in economic reform. When he later became the party secretary of Guangdong Province, the economy was vibrant under his leadership.[35] Wang is now one of the seven top leaders in China.

We next investigate in more detail the intuition that political leaders with a Maoist imprint would be more antagonistic toward business and market-related ideas. Since party secretaries and mayors are in charge of the socioeconomic affairs of their jurisdictions, their subjective feelings have objective consequences. Consistent with this, prior research shows patterns of probusiness and antibusiness behavior among local

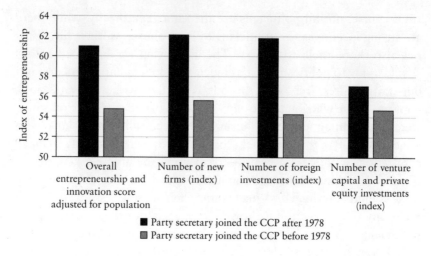

Figure 10.3 Business-Related Actions of Chinese City Leaders (Party Secretaries)
Data sources: Authors' hand-collection and the Enterprise Survey for Innovation and Entrepreneurship in China by Peking University. Calculated by the authors.

politicians who were imprinted by Maoism before and after the reform in 1978.[36] Since the CCP-government has a dyadic leadership structure, with the party secretary and mayor as the top leaders of the CCP committee and city government, respectively, we tracked both. As discussed earlier, the party sits above the government, so the party secretary is the most senior official in the jurisdiction.

We first examined data obtained from the National School of Development at Peking University. On average, party secretaries who joined the CCP before 1978 are more antagonistic toward entrepreneurship (as reflected in the index of number of new firms in their jurisdictions), foreign investment (as reflected in the index of number of foreign investments), and index of numbers of venture capital and private equity investments that incubate entrepreneurship (fig. 10.3). These individuals, based on our prior work, might still maintain a Maoist mindset that perceives private business, especially foreign investment, as at odds with communism. The overall index of entrepreneurship and innovation in their jurisdictions is also smaller (10.15 percent less) for party secretaries who joined the CCP before 1978.

We also determined the data pattern for mayors (fig. 10.4), which is consistent with that for party secretaries. On average, mayors who

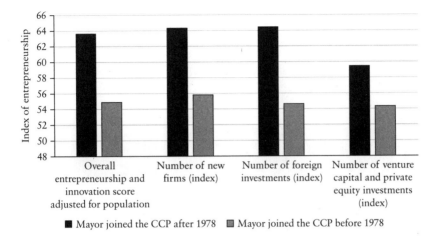

Figure 10.4 Business-Related Actions of Chinese City Leaders (Mayors)
Data sources: Authors' hand-collection and the Enterprise Survey for Innovation and Entrepreneurship in China by Peking University. Calculated by the authors.

joined the CCP before 1978 are also more antagonistic toward entrepreneurship, foreign investment, and venture capital and private equity investments. The overall index of entrepreneurship and innovation is also smaller for mayors who joined the CCP before 1978. Statistical analysis supports this pattern.[37]

Second, a typical probusiness policy is the establishment of development or tax-free zones (also called special economic zones) to attract the establishment of new firms, either domestic or foreign. Even the leaders of the small town of Sanzao in the city of Yancheng, Jiangsu Province, with around fifty thousand people, established such a zone.[38] Firms founded in these zones enjoy streamlined administrative procedures (for example, registration), better access to bank loans and other financial instruments, and tax rebates.[39] Party secretaries are 79.9 percent less likely ($= 2.72 / 13.5 - 1$) to implement probusiness policies such as establishing a special economic zone if they joined the CCP in the Maoist period than those who joined after 1978 (fig. 10.5). Similarly, mayors are around 81.1 percent less likely ($= 2.31 / 12.22 - 1$) to establish a special economic zone if they joined the CCP in the Maoist period than those who joined after 1978. Our statistical analysis also provides evidence for this phenomenon.[40]

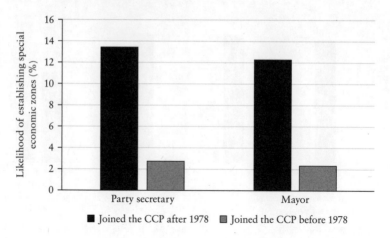

Figure 10.5 Political Leaders' Likelihood of Establishing Special Economic Zones
Data source: Authors' hand-collection of data from websites that report officials' characteristics and economic policies. Calculated by the authors.

Third, politicians can raise their profiles and attract new businesses to their jurisdictions by developing ties to the CEOs of publicly traded firms in their cities. One way to do this is to appoint successful businesspeople to the National People's Congress or the Chinese People's Political Consultative Conference.[41] The leaders of the city of Kunshan of Jiangsu Province attracted several businesspeople to invest there by giving away such memberships (this came to light because of a scandal: one of those leaders was the CEO of a metal-producing firm that failed to provide necessary safety measures; an explosion in their plant killed and wounded numerous workers).[42]

On average, party secretaries who joined the CCP before 1978 had 1.74 (or 48.3 percent) fewer business-government ties than those who joined the CCP after 1978. Similarly, mayors who joined the CCP before 1978 had 1.06 (or 33.2 percent) fewer business-government ties than those who joined the CCP after 1978 (fig. 10.6). Using statistical analysis, we found further supportive evidence for this phenomenon.[43]

Neoliberal economists typically portray governments, particularly communist governments with "command economies," as Hobbesian Leviathans, all-powerful political entities that must be tamed lest they destroy the businesses that they seek to control.[44] Governments lack the fine-grained data that are needed to allocate resources efficiently, and

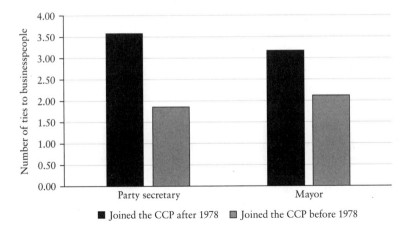

Figure 10.6 Number of Political Leaders' Business-Government Ties
Data source: Authors' hand-collection of data from websites that report officials' characteristics and the résumés of CEOs of publicly traded firms in China. Calculated by the authors.

they also focus on social objectives to the detriment of economic ones; any intervention in the market they undertake, these economists believe, can only distort it for the worse.[45] Corruption is the most predictable result, as we have seen during the market transitions in many former communist countries; a significant number of politicians take bribes and otherwise seek to benefit themselves.[46]

While there are many well-known cases of politicians who are indeed "grabbing hands," in the Chinese idiom, in many other cases, politicians play the role of a "helping hand." Doing so can serve their own interests as well as the businesses', as economic success is the most important metric for political success. But the neoliberal economists are not all wrong, either. China's model is in some respects a double-edged sword. Under the system of political centralization and economic decentralization, the central government's goals are paramount. In Mao's period, only political leaders whose performance was consistent with Mao's preferences would be promoted. During the Great Leap Forward, that meant increasing steel output and agricultural yields—or at least pretending to. Wang Qiancheng, a village manager, was quickly promoted to the county level when he issued misleading reports that pleased Mao (the reality was that millions of Chinese died of hunger during the subsequent

Great Famine). During the Cultural Revolution, Mao emphasized political loyalty and enthusiasm for the "revolution"—which officials could demonstrate by, for example, attacking senior leaders who might threaten Mao. Incompetent and corrupt leaders such as Wang Hongwen and Chen Yonggui thrived by doing just that. After Mao's death and the reform, the chief goal became the promotion of GDP growth.

But neo-Maoist movements are on the rise, and Xi Jinping has been pressing for greater regulation of and restrictions on the private sector. Not surprisingly, many entrepreneurs are worried that local political leaders will become more antagonistic toward private business. In a provocative 2021 speech, Jack Ma criticized the CCP-government, declaring that, "in fact, supervision and regulation are two things. Supervision is to watch your development, and regulation should happen only when there are problems. However, our current regulative capacity is too strong and that of supervision is not enough. Good innovation is not afraid of regulation, but we are afraid of yesterday's [outdated] regulation, we cannot regulate the airport the same way we regulate the railway station, and we cannot regulate the future with yesterday's method." Ma's speech, and other inflammatory statements—for example, he said that "working 9 A.M. to 9 P.M., six days a week is a gift" and "Chinese financial regulations still follow an outdated pawnshop logic"—solicited an equally strong reaction from Xi and the regulatory body.[47] Declaring that "the relationship between financial development, financial stability, and financial security must be properly handled" and that "supervision must be strengthened, financial activities must be fully incorporated into supervision in accordance with the law, and risks must be effectively prevented," the supervisory body suspended the initial public offering of Alibaba's payment platform Ant Financial.[48] Xi's anti-corruption campaign has caused thousands of high-ranking officials to be prosecuted and imprisoned. Looking ahead, it seems likely that loyalty to communism will eclipse GDP heroism as a measure predicting political success.

Under China's current regime, politicians have strong probusiness incentives and may even act like businesspeople themselves in order to recruit businesses and attract investment. But these incentives are not universal and those politicians' behavior is crucially dependent on their life histories—specifically, their early exposure to Maoism. Ironically, the overall system owes the flexibility that allowed for piecemeal liberalization to Mao—though hardcore Maoists like Bo were opposed to it.

Since there is such competition between localities for business, on the one hand, and there are such differences between politicians' attitudes toward it, on the other, entrepreneurs and foreign investors are advised to leverage that competition to their advantage, while at the same time carefully studying local politicians' backgrounds, the better to understand their potential attitudes to their business. However, we also caution that businesspeople should be especially attentive to the supreme leader's political goals.

Business is always controlled politically in China, though that hand is heavier at some times and lighter at others. In the West, capital can significantly influence the state and often fight with it; in China, entrepreneurs strive to have close relations with the government and do not strive to change the system.[49] Rather, they cooperate with it and are willing in many cases to be co-opted by it, assuming they continue to prosper economically. As we have argued, the idea that economic liberalization inevitably leads to political liberalization is simply false; the CCP-government has effectively incorporated and controlled business interests within the party-state apparatus all along.

Having a good relationship with local CCP-governments is critical to business success in China. Many Western firms tend to stay away from host governments and politics; doing so might even be a hard-and-fast rule. Google refused to cooperate with the Chinese government by censoring search results, and in 2010 it finally left the Chinese market.[50] In 2021 Microsoft's LinkedIn social network followed the same path. While some government mandates, such as censorship, may be fundamentally at odds with a firm's values and mission, firms can often find a modus vivendi. For example, when the Chinese government wanted to develop its automobile industry and invited foreign firms to enter the Chinese market, it required them to establish joint ventures with Chinese firms and transfer technologies to them. German and Japanese automakers such as Volkswagen, BMW, Toyota, and Honda have been particularly successful in this regard.

More recently, Elon Musk cultivated a good relationship with the Chinese government, which allowed Tesla to establish a wholly owned subsidiary (Gigafactory) in Shanghai rather than a mandated joint venture. The local government in Shanghai also provided loans with good terms (for example, low interest and little collateral) and a vast building site for the Gigafactory. Within one year, the factory was built and had produced its first set of cars.[51] Musk thanked the Chinese government and people emotionally while criticizing the US government and people.[52] Tesla also established its only non-US research facility in Shanghai. Many Chinese have reacted very positively to Tesla; some even worry that their local brands, such as NIO and Xpeng, will be in trouble.[53] Microsoft also actively cooperated with rather than defied the Chinese government and as a result has dominated the Chinese market for decades.[54] While their pliancy has earned them some critiques domestically, we think it is important to recognize them as examples of companies that have successfully entered and expanded in China. Understandably, some firms may not want to follow their example, although if that is the case, perhaps they should rethink their ambitions in China.

In the next chapter, we will explore how the socialist system manifests itself in private firms in China. We specifically focus on the two typical ways that the CCP-government controls the private sector—state ownership and party branches. These can also be traced back to the experiences and influence of Mao.

11 The Socialist Economy and Private Firms in China

The purpose of the socialist revolution is to liberate productive forces. The shift from private and individual ownership to the socialist collective one regarding agriculture and the handicraft industry and from capitalist ownership to socialist ownership of private industry and commerce inevitably greatly liberated productive forces. This creates social conditions for the development of industrial and agricultural production.

Establish a system of party organizations and party representatives at all levels, build party branches in the company (military units), set up party groups in shifts and platoons, set up party representatives above the company level, and set up party committees in regiments and battalions. Important issues must be decided by the party committee.

—Mao Zedong

WHILE DECENTRALIZATION WAS FOLLOWED politically, in the economic realm a key element of socialist institutions was state ownership of economic units and central planning through the so-called socialist transformation, which was the core component of China's first five-year plan. Mao Zedong stated that "it is a sound policy and method to complete the socialist transformation of private industry and commerce through state capitalism."[1] The approach was to use government funds to buy out commercial and service industries (or use threats and coercion if they were reluctant to sell), while also establishing manufacturing industries from scratch with the help of expertise and funds from the Soviet Union. Finally, the agriculture industry, as well as fishing and forestry, would be collectivized.

Mao and the Chinese Communist Party (CCP) did try to faithfully implement Marxist doctrine to eliminate private ownership.[2] A typical

Figure 11.1 Rong Yiren (*Left*) and Jiang Zemin
"China Obit Rong Yiren," Associated Press, March 16, 1998. AP Photo/Xinhua.

example was the famous banker Rong Yiren (fig. 11.1), who "voluntarily" relinquished his property to the CCP and later occupied important positions in the party-state system (for example, vice president). Rong was worried about his capitalist identity and asked Mao whether he was subject to class struggle. Mao said that "in the unique Chinese context, these contradictions could be nonconfrontational and solved in a peaceful way."[3] A major consequence of such transformation was that all service industries became state owned.

Mao was intensely focused on industrializing China. The country was so undeveloped in that respect, Mao reflected, that "China could not even manufacture matches or nails, as a result they were called 'foreign made' matches and nails."[4] Soviet aid was especially important in the early days of the People's Republic; at one point there were 156 major development projects under way that were approved and supported by Joseph Stalin. China's entire manufacturing industry was state owned.

A major slogan of the CCP was, "Attack despotic landowners and distribute their land to the poor peasants." By the end of 1953, most landowners had been expropriated and most peasants had their own land. But as the socialist transformation intensified, the peasants' land was itself collectivized so that the government owned and managed it directly. The socialist transformation was completed by the end of 1956, after which China formally began its second five-year plan.

Mao mandated that CCP branches be established in every state-owned firm, just as there were at every level of government and at all universities. These CCP branches acted as the firms' key decision-making bodies. Managers had to be CCP members and members of their CCP branches; otherwise, they had no way to exercise their power. For example, when Tong Ren Tang, a famous pharmaceutical company founded in 1669 and China's largest producer of traditional Chinese medicine, became nationalized in 1954, its owner, Le Songsheng, whose family had owned it for thirteen generations, was not a CCP member. Le became chief manager of the nationalized firm, but he could not participate in CCP branch activities. As a result, he could only implement decisions if the CCP branch made them, such as stopping profit distribution to employees and expanding the firm's capacity. Le also had to report to the CCP secretary Wang Su.[5]

Despite the massive privatization following Deng Xiaoping's reform, party-state control of the private economy has been persistent, reflecting Mao's ideal of having the CCP-government control the economy. State-owned enterprises (SOEs) are still important, and in October 2019, the Fourth Plenary Session of the Nineteenth Central Committee of the Chinese Communist Party defined the socialist system as "state ownership as the main body, while multiple ownership economies are developing at the same time."[6] Meanwhile, the role of CCP branches has been persistently emphasized in SOEs, and in recent years, the CCP-government has encouraged, and later mandated, private firms to establish CCP branches.[7] In this way, the CCP-government keeps private-sector and capitalist forces under control.

State ownership of private firms and CCP-government organizations in private firms have attracted significant media and academic attention. Through ownership (economic control) and CCP branch establishment (political control), the state power subdues, constrains, and co-opts capitalist forces. While there are costs to state ownership, firms benefit from ease of financing and protection from political harassment. Political control through the CCP branch also has pluses and minuses. While the branches help motivate employees, they distort the lines of command and authority.

Before we discuss the recent rise of state ownership and CCP branches in private firms, we first chart the history of private firms in the People's Republic of China.

BACKGROUND ON PRIVATE ENTERPRISES IN THE PEOPLE'S REPUBLIC OF CHINA

Planned economy, SOEs, and heavy state intervention (for example, five-year plans that map strategies for economic development and set growth targets) are likely the three most important concepts mentioned when discussing the Chinese economy. One of the most salient aspects of disagreements in US-China trade talks during the Trump and Biden administrations was the Chinese government's insistence on continuing to provide massive subsidies to SOEs.[8] Given the media's emphases, most Westerners may presume that the Chinese economy is largely state owned.[9] For example, Senator Tom Cotton, in his report published on February 16, 2021, claimed that almost all Chinese firms are ultimately controlled by the government or CCP.[10] However, this description misses the nuances of the Chinese economy and the types of organizations therein. While it was true for the period between 1956 and 1978, since 1978, the CCP-government has moved to establish a more market-oriented economy, significantly encouraging the development of private enterprises.

There have been big swings in the relationship between the government and private economy since the founding of the People's Republic of China in 1949. Mao actually allowed different types of private ownership to exist during the early period of the People's Republic. For example, the de facto interim constitution of China passed on September 29, 1949 (two days before the founding of the communist regime)—the Common Program of the Chinese People's Political Consultative Conference—stated that "the people's government should encourage the enthusiasm of business operations and support the development of private economic enterprises that are beneficial to the national economy and people's livelihood."[11] In addition, the decision to adopt the current Chinese national flag—the five-star red flag—on September 27, 1949, reflects this intention: the large star represents the CCP, while the four smaller stars represent people from the four social classes—the working class, the peasant class, and the urban and national bourgeoisie (capitalists)—all of them unified by the CCP.[12]

However, by the early 1950s, as Mao and the CCP leaned toward the Soviet Union, China became an active member of the global communist movement, starting the socialist transformation that nationalized all industry sectors. By 1956, agriculture was collectivized and owned by the CCP-government, the handcraft industry had become state owned, and manufacturing and commercial industries were claimed to have been "peacefully redeemed" and become government assets. For the next two decades, China's economy was fully planned—government bureaus determined the procurement of raw materials, production, price, and distribution, and private ownership disappeared.[13]

The planned economy continued until 1978, after which the CCP-government gradually established a market economy: it allowed a private economy to exist but did not legally acknowledge it until Deng Xiaoping's 1992 Southern Tour. The CCP-government also transformed many SOEs into private firms. Specifically, as some of our examples in this book will illustrate, the CCP-government invented an intermediary status between SOE and private ownership called collective-owned enterprise (COE). It did so to preempt objections from communist hardliners, as words that connoted "private" were taboo during Mao's period, especially after the 1950s, when China split with the Soviet Union because of the latter's so-called revisionist, capitalist reform. It was hoped that such a hybrid organizational form would facilitate a smoother transition of SOEs to private ownership. The government first sold ownership of SOEs to managers and employees, so these firms became owned "collectively." Later, managers or other individuals might purchase ownership shares from others and take them fully private.[14] Numerous firms, such as Haier (founded in 1984) and Huawei (founded in 1987), were initially registered as COEs, as the CCP-government would not issue licenses for private firms until 1992.

We summarize China's major sources of private firms and entrepreneurs (table 11.1).[15] There are three types: people who used to be farmers, former SOE or COE managers or people who bought SOEs or

Table 11.1 Sources of Private Enterprises in China since 1978

Source of private firms	Typical background of entrepreneurs	Example entrepreneurs (firms listed in parentheses)
Agricultural cooperatives, production teams, township-village enterprises	Leaders of teams, heads of village, or ordinary farmers	Lu Guanqiu (Wanxiang), Ye Huaneng (Baolihua), Nian Guangjiu (Shazi Melon Seeds), Wu Renbao (Huaxi Village Group)
SOEs or COEs	SOE and government employees (including managers) or individuals	Cao Dewang (Fuyao), Chen Dongsheng (Taikang Insurance), Luo Bangpeng (Zhejiang Hisoar Pharm), Zhu Xinli (Huiyuan Juice), Zong Qinghou (Wahaha)
Greenfield	Well-educated people (many with overseas experience)	Cui Genliang (Hengtong), Li Yanhong (a.k.a. Robin Li; Baidu), Liu Chuanzhi (Lenovo), Ma Yun (a.k.a. Jack Ma; Alibaba), Ma Huateng (a.k.a. Pony Ma; Tencent), Ren Zhengfei (Huawei), Shi Yuzhu (Giant Group), Wang Wenjing (Yongyou), Zhang Chaoyang (a.k.a. Charles Zhang; Sohu)

Source: Based on the authors' summary of examples of Chinese entrepreneurs. The list is by no means exhaustive; it merely contains some representative entrepreneurs.

COEs, and those who started their businesses from scratch (that is, greenfield).

The first source of private firms is farmers, leaders of agricultural production teams, and heads of villages who transformed their agricultural collectives into township-village enterprises.[16] Some of these enterprises later developed into gigantic business groups and multinational enterprises. For example, Lu Guanqiu was a farmer before he founded the Wanxiang Group—now the largest automotive components manufacturer in China—in 1969. In that year, the CCP-government allowed each township government (called people's communes then) to own one agricultural machinery factory, and Lu successfully won the bid. By 1988, he had gained full control of the township-village firm. Some scholars suggest that the unprecedented economic growth in

China starting in the 1980s was largely driven by these township-village firms.[17]

The second source of private enterprises is SOEs, which might indirectly become privatized as COEs. These SOEs were mostly small and operating in the red—the Chinese government's privatization strategy was articulated as "grasping the large and letting go of the small."[18] For example, Fuqing Gaoshan Special-Shaped Glass Factory had experienced seven years of significant losses. The government hoped to get rid of the negative assets and sell the factory through a competitive bidding process. Cao Dewang paid about $19,000 to be the new owner of the factory in 1983. He made several strategic changes, one of which was to manufacture auto glass. The end result was Fuyao Glass, one of the largest auto glass makers in the world (featured in the Oscar-winning documentary *American Factory*).[19]

As noted, SOEs may also be transformed into private firms indirectly, by becoming COEs first. For example, Luo Bangpeng became director of Taizhou Jiaojiang Second Chemical Factory in 1984. The factory was suffering great losses, and the CCP-government invited Luo and his subordinate employees to purchase shares. Luo agreed and managed the factory well. In 1998 the firm was fully privatized, and Luo became the main owner.

The third source is greenfield establishment. Because of the dubious legal status of private firms before 1992, entrepreneurs might register their firms as COEs, as noted earlier. Many had government or SOE work experience and are thus called *xiahai*—going into the (business) sea. For example, Liu Chuanzhi was a researcher at the Institute of Computing Technology, Chinese Academy of Sciences. Bored and, in his words, disinclined to "endure his inaction and wasting time," he resigned from his position and established Lenovo.[20]

After 1992, the Chinese government clarified the legal status of private firms, and many individuals registered their firms by leveraging new resources and entrepreneurial opportunities. This was further enabled by the CCP-government's deregulation of entry into many industries after it announced it would only control industries of national interest. For example, the internet and e-commerce gave rise to Alibaba, Baidu, Tencent, and others. Founders of these firms, such as Jack Ma, Robin Li, Pony Ma, and Charles Zhang, had intellectual backgrounds and some had overseas educational or work experience (for example, Li graduated from the University of Buffalo and worked on Wall Street, and Zhang graduated from MIT and worked for a US corporation), and they were thus able to recognize opportunities in the internet era, having seen them in the West.

Private businesses proliferated between 1992 and 2008, when the global financial crisis hit China and the government initiated a stimulus plan, allegedly pumping $600 billion into the economy. SOEs particularly benefited from the stimulus plan, leading to a period in which the "the state advance[d] and private sector retreat[ed]." Local governments were also significant players behind the scenes in promoting SOEs.[21]

More recently, Xi Jinping has explicitly called on governments and individuals to make SOEs stronger, larger, and better.[22] For instance, on August 25, 2021, Xi claimed that "state-owned enterprises in our country have made historic contributions to the economic and social development, scientific and technological progress, national defense construction, and people's livelihood improvement, and they have made outstanding meritorious service! Their contributions cannot be ignored!"[23] Indeed, as noted, one of the main issues of debate in the US-China trade talks was the massive subsidies paid to SOEs.[24] Meanwhile, state ownership has grown. Given the increasingly conservative political environment, that trend is likely to continue.

PRIVATE FIRMS AND STATE OWNERSHIP IN CHINA

We welcome state ownership in our firm; it helps us apply for [and receive] bank loans.

—Xiao Guoying, founder and CEO of
Zhejiang Huagang Dyeing and Weaving Group[25]

Since 2008, the CCP-government increasingly provided SOEs with large government procurements and massive subsidies, favored them in regulation, and helped them crowd out both foreign and domestic private competitors.[26] The state also invested heavily in privately owned enterprises.

The Zhejiang Huagang Dyeing and Weaving Group is a privately owned garment firm in the city of Shaoxing, Zhejiang Province, with $70 million in total assets. The firm was among the first of China's post-reform enterprises to welcome government investment. According to a survey conducted in Shaoxing, around 25 percent of China's private firms accepted government investment in 2009.[27]

Since Xi took office, the state-owned sector has grown more dominant and state purchases of shares in private firms have accelerated, in accordance with his view that the state can make private firms more active, healthy, and vibrant.[28] On November 23, 2015, Xi declared that "Comrade Mao Zedong creatively put forward . . . original views on the development of our country's economy" in that "the dominant role of state ownership cannot be changed, and the leading role of the state-owned economy cannot be changed." Xi Jinping Thought on Socialism with Chinese Characteristics for a New Era emphasizes that "without the important material foundation that state-owned enterprises have laid for China's development over a long period of time, without the major innovations and key core technologies achieved by state-owned enterprises, and without state-owned enterprises' long-term commitment to a large number of social responsibilities, there would be no economic independence and national security for China, no continuous improvement in people's lives, and no socialist China standing tall in the East of the world."[29]

After the 2008–9 financial crisis, the CCP-government had to bail out many private firms, such as Hualian Sanxin, the largest precise terephthalic acid (an important ingredient for production of plastics) producer in Asia. With a revenue of over $10 billion, it had become "too big to fail." As a government official claimed at the time, if Hualian Sanxin collapsed, the "economy of the city of Shaoxin will fall back by five to ten years."[30] Since 2003 under Hu Jintao, the CCP-government has increasingly funded SOEs to consolidate—with large government procurements and massive subsidies—favored them in regulation, and helped them crowd out both foreign and domestic private competitors. In recent years, the government's interest in the private sector has had a more coercive quality. As noted earlier, many entrepreneurs are concerned that they will be prosecuted and that their property will be confiscated. Because of these fears, some have proposed to eliminate the private economy altogether, turning their firms over to the government in exchange for guarantees of personal safety and espousing a recent slogan calling for the "exit of private economy."[31] Although these are extreme cases, in fact many private firms have received investments from SOEs.

For example, Mengniu—one of the largest dairy producers in China—required government bailout following a food safety scandal in 2009. Specifically, Mengniu had promoted its high-end product Milk Deluxe, saying that the osteoblast milk protein it contained "can effectively increase bone density and osteoblast vitality, and prevent osteoporosis." However, in 2009, China's Ministry of Health found that osteoblast milk protein could lead to cancer. Grocers took Milk Deluxe off their shelves, and Mengniu's brand was significantly affected. Worse still, people compared this scandal to the 2008 scandal in which milk and infant formula were adulterated with melamine and hundreds of thousands of babies were made ill and some even died.[32] Mengniu was also involved, and it had not yet recovered.[33] The founder of Mengniu, Niu Gensheng, asked the government for help, and the SOE China Oil and Foodstuffs Corporation purchased more than 20 percent of Mengniu for upward of $1 billion, becoming its largest owner and effectively nationalizing it.[34]

The nationalization of private firms—that is, changing private firms to state-owned ones through the acquisition of shares—has become more prevalent in recent years. In 2018, 2019, and 2020, twenty-four, forty-one, and forty-four publicly traded firms, respectively, became nationalized, amounting to more than $100 billion in total assets.[35] This resembles the wave of nationalization—that is, the socialist transformation—in the 1950s. For instance, in 2019 the CCP-government in Hangzhou acquired stock in large private firms such as the Alibaba Group and the $40 billion Geely Group, owner of Volvo and the largest shareholder of Daimler.[36] As mentioned previously, firms such as Anbang Insurance (worth more than $200 billion) and Hainan Airlines Group (worth more than $140 billion) were taken over by the government.[37] The state-owned investor Wangtou Chinese (Beijing) acquired 1 percent of the shares of ByteDance (owner of TikTok/Douyin) and the right to appoint its board of directors. The same investor also holds 1 percent of the shares of the parent firm of Sina Weibo (China's most popular microblogging website).[38] As mentioned in prior chapters, the CCP-government is acquiring shares with veto power in the vehicle-for-hire service DiDi.

There are both positive and negative aspects of state control. On the one hand, private firms and state investors might have fundamentally different priorities and assumptions, which could lead to conflict. State control emphasizes bureaucratic standards instituted by the government; economic objectives are not its primary concern. For example, the government emphasizes the maintenance of social stability and thus might ask SOEs to hire more employees than needed in order to reduce the unemployment rate. Almost all of Ant Financial's strategic investors are now state owned, such as the Social Security Fund, the China Investment Corporation, and several major national banks. As a result, its views on profit distribution may conflict with those of its original owners. For example, state owners request stability of the financial system and risk control, whereas private owners focus more on efficiency and better services, which might come at the cost of financial stability and increase risks.[39]

Our interview subjects noted this conflict. For example, subject 9 said, "State-owned capital takes up shares, and it does not care about gains or losses. It is equivalent to the money the government owes us, and then cannot return it to us. It is relatively difficult for state-owned capital and private capital to work together." He also said, "If private enterprises account for the majority of shares and state-owned capital is in it, we are shackled in some areas and cannot freely decide. This is also a contradiction, right? So, I do not think this matter is easy." He also concluded that "state-owned and privately owned . . . do not share the same goal and the same vision. Thus, the collaboration is necessarily difficult." Subject 22 said that "there are often ideological fights and collisions, because state-owned capital is determined based on the state system." He also suggested, "You see that this matter is right, you have to do it, but [the government complains] that your procedures are not in place. . . . When the registration procedures are in place, this opportunity has gone." Our statistical research also shows that private firms may have difficulty in reconciling the conflicting demands of both private and state owners.[40]

Furthermore, governments at different levels might impose different priorities and conflicting goals: local governments emphasize economic benefits provided to their jurisdictions, and the central government emphasizes political control and social stability, such as benefits to employees. Our own research shows that state ownership undermines firms' management of their stakeholders—as some accounts claimed, ownership by all of the people essentially means ownership by none of the people.[41]

On the other hand, state control provides benefits. Beyond helping private firms access credit and financing, it can help firms evade government entities' inefficient, overly bureaucratic procedures and provide political protection from harassment. The Hangzhou government sent one official to each of its hundred largest private firms as a "helper." As a manager of a private enterprise that earns a revenue of $150 million reflected, "The government official helps us not only in getting bank loans, but also dealing with other bureaucratic processes related to labor relations, environmental protection, and other areas. We would not be able to hire someone like this even if we paid hundreds of thousands of dollars!"[42] Another entrepreneur said, "Having government affairs representatives helps us better understand government policy, their administrative procedures, etc., and thus save us costs of time and communication. We welcome them!"[43] Our interviewed entrepreneurs also acknowledged this. For example, subject 8 admired SOEs for their financing capability, saying that they "can obtain loans" because the CCP-government "allows SOEs to lose money, as long as you guarantee the appreciation and preservation of state-owned assets," even without collateral and when suffering serious losses. He went on to say, "[Our] use of state-owned enterprises solved the financing problem." Subject 13 said that "the government has also provided us with a lot of resources and capital."

The Chinese Private Enterprise Survey data bear this out. Entrepreneurs were asked specific questions regarding the level of difficulty they encountered with financing (no difficulty, with some difficulty, and with a lot of difficulty) and the reason for difficulty in bank financing (restrictive credit rating, discrimination against private ownership, exorbitant interest rate, excessive requirement of collateral, overly short loan terms, and insufficient funds available).

Private firms with state ownership experience significantly less difficulty in financing than those that are entirely privately held—30.0 percent of entrepreneurs who receive state investment said that they did not have difficulty in financing, while the percentage for those without state investment is 24.5 percent (fig. 11.2). In contrast, 22.8 percent of entrepreneurs who receive state investment said that they had a lot of difficulty in financing, while 26.6 percent of those without state investment said they did. We also performed statistical analyses, finding that on average, entrepreneurs receiving state investment are less concerned about their financing.[44]

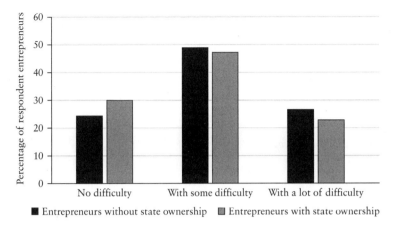

Figure 11.2 State Ownership and Level of Difficulty of Financing for Private Firms
Data source: Chinese Private Enterprise Survey. Calculated by the authors.

State ownership reduces the difficulty of financing in two main ways (fig. 11.3). First, it reduces discrimination by banks—14.8 percent of entrepreneurs who receive state investment said that they experienced discrimination for being privately owned, while the percentage was 19.9 percent for those without private investment. Second, state ownership helps mitigate the problem of having to provide excessive collateral—40.7 percent of entrepreneurs who receive state investment said that the main reason for their difficulty in obtaining bank financing was the collateral requirement, while the percentage for those without state investment was 50.5 percent.

State capital and investments might also provide some political protection for firms. Both our own research and that of many other social scientists have provided abundant evidence that firms in emerging economies are often subject to arbitrary harassment from government entities and others.[45] State ownership provides such firms with a sort of government imprimatur.[46] Subject 12 elaborated another benefit, saying that the state capital "has advantages. . . . If people want to mess with me, they will check my shareholders first. They might then evaluate whether they dare to mess with me as I have state capital backing me."

We again used the Chinese Private Enterprise Survey data to show this pattern. The questionnaires asked how much of a firm's profits were

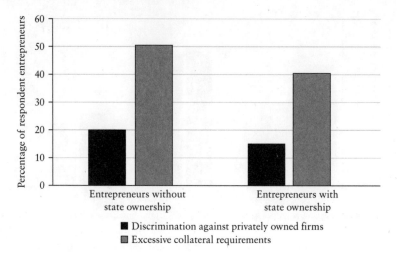

Figure 11.3 State Ownership and Reason for Difficulty of Securing Bank Financing for Private Firms
Data source: Chinese Private Enterprise Survey. Calculated by the authors.

appropriated by the government. Prior work—including our own research—also uses this measure to gauge harassment by the government due to weak institutions in China.[47] A lower ratio of profits was appropriated by the government from entrepreneurs who receive state investment (13.0 percent) than from those without state investment (14.2 percent) (fig. 11.4). Statistical evidence also bore this out.[48]

Why is the CCP-government so eager to control private companies with capital? First, as we have discussed, the Chinese government has placed state power over capital for thousands of years. This long statist tradition and Vladimir Lenin's successful experience of establishing the first communist regime in the USSR convinced Mao that the CCP-government should tightly control the economy—"The party leads everything."[49] Despite Deng's major economic reform, state capitalism and the CCP's control over the economy have been strictly adhered to—in every version of the official interpretation of the socialist economy with Chinese characteristics, the "dominant status of state ownership" has been emphasized. More recently, Xi further stressed that "we should unswervingly maintain the dominant status of state ownership" and that "our principles and policies for encouraging, supporting and guiding

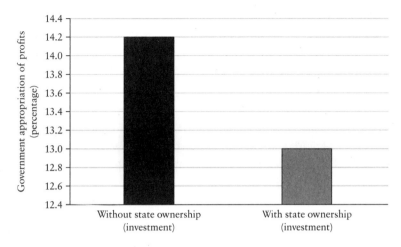

Figure 11.4 Government Appropriation of Profits
Data source: Chinese Private Enterprise Survey. Calculated by the authors.

the development of the private sector of the economy remain unchanged."[50] According to the recently elaborated Xi Jinping Thought
on Socialism with Chinese Characteristics for a New Era, "If the role
of SOEs is reduced or corroded and if these are enfeebled and destroyed,
then it would undermine the dominant position of public [state] ownership, the leading role of state-owned economy, the leading position of
the working class, the essential requirement of common prosperity, the
ruling foundation and the ruling position of the CCP and thereby undermine the system of socialism with Chinese characteristics."[51]

Recent economic crises in capitalist economies, such as the 1998 Asian
Financial Crisis and the 2008 worldwide crisis, have further convinced
the CCP's leadership of the virtues of state ownership. According to the
Marxist view, capitalist economies are subject to periodic crises.[52] The
leaders of the CCP-government believe that state ownership mitigates
the inherent risks within the capitalist system (such as an overheated
economy, asset bubbles, and overproduction). For example, Xi stated,
"We are developing a market economy under the major premise of the
leadership of the Chinese Communist Party and the socialist system. At
any time, we must not forget the attribute 'socialism.' The reason for
saying that it is a socialist market economy is to uphold the superiority
of our system and effectively prevent the drawbacks of the capitalist

market economy."[53] The trillion-dollar stimulus package in 2009 that effectively helped Chinese economic recovery further strengthened senior CCP-government leaders' confidence in a state-led economy.

A related concern is debt crises. Many local governments—for example, that of the city of Shaoxing—regularly monitor the financial health and operating statuses of private firms by asking them to report their key financial information to the government as an owner. The government pays particular attention to entrepreneurs who owe money but have limited assets and tries to prevent them from fleeing by sending "private enterprise helpers" or "government affairs representatives" to these firms.[54] Alibaba and Geely both accommodate such "helpers" within their operations.[55]

Setting aside the terrible human toll, the proportion of industrial output in the gross national product did in fact increase and the share of agricultural output dropped during the Mao era.[56] And like Mao, Xi has been obsessed with industrialization through CCP guidance—for example, the Made in China 2025 initiative—and believes the right approach to establish a strong and industrialized country is to resort to state capital.[57] This makes sense up to a point. While state ownership is helpful for reducing systematic risk to the whole economy through interventions—for example, closely monitoring firms and intervening in their decisions to avoid problems such as overproduction—it can also facilitate further industrialization in cases where it requires large-scale capital outlays but cannot generate immediate returns.

On the other hand, the efficiency of state capitalism is questionable. State investors might not be fully knowledgeable about the target industry or firm, and their procedures, priorities, and assumptions might clash with those of private owners. The historical precedents are alarming: after the socialist transformation in the 1950s, many reputable firms disappeared. For example, Chengzhu Lou, the most famous Cantonese restaurant, founded in 1746, went bankrupt due to poor management and the lack of incentives for employees. Relatedly, state investments might undermine entrepreneurs' incentives and do harm to the vibrant private economy. The legitimacy of the CCP's rule rests not on democracy but on economic performance, to which the booming private sector contributes a lot.

In time, the new wave of nationalization might undercut the CCP's rule and governance by choking the private economy.[58] Xi has begun acknowledging these risks, for instance saying in November 2018 that "for a period of time, some people in society have made some remarks that deny and doubt the private economy. For example, some people put forward the so-called 'the Exit of Private Economy,' saying that the private economy has fulfilled its mission and will withdraw from the stage of history; some people put forward the so-called 'new nationalization theory,' distorting the current mixed ownership reform in the new round and calling it the new nationalization movement. . . . These statements are completely wrong and do not conform to the CCP's major policies."[59] In the more recent elaboration of Xi Jinping Thought on Socialism with Chinese Characteristics for a New Era, "the status and role of the non-public economy in China's economic and social development has not changed; private enterprises and private entrepreneurs are our own people; the private economy can only grow and cannot be weakened . . . rather, it must move to a broader stage."[60]

But if Xi has tried to assure private entrepreneurs rhetorically, his actions to promote "common prosperity"—more equal distribution of wealth, combined with crackdowns on large private businesses—have had the opposite effect. It is still unclear how far the statist approach will go, but some Chinese are calling it "robbing the rich and helping the poor."[61]

In the next section, we will take a closer look at the role of party branches (or cells) in SOEs and privately owned firms.[62]

CCP BRANCHES IN PRIVATE COMPANIES

Activities of the [Chinese] Communist Party are a productive force for our firm.
—Zhou Haijiang, owner and CEO of the $7 billion Hongdou Group[63]

More and more private firms are following the CCP (fig 11.5). The Chinese government now mandates the establishment of CCP branches in private firms ("branch" is sometimes translated as "cell" or "organization"; we prefer "branch" and use it throughout this book). According to a recent report from China's Federation of Industry and Commerce, they now exist in more than half of China's private firms.[64] As noted earlier, CCP branches act to socialize new members and help the firm's

Figure 11.5 Follow Our Party, Start Your Business
"Tencent Headquarters as Asia's Largest Conglomerate Said to Face Broad China Clampdown on Fintech, Deals," Getty Images, March 20, 2021. Qilai Shen/Bloomberg via Getty Images.

leaders learn about government policies pertaining to their businesses. At Huawei, for example, there are more than three hundred CCP branches and tens of thousands of party members. Jack Ma claims to have based Alibaba's human resources management principles on Mao's idea of "building party branches on the company [military unit] level."[65] Recently the mandate has been extended to foreign firms as well.[66]

From the CCP-government's perspective, branches provide a counterbalance to the forces unleashed by capitalism during the first four decades of the reform and opening up, when the vast majority of Chinese firms learned from the modern Western enterprise system and established boards of directors, supervisors, and governing councils. Western values have been increasingly seeping into Chinese firms, so the CCP-government naturally wants to strengthen its own influence in order to maintain political control and realize its goal of "the Party leads everything."[67] Indeed, the basic approach of the CCP's control is to establish branches such that all institutions—government agencies, educational institutions, state-owned firms, and others—are under its purview. This has been an effort to tighten the CCP's control over all economic, civil, and political activities in China.[68] But as we have shown, that communist influence can undercut vibrancy, by introducing confusion regarding authority and imposing political tasks.[69]

Not surprisingly, the authors of most Western studies emphasize the CCP control aspects; they are wary of communist penetration of the private sector. The US government has expressed its concerns as well.[70] One report claims that the United States' current ban on Huawei was partially due to its complex and intricate relations with the CCP.[71] Likewise, in a 2020 speech at the Hudson Institute, FBI director Christopher Wray worried that "Chinese companies of any real size are legally required to have Communist Party 'cells' inside them to keep them in line. Even more alarmingly, Communist Party cells have reportedly been established in some American companies operating in China as a cost of doing business there."[72] CCP branches can clearly undermine a firm's independence, because they wield real executive power, even when they do not fully overlap with a firm's existing top management team. There could be undue political influence and mandatory tasks that firms have to perform—for example, poverty reduction and the provision of products and services to underserved regions, which might not be economical.[73]

While we do not disagree with these accounts and in no way discount their valid concerns, many are broad-brush and so miss the nuances of how and why companies may also find such branches to be worthwhile. At Alibaba's June 30, 2010, CCP conference, Jack Ma said his aim is to "make Alibaba's party branch the best and most advanced one in China," emphasized that "95 percent of CCP-member employees are scoring 'good' in their performance," and added that "CCP-member employees are the backbone of the enterprise."[74] Again, our focus is mainly to understand how these CCP branches function from the perspective of businesses themselves within the Chinese context, setting aside for the moment whatever legitimate political and national security concerns non-Chinese observers may have.

A valid question is, Do CCP branches have legitimate business functions? The specifics of the Chinese context provide a partial answer. First, the party branch is legally required for firms that have more than three CCP members.[75] Second, these organizations may actually provide useful business functions. As discussed earlier, private firms have to attend to government policies for their survival and success, and the CCP branch facilitates communication between the government and private firms. Plus, they serve a number of human resource functions.

One role of the CCP branches is to quickly socialize and train new members by trying to understand their needs and mapping a clear career path for them. Fuyao Glass provides comprehensive training for new employees and tries to incorporate them into its "family." The company's CCP branch performs a socioeconomic background check of new employees to understand their current status and provides bonuses, interest-free loans, and free medical and other services for those living in poverty.[76]

CCP branches also provide an avenue for individuals to interact with each other, nurturing a sense of belonging and solidarity. The Beijing Jing'aogang Group, a $1 billion business conglomerate, has a strong CCP branch that organizes entertainment activities to get employees together. It also provides free housing for employees living outside Beijing.[77] Our interviewed entrepreneurs agreed that the CCP branch enhances company cohesion. For example, subject 13 said, "Our company has also established a CCP branch. I think it leads to a sense of belongingness. . . . This should be a good thing."

Additionally, CCP branches tend to have a mentoring model in which more experienced CCP members help new employees. The Hengtong Group pairs three to five non-CCP and new employees with one CCP mentor, who meets with them on a regular basis for skill training. In this way, firms' technical experience can transmit from employees of older generations to those of new ones.[78]

CCP branches might also have a modeling effect: CCP members' devotion and hard work can incentivize others. The Hengtong Group's branch showcases highly productive employees and offers them bonuses as well.[79] Around twenty CCP members in Dongguan Zelong Cable, a private cable producer, worked under the leadership of the branch secretary Ye Zhide to obtain important patents, eating and sleeping in their offices until the push was successful, which incentivized hundreds of non-CCP members to do the same. Many other private firms in the city of Dongguan also use CCP members as "pioneers" to motivate other employees.[80]

Our interview subject 1 said, "I think it is precisely because of the CCP branch and the fact that a company has CCP members that we can use this core force to influence another group of people," and "I feel that it is precisely because our company has more than ten or twenty

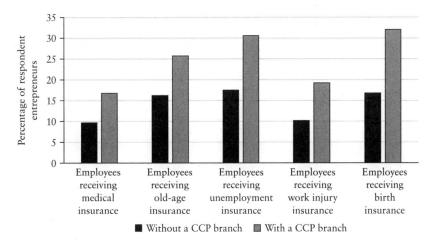

Figure 11.6 CCP Branch and Employee Insurance for Entrepreneurs
Data source: Chinese Private Enterprise Survey. Calculated by the authors.

CCP members, which has created a kind of righteousness in our company and shaped the whole company. This pioneering role model is good for the development of our enterprise." Subject 22 said, "I firmly insist that enterprises need to be managed by a party organization," and the "party committee can play an exemplary role in enterprises, and CCP members can play this modeling role to lead other employees." Subject 28 also emphasized the vanguard and exemplary role of the CCP members. Subject 15 claimed that "the advanced nature of the CCP must be reflected in the company."

We calculated differentials in employee insurance coverage by firms with and without CCP branches (fig. 11.6). Overall, firms with CCP branches offer more generous employee insurance for medical care, retirement, unemployment, injury, and birth and fertility—the five major benefit areas in China. Our statistical analysis confirms the positive relationship between the presence of a party branch and insurance benefits: firms with a CCP branch purchase medical insurance for 7.2 percent more employees, retirement care for 9.7 percent more employees, unemployment coverage for 13.1 percent more employees, disability for 9.2 percent more employees, and birth and fertility coverage for 15.5 percent more employees. These differences are substantial.[81]

Furthermore, as suggested by and consistent with other academic research in human resources, better employer-employee relations lead to improved financial performance.[82] To understand how CCP branches and financial performance are connected, we plotted a simple comparison of returns on total assets (profitability) of private ventures with and without CCP branches using the data from the Chinese Academy of Social Sciences. In general, private ventures with a CCP branch enjoy better financial performance: on average, the profitability of firms with CCP branches is 12.6 percent higher than that of those without CCP branches.[83]

A likely determinant of this performance is the help that CCP branches provide private firms in understanding government policies and thus fitting in with the changing institutional environment. Zhou Haijiang, chairman and CEO of the $7 billion Hongdou Group, actively attended to government policies and held CCP branch meetings regularly to study leaders' speeches. As Zhou reflected, "The key for our CCP branch is to follow the CCP's policy and Hongdou has done this in a solid way."[84] Similarly, the well-known Chinese venture capitalist and political scientist Eric Li (Li Shimo), who gained a lot of attention from his 2013 TED talk, is not a CCP member but says that he follows its leading journal, *Qiushi* (Seeking truth), specifically noting that it is the party branch of his firm that allows him to stay in the room to read these CCP journals, which identify promising areas for investment.[85] Our interview subject 22 also said that the CCP branch facilitated his habit of reading government reports and attending to government policies. "I will be keen to seize this window and do it immediately. Sometimes I take two steps earlier than others, and these two steps determine the success of our company."

Attending to government policies and responding to the rapidly changing institutional environment is important for many Chinese firms born in the internet era. The traditional big three in China's internet industry—Alibaba, Baidu, and Tencent—all have CCP branches. Tencent's branch, which was formally honored in 2016 as one of the one hundred best CCP branches in China, provides five platforms—a CCP activities hall, a CCP journal, a CCP documentary, a CCP WeChat channel, and an intranet for CCP members—for classes related to the CCP-government and its policies.[86] Likewise, new firms such as Mobike and oFo—bike-rental service companies that at one point were valued at tens of billions of dollars—regularly hold CCP meetings to understand the latest government policies.[87]

Our larger point is that foreign observers should not perceive the Chinese political and economic system through overly ideological lenses or take what may appear to be unusual features out of context. To understand the business environment in China, one should accept it as a whole and unique system, and aim to understand the roles of all its different elements.

In conclusion, while state ownership might make private firms' operations more complicated and subject to clashes with the government, many firms draw concrete benefits from it, as it improves their communications with the government and provides them with an endorsement that can smooth many financial and regulatory issues. A metaphorical way to understand the CCP-government is that it plays two roles—at the same time, it is both a competitor (that is, its SOEs and the private companies it invests in compete within the economy) and the referee who decides the winner of the competition.[88] State ownership is also a double-edged sword for the government. While it helps reduce systematic risks to the economy and facilitates further industrialization, it introduces conflicts and inefficiencies that can undermine the vibrancy of the private sector, which is crucial for China's economic performance and the CCP's rule and governance.

And while we acknowledge potential downsides, such as unclear authority and negative political influence—another of Mao's political legacies—we suggest that CCP branches also help firms in certain ways. In saying this, we want to emphasize that our aim is to understand, not to endorse the CCP or Chinese communism. Inadequate knowledge of the system, perhaps due to dismissing certain elements out of ideological concerns or an interest in stoking fear among Americans, has put American companies and the US government at a disadvantage and burdened them with significant costs.[89]

Looking into the future, we believe it is likely that the momentum of the nationalization wave will continue. Since 2008, China has become increasingly suspicious about the Western model and more avid to create a development model of its own. Ninety-five million Chinese belong to the CCP. It appears inevitable to us that within the next decade or so, almost all private firms in China will include CCP branches. That may be a source of discomfort for many Westerners, but if they want to do business in China, they will have to get used to it.

Conclusion

The longer you can look back, the farther you can look forward.
　　　　　　　　　　　　　　　　　　　—Winston Churchill

CHINA'S COMBINATION OF A COMMUNIST ideology and political system, on one hand, and a capitalist practice and economy, on the other, has been a long-standing puzzle—and challenge—for Western business and political leaders. How can the two seemingly incompatible ideologies shape business activity in China? According to many, as China's markets liberalized and its people were exposed to global ideas, its politics should have liberalized as well. But in fact, the opposite has happened; under President Xi Jinping, the country has become even more hardline communist.

To understand the unique political economy that has developed in China, we look to China's history and especially trace the legacy of early Chinese Communist Party (CCP) leader Mao Zedong, which deeply affects the politicians and private enterprise leaders who sit at the center of this seeming contradiction. While Western observers typically attribute China's current political economy to Deng Xiaoping's formulation of a socialist market economy, Mao's enduring effects on China's contemporary economic development have largely been ignored. Indeed, Maoism is the intellectual foundation for China's official ideology, and it has shaped the adaptations that were possible under the reform and opening-up period that began in 1978. In the spirit of the Winston Churchill quote that opens this chapter, the reason that so many commentators have been wrong about China's future over the years is that they have failed to account for its history—in particular the legacy of Mao.

Mao's effects on China and the Chinese population have been pervasive. Our perspective is built on imprinting theory, the ways that the ideas and experiences that individuals are exposed to at critical junctures in their lives shape their later development. We specifically apply this perspective to China's business leaders, showing that three key ideological principles that they were exposed to during Mao's reign—nationalism, frugality, and a devotion focus—persistently influence their ideas about internationalization, cost strategy, and social responsibility, while Mao's military strategies shaped their thinking about business strategy and organization. Mao's theory of socialist construction and the mass campaigns that applied it, such as the Great Leap Forward and the Cultural Revolution, influence entrepreneurs' attitude toward resource use and their institutional confidence to this day. Another key campaign from the Mao era, the Third Front Construction, has had lasting effects on regional entrepreneurship. Mao left his imprint on China's institutional structures, specifically its centralized political system and decentralized economic system. Overall, we stress that Mao and the CCP play the role of a fulcrum in China—all reforms and changes, be they to the state or to the market, stem from those systems. As both Mao and Xi have stated, "The CCP leads everything."

In this concluding chapter, we lay out at a macro level the "first principles" of Chinese governance, in both the business and political realms. This leads to the articulation of a "Chinese management model" derived from our examination of the lasting influence of Mao. After that, we summarize the policy implications for the United States and the West in general, and venture a view of China's future.

UNDERSTANDING THE CCP FROM "FIRST PRINCIPLES"

We all have our own sets of a priori assumptions that shape our decisions and approaches to different situations. The West's general reluctance to examine the long-standing effects of Chinese communism and socialism from a neutral social science perspective stems from such unconscious biases. In the United States, for instance, there have been two major "red scares." Throughout the Cold War with the Soviet Union, communist ideas were infused with negative connotations—a tendency that was reinforced by American culture (focused on individualism and anti-statism) and its strong religious traditions (aversion to atheism).[1] In the current hyperpolarized US political environment, anything associated with "socialism" or "communism" is demonized by the Right, further compromising politicians' and businesses' understanding of the Chinese model.

What was more palatable to the West and consistent with its ideas about how economies develop was the notion that liberalism, globalization, and the development of the internet were unstoppable forces that would expose authoritarian regimes like the CCP-government as illegitimate and cause their collapse.[2] Twenty years ago, Gordon Chang's *The Coming Collapse of China* topped the best-seller lists.[3] The Soviet collapse seemed to confirm the idea that communism was intrinsically unsustainable and that liberal democracy would sweep the world. Francis Fukuyama's *The End of History and the Last Man* argues that the world is converging on the modes of capitalism and electoral democracy. It is clear now that such assessments and the theories and analogies on which they are based are wrong, and that we will be dealing with CCP governance of China well into the future.

In China, the legitimacy of the CCP is deeply tied to Mao, and yet his legacy is profoundly mixed. Although his actions and ideas contributed to Chinese development in myriad ways, he was also responsible for disastrous policies that led to the persecution and deaths of tens of millions of Chinese. This provides a challenge for the CCP, leading to what Harvard government professor Elizabeth Perry describes as "tight Party control over the interpretation of Chinese history and politics."[4] As Jude Blanchette describes in his recent book *China's New Red Guards,* the CCP views its legitimacy as "inextricably" tied to Mao and thus carefully "polices the boundaries of Mao's legacy."[5] Xi's crackdown on so-called historical nihilism, which is to say criticism of the CCP and Mao, is a case in point. For example, to control the historical narrative, China's official online "Rumor Refutation Platform" was launched in summer 2021 to collect tips and reports of content that "smears Party history" and "slanders and discredits CCP leaders." A person found to have spread such rumors might face up to fifteen years in prison according to Chinese law.[6] The CCP-government has consistently discouraged the formal study of history, especially where Mao is concerned.[7] Yang Jisheng, an award-winning journalist whose monumental book

Tombstone identified Mao's Great Leap Forward as the root cause of the Great Famine and hence an estimated thirty-six million deaths, provides a case in point. Yang has been heavily criticized and monitored. He is not allowed to leave China, and his right to publish books has been revoked.[8]

Now more than ever, as China rises as both a business competitor and a potential military adversary, we need to base our decisions on a sound and nuanced understanding of its leaders' thinking. Westerners and Chinese alike would do well to follow one of Mao's key precepts—"seeking truth from facts." Americans need to remember that the Chinese historical and cultural context differs in key ways from those of the West and the Soviet Union, and we need to understand how it does so.

Since 2017, the US government has singled out China as its main strategic competitor, and in May 2022, Antony Blinken announced that competition with China is one of the three main pillars of the Biden Administration's China policy (the other two are fostering US innovation and aligning with allies). The current US president, Joe Biden, has articulated a "China doctrine," and he admitted, "I see stiff competition with China. China has an overall goal, and I don't criticize them for the goal, but they have an overall goal to become the leading country in the world, the wealthiest country in the world, and the most powerful country in the world. That's not going to happen on my watch because the United States are going to continue to grow and expand."[9] Meanwhile, containing China became a major topic at the 2021 G7 summit.[10] But the West's knowledge of China, particularly the CCP, is limited.

America's view of China in some ways resembles China's complacent and entirely wrong view of the West before the 1839 Opium War ushered in its century of humiliation. Much of what the West thinks it knows about China is outdated, inaccurate, and built on a number of wrong assumptions, as well as the misplaced analogy of the Soviet Union. There are many examples in American history of what a refusal to understand another country can lead to—from the beginnings of the Cold War in the 1940s to the Vietnam War in the 1960s and the conflicts in Afghanistan and Iraq in the 2000s. Additionally, the USSR's profound misunderstanding of Afghanistan likely contributed to its own collapse.[11]

The year 2021 was the centenary of the CCP, and the party is unlikely to lose power anytime soon. While there are some indications that

Xi's Mao revival may stifle business innovation and slow economic growth, given the size and scope of China's current economic position, the regime has a large margin for error.[12] We need to be prepared to coexist with this competitor, as US trade representative Katherine Tai argued in late 2021 and US secretary of state Blinken emphasized multiple times in his May 2022 speech.[13] Our perspective helps flesh out what Tai's model of "durable coexistence" might entail.

PRINCIPLES OF BUSINESS

The following set of principles constitutes a Chinese management model for the current age. Anyone who wants to do business in China needs to understand them. They are country over capital, resource consciousness, context consciousness, norms over rules, and persistence.

Country over Capital

The idea of country over capital—that is, the party state, as representative of the country, standing above and controlling economic forces (capital)—is in sharp contrast to capitalism as it is practiced in the West, which supposes that economic forces are separate from the state and to a large extent determine its politics. The CCP sits above both the state and the economy in China. This is manifested in its particular combination of nationalism, a devotion focus, and statism, which initially came from Mao and now forms a bedrock sentiment among the Chinese population. While China's culture traditionally prioritizes state and country above the individual, and its history breeds a strong nationalistic mindset, the historical situation that Mao harnessed is also important to understand. For example, the CCP-government sees China as a victim of the Western powers (for example, the hundred years of humiliation) and seeks to restore China's greatness.[14]

As such, Chinese brands are enjoying increasing success and popularity among the Chinese (for example, Li-Ning as a Chinese sports brand), while foreign firms that allegedly violate Chinese national interests (for example, Dolce & Gabbana's ad that was seen as racist and the NBA's and Nike's criticisms of China's policies regarding Hong Kong and Xinjiang) suffer a backlash. For many Chinese, the dignity and honor of their nation trumps their economic interests; some celebrities and businesspeople immediately cut their connections with those brands, even at the risk of being sued for breach of contract (for example, Dilraba Dilmurat, an Uighur actress born in Xinjiang who broke off her relationship with Dolce & Gabbana).[15] Chinese consumers and supply chain partners boycotted H&M, which endorsed the Better Cotton Initiative's boycott of cotton from Xinjiang.[16] We have shown through our statistical analyses that some entrepreneurs think foreign investors are unreliable and detrimental to their businesses. Firms doing business in China need to recognize and accept this feature of the Chinese market if they wish to stay there. Understandably, some Chinese beliefs may be at odds with Western companies' missions and values. In such cases firms should consider exiting the Chinese market, just as Google did in 2010.

The country-over-capital principle also means that many Chinese businesspeople maintain a devotion focus, as we have shown, in accordance with Mao's "mass line." Many entrepreneurs embraced Xi's "common prosperity" principle—for example, both Alibaba and Tencent promised to donate tens of billions of US dollars to the cause. Although this is likely driven by fear of government coercion in part, the rapid response and supportive words suggest that the devotion focus also plays a role.

This principle is consistent with many elements of Chinese culture, such as Confucianism and Maohism, which both emphasize selflessness and devotion to larger groups. Many entrepreneurs, especially those who are CCP members, participate in social programs initiated by the CCP-government and make philanthropic donations. While the formal concept of corporate social responsibility was invented in the West, it was quickly accepted by Chinese firms and consumers because of this historical background. Chinese expect foreign firms to contribute to their society, and not only economically—through products, taxes, and employment—but also socially, via engagement with the community and redistribution of profits through corporate giving. As noted earlier, many multinational firms suffered a backlash for their sluggish disaster relief following the 2008 Sichuan earthquake.[17] Firms aiming to do business in or with China should pay particular attention to this, as support for local communities can help them gain the trust of consumers and government leaders alike.

Further and relatedly, the country-over-capital principle also includes statism—that is, substantial state control over socioeconomic issues and political affairs. As we have elaborated, there has been a high and increasing level of party-state control of private business in China. This trend has been particularly salient since the 2008 financial crisis. The CCP-government controls private business through ownership investments (as a minority shareholder) and the CCP branches that it opens within them. Such state control necessarily creates conflicts of interest. For example, the CCP-government might focus more on increasing employment and reducing inequality through redistribution, which is at odds with most firms' traditional focus on increasing profits. The role of CCP branches may pose a challenge, as they confuse the lines of authority. But being owned by the state and having a CCP branch also confer benefits, such as better access to financing, political protection in an institutional environment where property right protection has been weak, employee motivation, and a better grasp of government policies. Firms must endeavor to strike a sustainable balance—though, once again, should that entail compromising their core missions and values, they might have to withdraw from the Chinese market.

An important ideological tool is the CCP's United Front Department, which, following Mao, Xi has called a "magic weapon" for the CCP. This organization is responsible for organizing and influencing Chinese citizens, overseas Chinese, and influential foreigners through intelligence gathering, the silencing of dissent, and cultural exchange. Xi said the department should unite people of Chinese origin around the world under a single world view and in a common cause.[18]

The bottom line is that it is important to establish and maintain good relations with the host government. As an old saying has it, when visiting China's capital, remember that humility can save your business's capital.

Resource Consciousness

Resource consciousness is also an important principle for doing business in China and with Chinese business partners. As we showed, Mao emphasized the principle of frugality, drawing on an important element of traditional Chinese culture that has persisted for thousands of years. Many Chinese entrepreneurs pay particular attention to cost cutting, a principle that is emphasized in Chinese business schools.[19] Although business education was only introduced to China after the reform, many Chinese entrepreneurs learned frugality through Mao's example.

Furthermore, the Great Leap Forward and the resulting famine made a generation of Chinese aware of the preciousness of resources, analogous to how the Great Depression inculcated a sense of thriftiness in the generation that came of age during it. China was resource poor in the 1970s, when the reform began and many Chinese entrepreneurs were starting out. While Ren Zhengfei of Huawei and Liu Yonghao of the New Hope Group are billionaires, they are notoriously thrifty and expect their firms to pay particular attention to cost cutting. Repurposing and transforming what seems useless into something valuable is another expression of resource consciousness. As we have seen, Lu Guanqiu of Wanxiang transformed scrap metals into an agricultural machine factory, and Cao Dewang adapted his facilities for auto-glass making. Furthermore, and as discussed in prior chapters, socialist institutions in China prioritize state-owned enterprises when allocating resources, especially better access to bank financing and government funding. Private entrepreneurs have to make the most of what they have, concentrating their weaker forces, in Mao's military formulation, to annihilate their enemies (win the competition).

Context Consciousness

A key argument of our book is that Western analysts try to understand China without context, ignoring its strong Maoist roots and other contextual factors. Since Mao and the CCP came to rule China in 1949, the CCP-government has emphasized its exceptionalism in the same ways that the United Kingdom and the United States have over the last two centuries. Mao departed from the Soviet Union's model, developing a socialist system and economy "with Chinese characteristics."

Consider the Maoist strategy, described in earlier chapters, of surrounding cities from the countryside, which recognizes the fundamentally rural nature of the Chinese population. Mobilizing farmers in villages was seen as an aberration of orthodox communism; Joseph Stalin and Chinese Bolsheviks scorned Mao for his ignorance of "real" Marxism-Leninism.

But just as the Chinese-specific military strategy allowed the CCP to win its war against the Kuomintang, firms that adopted the approach have enjoyed success. For example, Pinduoduo was founded in 2015 and grew rapidly to earn more than $200 billion by reaching out to what the company described as six hundred million underserved Chinese consumers in rural areas. The Maoist business strategy "Never fight an unprepared war" also emphasizes the importance of fully understanding the context before you undertake an operation.

KFC has been deeply aware of the local context in China since it entered the country in 1987. Famously, its menu incorporates a great number of Chinese food items, such as noodles and rice bowls, and its slogan is, "Changing menus for China and developing new items."[20] It even offers chicken prepared in the style of Peking duck.[21] Chinese outlets of McDonald's feature fried buns and soybean milk on their breakfast menus.[22] These firms have expanded tremendously throughout China.

In contrast, Amazon was not successful in China due to its lack of localization. For example, it refused to accept debit cards and China's payment system UnionPay, which were preferred by the Chinese before Alipay and WeChat Pay took off; instead, it required credit cards linked to Visa and Mastercard systems, which were mainly used in establishments such as high-end hotels that catered to foreigners. In addition, Amazon did not delegate power to its Chinese subsidiary, causing many decisions to be significantly delayed. Those concerning personnel recruitment, finance, technology, and other issues had to be referred to the US headquarters, and it took months and years to develop promotional projects, things Amazon China's competitors could do in days.[23] Liu Qiangdong, founder of China JD.com, Amazon's biggest local competitor, mocked Amazon, saying, "If the person in charge in China cannot decide anything, there is no need to talk about execution. You can ask Wang Hanhua [the then CEO of Amazon China], can he do what he wants?" In another example, Best Buy insisted on opening its stores in city centers, ignoring the large rural market, and it focused on high-end consumers. The firm suffered serious losses before it exited the Chinese market.[24]

Norms over Rules

As many academic studies and press accounts have noted, East Asian countries and regions are ruled as much by unwritten social norms as written laws and regulations.[25] These informal social relations form a basis of trust and are honored more than formal contracts by the Chinese people. For example, our research has shown that Chinese entrepreneurs tend to focus more on *guanxi* (the system of social connections and relationships that facilitates business and other dealings) in their businesses, sometimes even setting aside rivalries to respond to the interests of society as a whole. Archrivals Jack Ma and Pony Ma have cooperated on various philanthropic causes, for example.[26] Chinese and Japanese entrepreneurs tend to avoid litigation, preferring informal negotiations.[27] Shi Yuzhu utilized the social norm of filial devotion to popularize his famous melatonin product Brain Platinum.

The Cultural Revolution sabotaged China's institutions and respect for the rule of law; as we saw, many entrepreneurs who experienced it have sought to escape China to avoid legal sanctions. Indeed, the reform and opening up were enabled by a group of farmers who illegally broke up their agricultural collective. Similarly, private firms were technically illegal until 1992, but many successful firms were founded, such as TCL (founded in 1981), Haier (founded in 1984), Huawei and Wahaha (founded in 1987), and the Giant Group (founded in 1992).

Guanxi and personal connections are particularly important for business venturing in China, as we have shown in our discussion of the Third Front Construction. Social capital enables the high entrepreneurship rate in many Third Front cities, where many new businesses are funded informally by coworkers and potential customers.

Interestingly, many Chinese retain this deeply ingrained emphasis on informal norms even after immigrating to the United States. An example is the Abacus Federal Saving Bank, founded by Thomas Sung and his US-born daughters, which was the focus of an Oscar-nominated documentary.[28] It had become a norm in Sung's community to use cash in order to evade taxes, with the consequence that people did not have formal credit histories. Abacus utilized informal networks and connections to understand potential borrowers' creditworthiness. For example, when a restaurant owner came to Abacus to get a loan for refurnishing, Sung did not need to see any documents because he ate in the restaurant and so knew very well the borrower's risk of default. This became a serious legal issue when Abacus sold its mortgages to Fannie Mae, which had strict rules on loan qualifications.

The economic traditions of this Chinese community confused the jury when Abacus's case went to trial. In the community, many loans were not enforced by law but governed and managed by the social network. Some loan defaults were forgiven as gifts among friends or relatives.

Serious conflicts were arbitrated by "big men"—figures with high social status—rather than courts. Importantly, this norm runs deeper than Mao's influence, as the members of this community had mostly migrated to the United States when the Kuomintang was still the ruling party.

Persistence

Mao constantly elevated the need to be persistent—have grit, patience, a strong work ethic, diligence, and so on—and the doctrine is an important traditional value of the Chinese people as well. Many quotes from Mao, as we have shown, have become mottos of inspiration for entrepreneurs, especially those on hard work, diligence, and perseverance, such as "A single spark can start a prairie fire." Similarly, Mao's theory on protracted war also suggests being confident, perseverant, and patient. As discussed in earlier chapters, the US government became impatient during its initial negotiations with the CCP-government in the late 1970s, but it applied the principle of patience during the recent US-China trade talks. Potential Chinese business partners should consider trying to collect information, analyze details, and create long-term relationships before moving ahead. This might be time consuming and seemingly without purpose.[29] Overall, our own and others' research, such as Lucian Pye's, suggests that negotiators must practice patience, accept prolonged periods of no movement as normal, and discount Chinese rhetoric about the dire consequences of disagreement.[30]

Although China has become more and more globalized and many young people have overseas experience, as we have discussed, family socialization and intergenerational transmission ensure the persistence of both Mao's imprint and that of traditional Chinese culture. The Chinese educational system and red tourism both portray Mao as a saint, and his quotes have worked themselves into the Chinese language—much as turns of phrase from William Shakespeare and the King James Bible have implanted themselves in English—and so are powerful carriers of Mao's legacy for generations to come.

At the same time, socialist institutions and the CCP-government deliberately promote Maoism as a Chinese tradition. For example, in 2012, the then Chinese president, Hu Jintao, elaborated core socialist values based on traditional Chinese virtues such as harmony, patriotism, dedication, integrity, and friendship.[31] In February 2021 Xi stated, "Without the prosperity of Chinese culture, there would be no great rejuvenation of the Chinese nation," and "We must inherit and carry forward the content of traditional culture that is suitable for regulating social relations and encouraging people to move up and toward goodness in light of present conditions."[32]

PRINCIPLES OF GOVERNANCE

It is also critical to understand the Chinese governance model, given the importance of the CCP-government and the political environment in Chinese business and entrepreneurship. We summarize five principles of governance in China: politics at the center, economic decentralization, ideological pragmatism, historical existentialism, and moderatism.

Politics at the Center

As we have described in previous chapters, China has a long tradition of strong, centralized government with a strict top-down power structure. It was not surprising that Mao and the CCP-government established an unquestionable central authority after they settled in Yan'an after the Long March. Within the top-down power structure, the supervising authority tightly controls its subordinate CCP leaders through appointments and promotions. This contrasts with most Western democratic countries, which do not have superordinate-subordinate relationships between central and local governments. State governors in the United States do not formally report to the US president; they are responsible to and elected by constituents within their states.

Top-down mobilization is how the CCP-government deals with major socioeconomic and political issues, making five-year plans for economic development, launching major initiatives (for example, the Belt and Road Initiative and Made in China 2025), and promulgating new ideology by supreme leaders (for example, Xi Jinping Thought on Socialism with Chinese Characteristics for a New Era). Top-down mobilization is also how the CCP-government fought against the COVID-19 pandemic. Once Xi and other senior leaders declared a national emergency, provinces, then prefectures and cities, counties, towns, and villages quickly responded to the call. This clearly contrasts with the fights between former US president Donald Trump and several state governors regarding resource allocation and mandatory business and school closings.[33]

The top-down structure in China follows directly from Vladimir Lenin's ideas about political control.[34] Mao adapted them directly, proposing that "in the seven areas—industry, agriculture, commerce, education, military, politics, and different political parties, the CCP should lead everything." Xi reiterated Mao's quote in 2016, doubling down by saying, "Party, political, military, civil and academic, east, west, south, north and center, the Party leads everything," and wrote this statement into the CCP constitution in 2017.[35]

However, such political centralism might also make lower-level individuals risk averse; they may fear that their behaviors or ideas are at odds with supervising authorities.[36] This issue has special salience during leadership transitions, as lower-level officials are unsure about the ideas and ideology of new leaders. A well-known exception that proves the rule is Xie Gaohua, the party secretary of the county of Yiwu, who early in the reform period, like the Anhui farmers who reallocated their land, allowed and even encouraged individual entrepreneurs to sell their products at the risk of his political career. At the time this was not yet legal and could be labeled as a capitalist practice. Xie's actions laid the foundation for the future prosperity of Yiwu, which has now become the largest small-commodity wholesale market in the world.[37] Similarly, Xi Zhongxun—father of Xi Jinping—took risks while reforming the economy of Guangdong Province, where he promoted special economic zones as a de facto capitalist experiment.[38] These deviant officials were later praised as important reformers, but such innovations will likely be suppressed and deterred in the future, given the increased risks of being on the wrong side.[39]

Ironically, although Xi responded fast with top-down mobilization to combat COVID-19, local officials feared making mistakes, such as political leaders in Wuhan covering up early COVID cases, which medical staff mislabeled SARS II, to avoid a public panic. They even detained Li Wenliang, the physician who sounded early warnings about the virus (and was one of its early fatalities), for "spreading misinformation."[40]

Another important manifestation of politics being the center is the CCP's command of the military. Recent projects on military-civil fusion aim to develop a world-class, technologically advanced military with intellectual property, key basic research and development, and technological advances acquired from around the world.[41] Simply put, the CCP is trying to make its military and the Chinese economy more symbiotic and beneficial to each other. While it is not unusual to develop military technology to benefit the economy (many high-end technologies in the United States, including the internet, were originally developed for defense), what is unique in China is that the military is an arm not of the state but of the CCP. Advanced surveillance technology developed for the military also strengthens the CCP-government's high-tech authoritarian model.

Economic Decentralization

We have underlined the importance of economic decentralization in China, which gives local officials discretionary power to implement policies (provided they are consistent with the overarching ideology of the central government and supreme leaders). Unlike his rival Chiang Kai-shek, who was a micromanager, Mao delegated more power to his front-line commanders. Upon their retirement from the military, many became regional leaders and their troops staffed the regional and provincial bureaus.

While political decentralization makes lower-level officials wary when leadership transitions occur, economic decentralization emboldens them to implement local policies focused on the goals set by the central government. Research has shown that local leaders compete with one another to deliver economic results and the winner is likely to be promoted to the next level of government.[42] A negative example of this, discussed earlier, is that local officials who lied about agricultural yields to please Mao during the Great Leap Forward were often rewarded with promotions.

This setup in some ways resembles Western federalism. But a distinguishing characteristic in China is that local governments are still politically bound by their supervising authority, and thus political issues often trump economic ones. In addition, the intense economic competition among local officials can trigger negative spillover effects, such as pollution (officials have a tendency to promote growth by relaxing environmental regulations), internal trade barriers, and local protectionism.[43] Studies have found that fees for interprovincial trade are sometimes higher than international tariffs.[44] As we have elaborated, firms hoping to do business in China are advised to leverage the regional competition for economic growth.

Ideological Pragmatism

Mao's classic article "On Practice"—widely taught in party schools of the Soviet Union—establishes his idea of seeking truth from facts, which means that theory must fit with reality, and if not, theory needs to be changed. This pragmatic approach laid the groundwork for Deng Xiaoping's economic reforms.

Deng further developed Mao's doctrine, arguing that "socialism can have a market and capitalism can have a plan," and "a good cat can catch mice, regardless of whether it is black and white."[45] By calling "the market economy within the Chinese socialist system" a market economy, Chinese leaders have sought common ground with liberal democracies for economic cooperation (though Xi has increasingly emphasized the "socialist" attribute in his economic discussions).[46]

Another important aspect of ideological pragmatism is the CCP-government's response to public opinion. It is as likely to quash communist discussion that is too hard-line as it is capitalist discussion. For example, a famous leftist website called Wuyouzhixiang (Land of nothingness) was suspended for one month due to its promotion of a new Cultural Revolution; although Xi resembles Mao in many aspects, he also likely understands that a true Cultural Revolution, with massive persecutions and killings as well as nationalization of private property, would undercut the CCP's rule. At the same time, the CCP-government has been supportive of Wuyouzhixiang's propaganda against the West, which it deems is needed.[47]

To fuel nationalism and counter the Trump administration's "bullying" positions, the CCP-government popularized a recent movie, *The Battle at Lake Changjin,* in which the best corps of the Chinese army (with twelve divisions) surrounded the US Marines' legendary First Division during the Korean War. Though the marines ultimately escaped the siege, they were astonished to discover that some of the Chinese troops had frozen to death while still holding their rifles in the firing position. The movie was a powerful piece of the CCP's propaganda showing that China could stand up to even the most powerful enemies, that the war essentially ended the "century of humiliation," and that foreign powers need to respect China as an independent nation.[48] The movie has broken many records at Chinese box offices since its release on October 1, 2021—the seventy-second anniversary of the communist regime—and has become the biggest moneymaker in Chinese movie history, earning $750 million in its first two weeks and topping that year's box office worldwide with ticket sales of well over $900 million.[49] In contrast, movies criticizing hard-line Cultural Revolutionists were prevalent at the beginning of the reform and opening up in the late 1970s and early 1980s but have now been banned, in line with the CCP focus on historical nihilism. And when journalist Luo Changping questioned the righteousness of the Korean War and scoffed at the frozen-to-death Chinese troops as "idiots," his Weibo account was shut down and he was detained and sentenced for the crime of defaming political martyrs.[50]

Western audiences who try to understand China through an overly ideological lens tend to overemphasize the flexibility of the CCP.[51] The CCP is pragmatic, but within the constraint that the party is at the center of all activity. Desmond Shum's *Red Roulette* argues that the CCP's ideology has only bent in the 1980s when under significant economic pressure and, after stabilizing, reverted to the practices and policies set by communism and Maoism.

In any case, pragmatism is consistent with the Chinese philosophical tradition. Unlike the philosophical systems of ancient Greece and later Germany, which try to understand fundamental metaphysical questions, China's philosophical traditions, such as Confucianism, mostly concern political ideology and how to organize a state or country.[52] Hence, it is likely that the CCP-government will adopt whatever is useful for economic development, as long as it remains at the center.

Historical Existentialism

Mao was an enthusiastic student of Chinese history; as such, he based many of his ideas about governance on the experiences of Chinese emperors.[53] Mao was said to read *The Twenty-Four Histories* (that is, the *Orthodox Histories*), the dynastic histories spanning from 3000 BCE to the Ming dynasty of the seventeenth century, every day and published his comments on them.[54] In the same spirit, the CCP-government often uses history to justify and legitimize its rule and policies, a practice we label historical existentialism to contrast with historical nihilism, which the CCP-government defines as incorrect interpretations of history that criticize the CCP, its national leaders and heroes, and socialism.[55] Mao focused the CCP on the need to "stand up" and overcome the hundred years of humiliation following the Opium Wars. Xi evokes China's past glories as well (for example, the Chinese Dream, or "make China great again"). During the centenary speech for the CCP, he uttered the phrase "rejuvenation of the Chinese nation" twenty-six times, claiming it as the unswerving mission of the CCP.[56]

The CCP actively shapes interpretations of history, writing new official histories of the party and Mao and labeling any ideas that stray from them as "historical nihilism."[57] For example, on November 16, 2021, Xi officially stated the third historical resolution of the CCP's history during the Sixth Plenary Session of the Nineteenth CCP Central Committee, only the third such summation of the past in the CCP's one-hundred-year history. This placed Xi on par with Mao and Deng, who issued historical resolutions in 1945 and 1981, respectively. The resolution mentioned Mao eighteen times, Deng six times, and Xi twenty-two times. It portrays Mao as leading China to stand up against oppression, Deng leading China to prosperity, and Xi leading China to strength. Furthermore, while the previous two historical resolutions aimed to correct errors and so "rescue" the CCP from past critical mistakes, the new one serves to uphold Xi's leadership, extol the achievements of the CCP, and reinforce current CCP leaders' will.[58]

The hundred years of humiliation are constantly invoked to underline the idea that "only the CCP can save China." This exact phrase was also used in Xi's centenary speech, in which he emphasized that such periods were forever in the past because of CCP leadership. Mao is seen as the exalted figure that led the CCP to its current position, and his many sacrifices are said to underlie the legitimacy of its rule. The CCP's leaders are especially wary of the kind of historical revisionism that Nikita Khrushchev wielded against Stalin; they believe it sowed the seeds of the USSR's ultimate collapse.[59]

Some scholars suggest that Khrushchev's Secret Speech reflects the Russian philosophical tradition of nihilism more generally.[60] In any case, historical existentialism is consistent with the Chinese philosophical tradition that sees history as an important mirror for spotting and correcting damaging policies and behaviors.[61] The focus on China's glories raises morale and counters the criticisms of China and Mao in the Western media.[62] This book in many ways pays homage to the principle of studying history to understand the present, although our approach has been to take a social scientific perspective and delve into contemporaneous accounts, as opposed to relying on the CCP's recent politically driven interpretations.

Moderatism

The final elements of Chinese governance that we emphasize are moderation, harmony, and modesty, which stem from the guiding Confucian principle of "the Doctrine of the Mean."[63] It means to not bend to one extreme or another, to maintain balance and harmony, to be cautious and gentle, and to show no contempt for inferiors.[64] In his speaking and writing, Mao recognized this point, saying, "Being excessive is too left-leaning [hard-line communist] and being deficient means too right-leaning [capitalist]. We need to find an optimal status, which is what the Doctrine of the Mean suggests," and "this thought is indeed a great discovery of Confucius . . . a great achievement, an important category of philosophy, and it deserves a good explanation." However, Mao also attacked Confucianism for "lacking the idea of development and seeing objects as static."[65] Of course, Mao himself engaged in extremism, such as by initiating the Great Leap Forward and the Cultural Revolution. Accordingly, even the CCP-government's overly rosy assessment of Mao has labeled these campaigns as wrong decisions that violate the principle of moderatism.[66]

Moderatism has many applications for domestic affairs. Leaders are evaluated along a three-seven divide—that is, if 70 percent of a person's deeds contribute to the CCP-government and 30 percent are detrimental, then one's overall contributions dominate one's errors. The CCP-government has used this standard to judge Mao. In contrast, scholars have suggested that Russia's traditions are more inclined to extremism and that Russian words related to the Doctrine of the Mean (золотая середина) are seen as pejorative.[67]

Moderatism is also reflected in China's international relations and foreign policies, which have traditionally sought cooperation rather than confrontation. For example, since Deng's period in 1978, China has focused on economic development rather than exporting communist ideology to different countries.[68] This is reflected in Deng's famous quote, "Hide your strength and bide your time." China has made efforts to maintain good relationships with countries that are opposed to each other, such as those from the communist camp and the capitalist camp during the Cold War period, Israel and Arab countries, and others.

While Xi and other "Wolf Warrior" diplomats have become more confrontational, part of this may have been an effort to respond to Trump's provocations in kind, and we do believe that there are glimmers of moderation that can be capitalized on. For example, since the US-China trade war began on March 22, 2018, senior leaders on the Chinese side have claimed that the two countries should work together. In one instance, Xi said to Trump in their Osaka meeting on June 29, 2019, that "the United States and China would both benefit if they cooperate and suffer if they fight."[69] Current US president Biden has continued to enforce his predecessor's tariffs as of our writing in mid-2022, though as a seasoned politician, Biden's position is more predictable and consistent with Washington's long-term norms. Regardless, we do think the deep-seated principle of moderatism should be kept in mind, as well as the understanding that much of China's extreme discourse is meant more for domestic consumption and propaganda than as a guide to international relations. In today's environment, with its ease of global communications, making this distinction is a challenge for all countries when interpreting others' discourse. As a result, we think understanding history today is more important than ever, as it will help separate the true underlying sentiments from propaganda.

We hope the United States will find ways to constructively deal with the rise of China while protecting its national interests. Despite the CCP's confrontational rhetoric, China's history suggests that it would prefer to find a modus vivendi with the United States as well. Clearly cooperation is in both parties' interests.

AUTHORITARIAN COUNTRIES AND THE LIFE HISTORIES OF THEIR POLITICAL LEADERS

We believe our imprinting perspective can contribute to a greater understanding of other political leaders. While the danger of oversimplification and caricature is not to be ignored, all individuals are influenced by key events in their early lives that can help us understand—or at least provide a context for their later actions. We believe this is particularly the case in authoritarian countries, which typically have top-down power structures in which supreme leaders' decisions loom large. We look at several notable examples in China and the Soviet Union and then consider how Xi's own background can provide a lens into China's possible future.

Deng was trained in France through the Diligent Work-Frugal Study Movement. He recognized some of the useful aspects of capitalism, such as markets, and thus could understand why a socialist state might want to adopt a market economy. Moreover, he was in the Soviet Union when Lenin implemented his New Economic Policy, which was essentially a market-oriented reform. Deng's interest in adopting "capitalist measures" cropped up throughout his career and caused him to fall out of power during the Cultural Revolution twice. At the risk of oversimplifying, it is reasonable to conclude that had he not sincerely believed that markets and communism could coexist, he would have simply followed Mao.

Mikhail Gorbachev's paternal grandfather was exiled to Siberia and his maternal grandfather was arrested and investigated for fourteen years during Stalin's Great Purge, and he joined the communist party around the time of Khrushchev's Secret Speech. These early experiences contributed to his later disillusionment with doctrinaire Marxism-Leninism and his interest in new thinking and humanitarian socialism, which ultimately led him to relax the Soviet Union's authoritarian control.[70] In 1990 the Soviet constitution dropped its insistence on communist or Bolshevik leadership, and on December 26, 1991, Gorbachev announced the end of the Soviet Union.[71] Again, we do not want to be simplistic, but one wonders whether the USSR might not have ended the way that it did if Gorbachev had not had these negative experiences.

This perspective also provides some insights into the Chinese supreme leaders Jiang Zemin, Hu Jintao, and Xi. Jiang knew several Western languages and could play many musical instruments—he sang the classic song "One Day When We Were Young" and danced with the then mayor of San Francisco, Dianne Feinstein, in 1987, and he played the ukulele during his visit to Hawaii in 1997. His appreciation of the West made him approachable. In contrast, Hu began his career in a Third Front Construction project; he is generally portrayed as a hard-line communist, which explains the decade of "the state advances and the private sector retreats" that he presided over. Before he stepped down, Hu said, "We must clearly see that international hostile forces are stepping up their strategic plans to Westernize and divide our country" and that "we must alarm forever, stay vigilant, and take effective measures to prevent and respond."[72]

Perhaps most important to consider is what we can learn about Xi from his formative experiences. He was born in 1953 in Beijing when his father, Xi Zhongxun, was director of the Publicity Department of the CCP and a national-level leader who held a similar political rank as Deng. But in 1962, Xi Zhongxun was labeled as anticommunist, and he consequently fell out of power and was arrested. The family home was searched and their possessions confiscated. Xi Jinping graduated from middle school in 1968, when there were three typical paths for Chinese youths to follow. Those whose parents were still in high places could go to college or join the military, while those with questionable backgrounds had to go to rural areas as "sent-down youths." Given his father's fall from power, Xi was sent to Liangjiahe Village in Shaanxi Province.

As noted earlier, at first he could not endure the poor living conditions and tried to escape. Ultimately, he returned and dedicated himself to hard manual labor and the study of communist books such as *Capital*, *The Communist Manifesto*, the *Selected Works of Mao Zedong*, and *Collected Works on Military by Mao Zedong*. According to the book *Xi Jinping's Seven Years as a Sent-Down Youth*, Xi became a fervent communist, and with his father's encouragement, he set out to regain his power.[73] Our earlier analysis of how such experiences may lead individuals to disrespect Chinese institutions can also provide insight into Xi's violation of many recent governance rules and norms, such as eliminating presidential term limits.

Upon his father's release in 1975, Xi enrolled at Tsinghua University. By the time he graduated in 1979, his father had fully regained his power and become party secretary of Guangdong Province. Xi worked as a secretary of Minister of National Defense Gen Biao, who was a good friend of his father. With further help from his father, he was appointed to a position in Zhengding County, Hebei Province, in 1982 and was promoted to party secretary by the end of 1983. In 1988 he was promoted to party secretary of the city of Ningde in Fujian Province, where he prosecuted around four hundred officials for corruption. His political rank kept rising, to the provincial level in 1993 and the national level (as vice president to succeed Hu) in 2007. When he was the governor of Fujian Province, he obtained an on-the-job (part-time) PhD in Marxist theory and ideological and political education.[74] Chinese leaders commonly receive PhDs, and it is not clear to what extent they do the work themselves. But what is interesting in Xi's case is his focus on Marxist ideology as opposed to economics and management, which were much more popular among Chinese leaders at the time.

Many people have been surprised by Xi's neo-Maoism.[75] Perhaps they would not have been if they had considered his deep reading of Karl Marx and Mao as a sent-down youth, as well as his obsession with politics and the party as a provincial leader. Having experienced his father's ups and downs and his own years in the wilderness, he gained an appreciation of the need to secure and hold power. All of this helps explain the tightened controls on civil society, his creation of a cult of personality, and his pursuit of an extended presidential term.

Indeed, he has essentially reinvented Maoist ideological weapons in his efforts to establish complete control of the CCP-government. Due to his lack of strong political background, President Hu was unable to fully grasp power from his predecessor, Jiang. Some even referred to Hu as a "son emperor" of Jiang, who was the true (and shadow) emperor.[76] Once Xi became supreme leader, he was wary of becoming a puppet.[77] He was aware of rumors suggesting that his alleged political enemies—especially those belonging to the Jiang faction—wanted to replace him after his first five-year term with Bo Xilai.

Something similar had happened in the late 1980s when Deng was in charge. Deng was not the de jure but the de facto supreme leader of China, as he wielded paramount power and controlled the military. Hu Yaobang became the general secretary and succeeded Hua Guofeng in 1982 as the de jure top leader in China. But after Hu exhibited some liberal tendencies and did not offer a tough response to the 1986 Chinese student demonstrations, which were the prelude to the Tiananmen Square protests in 1989, Deng dethroned him and promoted Zhao Ziyang. Zhao also exhibited sympathy for the students in 1989 and was dethroned in his turn, to be replaced by Jiang. Even after Deng claimed to retire in 1989, his influence persisted. For example, during his famous Southern Tour in 1992, he said, "Whoever does not reform will step down," suggesting that he could replace Jiang just as he had Hu and Zhao.[78]

With these examples in mind, Xi focused on solidifying his power. Mao's Yan'an Rectification Movement, the Cultural Revolution, and other campaigns provided him with guidance on how to do so—Xi would reinvent Maoism. His anti-corruption efforts in Fujian Province had also taught him that a large campaign could further establish his authority. So he initiated a mass anti-corruption campaign that was targeted at Jiang's followers. By reinventing Maoism as a counterforce to Jiang and jailing his allies, Xi reshaped the political environment in China.[79] Within the first two years of Xi's term, Bo Xilai and Zhou Yongkang, the latter a former standing committee member of the Politburo of the CCP, had been disgraced and prosecuted, and the Chinese constitution was later amended to remove presidential term limits. Many other events contributed to Xi's perception that strongman leadership is a better approach than bottom-up decentralization, including the increasing factionalism within the CCP, rampant corruption, environmental pollution, economic slowdown, and increasing social unrest (such as the protests in Hong Kong). Thanks to this focus on power and control, Xi abandoned Deng's "hide your strength and bide your time" strategy, eagerly launching the Belt and Road Initiative and Made in China 2025, thus establishing China's own developmental model. As Antony Blinken said in his May 2022 China policy speech, it is clear now that "Beijing believes that its model is the better one; that a party-led centralized system is more efficient, less messy, ultimately superior to democracy."[80] Meanwhile, Xi's obsession with Maoism and communism and his deemphasis on economic liberalization explain his insistence on subsidizing the relatively less efficient state-owned enterprises and his imposition of party control on private enterprises, as discussed in earlier chapters.

How far will Xi go? The political environment is turning more and more conservative and hostile to the West. As noted in prior chapters and recorded in other accounts, he has even whitewashed the Cultural Revolution in the new version of the CCP's official history.[81] Rather than anticipating a more liberal, Westernized Chinese society and economy, we should be prepared to deal with a more Maoist, communist China.

Because of the chaos Mao unleashed on China at the end of his reign, leadership beyond two terms was prohibited in China. While Xi appears determined to stay for at least another five-year term, and possibly much longer, the stringent zero COVID policy, economic slowdown, and Xi's other policies have also solicited critiques within the CCP, all of which may block his ambitions. This will become clearer in late 2022, when the CCP holds its Twentieth National Congress. Importantly, as of this writing Xi and senior CCP leaders have not agreed on his successor, who according to tradition should be young (born in the 1960s or later) and appointed as a vice president during the national congress.[82]

Economically, gross domestic product growth is unlikely to return in the near future to the 10 percent annual rate that it had enjoyed for so long, and given the current size of China's economy, it may never do so in the near future. While systemic factors are contributing to the decline in the growth rate—for example, China's gradually disappearing low-cost advantage, the movement of the manufacturing industry to Vietnam and other countries, the trade war with the United States, a slow-down of investment, challenges from COVID and more—they also suggest that Xi's ideas and principles could be having negative effects. His anti-corruption movement and tightening up of political centralization are dampening local politicians' efforts to promote economic growth in their jurisdictions; lower-level officials are increasingly worried about making mistakes, as the consequences can be dire.

Entrepreneurs are also facing more uncertainty; many fear that their assets may be confiscated and that they may be imprisoned or worse. Recent examples include the Ant Financial and DiDi investigations and state takeovers of ByteDance and Sina Weibo. While it is unlikely that Xi will nationalize the entire private sector, the reform and privatization of state-owned enterprises that started in the early 2000s is likely to be further delayed and even reversed, and further controls may also be exerted on private firms.

Xi is clearly focused on Mao's idea of independence through industrial strength. While his 2021 crackdowns on Tencent's videogame Honor of Kings (calling it "spiritual opium") and China's private education sector (in order to make education more egalitarian) are seen as Maoist and antimarket, writers have also suggested that Xi wants to focus on developing industries that are more directly related to China's independence, such as semiconductors, electric vehicle batteries, commercial aircraft, and telecommunications equipment.[83]

Importantly, the private sector increasingly supports the CCP, which had grown stronger and may appear to Xi to be less vulnerable to capitalist forces. As we have shown through discussion of our interviews with Chinese entrepreneurs, they are generally supportive of the CCP and admire Mao. That makes sense to us, as their thoughts have been shaped by the CCP and Mao's ideas; such imprints are enduring and hard to change. In private discussions, many Chinese are supportive of Xi's strongman leadership. And as we have elaborated, whether entrepreneurs are communists or not, they recognize the benefits that CCP branches bring.

The CCP and the Chinese people are increasingly coupled, and the education system, state propaganda, and Xi's rhetoric linking traditional Chinese values and Maoism ensure that this will continue into the next generation. In Xi's words, "Cultivating and promoting the core values of socialism must be based on the excellent Chinese traditional culture."[84] Meanwhile, the CCP-government has equated Maoist doctrines such as the mass line with the wisdom of Lao Tzu ("Rulers should think from the perspective of the people") and Mencius ("To win support for a regime, one has to win the hearts of the people").[85]

Internationally, Xi is likely to maintain his hawkish posture. Biden has called Xi a "real rough guy" and said that he "doesn't have a democratic bone" in his body.[86] US academics and strategists have debated China's ambitions. For instance, some reject the idea that China has any grand strategy to replace the United States and rebuild an international order in favor of China, pointing out that China's overarching goals seem different from those of the Soviet Union in that the CCP has been refraining from spreading "Chinese-style" communism to other parts of the world.[87] Rather, China has focused on legitimizing its authoritarian, one-party rule, promoting it as more superior than liberal democracy, thus posing an ideological challenge to the West.[88]

Others doubt the veracity of Xi's and China's claims about China's lack of interest in international influence, suggesting instead that it is seeking to replace the United States in the international order. For example, Xi used a speech at the United Nations General Assembly to advance a "Chinese Model" as an alternative to the one developed by the United States and the West, promoting its "Global Development Initiative" to help developing countries with debt suspension and development aid and pledging $3 billion to support COVID-19 response and economic recovery in developing countries.[89] Meanwhile, Xi has been pressing China's influence in the developing world as the leader of a "community with a shared future for mankind." The concept has been used by the CCP to describe win-win situations through cooperation and to denigrate hegemonic politics and unilateralism, which is how the

CCP describes its Western rivals. Xi has also been encouraging the development of China-centric institutions and programs such as the Belt and Road Initiative, the Asian Infrastructure Investment Bank, the New Development Bank, and recent trade agreements such as the Regional Comprehensive Economic Partnership.[90] These points are somewhat reminiscent of a global "surround the cities from the countryside" strategy and suggest that Xi is clearly committed to developing a model for China that is independent of the West.

Indeed, the hegemonic provision of public goods such as defense, security, and health products is a common strategy in international politics.[91] Now that China is providing such public goods, and digital authoritarian tools, many people believe that it has the ambition to establish its hegemony; some analysts claim that China is using the United Nations to advance its foreign policy.[92] Writers have frequently reckoned with Xi's vision and ambition, suggesting that Xi hopes to place China on the central stage and may even attempt to fundamentally transform the international order rather than merely requesting more influence within the existing international system.[93] Meanwhile, there have been reports on how entities related to the Chinese government or the CCP are using money to infiltrate US institutions and shape academic and political conversation about China to make it more favorable.[94] Overall, its hawkish position, the establishment of China-centric institutions that might reshape the international order, the recent militarization of the South China Sea with an eye toward Taiwan, and other actions provide grounds for cynicism about China's claim of a strictly peaceful rise.[95]

In sum, to better understand this complex geopolitical situation and plan for the future, we do need to know China better, starting from the first principles of its ideology, which we elaborated earlier and argue were enduringly shaped by Mao.[96]

CONCLUDING REMARKS

Our motivation for writing this book is our belief that the United States and the West more generally need to come to grips with the fact that China, under CCP rule, will be an active competitor in economic and other realms well into the future and that, just as US trade representative Tai suggested, we must prepare for a period of "durable coexistence," a sentiment echoed by Blinken's frequent statements that we will need to "coexist," "cooperate," and "compete" with China. Our book advances the idea that to understand China's present place in the world, we must take a step back and understand its past—in particular, Mao's and Maoism's enduring effects on entrepreneurship, private enterprise, and market development in China. We want to dispel the illusion that China and the CCP will either evolve into Western-style capitalism or collapse, and we want to build a more realistic foundation for coexistence.

China's Maoist roots are deep; the changes that have occurred in China since the reform in the 1970s have occurred within Maoist guardrails, with the CCP guiding both the state and the market. This is a dramatic contrast to both how these sectors operate in the West and how people in the West think they operate. It is impossible to understand China's business environment without a sound understanding of its political environment and the fact that it is the party that sits at the center of all activities. As our research has shown, most Chinese businesspeople and government officials have not "awakened from Mao's dream," which is why they are so willing to shun foreign capital, even when doing so costs them profits.[97] The "Chinese management model" that we develop shows that the Western model, in which "state" and "market" are discrete and even opposing entities, is not universal for all countries.

For all that, we do believe that there are still enormous opportunities for Western firms in China. In 2019 Prime Minister Li Keqiang promised to open the Chinese financial market to foreign investors, and at the end of 2020, China signed important free trade agreements with fifteen Asia-Pacific countries and the European Union. In 2021, even in spite of the trade war, most US businesses operating in China reported record profits there and had an optimistic view of competing in China in the future.[98]

Foreign investors and firms need to develop a better appreciation of the importance of CCP branches. At the same time, they should check the résumés of politicians in the areas where they want to do business. They will be less likely to be welcomed by politicians who were born and raised red—for example, who joined the CCP and received communist indoctrination during Mao's period.

This book also has important implications for American and other Western policymakers. There have been many misjudgments and misunderstandings of China since its major economic reform began in 1978, and the situation has become even more fraught since the inauguration of President Xi in 2012.[99] Even the *New York Times* columnist Nicholas

Kristof, who lived in China for many years and knows the country well, and who won a Pulitzer Prize for his reporting on the Tiananmen Square Massacre in 1989, got it wrong. Back in 2013, he confidently predicted that "Xi Jinping will spearhead a resurgence of economic reform, and probably some political easing as well. Mao's body will be hauled out of Tiananmen Square on his watch, and Liu Xiaobo, the Nobel Peace Prize-winning writer, will be released from prison."[100] Kristof has certainly changed his tune; we only note this as an example of how wrong so many Western assumptions about China, even from those who are quite knowledgeable about the country, have proved to be. To truly understand China, we must set our ideological biases and our hopes aside and, in Mao's words, derive "truth from facts." We need to appreciate the context and the history of modern China, and the way that Mao has haunted it as an "infallible" ghost who will not go away.

Democracy is not coming to China; its institutions and its culture are deeply imbued with authoritarian socialism. While those born after Mao's reign, and especially during the US-China honeymoon period of 1979 to 1989, might be more liberal and cosmopolitan, neo-Maoist movements; the growth of the economy under the communist regime; the economic catastrophe of 2008 and 2009, which hit democracies heavily; and the United States' tougher posture all ensure that it will stay that way.[101] Beijing has strengthened its control and consolidated the power of the CCP in private firms. China's senior leaders and thought leaders are determined to follow a unique path—the "Chinese Model"—that is starkly different from that of Western democracies. Inspired by Xi, many Chinese have embraced the Chinese Dream, a dream to revive China's splendid past and make China great again.

A hawkish stance on China is one of the last areas of consensus between Democrats and Republicans. More and more US strategists, regardless of party affiliation, have converged on the idea of containing China. But their strategic thinking is based on a shallow and often wrong understanding of how China thinks and operates. By engaging with China's context and history, particularly Mao and the Maoist legacy, we have described China as it is rather than how those strategists want it to be. We do not claim to provide strategies for how to "beat China" but instead offer a better way to understand it—and, ultimately, to productively live with it.

Methodological Appendix

We conducted both qualitative and quantitative studies of Chinese entrepreneurs to examine our ideas about the lasting effects of Mao Zedong and his ideas on Chinese business and society. We used qualitative materials to bring our arguments about entrepreneurs and other important Chinese leaders to life and also analyzed large samples and big data with cutting-edge empirical methods to provide scientific evidence for these phenomena. Our initial investigations into these phenomena came from our peer-reviewed studies published in leading management journals, such as the following:

- Marquis, Christopher, and Kunyuan Qiao. 2020. "Waking from Mao's Dream: Communist Ideological Imprinting and the Internationalization of Entrepreneurial Ventures in China." *Administrative Science Quarterly* 65(3): 795–830.
- Zhang, Jianjun, Pei Sun, and Kunyuan Qiao. 2020. "Wining and Dining Government Officials: What Drives Political Networking in Chinese Private Ventures?" *Management and Organization Review* 16(5): 1084–1113.
- Wang, Danqing, Fei Du, and Christopher Marquis. 2019. "Defending Mao's Dream: Politicians' Ideological Imprinting and Firms' Political Appointment in China." *Academy of Management Journal* 62(4): 1111–36.
- Marquis, Christopher, and Yanhua Zhou Bird. 2018. "The Paradox of Responsive Authoritarianism: How Civic Activism Spurs Environmental Penalties in China." *Organization Science* 29(5): 948–68.

- Marquis, Christopher, Qi Li, and Kunyuan Qiao. 2017. "The Chinese Collectivist Model of Charity." *Stanford Social Innovation Review* 15(3): 40–47.
- Marquis, Christopher, Juelin Yin, and Dongning Yang. 2017. "State-Mediated Globalization Processes and the Adoption of Corporate Social Responsibility Reporting in China." *Management and Organization Review* 13(1): 167–91.
- Luo, Xiaowei Rose, Jianjun Zhang, and Christopher Marquis. 2016. "Mobilization in the Internet Age: Internet Activism and Corporate Response." *Academy of Management Journal* 59(6): 2045–68.
- Marquis, Christopher, Yanhua Zhou, and Zoe Yang. 2016. "The Emergence of Subversive Charities in China." *Stanford Social Innovation Review* 12(4): 42–47.
- Zhang, Jianjun, Christopher Marquis, and Kunyuan Qiao. 2016. "Do Political Connections Buffer Firms from or Bind Firms to the Government? A Study of Corporate Charitable Donations of Chinese Firms." *Organization Science* 27(5): 1307–24.
- Marquis, Christopher, Susan E. Jackson, and Yuan Li. 2015. "Building Sustainable Organizations in China." *Management and Organization Review* 11(3): 427–40.
- Marquis, Christopher, and Cuili Qian. 2014. "Corporate Social Responsibility Reporting in China: Symbol or Substance?" *Organization Science* 25(1): 127–48.
- Marquis, Christopher, Hongyu Zhang, and Lixuan Zhou. 2013. "China's Quest to Adopt Electric Vehicles." *Stanford Social Innovation Review* 11(2): 52–57.
- Marquis, Christopher, Jianjun Zhang, and Yanhua Zhou. 2011. "Regulatory Uncertainty and Corporate Responses to Environmental Protection in China." *California Management Review* 54(1): 39–63.

We also drew from our published Harvard teaching cases:

- Marquis, Christopher, and Yen Hsiang Wu. 2018. "Growing Home: Creating Institutional Change in China." Harvard Kennedy School Case 2119.0, May.
- Marquis, Christopher, and Xinghui Chen. 2017. "First Respond: The Challenges of Marketing Social Mission in China." Harvard Kennedy School Case 2103.0, August.
- Marquis, Christopher, and Qi Li. 2015. "Continental Hope Group." Harvard Business School Case 415050, January.
- Marquis, Christopher, Ying Zhang, and Shiyu Yang. 2015. "China Yintai: Developing Shared Value in China." Harvard Business School Case 415078, May.

- Marquis, Christopher, Laura Velez Villa, and Lynn Yin. 2012. "China Greentech Initiative (CGTI)." Harvard Business School Case 412105, February.
- Marquis, Christopher, Zucheng Zhou, Mo Chen, and Heng Fan. 2012. "Building a Community at Semiconductor Manufacturing International Corporation." Harvard Business School Case 413083, November.
- Marquis, Christopher, and Nancy Dai. 2011. "China Environment Fund: Doing Well by Doing Good." Harvard Business School Case 410142; Teaching Note 411098, May.
- Marquis, Christopher, Nancy Dai, Dongning Yang, and Hong Wu. 2011. "State Grid: Corporate Social Responsibility." Harvard Business School Case 410141; Teaching Note 412006, July.
- Marquis, Christopher, Nancy Hua Dai, and Lynn Yin. 2011. "Chairman Zhang and Broad Group: Growth Dilemmas." Harvard Business School Case 412095, December.
- Marquis, Christopher, Lynn Yin, and Dongning Yang. 2011. "COSCO: Implementing Sustainability." Harvard Business School Case 412081, November.
- Marquis, Christopher, G. A. Donovan, and Yi-Kwan Chu. 2010. "Swire Beverages: Implementing CSR in China." Harvard Business School Case 410021; Teaching Note 410129, April.

We presented our ideas at a number of public venues, including international conferences, symposia (some of which are listed here), podcasts, and foreign expert advisory panels for Chinese prime minister Li Keqiang in 2018 and 2020:

- Marquis, Christopher. 2019. "Red Guards to Red Entrepreneurs: How Mao Era Thought Seeps into Modern Chinese Business." In *China EconTalk,* podcast, edited by J. Schneider. https://supchina.com/podcast/chinaecontalk-with-special-guest-christopher-marquis/ [retrieved on April 15, 2022].
- Qiao, Kunyuan, and Christopher Marquis. 2019. "Internal Logics of Control: A Study of the Relationship between Internal and External CSR in China." Paper presented at the Academy of Management Annual Meeting Symposium, Boston, MA.
- Marquis, Christopher, and Kunyuan Qiao. 2018. "What Does Not Starve You Makes You More Economical: A Study of Resource Scarcity Imprint of Chinese Entrepreneurs." Paper presented at the Academy of Management Annual Meeting, Chicago, IL.
- Marquis, Christopher, Kunyuan Qiao, M. Diane Burton, Ryan Allen, Santiago Campero Molina, Prithwiraj Choudhury, and Aleksandra

Joanna Kacperczyk. 2018. "Individual Imprinting: Life History Matters." Paper presented at the Academy of Management Annual Meeting Symposium, Boston, MA.

• Marquis, Christopher, and Kunyuan Qiao. 2017. "Communist Ideological Imprinting and Internationalization: A Study of Chinese Entrepreneurs." Paper presented at the Academy of Management Annual Meeting, Atlanta, GA.

We have also presented our ideas during academic seminars at venues such as Harvard University, the University of Cambridge, London Business School, and the University of Texas–Dallas.

Our goal for this book was then to extend these arguments and also bring them to life through qualitatively presented case studies and examples.

QUALITATIVE MATERIALS

Our qualitative evidence comes from two main sources. First, in most of the chapters, we present short case studies of well-known entrepreneurs and other leaders in China that demonstrate many of the ideas we have developed from our larger-scale, quantitative research. We gathered information on these individuals from a wide range of online sources and news reports, including ones published by the BBC, CNN, the *New York Times,* the *Wall Street Journal,* and Chinese-language media such as Sina Finance and Sohu Finance.

In addition to these rich secondhand materials, we also recruited a sample of entrepreneurs and interviewed them to obtain unique firsthand insights into our area of research. We received approval from the Cornell Institutional Review Board for Human Participant Research Office (Protocol ID# 2004009526) before starting this process, and we notified participants that their identities would be kept confidential and they may choose not to answer some of the questions if they agreed to be interviewed.

We then began our sampling process, enlisting the help of the University of Electronic Science and Technology of China and chambers of commerce and business associations in different cities and provinces to recruit representative entrepreneurs. These entrepreneurs are all more than forty-four years old and thus may have experienced the Cultural Revolution. To ensure that these entrepreneurs are comparable, we restricted our sample to entrepreneurs whose businesses employed more than one hundred people with total assets of above 5 million Chinese yuan (US$720,000). Furthermore, their ventures should not be controlled by the government (that is, state investors or entities are not the controlling owners), and we did not recruit companies in the finance industry, which has a different mode of operation from manufacturing firms, consistent with most social science research. Our recruitment letter is provided in the next section.

Because most of the interviews were held following the COVID-19 outbreak and travel restrictions thus prevented us from traveling to China, we recruited research assistants to conduct the interviews in person. The interviews were all recorded and transcribed, and we met with the interview team before and after many of the interviews.

Interview Recruitment Letter

To Whom It May Concern / 尊敬的商会负责人：

I am a professor at Cornell University. Hope you and your family are well in this uncertain period.

我是康奈尔大学的一名教授。希望您和您的家人在这一段时间安康。

I am in the process of doing a book on the unique model of entrepreneurship that has developed in China, with the aim of communicating to global audiences this important aspect of the China development miracle. As current data show, there have been more than fifteen million entrepreneurs, who contribute over 50% tax revenue, 60% GDP, 70% innovation, 80% urban employment, and establish 90% of all firms in China. However, there have been relatively few systematic studies on private entrepreneurs in China, leaving us with a fragmented understanding of this important economic engine in the world.

我正在写一本关于中国企业家的书，希望向全球读者介绍中国发展奇迹的这一重要方面。正如现在的数据显示，中国有超过1500万位企业家，他们贡献了超过50%的税收、60%的国民生产总值、70%的税收和80%的城镇就业，并且90%以上的企业都是民营企业。但是当先鲜有对中国民营企业家系统的研究，阻碍了我们对这一世界经济引擎全面的了解。

The focus of the research will be on not just the importance of economic activity, but also how the political and party systems in China intersect with companies to provide a more sustainable and socially responsible economic system.

本研究不仅聚焦于企业家对于经济活动的重要性，而且希望从制度层面了解党和政府如何与民营企业合作，从而发展出一套可持续的、对社会负责的经济系统。因此，中国的经验和模式将对世界经济有重要的启示作用。

Briefly, we will ask the questions about their background, e.g., their self-image, motivation of becoming an entrepreneur, and important historical events in China they still remember. We also want to know a bit more about their firms, e.g., strategies they think important and how their life experience may play a role in these strategies. I have also attached a draft questionnaire. All their personal information will be kept strictly confidential, but we may share de-identified data in presentations of our research, e.g., stating their quotes.

简而言之，我们希望了解企业家的背景，比如他们如何描述自己、希望成为企业家的动机以及他们依旧记得的在中国发生的历史时刻。我们同时希望理解他们的企业，比如他们认为哪些战略重要、他们的生活经历如何影响这些战略的制定等。我在信末附上了问卷草稿。他们的所有信息将会被严格保密，但是我们可能会在书中引用除去他们身份信息之后的表述。

We are specifically interested in entrepreneurs / 我们具体希望采访如下的企业家：

1. Whose firms are still private (not controlled by State-owned Assets Supervision and Administration) and not in finance-related industries (e.g., online financing platform); 他们的企业依旧是民营的（并没有被国资委控股）并且不在金融行业（如融资平台）；
2. Employ more than 100 people or with an asset of above 5 million Chinese Yuan/RMB / 雇佣超过100名员工、总资产在500万元以上；
3. Whose age is above 44 年龄超过44岁

We hope that we can work with you to identify appropriate member entrepreneurs and help us gain access to them. Thank you for your consideration.
我们希望您能够帮助我们招募合适的商会成员企业家并作引荐以便我们采访。感谢您的时间。

If you have any questions or would like any further information, please feel free to contact me via email at cmarquis@cornell.edu.
如果您有任何疑问或者需要更多的信息，请不吝发邮件至cmarquis@cornell.edu垂询。

Sincerely,
此致
敬礼
Christopher Marquis / 孟睿思

In total, with the help of a research team at the University of Electronic Science and Technology of China, we interviewed thirty-two entrepreneurs (table A.1) face-to-face or online in Anhui, Chongqing, Guangdong, Heilongjiang, Hunan, Shanghai, Sichuan, and Zhejiang. These entrepreneurs represent a wide diversity of geographical locations, such as northeastern (for example, Heilongjiang), southeastern (for example, Guangdong, Shanghai, and Zhejiang), southwestern (for example, Chongqing and Sichuan), and central (Anhui and Hunan) provinces. The sample is also consistent with the distribution of entrepreneurship in China, as most private firms are located in these areas.[1]

During the interviews, we began with some basic questions about respondents' personal experiences. Our questions then covered issues such as the combination of a communist identity and the status of entrepreneur, Mao's quotes, principles, mass movements, and their firms' operations (for exam-

Table A.1 Summary of Interview Subjects

Number	Gender	Birth year/ cohort	CCP membership	Industry	Founding year
1	Male	1971	CCP member	Furniture	2005
2	Male	1964	Not a CCP member	Chemical fertilizer	2002
3	Female	1964	Not a CCP member	Agriculture	1985
4	Female	Early 1970s	Not a CCP member	Internet	2014
5	Female	1968	Not a CCP member	E-commerce	2010
6	Male	1968	CCP member	Hospital	2000
7	Male	1970	Not a CCP member	Food	2007
8	Male	1974	CCP member	Agriculture	2011
9	Male	1967	Not a CCP member	Conglomerate (real estate, tourism, and others)	1999
10	Male	1967	Not a CCP member	Shoe	1995
11	Male	1963	CCP member	Furniture	1998
12	Male	Late 1970s	CCP member	Internet	2013
13	Male	1975	Not a CCP member	Hospital	2004
14	Female	1960	CCP member	Culture	2015
15	Female	1964	Not a CCP member	Manufacturing	1991
16	Male	Early 1970s	Not a CCP member	Air conditioners	1999
17	Female	1966	CCP member	Education	2013
18	Male	1967	CCP member	Manufacturing	2014
19	Female	Late 1960s	Not a CCP member	Conglomerate	2003
20	Female	1962	Not a CCP member	Retail	2010
21	Female	1970	CCP member	Food	2000

(*Continued*)

Table A.1 (*Continued*)

Number	Gender	Birth year/ cohort	CCP membership	Industry	Founding year
22	Male	1965	Not a CCP member	Consulting	2004
23	Female	Early 1960s	Not a CCP member	Food	1999
24	Female	1974	Not a CCP member	Garment	2010
25	Male	Unknown	Not a CCP member	Hotel	2020
26	Female	Late 1960s	Not a CCP member	Culture	2005
27	Male	1971	Not a CCP member	Consulting	1999
28	Female	Late 1970s	Not a CCP member	Environment	2011
29	Male	1965	Not a CCP member	Sports	1987
30	Male	Late 1970s	Not a CCP member	Food	2009
31	Male	1970	CCP member	Glass	1999
32	Male	Late 1970s	Not a CCP member	Aviation	2021

ple, those regarding state ownership, internationalization, cost reduction, and philanthropic donation).

We report a selected set of anonymized interview quotes in our book and also performed content analysis of the text of the interviews.

The questionnaire for our interviews is provided in the next section.

Questionnaire for Interviews / 采访问卷

We are studying entrepreneurs' perception and their firms' involvement in areas of social contribution, stakeholder management, governance, innovation, internationalization, and cost reduction, in particular how these factors stem from China's unique socialist market economy with Chinese characteristics.

我们的问题将围绕企业家和他们的企业对于国际化、降低成本、社会责任和利益相关者管理、治理、创新以及对于中国特色社会主义市场经济的感知展开。

1. Could you describe yourself in three words and elaborate a bit?
   用三个词来形容您自己并且稍作展开?

2. Could you describe a typical day as an entrepreneur? 您如何描述作为企业家的一天?

3. Where did you get the idea of becoming an entrepreneur? 您是从何处得到要成为企业家的想法?

4. What's your greatest entrepreneurial achievement that you are proud of and toughest experience you still remember? 迄今您最骄傲的创业成就和最坎坷的经历是?

5. Do you think communist membership and entrepreneur identity is compatible or contradictory, and why? 您认为党员和企业家身份冲突还是兼容呢? 为什么?

6. Which one of these characteristics—independence and self-reliance, frugality, and devotion—most impresses you? 独立自主、自力更生, 节约和奉献中哪个给您印象最深?

7. Have you experienced and had memory of any of the three—the Great Chinese Famine, Send-down movement, and Third Front Construction? 您是否经历过或者还记得三年困难时期、上山下乡、和三线建设? What do you get from these experiences? 您从这些经历中学到了什么?

8. Do you have any particular memory of Chairman Mao, e.g., some impressive sentences and quotes of Chairman Mao you still remember? 毛主席有没有给您留下特别的回忆, 比如毛主席说的哪句话或者格言您还记得?

9. How does it relate to your business, e.g., what can you learn from Chairman Mao? 毛泽东思想如何影响您的企业呢, 比如您觉得您的企业可以从毛主席那里学到什么呢?

10. Does your firm receive investment or have owners that are state-owned? 您的企业是否有国有资本? [If yes] How would you balance interests of your private and state owners? 【如果是】您如何权衡民营和国营所有者的利益呢?

11. Have you considered or already internationalized your firm? 您是否考虑过对公司进行国际化?

    (1) [If yes] Do you receive foreign investments or are you investing in foreign firms/owning subsidiaries? 【如果是】您是收到外国资本还是向海外投资/拥有海外子公司?

    (2) [If no] Why not internalize your firm, do you have concerns of your foreign partners or your own firm? 【如果没有】为什么不进行国际化呢, 您对海外商业伙伴或者您的公司有何顾虑?

    (3) [If no] Have you ever declined such opportunities and why? Do you feel regretful? 【如果没有】您是否曾经拒绝过这些机会? 您是否因此感到后悔?

12. Do you think [cost reduction, CSR, corporate governance, and innovation] is important? 您认为【节约成本/社会责任/公司治理/创新】最重要?

(1) What exactly did you do in these aspects? 您在这一战略上具体做了什么?

(2) Do you think your experience plays a role? 您认为您的经历是否在这一决策过程中起到作用?

13. Do you have experiences of transforming seemingly useless products/strategies into profits? 您是否有过将看似无用的产品或者战略变成利润? [If so] Could you share with us that experience, especially how did you think about them? 【如果有】可否与我们分享您的经验，尤其是您如何思考的?

QUANTITATIVE DATABASES

We developed five databases to understand entrepreneurship and business and market development in China and to ground our ideas in evidence, drawing on state-of-the-art social scientific methods: survey data of private entrepreneurs and their ventures, data of publicly traded firms that are entrepreneur controlled, data on politicians' backgrounds, a database of newspaper articles and keywords, and city-level data on entrepreneurship and an innovation index.

Chinese Private Enterprise Survey

First, we subscribed to nationwide survey data on entrepreneurs in China—the Chinese Private Enterprise Survey—in 1993, 1995, 1997, 2000, 2002, 2004, 2006, 2008, 2010, and 2012 by the Chinese Academy of Social Sciences.[2] With the help of the Bureau of Industry and Commerce and Federation of Industry and Commerce, the Academy selects entrepreneurs from all thirty-one provinces in China, ensuring that the portion of the sampled entrepreneurs over the total population of entrepreneurs in China ranges between 0.03 percent and 0.05 percent. The team conducts multistage sampling. First, it determines the total number of entrepreneurs to be sampled and that of each province. Second, within each province, the team samples the capital city, a large city, and a small city. It also chooses three counties of varying levels of economic development—high, medium, and low. Third, according to the ratio of urban to rural population, the team determines the number of surveyed households in urban and rural areas. Moreover, it determines the number of surveyed households in each industry according to the distribution of urban and rural industries. It selects specific surveyed households according to the principle of equidistance.

The survey team uses long questionnaires to collect exhaustive personal information from entrepreneurs and financial indicators of their ventures in three aspects. The first concerns entrepreneurs' personal information and experience, such as age, gender, education, work experience before enterprising (for example, in the government, state-owned enterprises, and foreign enterprises), political and socioeconomic status (for example, Chinese Communist Party [CCP] membership, position in the government, National People's Congress membership, Chinese People's Political Consultative Conference membership, family income, and position in the social hierarchy).

The second part collects information on respondents' private ventures. It includes founding year, sources of funding, size, industry, financials (for example, revenue, tax, profit, finance, loans, and international cooperation), structure (for example, decision-making, board of directors, shareholder conference, workers' union, and CCP branch), human resources (employee salaries and insurance), and philanthropic donations (participation in disaster relief, poverty reduction, and environmental protection). The third section asks questions about the business environment, such as government policies and support and financing (for example, ease of receiving credit from banks).

Information from the waves of surveys is coded as datasets with numeric and string variables for quantitative analysis. We unified the datasets across different waves by standardizing the naming convention of different variables over the years and then performed quantitative analysis.

Data on Entrepreneur-Controlled, Publicly Traded Firms

We collected data on publicly traded firms that are still controlled by their founding entrepreneurs as a further set of data beyond the Chinese Private Enterprise Survey. We did so for two reasons. First, although the Chinese Private Enterprise Survey provides exhaustive information on private entrepreneurs and their ventures with structured interview questionnaires, the data do not provide any way to study entrepreneurs' use of language. According to the most recent social science research,[3] people's use of words can reflect their cognition and mental processes. Publicly traded firms' annual reports help us trace what entrepreneurs say about their firms. In contrast, firms in the Chinese Private Enterprise Survey are anonymized and most of them do not need to publish annual reports because they are not publicly traded.

Second, examining these entrepreneur-controlled, publicly traded firms enhances the representativeness of our evidence beyond the Chinese Private Enterprise Survey. To be listed on one of China's stock exchanges, firms have to be in relatively good standing (for example, with sustained capability of earning profits and without legal charges or tax fraud), with good governance (for example, a board of directors, a supervisory board, independent directors, an audit, and no misreporting or fraud), and of large size (with at least US$4 million market capitalization). By looking at these relatively large and well-run companies, we can better understand business and entrepreneurship in China.

The main datasets are from the Chinese Stock Market and Accounting Research Database, which is the most authoritative source for data on publicly traded firms in China. We specifically obtained financial datasets (balance sheets, income statements, and cash flow statements); databases of executives including their birth year, gender, nationality, educational background, salary, functional background (for example, production, research and development, human resources, management, marketing, finance, or law), overseas background, political background (for example, government work experience and whether they are delegates to the National People's Congress or the Chinese People's Political Consultative Conference), and their raw curricula vitae; and information on foreign direct investment.

We then used Python to mass-download annual reports of firms traded on the Shanghai and Shenzhen Stock Exchanges from the official websites of the two exchanges (http://www.sse.com.cn/disclosure/listedinfo/announcement/ and http://www.szse.cn/disclosure/listed/fixed/index.html). We used content analysis on the downloaded PDF files of firms' annual reports. Like statistical software that processes numeric data, content analysis is a way to analyze text data. Following the established methods,[4] we first generated a list of potential keywords from Mao's teaching, quotes, principles, and other sources based on existing studies. Then we asked three experts to validate the list for us. We left out some keywords with no representation. With the final list of keywords, we used Python to code occurrences of these words in firms' annual reports.

We merged the datasets from the Chinese Stock Market and Accounting Research Database and the annual report database, only keeping firms that are entrepreneur controlled. Although the financial data start in 1990 when the stock market in China was established, detailed data on CEOs regarding political background and foreign direct investment do not begin until 2007 and 2009, respectively. Hence, our sample starts in 2007 and ends in 2018.

Data on Politicians

We manually collected data on politicians' life, education, and employment at the city level, which is the finest-grained level that most existing studies use.[5]

We obtained data from Zecheng Net (http://www.hotelaah.com/liren/), Chinese Economy (http://district.ce.cn/), and Renmin Net reports on these officials' individual histories (for example, http://www.sh-pilots.com.cn /Party/showart.aspx?aid=3985&sid=29). We also used Wikipedia, Baidu

Baike, Xinhua Net, websites of different provinces and cities, Google, Baidu, and statistical yearbooks of different provinces to supplement the data when they were missing from the primary sources. The data include politicians' province, city, name, birth, hometown, years of inauguration and departure, next position, whether they were promoted or demoted, the year of joining the CCP, educational attainment, and their work experience in the provincial and central governments. Due to data availability, our city-level data start in 2000 and end in 2018.

We assembled two datasets, one that covers city party secretaries and one that covers city mayors.

Database of Chinese Newspapers

We gathered the full text of the *People's Daily,* the most authoritative newspaper controlled by the CCP, from 1949 to 2010. Many slogans, announcements, and important Maoist principles were first published in this outlet. We used this database to chart the ideological climate in China.

However, different provinces might exhibit variation in their embrace of Maoist principles. To track this variation, we hired two research assistants to search for keywords related to Maoist principles and ideology and code their occurrences year by year for each province's daily—the counterpart of the *People's Daily* in each province—from the Index Database of Chinese Newspapers (http://www.cnbksy.com). As we did for annual reports of firms, we first generated a list of keywords based on existing studies, which we report in the specific chapters. We checked the list with Python coding of the *People's Daily* and asked experts to help us validate the list. Then we derived a list of keywords for our research assistants to check. We verified the interrater reliability between the two research assistants. We also randomly checked these data ourselves to ensure accuracy.

City-Level Entrepreneurship Data

We obtained the entrepreneurship index in China from a research team at the National School of Development at Peking University. The data can be subscribed to at https://opendata.pku.edu.cn/dataset.xhtml?persistentId =doi:10.18170/DVN/DLBWAK. The research team surveyed Chinese firms of different sizes, industries, and ages in all cities in China and obtained data for numbers of new firms, foreign investments, venture capital and private equity investment, patents, and trademarks (standardized with indexes). Then, based on these data points, the team provided an overall index of entrepreneurship and innovation, as well as one adjusted for size of population and area. The sample period of the data in use is 2000 to 2018.

Notes

INTRODUCTION

1. Based on the World Bank data at https://data.worldbank.org/country/china [retrieved on July 1, 2021].

2. Cheng, Jonathan, "China Is the Only Major Economy to Report Economic Growth for 2020," https://www.wsj.com/articles/china-is-the-only-major-economy -to-report-economic-growth-for-2020-11610936187 [retrieved on July 1, 2021]; Yao, Kevin, and Gabriel Crossley, "China Tops Forecasts with 8.1% Growth in 2021 but Headwinds Loom," https://www.reuters.com/markets/asia/chinas-q4-2021-gdp -grow-faster-than-expected-2022-01-17/ [retrieved on January 18, 2022].

3. National Security Strategy 2017, https://nssarchive.us/national-security -strategy-2017/ [retrieved on July 1, 2021].

4. Hayashi, Yuka, "U.S. Trade Balance with China Improves, but Sources of Tension Linger," https://www.wsj.com/articles/u-s-trade-deficit-narrowed-in-december -as-exports-outpaced-imports-11612532757 [retrieved on July 1, 2021]; Arreddy, James, "Former Chinese Party Insider Calls U.S. Hopes of Engagement 'Naive,'" https://www.wsj.com/articles/former-chinese-party-insider-calls-u-s-hopes-of -engagement-naive-11624969800 [retrieved on January 22, 2022].

5. "Remarks as Prepared for Delivery of Ambassador Katherine Tai Outlining the Biden-Harris Administration's 'New Approach to the U.S.-China Trade Rela- tionship,'" https://ustr.gov/about-us/policy-offices/press-office/press-releases/2021 /october/remarks-prepared-delivery-ambassador-katherine-tai-outlining-biden -harris-administrations-new [retrieved on October 14, 2021]; Kurlantzick, Joshua, "Nonstop Party: The Surprising Persistence of Chinese Communism," http://archive .boston.com/bostonglobe/ideas/articles/2009/11/22/the_surprising_persistence_of _chinese_communism/ [retrieved on January 18, 2022].

6. Blinken, Antony J., "The Administration's Approach to the People's Republic of China," May 26, 2022, https://www.state.gov/the-administrations-approach-to-the -peoples-republic-of-china/ [retrieved on May 27, 2022].

7. "Is Biden's Foreign Policy Grade A Material?," https://foreignpolicy.com/2022 /01/20/biden-foreign-policy-report-card-russia-china-afghanistan/; Fontaine, Richard, "Washington's Missing China Strategy: To Counter Beijing, the Biden Administration Needs to Decide What It Wants," https://www.foreignaffairs.com/articles/china/2022 -01-14/washingtons-missing-china-strategy [retrieved on January 22, 2022].

8. Page, Jeremy, "How the U.S. Misread China's Xi: Hoping for a Globalist, It Got an Autocrat," https://www.wsj.com/articles/xi-jinping-globalist-autocrat -misread-11608735769 [retrieved on July 1, 2021]. We use the Chinese naming convention (surname followed by given name). While in Chinese the translation of Xi's title is typically "chairman" or "general secretary," in US media he is typically referred to as "president," which is the convention we follow.

9. Economy, Elizabeth, "China's Neo-Maoist Movement," https://www .foreignaffairs.com/articles/china/2019-10-01/chinas-neo-maoist-moment [retrieved on April 1, 2022]; "China's Xi Allowed to Remain 'President for Life' as Term Limits Removed," https://www.bbc.com/news/world-asia-china-43361276 [retrieved on July 1, 2021].

10. Bishop, Bill, "Xi Chairs Symposium with Business Leaders; 'Xi Thought' Coming? TikTok," https://sinocism.com/p/xi-chairs-symposium-with-entrepreneurs [retrieved on August 25, 2021]; He, Laura, "Xi Jinping Wants China's Private Companies to Fight Alongside the Communist Party," https://www.cnn.com/2020/09 /22/business/china-private-sector-intl-hnk/index.html [retrieved on April 1, 2022]; Wei, Lingling, "China's Xi Ramps Up Control of Private Sector. 'We Have No Choice but to Follow the Party,'" https://www.wsj.com/articles/china-xi-clampdown-private -sector-communist-party-11607612531 [retrieved on April 21, 2022]; Nagarajan, Shalini, "China's Xi Jinping Personally Halted Ant's Record-Breaking $37 Billion IPO after Boss Jack Ma Snubbed Government Leaders, Report Says," https://markets .businessinsider.com/news/stocks/ant-group-ipo-personally-halted-china-xi -jinping-jack-wsj-2020-11-1029800224 [retrieved on April 1, 2022]; Yang, Yingzhi, and Brenda Goh, "Beijing Took Stake and Board Seat in Key ByteDance Domestic Entity This Year," https://www.reuters.com/world/china/beijing-owns-stakes -bytedance-weibo-domestic-entities-records-show-2021-08-17/ [retrieved on August 22, 2021]; Webb, Quentin, and Lingling Wei, "Chinese Ride-Hailing Giant Didi Could Get State Investment," https://www.wsj.com/articles/city-of-beijing-leads -plan-for-state-investment-in-didi-the-embattled-ride-hailing-giant-11630681353 [retrieved on September 28, 2021].

11. "The Theory of Private Enterprises Withdrawing from the Market: State Advancement and Private Retreat Are Intensified, and the Panic of Chinese Private Enterprises Spreads," https://www.bbc.com/zhongwen/simp/chinese-news-45522113 [retrieved on July 1, 2021]. Unless otherwise noted, all translations of Chinese language sources are our own.

12. Bradsher, Keith, and Alexandra Stevenson, "Beijing Takes Over Anbang, Insurer That Owns Waldorf Astoria," https://www.nytimes.com/2018/02/22/business /china-anbang-waldorf-astoria.html [retrieved on July 1, 2021].

13. "Xi Jinping: Speech at the Celebration of the Centenary of the Founding of the Chinese Communist Party," http://www.gov.cn/xinwen/2021-07/01/content_5621847.htm [retrieved on July 10, 2021].

14. Wei, Lingling, "Xi Jinping Aims to Rein in Chinese Capitalism, Hew to Mao's Socialist Vision," https://www.wsj.com/articles/xi-jinping-aims-to-rein-in-chinese-capitalism-hew-to-maos-socialist-vision-11632150725 [retrieved on April 1, 2022]; McDonald, Joe, "China Chases 'Rejuvenation' with Control of Tycoons, Society," https://apnews.com/article/technology-lifestyle-asia-beijing-xi-jinping-1a03a0ad19397face74b2e2dd2130d33 [retrieved on September 28, 2021]. However, Xi also has established the Beijing Stock Exchange for small and medium-size enterprises, especially those specializing in technology and innovation. Tom Hancock, a seasoned Bloomberg reporter, voiced his suspicion: see https://twitter.com/hancocktom/status/1440183242208931850 [retrieved on September 28, 2021].

15. "Bernie Sanders on China," https://feelthebern.org/bernie-sanders-on-china/ [retrieved on April 1, 2022]; Sanders, Bernie, "Washington's Dangerous New Consensus on China," https://www.sanders.senate.gov/op-eds/washingtons-dangerous-new-consensus-on-china/ [retrieved on April 1, 2022]; Kai, Jin, "How Trump Fueled Anti-Asian Violence in America," https://thediplomat.com/2021/06/how-trump-fueled-anti-asian-violence-in-america/ [retrieved on April 1, 2022]; "Rubio Delivers Lecture on How the Bipartisan Economic Consensus Is Destroying American Greatness," https://www.rubio.senate.gov/public/index.cfm/2021/12/rubio-delivers-lecture-on-how-the-bipartisan-economic-consensus-is-destroying-american-greatness [retrieved on January 22, 2022]; Blinken, Antony J., 2022, "The Administration's Approach to the People's Republic of China," https://www.state.gov/the-administrations-approach-to-the-peoples-republic-of-china/ [retrieved on May 27, 2022].

16. Douthat, Ross, "James Bond Has No Time for China," https://www.nytimes.com/2021/10/16/opinion/james-bond-china.html [retrieved on November 20, 2021]; Farhi, Paul, and Jeremy Barr, "The Media Called the 'Lab Leak' Story a 'Conspiracy Theory.' Now It's Prompted Corrections—and Serious New Reporting," https://www.washingtonpost.com/lifestyle/media/the-media-called-the-lab-leak-story-a-conspiracy-theory-now-its-prompted-corrections--and-serious-new-reporting/2021/06/10/c93972e6-c7b2-11eb-a11b-6c6191ccd599_story.html [retrieved on April 1, 2022]; Devlin, Kat, Laura Silver, and Christine Huang, "U.S. Views of China Increasingly Negative amid Coronavirus Outbreak," https://www.pewresearch.org/global/2020/04/21/u-s-views-of-china-increasingly-negative-amid-coronavirus-outbreak/ [retrieved on April 1, 2022]; Yuan, Li, "The Army of Millions Who Enforce China's Zero-Covid Policy, at All Costs," https://www.nytimes.com/2022/01/12/business/china-zero-covid-policy-xian.html [retrieved on January 18, 2022].

17. Blinken, "The Administration's Approach to the People's Republic of China."

18. Li, Eric, "The CCP's Greatest Strength Is 'Self-Reinvention,'" https://foreignpolicy.com/2021/07/02/ccp-reinvention-anniversary-youth-popularity/ [retrieved on July 11, 2021].

19. For a summary, see Barboza, David, "Clyde Prestowitz on the China Fallacy," https://www.thewirechina.com/2021/06/13/clyde-prestowitz-on-the-china-fallacy/ [retrieved on July 10, 2021].

20. Quoted on p. 4 of Mitter, Rana, and Elsbeth Johnson, "What the West Gets Wrong about China: Three Fundamental Misconceptions," *Harvard Business Review* 99, no. 3 (2021): 2–8.

21. Osnos, Evan, "Huntsman, China, and the Bears," https://www.newyorker.com/news/evan-osnos/huntsman-china-and-the-bears [retrieved on September 29, 2021].

22. Mitter and Johnson, "What the West Gets Wrong." Also see Li, Eric, "CCP's Greatest Strength."

23. Mamta, Badkar, "This Chart Busts the Myth That China's Economy Is Driven by Gov't-Owned Businesses," https://www.businessinsider.com/chart-debunks-state-owned-enterprises-myth-2012-4 [retrieved on July 1, 2021].

24. "China Focus: Private Enterprises Help Bolster China's High-Quality Growth," http://www.xinhuanet.com/english/2019-08/27/c_138342609.htm [retrieved on July 1, 2021].

25. He, Amy, "Tencent Named One of Most Innovative Companies," http://usa.chinadaily.com.cn/epaper/2015-12/03/content_22617535.htm [retrieved on July 1, 2021].

26. Wright, Arthur F., *Confucianism and Chinese Civilization* (Stanford, CA: Stanford University Press, 1975); Pan, Zhongdang, Steven H. Chaffee, Godwin C. Chu, and Yanan Ju (eds.), *To See Ourselves: Comparing Traditional Chinese and American Cultural Values* (New York: Routledge, 2019); Levenson, Joseph Richmond, *Confucian China and Its Modern Fate* (Berkeley: University of California Press, 1972); Jacobs, L., G. Guopei, and P. Herbig, "Confucian Roots in China: A Force for Today's Business," *Management Decision* 33, no. 10 (1995): 29–34.

27. The original sentence is, "A spectre is haunting Europe—the spectre of communism." Marx, Karl, and Friedrich Engels, *Manifest Der Kommunistischen Partei/ Manifesto of the Communist Party,* translated by Samuel Moore (Waiheke Island, UK: Floating Press, 1848/1888), 1.

28. "Ren Zhengfei: Huawei Culture Is the CCP Culture," https://www.dwnews.com/%E4%B8%AD%E5%9B%BD/59724653/%E4%BB%BB%E6%AD%A3%E9%9D%9E%E5%8D%8E%E4%B8%BA%E6%96%87%E5%8C%96%E5%B0%B1%E6%98%AF%E5%85%B1%E4%BA%A7%E5%85%9A%E6%96%87%E5%8C%96 [retrieved on July 1, 2021].

29. "Summary of Zhengfei Ren's Interview with a German TV Station: I Have Put Life and Death Aside," http://m.us.sina.com/gb/finance/sinacn/2019-09-23/detail-ifzpekac4630761.shtml [retrieved on July 1, 2021].

30. Ren, Zhengfei, "My Father and Mother," 2001, https://www.douban.com/note/187496301/ [retrieved on July 1, 2021].

31. Ren, Zhengfei, "My Father and Mother."

32. "Demystify Ren Zhengfei's First Marriage," https://www.sohu.com/a/344946647_654590 [retrieved on July 1, 2021].

33. "What Kind of Person Is Ren Zhengfei?" https://www.zhihu.com/question/52941324 [retrieved on July 1, 2021]. .

34. "EU Ranks Huawei as the World's 2nd Highest Investor in R&D," https://www.huawei.com/en/news/2021/12/european-commission-huawei-investor [retrieved on April 4, 2022]; Li Na, "Huawei to Spend More Than USD20 Billion on

R&D in 2021 with Cloud Focus," https://www.yicaiglobal.com/news/huawei-to-spend-more-than-usd20-billion-on-rd-in-2021-with-cloud-focus- [retrieved on April 4, 2022]; "2022 Patent 300 List," https://harrityllp.com/patent300/ [retrieved on January 18, 2022].

35. "Ren Zhengfei: I Am a CCP Member, and I Will Fight for Communism for All My Life and Will Never Betray," https://user.guancha.cn/main/content?id=162048&s=fwzwyzzwzbt [retrieved on July 1, 2021].

36. "Ren Zhengfei: My Spiritual Mentor Is Chairman Mao," https://www.sohu.com/a/316888766_764234 [retrieved on July 1, 2021].

37. "Ren Zhengfei on Why Join CCP: All Excellent People Would Join Them," http://news.sina.com.cn/c/2013-05-10/093327082310.shtml [retrieved on July 1, 2021].

38. "Ren Zhengfei: I Am a CCP Member."

39. "A Model of Learning Maoism—Zhengfei Ren of Huawei: Maoism Is the Guiding Principle (and Soul) of Huawei," https://www.kunlunce.com/ssjj/guoji pinglun/2019-03-20/132058.html [retrieved on July 1, 2021].

40. For more elaboration of Ren's management and strategy, see "Ren Zhengfei of Huawei, His Spiritual Mentor Is Mao Zedong," https://zhuanlan.zhihu.com/p/52515236 [retrieved on July 1, 2021].

41. Other examples include Pinduoduo (the largest agriculture-focused technology platform in China), Alibaba (one of the largest technology firms in China), Giant Group (a firm selling a melatonin product that is the best-selling health product in China), Biguiyuan (a gigantic real estate company), and SAIC-GM-Wuling (one of the largest automobile makers in China). We discuss this strategy later.

42. "Ren Zhengfei: A Model Student of Maoism among Chinese Entrepreneurs," http://tech.ifeng.com/telecom/special/huaweifeichangdao/detail_2010_10/27/2918621_1.shtml [retrieved on July 1, 2021].

43. "Li Keqiang Talked to Jack Ma, Indicating That He Searched on Taobao and Praised Entrepreneurs Born in 1980s and 1990s for Their Diligence," http://www.ce.cn/xwzx/gnsz/szyw/201311/10/t20131110_1729850.shtml [retrieved on April 21, 2022]. Note that communists call each other "comrade" officially, suggesting that Jack Ma is a communist like Prime Minister Li.

44. "An Analysis Report on the Current Situation of Party Organization Construction in My Country's Private Enterprises," http://www.acfic.org.cn/fgdt1/zjgd/201905/t20190523_125262.html [retrieved on July 23, 2021].

45. There are some differences between these two groups that influence China's current model of private enterprise. Having gone through CCP indoctrination earlier in life, the CCP-to-entrepreneur population has a deeper ideological commitment to Mao's ideas and is more deeply embedded in the CCP-government system. The communist identities of entrepreneurs who later joined the CCP are likely more transactional—e.g., a way to seek governmental protection (a supposition that is borne out by academic research and many media accounts)—though most were also steeped in Maoist thought as young people.

46. See, e.g., Chen, Zhiqiang, https://www.jfdaily.com/news/detail?id=119488 [retrieved on July 1, 2021]; Dickson, Bruce J., *Red Capitalists in China: The Party, Private Entrepreneurs, and Prospects for Political Change* (Cambridge: Cambridge

University Press, 2003); and Marquis, Christopher, and Kunyuan Qiao, "Waking from Mao's Dream: Communist Ideological Imprinting and the Internationalization of Entrepreneurial Ventures in China," *Administrative Science Quarterly* 65, no. 3 (2020): 795–830. However, Dickson did not find significant differences in their political opinions. Yanfei Sun, "Private Entrepreneurs Are in a Historical Turning Point and Might Become Nova in Political Realm," http://finance.sina.com.cn/g /20031121/1445529948.shtml [retrieved on July 1, 2021]. We calculated this number as a product of 8.4 million entrepreneurs in China and approximately 40 percent of them being CCP members according to Chinese Private Enterprise Survey data.

47. "Summarizing Internet Companies with Communist Party Branches: There Are Many Actually Besides Baidu, Alibaba, and Tencent," http://tech.sina.com.cn/i /2017-07-01/doc-ifyhrxtp6420838.shtml [retrieved on July 1, 2021].

48. "Analysis Report."

49. Thomas, Neil, "Party Committees in the Private Sector: Rising Presence, Moderate Prevalence," https://macropolo.org/party-committees-private-sector-china /?rp=m&fbclid=IwAR1bDHDjgNqDp9J8GwNLAbRo3hMHTktQocwJXbUb7T ho8ZuoObJ9bDuctL8 [retrieved on May 8, 2022].

50. "Path of Entrepreneurship and Innovation of a Communist Entrepreneur—Cui Genliang, Party Secretary and Chairman of Hengtong Group," http://dangjian .people.com.cn/n1/2016/0509/c117092-28336175.html [retrieved on July 2, 2021].

51. Borst, Nicholas, "The Party on the Inside: The CCP and Chinese Companies," https://www.thewirechina.com/2021/05/09/the-party-on-the-inside-the-ccp -and-chinese-companies/ [retrieved on July 1, 2021].

52. Li, Hongbin, Lingsheng Meng, Qian Wang, and Li-An Zhou, "Political Connections, Financing and Firm Performance: Evidence from Chinese Private Firms," *Journal of Development Economics* 87, no. 2 (2008): 283–99; Truex, Rory, "The Returns to Office in a 'Rubber Stamp' Parliament," *American Political Science Review* 108, no. 2 (2014): 235–51.

53. Li, Hongbin, Pak Wai Liu, Junsen Zhang, and Ning Ma, "Economic Returns to Communist Party Membership: Evidence from Urban Chinese Twins," *Economic Journal* 117, no. 523 (2007): 1504–20.

54. "Twenty Years of Political Recognition of Private Entrepreneurs, Who Are Hoping to Further Improve Their Political and Economic Status," http://finance.sina .com.cn/china/hgjj/20121106/144313591956.shtml [retrieved on July 1, 2021].

55. Marquis and Kunyuan, "Waking from Mao's Dream."

56. "Ren Zhengfei: I Am a CCP Member"; "Jack Ma Said to Surrender Alipay to the Government," http://news.ifeng.com/a/20180112/55059108_0.shtml [retrieved on July 1, 2021]. In this book, "CCP-government" refers to the coupled entity representing both the CCP as a party and the Chinese government, given China's party-state system.

57. Sun, Yanfei, "The Rise of Protestantism in Post-Mao China: State and Religion in Historical Perspective," *American Journal of Sociology* 122, no. 6 (2017): 1664–725.

58. We use the terms "socialism" and "communism" interchangeably. According to the CCP's teaching, socialism is a specific, primitive stage of communism, which

can refer to the end state of the utopian society Marx described or a consistent ideology.

59. "Xi Jinping Talks about Market Economy: The Attribute 'Socialism' Must Not Be Forgotten," http://cpc.people.com.cn/xuexi/n1/2019/0128/c385476 -30592929.html [retrieved on August 7, 2021].

60. Malmendier, Ulrike, and Stefan Nagel, "Depression Babies: Do Macroeconomic Experiences Affect Risk Taking?," *Quarterly Journal of Economics* 126, no. 1 (2011): 373–416; Giuliano, Paola, and Antonio Spilimbergo, "Growing Up in a Recession," *Review of Economic Studies* 81, no. 2 (2014): 787–817; Schoar, Antoinette, and Luo Zuo, "Shaped by Booms and Busts: How the Economy Impacts CEO Careers and Management Styles," *Review of Financial Studies* 30, no. 5 (2017): 1425–56.

61. See, for example, "Nan Cunhui Questions Schneider Electric and Delixi Group Company Limited Merger," https://business.sohu.com/20070108/n2474 69516.shtml [retrieved on July 1, 2021].

62. Johnson, Victoria, "What Is Organizational Imprinting? Cultural Entrepreneurship in the Founding of the Paris Opera," *American Journal of Sociology* 113, no. 1 (2007): 97–127; Meacham, Jon, *American Gospel: God, the Founding Fathers, and the Making of a Nation* (New York: Random House, 2007).

63. Raynard, Mia, Michael Lounsbury, and Royston Greenwood, "Legacies of Logics: Sources of Community Variation in CSR Implementation in China," in *Research in the Sociology of Organizations,* edited by Michael Lounsbury and Eva Boxenbaum, 243–76 (Bingley, West Yorkshire, UK: Emerald Group, 2013).

64. "Study Outline of Xi Jinping's Thought of Socialism with Chinese Characteristics for a New Era," http://theory.people.com.cn/GB/68294/428935/index.html [retrieved on Apr 21, 2022].

65. Stahl, Günter K., and Rosalie L. Tung, "Towards a More Balanced Treatment of Culture in International Business Studies: The Need for Positive Cross-Cultural Scholarship," *Journal of International Business Studies* 46, no. 4 (2015): 391–414; Nisbett, Richard, *The Geography of Thought: How Asians and Westerners Think Differently . . . and Why* (New York: Simon and Schuster, 2004).

66. "A Little More Plan or a Little More Market Is Not the Fundamental Difference between Socialism and Capitalism," http://cpc.people.com.cn/n/2013/0819 /c69710-22616543.html [retrieved April 21, 2022].

67. "Xinhua Insight: China Embraces New 'Principal Contradiction' When Embarking on New Journey," http://www.xinhuanet.com/english/2017-10/20/c _136694592.htm [retrieved on July 26, 2021].

68. Weber, Max, *The Religion of China: Confucianism and Taoism,* translated by Hans H. Gerth (New York: Free Press, 1915/1951).

69. Fairbank, John King, *The United States and China,* 4th ed. (Cambridge, MA: Harvard University Press, 1983).

70. Marquis and Qiao, "Waking from Mao's Dream."

71. Quoted in Crane, Brent, "The China Bull," https://www.thewirechina.com /2021/10/24/the-china-bull/ [retrieved on November 20, 2021].

72. Fukuyama, Francis, *The End of History and the Last Man* (New York: Free Press, 1992).

73. Hochuli, Alex, and George Hoare, *The End of the End of History: Politics in the Twenty-First Century* (Winchester, UK: Zero Books, 2021).

74. Chang, Gordon G., *The Coming Collapse of China* (New York: Random House, 2001); Chang, Gordon G., "The Coming Collapse of China: 2012 Edition," *Foreign Policy,* December 29, 2011; Beckley, Michael, and Hal Brands, "The End of China's Rise: Beijing Is Running Out of Time to Remake the World," https://www.foreignaffairs.com/articles/china/2021-10-01/end-chinas-rise [retrieved on January 1, 2022].

75. Dickson, Bruce J., *The Party and the People: Chinese Politics in the 21st Century* (Princeton, NJ: Princeton University Press, 2021); Orville, Schell, "Life of the Party: How Secure Is the CCP?," https://www.foreignaffairs.com/reviews/review-essay/2021-06-22/life-party [retrieved April 4, 2022].

76. Marquis, Christopher, and Yanhua Zhou Bird, "The Paradox of Responsive Authoritarianism: How Civic Activism Spurs Environmental Penalties in China," *Organization Science* 29, no. 5 (2018): 948–68; Heurlin, Christopher, *Responsive Authoritarianism in China: Land, Protests, and Policy Making* (Cambridge: Cambridge University Press, 2017).

77. Huntington, Samuel P., *The Third Wave: Democratization in the Late Twentieth Century* (Norman: University of Oklahoma Press, 1991).

78. Wang, Zhenmin, "Constitutional Politics: The Road to Permanent Peace and Stability on How the Communist Party Can Escape from the Historical Cycle," *Tsinghua China Law Review* 6, no. 1 (2013): 1–22.

79. "Xi Jinping: We Should Not Simply Use GDP to Determine Heroes," http://www.xinhuanet.com//world/2013-10/07/c_117609149.htm [retrieved on June 24, 2021]; Blanchette, Jude, "Xi's Confidence Game: Beijing's Actions Show Determination, Not Insecurity," https://www.foreignaffairs.com/articles/asia/2021-11-23/xis-confidence-game [retrieved on January 1, 2022].

80. Kygne, James, and Yu Sun, "China and Big Tech: Xi's Blueprint for a Digital Dictatorship," https://www.ft.com/content/9ef38be2-9b4d-49a4-a812-97ad6d70ea6f [retrieved on October 1, 2021].

81. Chen, Qingqing, and Yuzhu Yan, "Sullivan's Remarks Suggest Softer Tone on US-China Ties, but 'Words Alone Are Not Enough,'" https://www.globaltimes.cn/page/202111/1238448.shtml [retrieved on November 20, 2021].

82. Their theory argues that human society was initially organized in a primitive egalitarian form. With the advancement of technology, people started to save and private ownership of the means of production emerged. At the same time, prisoners of wars from different residential groups became slaves and a slavery system emerged. The further advancement of iron products and the plow required free labor, and more people were incentivized to own land for agricultural production, giving rise to feudalism. The Industrial Revolution then led labor to work in factories and thus capitalism emerged. Capitalists' exploitation of labor fueled class struggle, and with the advancement of technology, society would finally evolve into a utopian communist one in which people could get whatever they wanted and private ownership would disappear. Marx and Engels, *Manifest Der Kommunistischen Partei.* See also Engels, Friedrich, *The Origin of the Family, Private Property, and the State: In the Light of the Researches of Lewis H. Morgan* (Chicago: Charles H.

Kerr, 1884/1902); and Marx, Karl, and Friedrich Engels, *Die Deutsche Ideologie/ The German Ideology*, edited by Christopher John Arthur (New York: International Publishers, 1846/1970).

83. In Chinese textbooks, absolute monarchy with political centralization that lasts for thousands of years is actually still called "feudalism." However, a key distinction is that such Chinese feudalism only grants titles rather than fiefs to lords to prevent development of independent power and possible rebellion. Periods with granted fiefs were very short (e.g., 206–154 BCE).

84. "Xi Jinping: A Clear-Cut Stand against Historical Nihilism," https://www.hrbmu.edu.cn/dsxx/info/1033/1132.htm [retrieved on November 20, 2021].

85. "National People's Congress Closing: Xi Jinping's Speech Emphasizes 'the Party Leads Everything,'" https://www.bbc.com/zhongwen/simp/chinese-news-43468026 [retrieved on July 26, 2021].

86. "'Questions and Answers on the Party's Mass Line Study' Series 1," http://qzlx.people.com.cn/n/2014/0221/c376102-24429902.html [retrieved on July 26, 2021].

87. "Deng Xiaoping: Let Some People Get Rich First," http://cpc.people.com.cn/GB/34136/2569304.html [retrieved on May 23, 2022].

88. "Xi Jinping: Decisive Victory to Build a Moderately Prosperous Society in an All-Round Way and Win the Great Victory of Socialism with Chinese Characteristics for a New Era—Report at the 19th National Congress of the Communist Party," http://www.xinhuanet.com//politics/2017-10/27/c_1121867529.htm [retrieved on July 11, 2021].

89. "'Do Not Forget the Original Intention, Keep in Mind the Mission' Theme Education Summary Conference Held," http://www.xinhuanet.com/politics/bwcxljsm/ [retrieved on April 21, 2022]; "Xi Jinping: Speech at the Educational Summary Conference on the Theme of 'Do Not Forget the Original Intention, Keep in Mind the Mission," http://www.xinhuanet.com/politics/leaders/2020-06/30/c_1126177651.htm [retrieved on July 26, 2021].

90. "Xi Jinping: Speech at the Celebration"; Mitter and Johnson, "What the West Gets Wrong."

91. Gruin, *Communists Constructing Capitalism;* Gruin, "Communists Constructing Capitalism."

92. "The New Version of 'The History of the CCP' Downplays the Cultural Revolution, and the Content of Extolling Xi Accounts for a Quarter," https://www.rfa.org/mandarin/yataibaodao/zhengzhi/xx-04142021124852.html [retrieved on July 1, 2021].

93. "Xi Jinping: Speech at the Celebration."

94. Mai, Jun, "Xi Jinping Asks: Why Do Chinese Officials Lack Initiative and Wait for Orders from the Top?," https://sg.news.yahoo.com/xi-jinping-asks-why-chinese-042938587.html [retrieved on July 23, 2021].

95. Magnier, Mark, "The Underrated Influence of Modern Neo-Maoists on China's Communist Party," https://www.scmp.com/culture/article/3016066/still-alive-and-kicking-underrated-influence-neo-maoists-todays-china [retrieved on April 4, 2022]; Shephard, Christian, "China's Neo-Maoists Welcome Xi's New Era, but Say He Is Not the New Mao," https://www.reuters.com/article/us-china-congress

-maoists/chinas-neo-maoists-welcome-xis-new-era-but-say-he-is-not-the-new-mao
-idUSKBN1CX005 [retrieved on April 4, 2022]; Wu, Zuolai, "Comment on China:
Is Xi Jinping the Version 2.0 of Mao Zedong?," https://www.bbc.com/zhongwen
/simp/focus_on_china/2013/10/131007_cr_xijinping_maozedong [retrieved on July 1,
2021].

96. Malmendier and Nagel, "Depression Babies"; Giuliano and Spilimbergo,
"Growing Up in a Recession"; Marquis, Christopher, and Kunyuan Qiao, "Com-
munist Ideological Imprinting and Internationalization: A Study of Chinese Entre-
preneurs," paper presented at the Academy of Management Proceedings, Atlanta,
GA, 2017; Marquis, Christopher, and Kunyuan Qiao, "What Does Not Starve You
Makes You More Economical: A Study of Resource Scarcity Imprint of Chinese
Entrepreneurs," paper presented at the Academy of Management, Chicago, IL, 2018;
Marquis and Qiao, "Waking from Mao's Dream"; Marquis, Christopher, Kunyuan
Qiao, M. Diane Burton, Ryan Allen, Santiago Campero Molina, Prithwiraj Choud-
hury, and Aleksandra Joanna Kacperczyk, "Individual Imprinting: Life History
Matters," *Academy of Management Proceedings* 2018, no. 1 (2018): 14868; Wang,
Danqing, Fei Du, and Christopher Marquis, "Defending Mao's Dream: Politicians'
Ideological Imprinting and Firms' Political Appointment in China," *Academy of
Management Journal* 62, no. 4 (2019): 1111–36.

97. "Regional Distribution of Best Private Enterprises in China: Jiangsu and Zhejiang Took the Lead and Chongqing Surpassed Tianjin," https://finance.sina.com
.cn/china/2019-08-29/doc-iicezueu2028692.shtml [retrieved on July 1, 2021].

98. Blinken, "The Administration's Approach to the People's Republic of China."

99. Another example is Xi's reversal of Deng's isolationist policy of "hiding strength
and biding time." Rather, Xi focused on enhancing China's influence by initiating the
Belt and Road Initiative, which is also reminiscent of Mao's ideal of exporting communist revolution and China's influence to developing areas like Africa.

PART I: MAO ZEDONG, MAOIST PRINCIPLES, AND PRIVATE
BUSINESS IN CHINA

Epigraphs: "Looking Back on the Cultural Revolution: Mao Zedong as the Artificial
Sun," https://www.voachinese.com/a/a-21-w2007-01-05-voa53-63061687/1045787
.html [retrieved on July 1, 2021]; Mao, Zedong [毛泽东], 毛泽东选集（第一卷）/
Selected Works of Mao Tse-Tung [in Chinese], vol. 2 (Beijing: People's Press [人民出版社],
1991), 349.

CHAPTER 1: MAOISM—COMMUNISM, CHINESE-STYLE

Epigraph: "Looking Back on the Cultural Revolution: Mao Zedong as the Artificial Sun," https://www.voachinese.com/a/a-21-w2007-01-05-voa53-63061687
/1045787.html [retrieved on July 1, 2021].

1. Buckley, Chris, "China's History Is Revised, to the Glory of Xi Jinping,"
https://www.nytimes.com/2021/11/16/world/asia/china-history-xi-jinping.html [re-
trieved on November 20, 2021].

2. Naughton, Barry, and Susan Shirk, "China Policy and the American Presidency," in *Sinica*, podcast, edited by Kaiser Kuo, SupChina, Brooklyn, aired February 6, 2020, https://supchina.com/podcast/china-policy-and-the-american-presidency/ [retrieved April 4, 2022].

3. "To Understand Today's China, One Must Understand the Chinese Communist Party," http://www.qstheory.cn/qshyjx/2021-12/03/c_1128127015.htm [retrieved on January 22, 2022].

4. "Mao Zedong in the Eyes of Xi Jinping," http://dangjian.com/gcsy/djxx /201701/t20170105_3991430.shtml [retrieved on January 29, 2022].

5. The Wolf Warrior style is concentrated in Chinese diplomats. See Martin, Peter, *China's Civilian Army: The Making of Wolf Warrior Diplomacy* (Oxford: Oxford University Press, 2021). For communist countries and many other countries around the world, foreign affairs are reflections of their domestic issues. The tough Wolf Warrior style is related to the CCP-government's intention to contain the threat of the capitalist world.

6. "Xi Jinping: Speech at the Celebration of the Centenary of the Founding of the Chinese Communist Party," http://www.gov.cn/xinwen/2021-07/01/content _5621847.htm [retrieved on July 10, 2021].

7. Gao Hua [高华], 红太阳是怎样升起的——延安整风运动的来龙去脉 / *How the Red Sun Rises: The Origin of Yan'an Rectification Movement* (Hong Kong: Chinese University of Hong Kong Press, 2000).

8. Levine, Marilyn A., *The Found Generation: Chinese Communists in Europe during the Twenties* (Seattle: University of Washington Press, 2017). Many CCP leaders, such as Deng Xiaoping, were involved in this program.

9. The anniversary was then moved to July 1 since Mao had misremembered the actual date of the first meeting of the CCP. He remembered it as a day in July, and for convenience, when it settled in Shaanxi Province, the CCP celebrated its anniversary on July 1. Later, some CCP members investigated the founding and discovered the exact date.

10. Many communist leaders used aliases in case authorities arrested them. Mao Zedong also went by Li Desheng, Yang Ziren, and twenty-four less-known aliases.

11. "How Mao Zedong Broke 'Marxism-Leninism Cannot Come out from the Poor Ravines,'" http://www.zgdsw.com/mobile/newsx.asp?id=572 [retrieved on October 2, 2021].

12. See the recent confusion at Yeung, Jessica, "US Lawmakers Want to Stop Calling Xi Jinping a President. But Will He Care?," https://www.cnn.com/2020/09 /08/asia/xi-jinping-title-us-bill-intl-dst-hnk/index.html.

13. Dwivedi, G. G., "An Expert Explains: The PLA and Its Relationship with China's Communist Party," https://indianexpress.com/article/explained/peoples -liberation-army-communist-party-of-china-6562035/ [retrieved on October 16, 2021].

14. "CPC 'Commands the Gun,' Says Xi as He Asks Chinese Military to Expedite Modernisation Process," https://economictimes.indiatimes.com/news/defence/cpc -commands-the-gun-says-xi-as-he-asks-chinese-military-to-expedite -modernisation-process/articleshow/84924462.cms?from=mdr [retrieved on October 16, 2021].

15. Gao, *How the Red Sun Rises*.

16. Engels, Friedrich, *Anti-Dühring/Herr Eugen Dühring's Revolution in Science* (Beijing: Foreign Language Press, 1878/1976), 158.

17. Some authors questioned Mao's self-taught communism—e.g., Schwartz, Benjamin, "On the 'Originality' of Mao Tse-Tung," https://www.foreignaffairs.com /articles/china/1955-10-01/originality-mao-tse-tung [retrieved on July 1, 2021].

18. Maddison Historical Statistics, GDP data, https://www.rug.nl/ggdc /historicaldevelopment/maddison/ [retrieved on July 1, 2021].

19. Before the Qin dynasty, the central government was relatively weak, and the entity was called a kingdom. Hence, the head of the government was called the king. After the Qin dynasty, the central government became strong, and China entered the imperial era.

20. Dubuisson, Daniel, *The Western Construction of Religion: Myths, Knowledge, and Ideology* (Baltimore: Johns Hopkins University Press, 2007).

21. Harris, Nigel, *The Mandate of Heaven: Marx and Mao in Modern China* (Chicago: Haymarket Books, 2015); Zhao, Dingxin, "The Mandate of Heaven and Performance Legitimation in Historical and Contemporary China," *American Behavioral Scientist* 53, no. 3 (2009): 416–33.

22. Chen, Qiang, "Climate Shocks, Dynastic Cycles and Nomadic Conquests: Evidence from Historical China," *Oxford Economic Papers* 67, no. 2 (2014): 185–204; Chu, C. Y. Cyrus, and Ronald D. Lee, "Famine, Revolt, and the Dynastic Cycle," *Journal of Population Economics* 7, no. 4 (1994): 351–78; Fan, Ka-wai, "Climatic Change and Dynastic Cycles in Chinese History: A Review Essay," *Climatic Change* 101, no. 3 (2010): 565–73.

23. "How Much Money Did the Four Big Families Grab? Japanese Spy: US$20 Million, Ma Yinchu: Can't Say," https://kknews.cc/zh-my/history/9vokx6l.html [retrieved on April 23, 2022]; "To What Extent Was the Government of the Republic of China 'Corrupted' during the Anti-Japanese War?," https://history.sohu.com /20171105/n521533846.shtml [retrieved on October 2, 2021].

24. Zhang, Jiakang, "Chongqing Peace Talks—Mao Zedong and Chiang Kai-shek's Face-to-Face Contest," http://cpc.people.com.cn/GB/64162/64172/85037 /85038/7055791.html [retrieved on April 23, 2022]; "Greet a Bright Future in a Historic Choice: How Did the Chinese Communist Party Turn Crises into Opportunities to Win the War of Liberation," https://www.shou.org.cn/bwcx/2020/0811 /c8348a68654/page.htm [retrieved on July 12, 2021].

25. "Patio Spring Snow," https://www.shicimingju.com/chaxun/list/48905.html [retrieved on April 23, 2022].

26. Chinese typically would deem Genghis Khan a monarch of China.

27. Freeman, Chase W., "Mao Zedong: Nationalist in Spite of Himself," https:// mepc.org/speeches/mao-zedong-nationalist-spite-himself [retrieved on April 4, 2022]; "'Patio Spring Snow' Alarmed Chiang Kai-shek, So a Well-Planned Cultural Encirclement and Suppression Began," https://www.163.com/dy/article/G3JPHKEQ 0542OQ8T.html [retrieved on July 1, 2021].

28. Based on various papers, books, and other resources. We elaborated these characteristics in an "ideal-typical" way, presenting a pure model to better contrast the two ideologies, although as usual, reality diverges from theory—e.g., govern-

ments in capitalist countries may also intervene in their markets like Franklin D. Roosevelt's New Deal.

29. "Resolutions on Several Historical Issues of the Party since the Founding of the People's Republic of China," http://www.people.com.cn/item/20years/newfiles/b1040.html [retrieved on April 23, 2022]; "Maoism," http://www.xinhuanet.com/politics/yj18d/mzdsx.htm [retrieved on April 23, 2022]; "Eternal Monument • Red Memory: The Scientific System of Mao Zedong Thought (Part 1)," http://www.gov.cn/test/2007-09/06/content_739169.htm [retrieved on April 23, 2022]; "Eternal Monument • Red Memory: The Scientific System of Mao Zedong Thought (Part 2)," http://www.gov.cn/test/2007-09/06/content_739161.htm [retrieved on April 23, 2022]; "The Central Committee of the Chinese Communist Party and the State Council Issued the 'Opinions on Strengthening and Improving Ideological and Political Work in the New Era,'" http://www.gov.cn/zhengce/2021-07/12/content_5624392.htm [retrieved on July 23, 2021]. These three major aspects have six major applications. The first concerns approaches for communist revolutions in China, which Mao developed based on the special characteristics of China and focused on mobilizing farmers, who constitute the majority of Chinese people. The second concerns socialist institutions and construction, such as the frugality principle and the politically centralized and economically decentralized structure. The third application concerns military strategies, which many Chinese entrepreneurs adopt. The fourth application concerns policy for socialist institutions, including agricultural collectivization during the Great Leap Forward, class struggle during the Cultural Revolution, and industrial relocation during the Third Front Construction. The principle that ideological and political work should adhere to the CCP ideology and serve the people or popular masses is the fifth application, which concerns the ideological environment. The sixth application is the construction of communism and management of the CCP, including the principle of responding to the CCP's call and adhering to key rules such as serve the people, closely connect to the popular masses, work hard, be frugal, and resist erosion by capitalist thoughts.

30. "CCP Member: Today in History," https://news.ruc.edu.cn/archives/320670 [retrieved on April 23, 2022].

31. Quoted on pages 159, 166 of Mao, Zedong, *Quotations from Chairman Mao Zedong* [in Chinese] (Beijing, China: People's Liberation Army General Political Department, 1966).

32. Mao, Tse-tung, *Quotations from Chairman Mao Tse-Tung* (Worcestershire, UK: Read Books, 2013).

33. Mao, *Quotations from Chairman Mao Zedong*, 160–61.

34. Mao, *Quotations from Chairman Mao Zedong*, 160.

35. "The Essence and Characteristics of Mao Zedong's Mass Line Thought," http://theory.people.com.cn/n/2013/1225/c40531-23946088.html [retrieved on February 1, 2022].

36. Mao, Zedong [毛泽东], 毛泽东军事文集 / *Collected Works on Military by Mao Zedong* [in Chinese], vols. 1–6 (Beijing: Military Science Press/Central Party Literature Press, 1927–1972); Mao, Zedong [毛泽东], 毛泽东选集 (第四卷) / *Selected Works of Mao Tse-Tung* [in Chinese], vol. 4 (Beijing: People's Press [人民出版社], 1960). See also summaries such as "Mao Zedong Military Thought," http://www

.cdsndu.org/html_ch/to_articleContent_article.id=8a28e6d84a9a04ff014a9b359d a60228.html [retrieved on July 24, 2021].

37. "The Basic Characteristics of Mao Zedong's Military Thought," https://www .1921.org.cn/chapter.html?id=5a9535be947f3212c37b3c24&c=53 [retrieved on February 1, 2022].

38. Most countries use the Gregorian calendar, whereas Russia uses the Julian calendar, the former being fourteen days ahead of the latter. So the October Revolution took place on November 7, 1917 (Gregorian calendar) or October 25, 1917 (Julian calendar). Meanwhile, according to more recently disclosed documents and published books, Mao's true benchmark might be the Soviet Union, as he wanted to replace Khrushchev and the Soviet Union as the leader of the global communist camp. See, for example, Shen, Zhihua [沈志华], 中苏关系史纲 / A Brief History of Sino-Soviet Relations [in Chinese] (Beijing: Social Science Academic Press [社会科 学文献出版社], 2016).

39. Meng, Xin, Nancy Qian, and Pierre Yared, "The Institutional Causes of China's Great Famine, 1959–1961," *Review of Economic Studies* 82, no. 4 (2015): 1568–611.

40. "Resolutions on Several Historical Issues of the Party since the Founding of the People's Republic of China," https://news.sina.com.cn/c/nd/2016-05-16/doc -ifxsenvn7202369.shtml [retrieved on July 12, 2021].

41. At that time, there were three main options for youths: going to college and becoming a Worker-Peasant-Soldier student, joining the military, and going to the countryside and becoming a sent-down youth. Only very few could go to college or join the military, typically youths whose parents were high-ranking officials or who performed very well in the send-down movement. For example, Xi Jinping was first sent down when his father lost power. Then, because of his relatively good performance and his father's regained power, he became a Worker-Peasant-Soldier student in Tsinghua University.

42. Shen, *Brief History*.

43. Niu, Jun, "Reevaluation of the U.S.-China Relationship in the 1960s," http://cn3.uscnpm.org/model_item.html?action=view&table=article&id=20364 [retrieved on July 1, 2021].

44. Xia, Fei, "Third Front Construction: A Major Strategic Decision of Mao Zedong," http://cpc.people.com.cn/GB/85037/8627645.html [retrieved on July 1, 2021].

45. Fan, Jingting, and Ben Zou, "Industrialization from Scratch: The 'Construction of the Third Front' and Local Economic Development in China's Hinterland," *Journal of Development Economics* 152 (2021): 102698.

46. Xu, Chenggang, "The Fundamental Institutions of China's Reforms and Development," *Journal of Economic Literature* 49, no. 4 (2011): 1076–151. We also are familiar with economists' approach to measuring (fiscal) decentralization with the share of fiscal revenue to be distributed to the central and local governments. The rationale is that if the local government retains more revenue, then there is indication of decentralization. Then, looking historically, the trend of decentralization had gained momentum since 1958 and particularly from 1970 to 1993 when the central and provincial governments retained 20 percent and 80 percent of fiscal revenues, respectively, indicating decentralization. However, we believe a better measure of decentral-

ization accounts for the deep structural relations between the central and provincial governments rather than temporary distribution of fiscal revenue between these two levels of government, which are subject to negotiations. For example, the fact that local political leaders (party secretaries) appoint their bureau leaders clearly indicates a decentralized structure. See, for example, "Changes in the Relationship between the Central and Local Governments in the Mao Zedong Era," http://theory.people.com .cn/n/2014/0825/c388253-25532921.html [retrieved on October 2, 2021]; Guan, Hanhui [管汉晖], "The Financial Relations between the Central and Local Governments in China since the Qin and Han Dynasties," *Economic Sciences* [in Chinese] 5, no. 4 (2017): 109–24; Chen, Ye, Hongbin Li, and Li-An Zhou, "Relative Performance Evaluation and the Turnover of Provincial Leaders in China," *Economics Letters* 88, no. 3 (2005): 421–25; Li, Hongbin, and Li-An Zhou, "Political Turnover and Economic Performance: The Incentive Role of Personnel Control in China," *Journal of Public Economics* 89, no. 9 (2005): 1743–62; and Jin, Hehui, Yingyi Qian, and Barry R. Weingast, "Regional Decentralization and Fiscal Incentives: Federalism, Chinese Style," *Journal of Public Economics* 89, no. 9 (2005): 1719–42.

47. Montinola, Gabriella, Yingyi Qian, and Barry R. Weingast, "Federalism, Chinese Style: The Political Basis for Economic Success in China," *World Politics* 48, no. 1 (1995): 50–81; Qian, Yingyi, Gérard Roland, and Chenggang Xu, "Why Is China Different from Eastern Europe? Perspectives from Organization Theory," *European Economic Review* 43, no. 4 (1999): 1085–94; Qian, Yingyi, and Chenggang Xu, "The M-Form Hierarchy and China's Economic Reform," *European Economic Review* 37, no. 2 (1993): 541–48.

48. Freedman, Josh, "China Takes Federalism Way Further Than the US, and Is Paying the Price for It," https://www.vox.com/2015/8/31/9228723/china-safety-net -inequality [retrieved on July 1, 2021]; Montinola, Qian, and Weingast, "Federalism, Chinese Style."

49. Mao, Zedong, "On Ten Major Relationships," April 25, 1956, https://www .marxists.org/chinese/maozedong/marxist.org-chinese-mao-19560425.htm [retrieved on August 7, 2021].

50. "Xi Jinping: We Should Not Simply Use GDP to Determine Heroes," http:// www.xinhuanet.com//world/2013-10/07/c_117609149.htm [retrieved on June 24, 2021].

51. Kelly, Jason M., *Market Maoists: The Communist Origins of China's Capitalist Ascent* (Cambridge, MA: Harvard University Press, 2021).

52. "What Does a Communist Party Branch Mean to Private Firms?," http:// www.fgdjw.gov.cn/fgdjw/system/2014/02/20/017702760.shtml [retrieved on April 23, 2022]; "Why Should Private Firms Strengthen the Communist Party Influence?," http://politics.people.com.cn/n1/2019/1015/c429373-31400444.html [retrieved on June 24, 2021].

CHAPTER 2: MAO'S LASTING INFLUENCE ON CHINA

Epigraphs: "Zhengfei Ren of Huawei: My Mentor Is Mao Zedong," https://zhuanlan .zhihu.com/p/67175095 [retrieved on July 1, 2021]; Tang Shuangning, "The Useful Enlightenment of Mao Zedong's Way of Thinking to My Financial Work," http://

fgw.hunan.gov.cn/tslm_77952/hgzh/201312/t20131217_2893634.html [retrieved on August 27, 2021].

1. "What Is the Main Content of Deng Xiaoping Theory System?," http://fuwu .12371.cn/2012/06/18/ARTI1340016571673537.shtml [retrieved on July 25, 2021].

2. "Jiang Zemin's Speech at the Meeting Celebrating the 80th Anniversary of the Founding of the Chinese Communist Party," http://www.china-un.ch/eng/zgbd /smwx/t85789.htm [retrieved on July 25, 2021].

3. Leng, Rong, "Fully Understand the Historical Status and Guiding Significance of the Scientific Outlook on Development," https://theory.gmw.cn/2018-10 /23/content_31806865.htm [retrieved on July 10, 2021].

4. For example, see Blanchette, Jude, *China's New Red Guards: The Return of Radicalism and the Rebirth of Mao Zedong* (Oxford: Oxford University Press, 2019); and "Xi Jinping Traced Political Roots and Tried the Red Flag Based on Mao Zedong," https://www.dw.com/zh/%E4%B9%A0%E8%BF%91%E5%B9%B3% E6%94%BF%E6%B2%BB%E5%AF%BB%E6%A0%B9%E7%A5%AD%E5 %87%BA%E6%AF%9B%E6%B3%BD%E4%B8%9C%E7%BA%A2%E8%8 9%B2%E5%A4%A7%E6%97%97/a-16953110 [retrieved on July 1, 2021].

5. See, for example, Cable, Vince, "Is China a Capitalist or Communist Country?," https://www.futurelearn.com/info/courses/politics-of-economics/0/steps/30823 [retrieved on July 1, 2021]. Such a broad-brush perception emerges from time to time in both academia and industry. For example, during the review process of one of our papers, several reviewers questioned us about the communist values of a certain group of entrepreneurs; they thought that all Chinese have communist values and there would be no variation among them in this regard.

6. The CCP membership data are from "Up to Date! The Total Number of Members of the Chinese Communist Party Is 95.148 Million," https://web.archive .org/web/20210630033240/https://mp.weixin.qq.com/s/CVmzqS1to5VuCBGoujc-lYA [retrieved on July 12, 2021]; and the Chinese population data are from the Seventh National Population Census of the People's Republic of China. http:// www.stats.gov.cn/tjsj/zxfb/202105/t20210510_1817176.html [retrieved on April 23, 2022].

7. Heim, Christine, and Elisabeth B. Binder, "Current Research Trends in Early Life Stress and Depression: Review of Human Studies on Sensitive Periods, Gene–Environment Interactions, and Epigenetics," *Experimental Neurology* 233, no. 1 (2012): 102–11; Greenberg, Mark T., Roger P. Weissberg, Mary Utne O'Brien, Joseph E. Zins, Linda Fredericks, Hank Resnik, and Maurice J. Elias, "Enhancing School-Based Prevention and Youth Development through Coordinated Social, Emotional, and Academic Learning," *American Psychologist* 58, no. 6–7 (2003): 466–74; Turnbull, Ann P., *Exceptional Lives: Special Education in Today's Schools* (Old Tappan, NJ: ERIC, 1995); Droit-Volet, Sylvie, Angélique Clément, and John Wearden, "Temporal Generalization in 3- to 8-Year-Old Children," *Journal of Experimental Child Psychology* 80, no. 3 (2001): 271–88.

8. Bredekamp, Sue, *Developmentally Appropriate Practice* (Washington, DC: ERIC, 1986); Bogard, Kimber, and Ruby Takanishi, "Pk-3: An Aligned and Coordinated Approach to Education for Children 3 to 8 Years Old," *Social Policy*

Report 19, no. 3 (2005): 1–24; Arnett, Jeffrey Jensen, "Emerging Adulthood: A Theory of Development from the Late Teens through the Twenties," *American Psychologist* 55, no. 5 (2000): 469–80; Arnett, Jeffrey Jensen, and Jennifer Lynn Tanner, "The Emergence of Emerging Adulthood: The New Life Stage between Adolescence and Young Adulthood," in *Routledge Handbook of Youth and Young Adulthood,* edited by Andy Furlong, 50–56 (London: Routledge, 2016).

9. Cunha, Flavio, and James J. Heckman, "The Technology of Skill Formation," *American Economic Review* 97, no. 2 (2007): 31–47; Cunha, Flavio, James J. Heckman, Lance Lochner, and Dimitriy V. Masterov, "Interpreting the Evidence on Life Cycle Skill Formation," in *Handbook of the Economics of Education,* vol. 1, edited by E. Hanushek and F. Welch, 697–812 (Amsterdam: Elsevier, 2005); Luby, Joan L., Andy Belden, Michael P. Harms, Rebecca Tillman, and Deanna M. Barch, "Preschool Is a Sensitive Period for the Influence of Maternal Support on the Trajectory of Hippocampal Development," *Proceedings of the National Academy of Sciences* 113, no. 20 (2016): 5742–47; Lupien, Sonia J., Sophie Parent, Alan C. Evans, Richard E. Tremblay, Philip David Zelazo, Vincent Corbo, Jens C. Pruessner, and Jean R. Séguin, "Larger Amygdala but No Change in Hippocampal Volume in 10-Year-Old Children Exposed to Maternal Depressive Symptomatology since Birth," *Proceedings of the National Academy of Sciences* 108, no. 34 (2011): 14324–29; Penhune, Virginia B., "Sensitive Periods in Human Development: Evidence from Musical Training," *Cortex* 47, no. 9 (2011): 1126–37.

10. Arnett, Jeffrey J., Rita Žukauskienė, and Kazumi Sugimura, "The New Life Stage of Emerging Adulthood at Ages 18–29 Years: Implications for Mental Health," *Lancet Psychiatry* 1, no. 7 (2014): 569–76; Nelson, Larry, Sarah Badger, and Bo Wu, "The Influence of Culture in Emerging Adulthood: Perspectives of Chinese College Students," *International Journal of Behavioral Development* 28, no. 1 (2004): 26–36; Nelson, Larry J., Xin xing Duan, Laura M. Padilla-Walker, and Stephanie S. Luster, "Facing Adulthood: Comparing the Criteria That Chinese Emerging Adults and Their Parents Have for Adulthood," *Journal of Adolescent Research* 28, no. 2 (2013): 189–208.

11. Malmendier, Ulrike, and Stefan Nagel, "Depression Babies: Do Macroeconomic Experiences Affect Risk Taking?," *Quarterly Journal of Economics* 126, no. 1 (2011): 373–416; Giuliano, Paola, and Antonio Spilimbergo, "Growing Up in a Recession," *Review of Economic Studies* 81, no. 2 (2014): 787–817.

12. Marquis, Christopher, and Kunyuan Qiao, "Communist Ideological Imprinting and Internationalization: A Study of Chinese Entrepreneurs," paper presented at the Academy of Management Proceedings, Atlanta, GA, 2017; Marquis, Christopher, and Kunyuan Qiao, "What Does Not Starve You Makes You More Economical: A Study of Resource Scarcity Imprint of Chinese Entrepreneurs," paper presented at the Academy of Management, Chicago, IL, 2018; Marquis, Christopher, and Kunyuan Qiao, "Waking from Mao's Dream: Communist Ideological Imprinting and the Internationalization of Entrepreneurial Ventures in China," *Administrative Science Quarterly* 65, no. 3 (2020): 795–830; Marquis, Christopher, Kunyuan Qiao, M. Diane Burton, Ryan Allen, Santiago Campero Molina, Prithwiraj Choudhury, and Aleksandra Joanna Kacperczyk, "Individual Imprinting: Life History Matters," *Academy of Management Proceedings* 2018, no. 1 (2018): 14868.

13. "Zhengfei Ren of Huawei: My Mentor Is Mao Zedong," https://zhuanlan
.zhihu.com/p/67175095 [retrieved on July 1, 2021].

14. See a summary of Chinese entrepreneurs' Maoist imprint at "Entrepreneurs
under the Influence of *Selected Works of Mao Zedong,*" https://zhuanlan.zhihu.com
/p/146592060 [retrieved on July 1, 2021].

15. "Entrepreneurs under the Influence."

16. "Put an End to These Communist Stereotypes," https://www.scmp.com
/article/567365/put-end-these-communist-stereotypes [retrieved on July 1, 2021].

17. This might reflect the traditional thinking that offspring of a criminal might
hate the regime and thus develop into criminals. Hence, in the ancient period, the
Chinese government would kill all family members of some felons (metaphorically
"chopping the weeds and eradicating their roots"). Those whose ancestors supported the CCP or who are members of the social classes (e.g., poor farmers) that
the CCP thinks reliable are called "integrity in its red roots and red in its seedling"
and are seen as reliable by the CCP.

18. "Xi Jinping's Firm but Tortuous Road to CCP," https://china.huanqiu.com
/article/9CaKrnK9Yvp [retrieved on July 1, 2021].

19. Emphasis might differ depending on when they go through the process, as the
CCP keeps adding the thoughts of new leaders. For example, if they went through
the process before Mao's death, the focus would have been Maoism; if they went
through the process more recently, Xi's thoughts would have been the main focus.

20. "Mao Announced in 1949 That Chinese People Now Stand Up with Dignity," http://news.sina.com.cn/c/sd/2009-09-23/095218709329.shtml [retrieved on
July 1, 2021].

21. Blanchette, *China's New Red Guards,* 36.

22. Wong, Chun Han, and Keith Zhai, "China Repackages Its History in Support of Xi's National Vision," https://www.wsj.com/articles/china-repackages-history
-xi-propaganda-communist-party-centenary-11623767590 [retrieved on July 13,
2021].

23. Marquis and Qiao, "Waking from Mao's Dream."

24. "Promoting Entrepreneurial Spirit, Listen to and Closely Follow CCP: On
the Celebration Event of the Seventy-Ninth Birthday of CCP by Association of
Female Entrepreneurs in Beijing," http://beijing.qianlong.com/2018/0706/2682705
.shtml [retrieved on July 1, 2021].

25. "General Secretary Xi Jinping Leads the Politburo Standing Committee
Members to Revisit the Party Oath," http://www.xinhuanet.com//politics/2017-10
/31/c_1121886075.htm [retrieved on July 25, 2021].

26. "Path of Entrepreneurship and Innovation of a Communist Entrepreneur—
Cui Genliang, Party Secretary and Chairman of Hengtong Group," http://dangjian
.people.com.cn/n1/2016/0509/c117092-28336175.html [retrieved on April 23,
2022].

27. "Path of Entrepreneurship and Innovation of a Communist Entrepreneur—
Cui Genliang, Party Secretary and Chairman of Hengtong Group"; "Build a Strong
Party to Make the Enterprise Stronger—Cui Genliang, Secretary of the Party Committee and Chairman of Jiangsu Hengtong Group," https://www.ccdi.gov.cn/lswh
/renwu/201604/t20160428_120623.html [retrieved on July 1, 2021].

28. Paine, Thomas, *Common Sense* (Philadelphia: Printed and Sold by R. BELLin Third Street, 1776); Chandler, Alfred Dupont, and Bruce Mazlish, *Leviathans: Multinational Corporations and the New Global History* (Cambridge: Cambridge University Press, 2005); Hobbes, Thomas, *Leviathan* (Oxford: Basil Blackwell, 1651/1947).

29. We will elaborate this idea further later; briefly, the Chinese culture has a strong tradition of "the spirit of shidafu (士大夫)," which emphasizes a sense of national pride and service to the nation.

30. Of course, this obedience is not unconditional, as there have been dynastic transitions and also uprisings such as the Taiping Rebellion. As we elaborated in the last chapter, the central government's legitimacy rests on the Mandate of Heaven, and people have the right to rebel. See Dingxin Zhao's recent work on how China came into being as a unified state after highly intensive wars: Zhao, Dingxin, *Eastern Zhou China Warfare and the Formation of the Confucian-Legalist State* (Shanghai: Sanlian, 2006); Zhao, Dingxin, *The Confucian-Legalist State: A New Theory for Chinese History* (New York: Oxford University Press, 2015); Zhao, Dingxin, *State and War: A Comparative Analysis of the Chinese and European Historical Development* (Hangzhou, China: Zhejiang University Press, 2015).

31. Quoted in Li, Xu-Hong, and Xiaoya Liang, "A Confucian Social Model of Political Appointments among Chinese Private-Firm Entrepreneurs," *Academy of Management Journal* 58, no. 2 (2015): 592.

32. Zhang, Jianjun, Christopher Marquis, and Kunyuan Qiao, "Do Political Connections Buffer Firms from or Bind Firms to the Government? A Study of Corporate Charitable Donations of Chinese Firms," *Organization Science* 27, no. 5 (2016): 1307–24; Ma, Dali, and William L. Parish, "Tocquevillian Moments: Charitable Contributions by Chinese Private Entrepreneurs," *Social Forces* 85, no. 2 (2006): 943–64.

33. "Over the Entire Chinese History, Who Do You Think Is the Greatest Person?" https://zhuanlan.zhihu.com/p/37413998 [retrieved on July 1, 2021].

34. Peony Hirwani, "Jackie Chan Says He Wants to Join the Ruling Communist Party of China," https://www.independent.co.uk/arts-entertainment/films/news/jackie -chan-communist-party-china-b1882991.html [retrieved on April 5, 2022].

35. "Chinese Gold Medalists Face Investigation over Mao Badges," https://www .bbc.com/news/world-asia-china-58075743 [retrieved on August 25, 2021]; Bishop, Bill, "Badges of Chairman Mao Zedong," Master's thesis, Johns Hopkins University, 1996, http://museums.cnd.org/CR/old/maobadge/ [retrieved on April 23, 2022].

36. "Off Track . . . Chairman Mao Badge Was Lin's Lucky Charm," http://www .chinadaily.com.cn/cndy/2008-08/19/content_6948348.htm [retrieved on August 25, 2021].

37. Long, Qiao, "China's Maoists Mark Death of Great Helmsman with Tributes, Street Events," https://www.rfa.org/english/news/china/mao-death-09082021080836 .html [retrieved on September 28, 2021].

38. "Relive the History of Revolution and Inherit the Red Gene," https://article .xuexi.cn/articles/index.html?art_id=17623575101621910565&item_id=1762357 5101621910565 [retrieved on July 1, 2021].

39. Hua, Shen, "Starting from the Baby: The CCP Strives to Ensure the 'Red Gene' Is Passed on from Generation to Generation," https://www.voachinese.com /a/CCP-brainwashing-youth-20201104/5647976.html [retrieved on July 1, 2021].

40. Before 1978, high school students had to be vetted for political loyalty before they were eligible to enter college—hence, good performance in political courses was critical in that period. Even the granddaughter of Sun Yat-sen, Sun Huifang, could not enter college because she failed the political review. Deng Xiaoping suspended it in 1978, yet in 2018, it was reinstituted. See Zheng, Qingjun, "The Cultural Revolution Ended for 40 Years, Yet the Political Review Came Back," https://bnn.co/news/gb/pubvp/2018/11/201811090431.shtml [retrieved on July 1, 2021].

41. Cantoni, Davide, Yuyu Chen, David Y. Yang, Noam Yuchtman, and Y. Jane Zhang, "Curriculum and Ideology," *Journal of Political Economy* 125, no. 2 (2017): 338–92.

42. "The Ministry of Education Held a Press Conference on the Measures for Educational Supervision and Accountability," http://www.scio.gov.cn/m/xwfbh /gbwxwfbh/xwfbh/jyb/Document/1711681/1711681.htm [retrieved on September 28, 2021].

43. Hsia, Hsiao-hwa, "China's Top Universities Get Poor Grades for Party Propaganda," https://www.rfa.org/english/news/china/grades-09072021134539.html; Zheng, William, "China's Top Universities Told to Stop Slacking Off on Communist Party Ideology," https://www.scmp.com/news/china/politics/article/3147779 /chinas-top-universities-told-stop-slacking-communist-party [retrieved on September 28, 2021].

44. Feng, Jiayun, "Why There Are So Few Women in Chinese Politics," https:// supchina.com/2021/07/01/why-there-are-so-few-women-in-chinese-politics/ [retrieved on July 12, 2021].

45. Hoonhout, Tobias, "Biden Quotes Mao Zedong to Explain Kamala Harris Pick," https://www.yahoo.com/now/biden-quotes-mao-zedong-explain-132820570 .html [retrieved on July 1, 2021].

46. "Foreign Media: Chinese Private Entrepreneurs Take Party History Class to Learn and Follow the Party Together," https://www.6parknews.com/newspark/view .php?app=news&act=view&nid=511916 [retrieved on April 23, 2022]; "The First Session of the Seminar on 'Not Forgetting the Original Intention and Remembering the Mission' for Communist Entrepreneurs Started," http://www.sh.chinanews .com.cn/dangjian/2019-10-24/65170.shtml [retrieved on January 24, 2022].

47. "'Teenage Mao Zedong' Micro-film Released, Initiating the 'First Summer Lesson' of the CCP History Study and Education for the Youth," http://www.hunan .gov.cn/topic/fdbnlqhxzc/bsskxjsz/202107/t20210711_19893511.html [retrieved on July 26, 2021].

48. "Watch Movies and Learn Party History! Have You Seen These Movies?," https://www.thepaper.cn/newsDetail_forward_11779151 [retrieved on July 26, 2021].

49. "China Film Bureau Launches Party Celebration Film Festival, at Least Two Red Films Are Shown in Each Theater Every Week," https://www.rfa.org/mandarin /yataibaodao/meiti/ql1-04062021044330.html [retrieved on July 26, 2021].

50. "Launch of the Theme 'Learning Party History, Celebrating One Hundred Years-2021 My Movie Party Class,'" http://sh.xinhuanet.com/2021-05/01/c_139918496.htm [retrieved on July 26, 2021].

51. "Watching Movies, Learning the CCP History," http://dangshi.people.com.cn/n1/2021/0625/c436975-32140983.html [retrieved on July 26, 2021].

52. "List of National Red Tourism Classic Scenic Spots Announced, 300 Scenic Spots Selected," http://www.xinhuanet.com/politics/2016-12/29/c_1120214541.htm [retrieved on April 23, 2022]; "Red Tourism: How to Exploit the Cultural Connotation of Red Gene," http://www.qstheory.cn/llwx/2019-07/07/c_1124720244.htm [retrieved on July 1, 2021].

53. "During the 'May 1st' Holiday, Red Tourism Booms All Over the Country—Remember the History of the Revolution, Inherit the Red Gene," http://society.people.com.cn/n1/2021/0505/c1008-32094620.html [retrieved on July 1, 2021].

54. Mahoney, James, *The Legacies of Liberalism: Path Dependence and Political Regimes in Central America* (Baltimore: Johns Hopkins University Press, 2001).

55. Rowen, Herbert H., "'L'état c'est à moi': Louis XIV and the State," *French Historical Studies* 2, no. 1 (1961): 83–98.

56. Meacham, Jon, *American Gospel: God, the Founding Fathers, and the Making of a Nation* (New York: Random House, 2007).

57. Tumarkin, Nina, *Lenin Lives! The Lenin Cult in Soviet Russia* (Cambridge, MA: Harvard University Press, 1997).

58. Hasou, Tawfig Y., *The Struggle for the Arab World: Egypt's Nasser and the Arab League* (Oxfordshire, UK: Routledge, 1985).

59. Raynard, Mia, Michael Lounsbury, and Royston Greenwood, "Legacies of Logics: Sources of Community Variation in CSR Implementation in China," in *Research in the Sociology of Organizations,* edited by Michael Lounsbury and Eva Boxenbaum, 243–76 (Bingley, West Yorkshire, UK: Emerald Group, 2013).

60. As we mentioned earlier, Mao and the CCP were not totally antagonistic toward capitalist forces; rather, they wanted to control these forces for their own benefit. See Kelly, Jason M., *Market Maoists: The Communist Origins of China's Capitalist Ascent* (Cambridge, MA: Harvard University Press, 2021).

61. Talk of Deng Xiaoping's South Tour (full text), http://news.12371.cn/2016/01/21/ARTI1453342674674143.shtml [retrieved on July 1, 2021].

62. Efron, Sonni, "Profile: A Reformist Alternative to Yeltsin: Economist Grigory Yavlinsky, the Liberals' Choice, Outpolls the Russian Leader in Popularity," https://www.latimes.com/archives/la-xpm-1993-10-12-wr-45027-story.html [retrieved on July 1, 2021].

63. Zubok, Vladislav M., *A Failed Empire: The Soviet Union in the Cold War from Stalin to Gorbachev* (Chapel Hill: University of North Carolina Press, 2009).

64. Kushner, Tony, *Angels in America, Part 2: Perestroika* (New York: Theatre Communications Group, 1991), 138.

65. Henderson, Jane, "Making a Drama Out of a Crisis: The Russian Constitutional Court and the Case of the Communist Party of the Soviet Union," *King's Law Journal* 19, no. 3 (2008): 489–506, quote on page 490; Tumarkin, *Lenin Lives!*

66. See Doshi, Rush, *The Long Game: China's Grand Strategy to Displace American Order* (Oxford: Oxford University Press, 2021). He also suggests that

Nazi Germany had a grand strategy with a nationalist focus and used the Leninist approach of state investment to quickly recover the German economy. Deng also warned about the issues of Gorbachev's reforms. See "The Major Change in the Soviet Union and Eastern Europe: Listen to What Xiaoping Said!," http://fenke .gzxjw.org.cn/fenke/makesizhuyi/maxxxd/1387.shtml [retrieved on August 25, 2021].

67. Weber, Isabella M., *How China Escaped Shock Therapy: The Market Reform Debate* (Oxfordshire, UK: Routledge, 2021). We focus more on structural factors than Weber, suggesting that in addition to the rhetorical strategy that the CCP adopted (discussed in the next section), its socialist institutions, which better enabled reforms region by region, are also important. In the conclusion we also discuss cultural factors.

68. Xu, Dean, Jane W. Lu, and Qian Gu, "Organizational Forms and Multi-population Dynamics: Economic Transition in China," *Administrative Science Quarterly* 59, no. 3 (2014): 517–47.

69. Chernyaev, Anatoly Sergeevich, *My Six Years with Gorbachev,* edited by Robert English and Elizabeth Tucker (University Park: Pennsylvania State University Press, 2012). See also Ma, Xiaoming, "Scholars on Soviet Union Talked about the Impact of the 20th Congress of the Communist Party of the Soviet Union on People in 1960s," http://dangshi.people.com.cn/n/2013/0809/c367826-22509236 .html [retrieved on July 1, 2021].

70. "Mao Zedong Has Made Three Faults and Seven Achievements, and Respecting the Founders of the Country Is China's Collective Self-Esteem," https://mil .huanqiu.com/article/9CaKrnJymmY [retrieved on July 1, 2021].

71. Weber, *How China Escaped.* The same situation occurred in the Soviet Union, where the more conservative Soviet leaders strongly opposed liberal and market-related rhetoric. As we mentioned in the foregoing section, the radical rhetoric—especially that ridiculing communism, Soviet leaders, and Soviet heroes—was also responsible for the disintegration of the USSR.

72. The careful and gradual economic liberalization is organically connected to its tight political control. For example, Deng suggested that the CCP can always stop and reverse any economic reforms—e.g., those concerning securities and the stock market—that might threaten its governance. See "The Origin of Chinese Stock Market," http://www.people.com.cn/GB/shizheng/8198/36907/36908/2731887 .html [retrieved on July 1, 2021].

73. Wu, Wei, "Door Opened and Window Closed by Deng Xiaoping," http:// www.ftchinese.com/story/001058956?archive [retrieved on July 1, 2021].

74. Marquis, Christopher, Qi Li, and Kunyuan Qiao, "The Chinese Collectivist Model of Charity," *Stanford Social Innovation Review* 15, no. 3 (2017): 40–47; Marquis and Qiao, "Waking from Mao's Dream."

75. "What Is the Difference between Privately Owned and People-Owned Enterprises," https://www.zhihu.com/question/21163786 [retrieved on July 12, 2021].

76. Blanchette, *China's New Red Guards,* 46.

77. Hua, Min, "Entrepreneurs Are Different from Capitalists," http://www .people.com.cn/GB/jingji/1045/1913158.html [retrieved on July 1, 2021].

78. Marquis and Qiao, "Waking from Mao's Dream"; Marquis, Christopher, and András Tilcsik, "Imprinting: Toward a Multilevel Theory," *Academy of Management Annals* 7, no. 1 (2013): 195–245.

79. Martin, Peter, *China's Civilian Army: The Making of Wolf Warrior Diplomacy* (Oxford: Oxford University Press, 2021).

80. Beech, Hannah, "China's Chairman Builds a Cult of Personality," https://time.com/4277504/chinas-chairman/ [retrieved on July 1, 2021].

81. "Xi Jinping: Speech at the Celebration of the Centenary of the Founding of the Chinese Communist Party," http://www.gov.cn/xinwen/2021-07-01/content_5621847.htm [retrieved on July 10, 2021].

82. The suit style originated in the West, but Sun Yat-sen (Sun Zhongshan) adapted it (creating the Zhongshan suit), and Mao adapted it again (creating the Zhongshan suit of Maoist style).

83. Blanchette, *China's New Red Guards*.

84. Wang, Shiming, and Yongyue Yu, "On the Theoretical Source and Development of Deng Xiaoping's Thought of Common Prosperity," http://cpc.people.com.cn/n/2013/1126/c69113-23659040.html [retrieved on October 15, 2021]; Xi Jinping, "Solidly Promote Common Prosperity," http://www.qstheory.cn/dukan/qs/2021-10/15/c_1127959365.htm; Vaswani, Karishma, "China Watch: How Xi Jinping's 'Common Prosperity' Will Affect the World," https://www.bbc.com/zhongwen/simp/chinese-news-58830610; Buckley, Chris Alexandra Stevenson, and Cao Li, "Warning of Income Gap, Xi Tells China's Tycoons to Share Wealth," https://www.nytimes.com/2021/09/07/world/asia/china-xi-common-prosperity.html [retrieved on October 15, 2021].

85. Martin, *China's Civilian Army*.

86. Yan, Xuetong, "Becoming Strong—the New Chinese Foreign Policy," https://www.foreignaffairs.com/articles/united-states/2021-06-22/becoming-strong [retrieved on July 11, 2021].

87. "People's Liberation Army Daily: You Must Not Eat the CCP's Meals and Smash the CCP's Pot," http://cpc.people.com.cn/n/2014/1224/c78779-26268924.html [retrieved on July 27, 2021].

88. Yuan, Li, "'Who Are Our Enemies?' China's Bitter Youths Embrace Mao," https://www.nytimes.com/2021/07/08/business/china-mao.html [retrieved on July 13, 2021].

89. For example, "*Selected Works of Mao Zedong*, vol. 1," https://book.douban.com/subject/2224879/ [retrieved on July 13, 2021]; "*Selected Works of Mao Zedong*, vol. 4," https://book.douban.com/subject/1085872/ [retrieved on July 13, 2021]; "*Selected Works of Mao Zedong*, vol. 5," https://book.douban.com/subject/1916533/ [retrieved on July 13, 2021].

90. Blanchette, *China's New Red Guards*, 10–11, 94–96.

91. See, for example, "Zhao Dingqi: The Class Issue Has Become a Race Issue. No Wonder Black Americans Cannot Find a Way Out—to discuss with Dr. Lin Yao," https://www.guancha.cn/zhaodingqi/2020_07_27_559050.shtml [retrieved on July 13, 2021]; "The Death of the Black Is a Manifestation of Increasingly Acute Class Contradictions in the United States," http://zhurengong.net/index.php?m=content&c=index&a=show&catid=3&id=8531 [retrieved on July 13, 2021].

PART II: MAO'S IDEOLOGICAL AND MILITARY PRINCIPLES
AND PRIVATE ENTERPRISE

Epigraphs: Mao, Zedong, *Quotations from Chairman Mao Zedong* [in Chinese] (Beijing, China: People's Liberation Army General Political Department, 1966), pp. 166, 161, 228–229, 181.

CHAPTER 3: NATIONALISM AND INTERNATIONALIZATION

Epigraph: Yin, Mingshan, "Embracing Globalization but We Shall Not Forget Our Nation," http://auto.sina.com.cn/news/2007-03-01/1817253661.shtml [retrieved on July 2, 2021].

1. "Looking Back on the Cultural Revolution (19): The Scam of the Send-Down Movement," https://www.voachinese.com/a/a-21-w2007-02-17-voa1-58417257/1083346.html [retrieved on July 2, 2021].

2. Mao, Yarong, "Zong Qinghou, the Founder of 'Wahaha' in 1978: From 'Active Activist in the Mountains to the Countryside' to the Head of the Beverage Empire—40 People in 40 Years," https://www.yicai.com/news/100022325.html [retrieved on August 9, 2021].

3. See Hamilton, Stewart, and Jinxuan Zhang, *Danone & Wahaha: A Bittersweet Partnership* (Lausanne, Switzerland: IMD Business Case, 2008); Krug, Barbara, and Stephen Rothlin, *Match and Mismatch: The Wahaha-Danone Dispute* (Rotterdam School of Management Business Case, 2010); "Conflict between Danone and Wahaha: The Victory That Belongs to Zong Qinghou Alone," https://zhuanlan.zhihu.com/p/56298921 [retrieved on April 23, 2022]; Yang, Mei, "The 'Divorcement' between Danone and Wahaha in Both Chinese and Western Styles," http://news.sohu.com/20070716/n251071497.shtml [retrieved on April 23, 2022].

4. "Yin Mingshan: Fighting for the Renaissance of the Chinese Nation and to Realize the Chinese Dream," http://www.zytzb.gov.cn/xzgytyzx7onxs/318220.jhtml [retrieved on July 2, 2021].

5. "The Communist Entrepreneur—Yin Mingshan Shows How to Make Profits and Political Friends in China," http://www.economist.com/node/1666584 [retrieved on July 2, 2021].

6. "The Intricate IPO of Lifan," http://www.chinatimes.net.cn/article/13023.html [retrieved on July 2, 2021].

7. "The Crisis at a Late Age for the Richest Man of Chongqing Yin Mingshan: Hundreds of Millions Chinese Yuan/Yuan/RMB Financing Freezes Equity His Family Holds," https://finance.sina.com.cn/money/cfgs/2019-06-27/doc-ihytcerk9569132.shtml [retrieved on July 2, 2021].

8. See, e.g., World Bank, "The Winners and Losers of Globalization: Finding a Path to Shared Prosperity," https://www.worldbank.org/en/news/feature/2013/10/25/The-Winners-and-Losers-of-Globalization-Finding-a-Path-to-Shared-Prosperity [retrieved on July 2, 2021].

9. "Mao Zedong Announced in 1949 That the Chinese People Stood Up," http://news.sina.com.cn/c/sd/2009-09-23/095218709329.shtml [retrieved on July 2, 2021].

10. "Xi Jinping: Speech at the Celebration of the Centenary of the Founding of the Chinese Communist Party," http://www.gov.cn/xinwen/2021-07/01/content _5621847.htm [retrieved on July 10, 2021].

11. "CCP Member: Today in History," https://news.ruc.edu.cn/archives/320670 [retrieved on April 23, 2022].

12. Mao, Zedong, *Quotations from Chairman Mao Zedong* [in Chinese] (Beijing, China: People's Liberation Army General Political Department, 1966), 159, 166.

13. "India Asked Chiang Kai-shek for Help during the Sino-Indian War but Was Refused," https://www.sohu.com/a/317596996_100248928 [retrieved on July 2, 2021].

14. Maddison Historical Statistics, https://www.rug.nl/ggdc/historicaldevelopment/maddison/?lang=en [retrieved on July 2, 2021].

15. Kennedy, Andrew Bingham, "Dreams Undeferred: Mao, Nehru, and the Strategic Choices of Rising Powers," PhD diss., Harvard University, 2007.

16. Ash, Alec, "China's New Nationalism," https://www.thewirechina.com/2021 /08/08/chinas-new-nationalism/ [retrieved on August 26, 2021].

17. "Mao's Visit to Soviet Union in 1949: Enthusiastic to Go but Dismal to Return," http://news.ifeng.com/special/60nianjiaguo/60biaozhirenwu/renwuziliao /200908/0817_7766_1305972.shtml [retrieved on July 2, 2021].

18. Acheson, Dean, "Speech on the Far East," https://teachingamericanhistory .org/document/speech-on-the-far-east/ [retrieved on October 16, 2021].

19. We provide this simplified description of the Sino-Soviet alliance as just one detail of the historical backdrop of our study.

20. "Mao's Visit to Soviet Union." However, Mao and the CCP had been defending Stalin to some extent. Chen, Jian, *Mao's China and the Cold War* (Chapel Hill: University of North Carolina Press, 2010).

21. *Encyclopedia Britannica,* s.v. "Holomodor," https://www.britannica.com /event/Holodomor [retrieved on July 5, 2021].

22. The reasons for the Sino-Soviet split are detailed and complex. For a fuller summary and analysis, see Li, Mingjiang, *Mao's China and the Sino-Soviet Split: Ideological Dilemma* (Oxfordshire, UK: Taylor and Francis, 2013); and Chen, *Mao's China.* We come back to this issue in later chapters.

23. *Merriam-Webster's Dictionary,* s.v. "paper tiger," https://www.merriam -webster.com/dictionary/paper%20tiger [retrieved on July 2, 2021].

24. Mao, *Quotations from Chairman Mao Zedong,* 159, 166.

25. Liang, Hao, Rong Wang, and Haikun Zhu, "Growing Up under Mao and Deng: On the Ideological Determinants of Corporate Policies," SSRN, 2019, https:// papers.ssrn.com/sol3/papers.cfm?abstract_id=3494916 [retrieved on April 7, 2022].

26. Mao, *Quotations from Chairman Mao Zedong,* 166–67.

27. "Interview with American Journalist Anna Louise Strong," https://www .marxists.org/chinese/maozedong/marxist.org-chinese-mao-19460806.htm [retrieved on April 23, 2022].

28. Duriau, Vincent J., Rhonda K. Reger, and Michael D. Pfarrer, "A Content Analysis of the Content Analysis Literature in Organization Studies: Research Themes, Data Sources, and Methodological Refinements," *Organizational Research Methods* 10, no. 1 (2007): 5–34; Hannigan, Timothy R., Richard F. J. Haans, Keyvan Vakili, Hovig Tchalian, Vern L. Glaser, Milo Shaoqing Wang, Sarah Kaplan,

and P. Devereaux Jennings, "Topic Modeling in Management Research: Rendering New Theory from Textual Data," *Academy of Management Annals* 13, no. 2 (2019): 586–632.

29. The approach we followed thus ensures that our list has face validity (based on prior work) and content validity (based on experts).

30. Page 10 of Zhang, Chenjian, "Formal and Informal Institutional Legacies and Inward Foreign Direct Investment into Firms: Evidence from China," *Journal of International Business Studies,* published online ahead of print, September 23, 2020, https://doi.org/10.1057/s41267-020-00359-1.

31. Deng, Zhong, and Donald J. Treiman, "The Impact of the Cultural Revolution on Trends in Educational Attainment in the People's Republic of China," *American Journal of Sociology* 103, no. 2 (1997): 391–428.

32. Gao, Yi, "A Commentary on Deng Xiaoping's Diplomatic Strategy Thought in the New Era," http://cpc.people.com.cn/GB/33839/34943/34983/2641962.html [retrieved on April 23, 2022]. Zhang, Chenjian, "Formal and Informal Institutional Legacies and Inward Foreign Direct Investment into Firms: Evidence from China," *Journal of International Business Studies,* published online ahead of print, September 23, 2020, https://doi.org/10.1057/s41267-020-00359-1.

33. CNN Wire Staff, "China Sees Culture as a Crucial Battleground," http://www.cnn.com/2012/01/05/world/asia/china-western-culture/ [retrieved on July 2, 2021].

34. "The Origins of the Name Huawei," https://kknews.cc/tech/5mbyxa2.html [retrieved on July 2, 2021].

35. "Key to Huawei's Success Is Its Insistence and Development of Maoism," https://zhuanlan.zhihu.com/p/88971588 [retrieved on July 2, 2021].

36. For more elaboration of Ren's management and strategy, see "Ren Zhengfei of Huawei, His Spiritual Mentor Is Mao Zedong," https://zhuanlan.zhihu.com/p/52515236 [retrieved on July 2, 2021].

37. Yuan, Li, "Huawei's CCP Culture Curbs Its Global Expansion," https://cn.nytimes.com/technology/20190506/huawei-china-communist-party/ [retrieved on July 2, 2021].

38. Pearlstine, Norman, David Pierson, Robyn Dixon, David S. Cloud, Alice Su, and Max Hao Lu, "The man behind Huawei," https://www.latimes.com/projects/la-fi-tn-huawei-5g-trade-war/ [retrieved on July 2, 2021]. There are numerous examples, such as Nan Cunhui—CEO and chairperson of business giant Chint Group, which has a market cap at US$8 billion—who warned in 2007 that "foreign capital was threatening the economic safety and political stability of China." "Nan Cunhui Questions Schneider Electric and Delixi Group Company Limited Merger," https://business.sohu.com/20070108/n247469516.shtml [retrieved on July 2, 2021]. There are many other accounts, such as Meng, Baole, "To Back Up Domestic Chips, the Chinese Authority Is Playing Both Hard and Soft," https://cn.nytimes.com/technology/20141028/c28qualcomm/ [retrieved on July 2, 2021]; and Kazer, William, "U.S. Firms in China See Rising Anti-foreign Sentiment," https://www.wsj.com/articles/u-s-firms-in-china-see-rising-anti-foreign-sentiment-1423618180 [retrieved on July 2, 2021]. See also "Notice of the General Office of the State Council on Establishing a Safety Review System for Foreign Investors' Mergers and Acquisitions of Domestic Enterprises,"

http://www.mofcom.gov.cn/aarticle/b/f/201102/20110207403117.html [retrieved on July 2, 2021]; and others suggesting that foreign firms might endanger forestry industry ("Be Alert to How Foreign Investment Intervenes Our Forestry Industry and Harms National Security," http://lvse.sohu.com/s2008/foresthazard/ [retrieved on April 23, 2022]) and the legal profession ("Chinese Lawyers' Service Was Taken by Foreigners and This Might Endanger National Security," http://world.huanqiu.com /exclusive/2013-12/4652044.html [retrieved on July 2, 2021]).

39. Li, Bingheng, "Hubei Capital Market," http://www.sfahb.net/Upload_My /UEupload/upload/file/20190103/636821138319059080678618 6.pdf [retrieved on July 2, 2021].

40. Marquis, Christopher, and Kunyuan Qiao, "Waking from Mao's Dream: Communist Ideological Imprinting and the Internationalization of Entrepreneurial Ventures in China," *Administrative Science Quarterly* 65, no. 3 (2020): 795–830.

41. We used ordinary least squares to perform our analysis. First, other things being equal, entrepreneurs who are CCP members on average use 0.257 more nationalism-related words, and the effect is statistically significant ($p = .000$). The effect amounts to 19.7 percent of the mean level of the usage of nationalism-related words (1.303). Second, entrepreneurs' sense of nationalism is negatively related to firms' internationalization—both attracting foreign investors and going abroad to explore foreign markets. Third, CCP membership not only affects firms' internationalization through the nationalist mindset but also shapes firms' internationalization directly. Our published work, a recent finance study, and the new evidence presented here together show that CCP indoctrination leads to a more nationalist mindset, which to some extent hinders firms' internationalization. Liang, Wang, and Zhu, "Growing Up under Mao"; Marquis and Qiao, "Waking from Mao's Dream."

42. Liang, Wang, and Zhu, "Growing Up under Mao"; Marquis and Qiao, "Waking from Mao's Dream."

43. Marquis and Qiao, "Waking from Mao's Dream."

44. "People of Jiangsu: Fight to Break the Technological Monopolization by Foreign Countries, and Optical Fiber Industry and Its Development in China Is Closely Related to Cui," http://www.ourjiangsu.com/a/20191106/1573008386330.shtml [retrieved on July 2, 2021].

45. "The Tenth Five-Year Plan of National Economic and Social Development: Precis," http://www.people.com.cn/GB/shizheng/16/20010318/419582.html [retrieved on July 2, 2021].

46. "Vice Minister Wang Bingnan Meets with Founder of the Alibaba Group Jack Ma," http://wangbingnan.mofcom.gov.cn/article/activities/201801/20180102 696593.shtml [retrieved on July 2, 2021]; "Creativity and Imagination Are the New Economy," http://www.ce.cn/xwzx/gnsz/gdxw/201712/05/t20171205_27109475.shtml [retrieved on July 2, 2021].

47. Research team of the CCP Jiangsu Committee's United Front Department, "Ideological Status and Strategies to Deal with in the Private Economic Sector," http://www.cssn.cn/mkszy/mkszyzgh/201606/t20160615_3071008_7.shtml [retrieved on July 2, 2021].

48. Huntington, Samuel P., *The Clash of Civilizations and the Remaking of World Order* (New York: Simon and Schuster, 1996).

49. Meisner, Maurice, *Mao's China and After: A History of the People's Republic* (New York: Free Press, 1999); Wang, Xinzhe, "The Leadership of the Party Is the Fundamental Guarantee for Taking a New Road of Industrialization with Chinese Characteristics," https://www.ccdi.gov.cn/lswh/lilun/202104/t20210421_240032 .html [retrieved on August 7, 2021].

50. "Xi Jinping and the Chinese Dream," https://web.archive.org/web/2016 0510092423/http://www.economist.com/news/leaders/21577070-vision-chinas-new -president-should-serve-his-people-not-nationalist-state-xi-jinping [retrieved on July 2, 2021]; "'Chinese Dream' Thought: From Mao Zedong to Xi Jinping—Commemorate the 120th Anniversary of Comrade Mao Zedong's Birth," http://theory.people.com.cn /n/2013/1223/c40531-23922267.html [retrieved on August 10, 2021].

51. Ferdinand, Peter, "Westward Ho—the China Dream and 'One Belt, One Road': Chinese Foreign Policy under Xi Jinping," *International Affairs* 92, no. 4 (2016): 941–57.

52. "Xi Jinping: Speech at the Celebration."

53. "The Core Meaning of Constructing Contemporary Chinese Discourse System," http://www.xinhuanet.com/politics/2017-05/16/c_1120977542.htm [retrieved on July 4, 2021]; Clover, Charles, "Xi Jinping Signals Departure from Low-Profile Policy," https://www.ft.com/content/05cd86a6-b552-11e7-a398-73d59db9e399 [retrieved on August 10, 2021].

54. King, Gary, Jennifer Pan, and Margaret E. Roberts, "How the Chinese Government Fabricates Social Media Posts for Strategic Distraction, Not Engaged Argument," *American Political Science Review* 111, no. 3 (2017): 484–501.

55. "'Fifty-Cent Party Members' Have Been Out. China Now Depends on More Than 20 Million 'Internet Volunteers,'" https://www.rfa.org/mandarin/yataibaodao /meiti/hc-04142021111449.html [retrieved on October 16, 2021].

56. "Who Stinks Public Intellectuals?," http://news.sohu.com/s2012/dianji-1044/ [retrieved on July 2, 2021].

57. "After a Lapse of Many Years, I Saw the Publicly Known Intellectuals and Influencers Being Arrested!," https://freewechat.com/a/MzA4NDk4MDkzMw== /2651408231/2 [retrieved on August 10, 2021].

58. "'Clarify Origins, Sources, Reasons to Increase Trustworthiness' Officially Released," https://www.piyao.org.cn/2021-07/15/c_1211241937.htm [retrieved on November 20, 2021].

59. Zhou, Laura, "Chinese Actor Zhang Zhehan Faces Domestic Boycott over 2018 Photos at Japan's Yasukuni Shrine," https://www.scmp.com/news/china /diplomacy/article/3145113/chinese-actor-zhang-zhehan-faces-domestic-boycott -over-2018 [retrieved on August 27, 2021].

60. Cole, J. Michael, "Does China Have a 'Blacklist' of Taiwan 'Separatists'?," https://thediplomat.com/2018/05/does-china-have-a-blacklist-of-taiwan -separatists/ [retrieved on April 7, 2022]; "Nationalism Shrouds Taiwanese Artists across the Strait 'a Dilemma,'" https://www.dw.com/zh/%E6%B0%91%E6%97%8F %E4%B8%BB%E4%B9%89%E7%AC%BC%E7%BD%A9-%E8%B7%A8%E 8%B6%B3%E4%B8%A4%E5%B2%B8%E7%9A%84%E5%8F%B0%E6%B 9%BE%E8%89%BA%E4%BA%BA%E8%BF%9B%E9%80%80 %E4%B8%A4%E9%9A%BE/a-58815291 [retrieved on August 27, 2021].

61. Yuan, Li, "When Patriotism Becomes a Selling Point: Local Brands See Opportunities amid the Wave of Boycott," https://cn.nytimes.com/china/20210406/china-xinjiang-local-brands/ [retrieved on July 2, 2021].

62. "Meet NIO, Fall in Love with the Future," https://www.nio.cn/testimonials/20200904009?noredirect= [retrieved on April 23, 2022].

63. Kygne, James, and Yu Sun, "China and Big Tech: Xi's Blueprint for a Digital Dictatorship," https://www.ft.com/content/9ef38be2-9b4d-49a4-a812-97ad6d70ea6f [retrieved on October 1, 2021].

64. Candelon, François, Michael G. Jacobides, Stefano Brusconi, and Matthieu Gombreaud, "China's Business 'Ecosystems' Are Helping It Win the Global A.I. Race," https://fortune.com/2021/07/02/china-artificial-intelligence-ai-business-ecosystems-tencent-baidu-alibaba/ [retrieved on October 3, 2021].

65. Mozur, Paul, Jonah M. Kessel, and Melissa Chan, "Made in China, Exported to the World: The Surveillance State," https://www.nytimes.com/2019/04/24/technology/ecuador-surveillance-cameras-police-government.html [retrieved on October 3, 2021].

66. Ash, "China's New Nationalism."

67. Johnson, Ian, and Thom Shanker, "Anti-Japanese Demonstrations Broke Out in Many Places in China," https://cn.nytimes.com/china/20120917/c17protests/ [retrieved on July 2, 2021].

68. Wang, Yiqing, "D&G Caught in 'Humiliating China' Storm, Zhang Ziyi and Other Chinese Celebrities Collectively Boycott," https://www.bbc.com/zhongwen/simp/chinese-news-46293409 [retrieved on July 2, 2021].

69. "The Government Encourages People to Boycott Foreign Brands? Zhao Lijian Refutes: Does This Still Need to Be 'Encouraged'?," https://www.163.com/dy/article/G69VUDG90539LWPU.html [retrieved on July 17, 2021].

70. Bishop, Bill, "Xi Chairs Symposium with Business Leaders; 'Xi Thought' Coming?; TikTok," https://sinocism.com/p/xi-chairs-symposium-with-entrepreneurs [retrieved on April 7, 2022].

71. Bishop, Bill, "Xi's Pudong Speech; Peaceful China and the Knife Handle; Did Xi Kill the Ant IPO?; Hong Kong," https://sinocism.com/p/xis-pudong-speech-peaceful-china [retrieved on August 25, 2021].

72. Zhang, Raymond, "TikTok Owner's Big Reason to Strike a U.S. Deal: China Is Slowing," https://cn.nytimes.com/technology/20200915/china-bytedance-tiktok-sale/dual/ [retrieved on August 26, 2021].

73. Zhang, Raymond, "China's Crackdown on Didi Is a Reminder That Beijing Is in Charge," https://cn.nytimes.com/technology/20210706/china-didi-crackdown/dual/ [retrieved on August 26, 2021].

74. He, Laura, "Xi Jinping Wants China's Private Companies to Fight Alongside the Communist Party," https://www.cnn.com/2020/09/22/business/china-private-sector-intl-hnk/index.html [retrieved on April 7, 2022]; Wei, Lingling, "China's Xi Ramps Up Control of Private Sector. 'We Have No Choice but to Follow the Party,'" https://www.wsj.com/articles/china-xi-clampdown-private-sector-communist-party-11607612531 [retrieved on April 7, 2022]; Nagarajan, Shalini, "China's Xi Jinping Personally Halted Ant's Record-Breaking $37 Billion IPO after Boss Jack Ma Snubbed Government Leaders, Report Says," https://markets.businessinsider

.com/news/stocks/ant-group-ipo-personally-halted-china-xi-jinping-jack-wsj-2020 -11-1029800224 [retrieved on April 7, 2022]; Yang, Yingzhi, and Brenda Goh, "Beijing Took Stake and Board Seat in Key ByteDance Domestic Entity This Year," https:// www.reuters.com/world/china/beijing-owns-stakes-bytedance-weibo-domestic -entities-records-show-2021-08-17/ [retrieved on August 22, 2021]; Webb, Quentin, and Lingling Wei, "Chinese Ride-Hailing Giant Didi Could Get State Investment," https://www.wsj.com/articles/city-of-beijing-leads-plan-for-state-investment-in-didi -the-embattled-ride-hailing-giant-11630681353 [retrieved on September 28, 2021].

75. "Xi Jinping Once Again Raised the Concept of 'Domestic Cycle' to Deal with the 'Unprecedented Pressure' of the Chinese Economy," https://www.bbc.com /zhongwen/simp/chinese-news-53511847 [retrieved on August 26, 2021].

76. Wen, Tiejun [温铁军], and Xiaodan Dong [董筱丹], 去依附——中国化解第一次经济危机的真实经验 / De-attachment: China's Real Experience in Resolving the First Economic Crisis [in Chinese] (Beijing: People's Oriental Publishing [中国东方出版社], 2019).

77. Liang, Yan, "The US, China, and the Perils of Post-COVID Decoupling," https://thediplomat.com/2020/05/the-us-china-and-the-perils-of-post-covid -decoupling/ [retrieved on July 2, 2021].

78. "No Force Can Stop the Chinese People from Achieving Their Dreams," http:// www.xinhuanet.com/2019-05/17/c_1124505469.htm [retrieved on July 2, 2021].

79. "The Sino-U.S. Trade War Is in Full Swing; China Takes a Strong Stand and Pledges to Accompany to the End," https://hotspot.com.my/article/96402/%E4%B 8%AD%E7%BE%8E%E8%B4%B8%E6%98%93%E6%88%98%E5%85%A 8%E9%9D%A2%E5%BC%80%E6%89%93-%E4%B8%AD%E5%9B%BD% E7%AB%8B%E5%9C%BA%E5%BC%BA%E7%A1%AC%E8%AA%93%E5 %A5%89%E9%99%AA%E5%88%B0%E5%BA%95 [retrieved on July 2, 2021].

80. Su, Ma, "How Chairman Mao Copes with External Pressure," http://cpc .people.com.cn/n1/2018/1130/c223633-30434843.html [retrieved on July 2, 2021].

81. See, e.g., "The Third Sino-American Confrontation: Revisiting 'Mao Zedong Thought' and Looking for a Good Way to Break through the U.S.-China Trade War," https://m.gelonghui.com/p/171405 [retrieved on July 2, 2021].

82. Yuan, Li, "After the Floods, China Found a Target for Its Pain: Foreign Media," https://www.nytimes.com/2021/07/28/business/china-floods-foreign-media .html [retrieved on August 26, 2021].

83. "'A Coup for China': Analysts React to the World's Largest Trade Deal That Excludes the U.S.," https://www.cnbc.com/2020/11/16/rcep-15-asia-pacific-countries -including-china-sign-worlds-largest-trade-deal.html [retrieved on August 10, 2021].

84. Dogachan, Dagi, "EU's Refugee Crisis: From Supra-nationalism to Nationalism?," *Journal of Liberty and International Affairs* 3, no. 3 (2018): 9–19.

85. Muis, Jasper, and Tim Immerzeel, "Causes and Consequences of the Rise of Populist Radical Right Parties and Movements in Europe," *Current Sociology* 65, no. 6 (2017): 909–30.

86. "Foreign Companies in China Making It Big," https://www.laowaicareer.com /blog/foreign-companies-in-china-making-it-big/ [retrieved on July 2, 2021].

87. For example, Kai-Fu Lee, in *AI Superpowers: China, Silicon Valley, and the New World Order* (Boston: Mariner Books, 2018), uses Google as an example of a company with a lack of countrification in China that thus failed in the Chinese market.

88. Germano, Sara, "Nike Chief Executive Says Brand Is 'of China and for China,'" http://www.ftchinese.com/story/001092985/en?archive [retrieved on August 10, 2021].

CHAPTER 4: FRUGALITY AND COST REDUCTION

Epigraph: "On the Spirit of Frugality and Entrepreneurs' Thrift," http://www.gototsinghua.org.cn/wenku/qiyewenhua/mba_89677.html [retrieved on July 2, 2021].

1. "Chinese Henry Ford: From a Son of Farmers to an Automobile Tycoon," https://www.bbc.com/zhongwen/simp/chinese-news-43519812 [retrieved on April 23, 2022]; "Billionaire Li Shufu Was Not Allowed to Enter by Security Guard of His Subsidiary," https://www.sohu.com/a/70697668_310913 [retrieved on July 2, 2021].

2. "Li Changchun: Geely's Investment in Hunan Is Right and Should Construct Chairman Mao's Hometown Well," http://www.shufuli.com/media_info.php?401 [retrieved on July 2, 2021].

3. Chi, Yuzhou, "This Book Affects the Whole Life of Zong Qinghou," http://finance.sina.com.cn/zl/lifestyle/2016-03-02/zl-ifxpvysv5099512.shtml [retrieved on July 2, 2021].

4. "Comment: What Did Entrepreneurs Who Worship Mao Learn from Mao Zedong," http://finance.sina.com.cn/review/hgds/20130320/074714889970.shtml [retrieved on July 2, 2021].

5. "Stories of Venturing: Frugal Stories of Chinese Entrepreneurs," https://www.sohu.com/a/123926798_379366 [retrieved on July 1, 2021]; "A List of Nine Most Frugal Business Tycoons in China: Zhengfei Ren and Jack Ma Were Not in It," https://www.sohu.com/a/149659951_453997 [retrieved on July 2, 2021].

6. Mao, Zedong, *Quotations from Chairman Mao Zedong* [in Chinese] (Beijing: People's Liberation Army General Political Department, 1966), 160–61.

7. Mao, *Quotations from Chairman Mao Zedong*, 160.

8. "Chairman Mao Admired Mozi Very Highly and Spoke Highly of Him: 'He Is a Sage Better Than Confucius,'" https://k.sina.cn/article_2996164967_b295d9 6700100r8vo.html?wm=3049_0047 [retrieved on August 10, 2021]. As we mentioned in early chapters, Mao, in his 1936 poem, wrote hopefully that he would be better than the emperors in China's Qin, Han, Tang, Song, and Yuan dynasties, when China was one of the most powerful countries in the world.

9. One of the most important political theses was "Ten Crimes of Qin," by Jia Yi.

10. "How Frugal Was Emperor Wen of Han Dynasty: Grave Robbers Would Want to Avoid His Cemetery," https://www.sohu.com/a/398755615_120150719 [retrieved on July 2, 2021].

11. "Frugality by Emperor Wen of Han Dynasty Made Fiscal Plenty," http://www.um07.com/china/xihan/2017/1021/705.html [retrieved on April 23, 2022]; "The Most Frugal Emperor in Chinese History: Emperor Wen of Han Dynasty," https://kknews.cc/history/4llqzeq.html [retrieved on July 2, 2021].

12. Lu, Zhidan [卢志丹], 毛泽东点评历史人物 / Mao Zedong's Comments on Historical Figures [in Chinese] (Beijing: People's Daily Press [人民日报出版社], 2016).

13. "Mao's Frugality Is Moving: His Pajamas Were Not Changed for Twenty Years but with Seventy-Three Patches," https://www.kunlunce.com/jczc/mzdsx/2017-12-04/121345.html [retrieved on July 2, 2021].

14. "Kung Hsiang-his: The Life of the Greediest in the Republic of China," https://www.bilibili.com/read/cv7854502 [retrieved on October 4, 2021]. Ironically, Kung was the seventy-fifth-generation descendant of Confucius.

15. "Only Use Her Silk Bed Products in the White House? Why Soong Mei-ling Loves Silk Products So Much," https://kknews.cc/history/gmzpvll.html [retrieved on July 2, 2021].

16. "Know China and Promote Frugality," http://book.people.com.cn/GB/69399/107423/160282/9600402.html [retrieved on April 23, 2022]; "Yan'an Stories," http://theory.people.com.cn/n1/2016/1009/c40531-28762166.html [retrieved on July 2, 2021].

17. "It Was Because We Tightened Our Belt That We Developed Atomic Bomb and Realized Our Industrialization," https://jmqmil.sina.cn/ifeng/doc-ifymuukv2247452.d.html [retrieved on July 2, 2021].

18. Zhang, Hua, "Mao Zedong and the Basis of Industrialization of the People's Republic of China," http://www.dswxyjy.org.cn/n/2014/0815/c218997-25475431.html [retrieved on July 2, 2021].

19. Song, Guiwu, "Frugality Should Be One of the Core Values of Socialism," http://sgwjjx.blog.sohu.com/307923635.html [retrieved on July 2, 2021].

20. "Hu Jintao on Enhancing Three Types of Awareness and Improving Cadres' Work Construction," http://cpc.people.com.cn/GB/67481/80541/index.html [retrieved on July 2, 2021]; "Xi Focus: Xi Stresses Stopping Wasting Food, Promoting Thrift," http://www.xinhuanet.com/english/2020-08/11/c_139282457.htm [retrieved on July 2, 2021].

21. Tidy, Joe, "Mukbang: Why Is China Clamping Down on Eating Influencers?," https://www.bbc.com/news/technology-53840167 [retrieved on July 2, 2021].

22. "Deng Xiaoping: Everything Should Follow the Frugality Principle," http://cpc.people.com.cn/n1/2018/1010/c69113-30332596.html [retrieved on July 2, 2021].

23. "Stories of Celebrity Entrepreneurs: The Stingy Ren Zhengfei," https://www.jmyhu.com/141945.html [retrieved on July 2, 2021].

24. "Begin with a Borrowed Hen for Eggs, and Become a Top 500 Private Enterprise in China 23 Years Later," https://cj.sina.com.cn/article/detail/2268916473/463823 [retrieved on July 2, 2021].

25. "Wise Lectures of Entrepreneurs: Liu Yonghao Recalled His Interesting Stories in Meeting with Chairman Mao in Person," https://biz.ifeng.com/c/7lwTFoMG2Fs [retrieved on July 2, 2021]; "Founding His Firm since He Could Not Afford Buy-

ing Meat for His Daughter: Starting from Scratch and Now One of the Richest Persons in China," https://zhuanlan.zhihu.com/p/27747970 [retrieved on July 2, 2021].

26. "The Seven Years' Experience in Countryside Was the Starting Point of Xi Jinping's Political Career and Mindset," http://cpc.people.com.cn/n1/2017/0310 /c64387-29135456.html [retrieved on July 2, 2021].

27. Marquis, Christopher, and Kunyuan Qiao, "Will COVID-19 Forge a New Generation of Gritty Chinese Entrepreneurs?," https://supchina.com/2020/07/20 /will-covid-19-forge-a-new-generation-of-gritty-chinese-entrepreneurs/ [retrieved on April 8, 2022].

28. Marquis, Christopher, Kunyuan Qiao, M. Diane Burton, Ryan Allen, Santiago Campero Molina, Prithwiraj Choudhury, and Aleksandra Joanna Kacperczyk, "Individual Imprinting: Life History Matters," *Academy of Management Proceedings* 2018, no. 1 (2018): 14868.

29. "Stories of Venturing."

30. We used regression analysis (ordinary least squares) to estimate the data and found that, first, CCP membership is more positively related to entrepreneurs' mindset of frugality, which is reflected in their use of related words. Other things being equal, entrepreneurs who are CCP members on average use 0.35 more frugality-related words, and the effect is statistically significant ($p = .000$). The effect amounts to 31.6 percent of the mean level of the usage of frugality-related words (1.107). Similarly, entrepreneurs who are CCP members on average cut down on cost by around 20 percent more, and the effect is statistically significant ($p = .000$). Second, entrepreneurs' frugal practices—discourse and actual cost-cutting behavior—are positively related to firms' performance. The total effect amounts to around 7 percent of performance increase. Third, CCP membership is directly and positively related to firm performance: on average, communist entrepreneurs earn 4.4 percent more profits than noncommunist entrepreneurs, and the effect is substantial.

31. Li, Hongbin, Pak Wai Liu, Junsen Zhang, and Ning Ma, "Economic Returns to Communist Party Membership: Evidence from Urban Chinese Twins," *Economic Journal* 117, no. 523 (2007): 1504–20.

32. Marquis, Christopher, and Kunyuan Qiao, "What Does Not Starve You Makes You More Economical: A Study of Resource Scarcity Imprint of Chinese Entrepreneurs," paper presented at the Academy of Management, Chicago, IL, 2018.

33. "On the Spirit of Frugality and Entrepreneurs' Thrift," http://www .gototsinghua.org.cn/wenku/qiyewenhua/mba_89677.html [retrieved on July 2, 2021].

34. Weber, Max, *The Protestant Ethic and the Spirit of Capitalism*, translated by Talcott Parsons (New York: Penguin, 1905/2002).

35. Lewis, William Arthur, "Economic Development with Unlimited Supplies of Labour," *Manchester School* 22, no. 2 (1954): 139–91.

36. Lee, Clive Howard, *A Cotton Enterprise, 1795–1840: A History of M'connel & Kennedy Fine Cotton Spinners* (Manchester: Manchester University Press, 1972).

37. Crouzet, Francois, *The First Industrialists: The Problem of Origins* (Cambridge: Cambridge University Press, 1985), 5.

38. Montag, Ali, "Here's Why Jeff Bezos Still Drove a Honda Long after He Was a Billionaire," https://www.cnbc.com/2018/01/18/why-amazons-jeff-bezos-drove -a-honda-after-he-was-a-billionaire.html [retrieved on July 2, 2021].

39. Hoffower, Hillary, and Taylor Nicole Rogers, "Mark Zuckerberg Was Just Spotted Shopping at Costco. Look Inside the Lives of Surprisingly Frugal Million-aires and Billionaires, from Businessmen like Warren Buffett to A-List Celebs like Jennifer Lawrence," https://www.businessinsider.com/frugal-billionaires-millionaires -lifestyle-money-car-house-habits-net-worth-2019-2 [retrieved on July 2, 2021].

40. "Bite Dalu and Ge Yuesheng Became the Richest Persons of the Post-90s Generation, and Hurun Claimed That the Average Age of Entrepreneur in China Is 29 Years Old," http://tech.163.com/18/1010/11/DTOL3SV9000998GP.html [re-trieved on July 2, 2021]; Mai, Jun, "China's Communist Party Revisits the Past to Regroup for Future," https://www.scmp.com/news/china/politics/article/3122688 /chinas-communist-party-revisits-past-regroup-future [retrieved on July 2, 2021].

41. "Sons of the Former Richest Persons in China," https://kuaibao.qq.com/s /20191114A0B15J00?refer=spider [retrieved on July 2, 2021].

42. Wang, Tao, "Unraveling the Puzzle of Inheritance and Governance of Chi-nese Family Businesses," https://www.huxiu.com/article/340719.html [retrieved on April 23, 2022]; Zhou, Ying, and Yongqian Chen, "The Inheritance Test: How to Escape from the Curse of Wealth Cannot Last over Three Generations," http:// finance.sina.com.cn/leadership/mroll/20120515/223712071529.shtml   [retrieved on July 2, 2021].

43. "Zong Qinghou: My Daughter Is as Thrifty and Frugal as Me," http://finance .sina.com.cn/leadership/crz/20110310/16229507248.shtml [retrieved on August 10, 2021].

44. "The Abacus of oFo's Small Yellow Car: Through Shopping Cash Back Re-fund Deposit, Further Squeeze Users," https://www.sohu.com/a/407301177_128339 [retrieved on August 10, 2021].

45. Busenitz, Lowell W., and Jay B. Barney, "Differences between Entrepreneurs and Managers in Large Organizations: Biases and Heuristics in Strategic Decision-Making," *Journal of Business Venturing* 12, no. 1 (1997): 9–30; "5 Good Reasons for Being Frugal That Entrepreneurs Need to Remember When They Succeed," https://www.completecontroller.com/5-good-reasons-for-being-frugal-that -entrepreneurs-need-to-remember-when-they-succeed/ [retrieved on July 2, 2021].

46. Kachaner, Nicolas, George Stalker, and Alain Bloch, "What You Can Learn from Family Business," *Harvard Business Review* 90, no. 4 (November 2012): 1–5.

47. Iaquinto, Anthony, and Stephen Spinelli, *Never Bet the Farm: How Entre-preneurs Take Risks, Make Decisions—and How You Can, Too* (Hoboken, NJ: John Wiley and Sons, 2010).

48. "Lost China's Richest Man Status in 20 Minutes! The 300 Billion Giants Cannot Even Afford 730,000 Yuan/Yuan/RMB. They Sell the 'Money Printing Ma-chine' That Makes a Daily Profit of Tens of Millions, and Li Hejun Failed to Keep Hanergy," https://www.163.com/dy/article/G733SQMH0534A5GP.html [retrieved on July 2, 2021].

49. Topping this list seems to be a curse—prior richest people such as Mou Qizhong, Tang Wanxin, Lan Shili, Gu Chujun, Zhou Yiming, and Huang Guangyu

all either went bankrupt or were imprisoned. For example, Huang lost hundreds of millions of US dollars in casinos, bribed officials, and embezzled funds. He was imprisoned for thirteen years.

CHAPTER 5: DEVOTION AND SOCIAL CONTRIBUTION

Epigraph: "Based on the People and Devote to the People: An Interview of Delegate Wang Jinduo to the Provincial People's Congress," http://gmyfz.yzdb.cn/2006/10/genzhi.htm [retrieved on July 2, 2021].

1. "Struggle Is Always on the Road—33 Years of Hebei Shuntian Group's Establishment," https://freewechat.com/a/MzIoMzM3ODc2OQ==/2247504242/3/ [retrieved on July 2, 2021].

2. "More Than 45.5 Million Party Members Have Paid 'Special Party Dues' of 9.73 Billion Yuan/Yuan/RMB to the Disaster Area," http://www.xinhuanet.com/politics/2016-06/02/c_129034960.htm [retrieved on July 2, 2021].

3. Ma, Li, "Wang Jinduo: Corporate Social Responsibility of a Communist Entrepreneur," http://www.beijingreview.com.cn/2009news/renwu/2011-06/24/content_371474.htm [retrieved on July 2, 2021].

4. "Jack Ma Opens a Twitter Account to Do Philanthropy," https://cn.nytimes.com/technology/20190506/huawei-china-communist-party/ [retrieved on July 2, 2021].

5. Wang, Shiming, and Yongyue Yu, "On the Theoretical Source and Development of Deng Xiaoping's Thought of Common Prosperity," http://cpc.people.com.cn/n/2013/1126/c69113-23659040.html [retrieved on October 15, 2021]; Xi, Jinping, "Solidly Promote Common Prosperity," http://www.qstheory.cn/dukan/qs/2021-10/15/c_1127959365.htm [retrieved on April 24, 2022]; Vaswani, Karishma, "China Watch: How Xi Jinping's 'Common Prosperity' Will Affect the World," https://www.bbc.com/zhongwen/simp/chinese-news-58830610 [retrieved on April 24, 2022]; Buckley, Chris, Alexandra Stevenson, and Cao Li, "Warning of Income Gap, Xi Tells China's Tycoons to Share Wealth," https://www.nytimes.com/2021/09/07/world/asia/china-xi-common-prosperity.html [retrieved on October 15, 2021].

6. Huang, Zheping, "Tencent Doubles Social Aid to $15 Billion as Scrutiny Grows," https://www.bloomberg.com/news/articles/2021-08-19/tencent-doubles-social-aid-to-15-billion-as-scrutiny-grows [retrieved on August 26, 2021]. We by no means claim that CCP status and influence are the sole factors and acknowledge that this move might be driven by recent crackdowns on big tech firms in China.

7. Sun then collaborated with Chiang Kai-shek to establish the Republic of China Military Academy, which became an important military school for the Kuomintang troops. However, some CCP generals were also trained there, such as Lin Biao (later vice president who was designated to succeed Mao), Xu Xiangqian (one of the ten marshals of the communist regime), and Chen Geng (one of ten grand generals of the communist regime).

8. Mao, Zedong, *Quotations from Chairman Mao Zedong* [in Chinese] (Beijing: People's Liberation Army General Political Department, 1966), 232, 234.

9. "Path of Entrepreneurship and Innovation of a Communist Entrepreneur—Cui Genliang, Party Secretary and Chairman of Hengtong Group," http://dangjian.people.com.cn/n1/2016/0509/c117092-28336175.html [retrieved on July 2, 2021].

10. "How Many Provinces Announced Independence in Xinhai Revolution in 1911?," https://www.zhihu.com/question/316259690 [retrieved on July 2, 2021].

11. Mao Zedong, "Anti-liberalism," https://www.marxists.org/chinese/maozedong/marxist.org-chinese-mao-19370907.htm [retrieved on April 23, 2022].

12. "The First Session of Communist Entrepreneurs' Conference on Do Not Forget the Original Oath and Remember Mission," http://www.chinanews.com/gn/2019/10-24/8987994.shtml [retrieved on July 2, 2021].

13. "The Spirit of Shidafu of Traditional Culture in China: Interview of Senior Professor Lin Peng at Tsinghua University," http://www.ccdi.gov.cn/yaowen/201906/t20190614_195462.html [retrieved on July 2, 2021].

14. Mao, Zedong, "On Agricultural Collectivization," https://www.marxists.org/chinese/maozedong/marxist.org-chinese-mao-19550731.htm [retrieved on April 23, 2022].

15. Fan, Ziying, Wei Xiong, and Li-An Zhou, "Information Distortion in Hierarchical Organizations: A Study of China's Great Famine," working paper, Princeton University, 2016.

16. Mao, Zedong, "On the Correct Handling of Contradictions among the People," https://www.marxists.org/chinese/maozedong/marxist.org-chinese-mao-19570227AA.htm [retrieved on April 23, 2022].

17. "Path of Entrepreneurship and Innovation of a Communist Entrepreneur—Cui Genliang, Party Secretary and Chairman of Hengtong Group," http://dangjian.people.com.cn/n1/2016/0509/c117092-28336175.html [retrieved on April 24, 2022]; "Ren Zhengfei Explains Why He Joined CCP: All Excellent People Would Join the CCP," http://news.sina.com.cn/c/2013-05-10/093327082310.shtml [retrieved on May 22, 2022]; "Jack Ma Opens"; Ma, "Wang Jinduo."

18. Marquis, Christopher, Qi Li, and Kunyuan Qiao, "The Chinese Collectivist Model of Charity," *Stanford Social Innovation Review* 15, no. 3 (2017): 40–47; *Oxford English Dictionary*, s.v. "guanxi," https://www.oed.com/view/Entry/47070883 [retrieved on April 8, 2022].

19. See members of the club at http://www.daonong.com/members/ [retrieved on August 10, 2021].

20. "Xu Jingxin, Founder CEO of Jianhua Building Materials, Donated 15 U.S. Dollars Million More in His Own Name," http://www.dgaibijini.com/xinwen/253.html [retrieved on July 2, 2021].

21. "Heart Together and Fight Disease Jointly," http://cpc.people.com.cn/n1/2020/0206/c431601-31574237.html [retrieved on July 2, 2021].

22. Lu, Xiaobo, and Elizabeth J. Perry, *Danwei: The Changing Chinese Workplace in Historical and Comparative Perspective* (Armonk, NY: M. E. Sharpe, 1997).

23. "Be Wary of Non-governmental Organizations with Foreign Political Backgrounds Infiltrating China," http://www.chinahaoren.cn/Articlebody-detail-id-37005.html [retrieved on July 2, 2021].

24. Gao, Lei, and Wang, Qi, "Private Enterprises' Glorious Chapter: Summary of 25 Years' Achievements of the Guangcai Initiative in China," http://www.gov.cn/xinwen/2019-10/20/content_5442563.htm [retrieved on July 2, 2021].

25. "Cui Genliang: A Communist Entrepreneur Who Dedicated 30 Years to Poverty Reduction," http://www.jiangsu.gov.cn/art/2018/10/19/art_64354_7844686.html [retrieved on July 2, 2021].

26. "Model of the Time for Jiangsu, and Stronger Communist Construction Leads to Stronger Firms: Interviewing Chairman, CEO Zhou Haijiang," http://www.xhby.net/js/jj/201907/t20190722_6272190.shtml [retrieved on April 24, 2022]; "Zhou Haijiang Participated in the Symposium Celebrating the Twenty-Fifth Anniversary of the Guangcai Project," http://www.chinanews.com/business/2019/10-22/8986207.shtml [retrieved on July 2, 2021].

27. "Ren Zhengfei: I Am a CCP Member Who Will Fight for Communism for All My Life and I Will Never Betray," https://user.guancha.cn/main/content?id=162048 [retrieved on July 2, 2021].

28. "CCP Representatives' Conference: Old CCP Member Zong Qinghou—Want to Build Homes for Employees," https://zj.zjol.com.cn/news/668818.html [retrieved on July 2, 2021].

29. "Jinke Real Estate: A Model of China," http://www.hsmrt.com/huanghongyun/614.html [retrieved on July 2, 2021].

30. "Jinke Group Donated 110 Million Yuan/Yuan/RMB Again, Adding to Precise Poverty Reduction," http://www.cq.xinhuanet.com/2019-08/21/c_1124903791.htm [retrieved on July 2, 2021].

31. Results show that CCP membership is positively related to entrepreneurs' focus on devotion, which is reflected in their use of related words. Other things being equal, entrepreneurs who are CCP members on average use 0.041 more devotion-related words, and the effect is statistically significant ($p = .000$). The effect amounts to 53.6 percent of the mean level of the usage of devotion-related words (0.077). Additionally, CCP membership is positively related to donation over total revenue: on average, communist entrepreneurs' donation over revenue is 0.020 percent more than noncommunist entrepreneurs' in absolute value and around 17.7 percent in relative terms. We used the Chinese Private Enterprise Survey to provide further evidence. In this dataset there is no way to measure the language of entrepreneurs, so we only directly tested the relationship between CCP membership and donation over revenue. The results are consistent with those from the Chinese Stock Market and Accounting Research Database: CCP membership is positively related to donation over total revenue; on average, communist entrepreneurs' donation over revenue is 0.188 percent more than noncommunist entrepreneurs', and the effect accounts for around 74.5 percent of the mean level of donation over revenue.

32. Liang, Hao, Rong Wang, and Haikun Zhu, "Growing Up under Mao and Deng: On the Ideological Determinants of Corporate Policies," SSRN, 2019, https://papers.ssrn.com/sol3/papers.cfm?abstract_id=3494916 [retrieved on April 7, 2022]; Marquis, Christopher, and Kunyuan Qiao, "Waking from Mao's Dream: Communist Ideological Imprinting and the Internationalization of Entrepreneurial Ventures in China," *Administrative Science Quarterly* 65, no. 3 (2020): 795–830.

33. Wang, Shiming, and Yu, "On the Theoretical Source."

34. Xi, "Solidly Promote Common Prosperity"; Vaswani, Karishma, "China Watch: How Xi Jinping's 'Common Prosperity' Will Affect the World," https://www.bbc.com/zhongwen/simp/chinese-news-58830610 [retrieved on April 23, 2022]; Buckley, Stevenson, and Li, "Warning of Income Gap."

35. Bradsher, Keith, "China Sets Aside Push to Spread Wealth in Pivotal Year for Xi," https://www.nytimes.com/2022/04/12/business/china-economy-covid.html [retrieved on April 23, 2022].

36. "Zong Qinghou: Common Prosperity Is the Responsibility of Private Entrepreneurs," http://i.cztv.com/view/11954758.html [retrieved on October 15, 2021]; Zhou, Haijiang, "The Historical Responsibility of Private Enterprises in Promoting Common Prosperity," http://www.gbq.gov.cn/xxgk/bmdt/t10890280.shtml [retrieved on April 24, 2022]; "Helping Common Prosperity Is Entrepreneurs' Responsibility—Hu Yulin, CEO of Hongda Thermal Power Co., Ltd.," http://www.tjcharity.org.cn/News/202112/202112161440056.htm [retrieved on January 22, 2022].

37. Blanchette, Jude, *China's New Red Guards: The Return of Radicalism and the Rebirth of Mao Zedong* (Oxford: Oxford University Press, 2019); Dikötter, Frank, *Mao's Great Famine: The History of China's Most Devastating Catastrophe, 1958–1962* (London: Bloomsbury, 2010); Godement, François, *Contemporary China: Between Mao and Market* (Lanham, MD: Rowman and Littlefield, 2015).

38. Dickson, Bruce J., *Red Capitalists in China: The Party, Private Entrepreneurs, and Prospects for Political Change* (Cambridge: Cambridge University Press, 2003).

39. Wang, Heli, and Cuili Qian, "Corporate Philanthropy and Corporate Financial Performance: The Roles of Stakeholder Response and Political Access," *Academy of Management Journal* 54, no. 6 (2011): 1159–81.

40. Marquis, Christopher, *Better Business: How the B Corp Movement Is Remaking Capitalism* (New Haven, CT: Yale University Press, 2020).

41. "Multinational Companies Have No Choice but to Make Donations, and the CEOs Are Frustrated," https://news.creaders.net/china/2008/05/31/803636.html [retrieved on August 10, 2021]; Luo, Xiaowei Rose, Jianjun Zhang, and Christopher Marquis, "Mobilization in the Internet Age: Internet Activism and Corporate Response," *Academy of Management Journal* 59, no. 6 (2016): 2045–68; Zhang, Jianjun, and Xiaowei Rose Luo, "Dared to Care: Organizational Vulnerability, Institutional Logics, and MNCs' Social Responsiveness in Emerging Markets," *Organization Science* 24, no. 6 (2013): 1742–64; Zhang, Jianjun, Christopher Marquis, and Kunyuan Qiao, "Do Political Connections Buffer Firms from or Bind Firms to the Government? A Study of Corporate Charitable Donations of Chinese Firms," *Organization Science* 27, no. 5 (2016): 1307–24.

42. McGinnis, Ariel, James Pellegrin, Yin Shum, Jason Teo, and Judy Wu, "The Sichuan Earthquake and the Changing Landscape of CSR in China," *Knowledge@Wharton*, April 20, 2009; Luo, Zhang, and Marquis, "Mobilization in the Internet Age"; Zhang and Luo, "Dared to Care."

CHAPTER 6: MAO'S MILITARY THOUGHT AND BUSINESS
STRATEGY AND MANAGEMENT

Epigraph: "Shi Yuzhu Recommends *Selected Works of Mao:* I Can Recite It," http://www.iceo.com.cn/idea2013/144/2013/1126/272844.shtml [retrieved on July 1, 2021].

1. "The Ups and Downs of Melatonin Brain Platinum for 22 Years: It Sells 100 Million in 30 Days with 10-Second Advertising, and Has Not Updated Sales Data in the Past Three Years," https://new.qq.com/omn/20200130/20200130A040JW00.html [retrieved on July 1, 2021].

2. "Ren Zhengfei: My Spiritual Mentor Is Chairman Mao," https://www.sohu.com/a/316888766_764234 [retrieved on July 1, 2021].

3. Von Ghyczy, Tina, Bolko von Oetinger, and Christopher Bassford, *Clausewitz on Strategy: Inspiration and Insight from a Master Strategist* (Hoboken, NJ: John Wiley and Sons, 2002).

4. "Big Guy's Remarks | Lei Jun: Xiaomi Continues to Rely on Guerrillas to Play Will Have Big Problems," https://www.36kr.com/p/1722831028225 [retrieved on July 1, 2021].

5. Mao, Zedong [毛泽东], 毛泽东军事文集 / *Collected Works on Military by Mao Zedong* [in Chinese], vols. 1–6 (Beijing: Military Science Press/Central Party Literature Press, 1927–1972); Mao, Zedong [毛泽东], 毛泽东选集（第四卷）/ *Selected Works of Mao Tse-Tung* [in Chinese], vol. 4 (Beijing: People's Press [人民出版社], 1960). See also summaries such as "Mao Zedong Military Thought," http://www.cdsndu.org/html_ch/to_articleContent_article.id=8a28e6d84a9a04ff014a9b359da60228.html [retrieved on July 24, 2021].

6. Mao, Zedong [毛泽东], 毛泽东选集（第一卷）/ *Selected Works of Mao Tse-Tung* [in Chinese], vol. 1 (Beijing: People's Press [人民出版社], 1951), 136.

7. Luo, Wendong, "The Foundation of Winning the People's War for Epidemic Prevention and Control," http://theory.people.com.cn/n1/2020/0928/c40531-31877669.html [retrieved on August 15, 2021].

8. Wang, Jianzhu, "Mao Zedong and the Third Front Construction," http://dangshi.people.com.cn/n/2015/0615/c85037-27156999.html [retrieved on July 24, 2021].

9. "Why Mao Zedong Emphasizes Never Fight an Unprepared War," http://www.jfdaily.com.cn/news/detail?id=218515 [retrieved on July 1, 2021].

10. "Shi Yuzhu: Naobaijin/Brain Platinum Became Popular Because of This Marketing Strategy," https://zhuanlan.zhihu.com/p/370147199 [retrieved on July 1, 2021].

11. Cai, Maoquan, "Core Theory of Shi Yuzhu's Business Strategy," https://mp.weixin.qq.com/s/ORNqdxsSdKUhlPCxpuCtIg [retrieved on April 23, 2022].

12. "Entrepreneurial Hero Chai Xinjian: From Sea Turtle to Tortoise," http://www.chinaqw.com/news/2006/0124/68/14306.shtml [retrieved on July 1, 2021].

13. "Zhou Zhonghua: A Single Spark Can Start a Prairie Fire," http://finance.sina.com.cn/meeting/2017-09-09/doc-ifykusey6088373.shtml [retrieved on July 1, 2021].

14. "Big Bowl Tea—Peer of the Reform and Opening-Up," http://www.xinhuanet .com/fortune/2018-09/29/c_1123503217.htm [retrieved on July 1, 2021].

15. "How to Surround Cities from the Countryside, Seize Power with Military Forces," http://epaper.gmw.cn/gmrb/html/2012-09/07/nw.D110000gmrb_20120907 _5-09.htm [retrieved on July 1, 2021].

16. Yang, Lingling, "Hellobike Obtained Quotes in Beijing, Shanghai, Guangzhou, and Shenzhen and Its Sieging Cities from Villages Strategy Was the Gamechanger," https://www.sohu.com/a/461387492_237556 [retrieved on July 1, 2021].

17. Doshi, Rush, *The Long Game: China's Grand Strategy to Displace American Order* (Oxford: Oxford University Press, 2021).

18. "Concentrate Advantageous Forces, Annihilate Enemy One by One," https:// www.marxists.org/chinese/maozedong/marxist.org-chinese-mao-19460916.htm [retrieved on July 1, 2021].

19. "Application of Concentrate Advantageous Force to Annihilate Enemy in Corporate Management," https://www.sohu.com/a/274066432_100184887 [retrieved on July 1, 2021].

20. Cai, "Core Theory."

21. "Huawei's Militarized Management Strategy and Tactics II: Concentrate Advantageous Forces," https://www.shangyexinzhi.com/article/514592.html [retrieved on July 1, 2021].

22. Mao, Zedong, "On Protracted War," https://www.marxists.org/chinese /maozedong/marxist.org-chinese-mao-193805b.htm [retrieved on July 1, 2021].

23. Cai, "Core Theory."

24. "A Summary of Maoist Entrepreneurs: Li Dongsheng on the Protracted War and Ren Zhengfei Are Role Models of Learning Mao," https://www.163.com/money /article/9E9BBGM100253G87.html [retrieved on July 1, 2021].

25. "The Protracted War of TCL," http://finance.sina.com.cn/leadership/case /20060427/10392535296.shtml [retrieved on April 24, 2022]; "Li Dongsheng on Protracted War," https://zhuanlan.zhihu.com/p/87931716 [retrieved on July 1, 2021].

26. "Lei Jun's Internal Speech Was Exposed: Fighting a Protracted War Firmly, Looking Down on Life and Death, Just Do It," https://www.sohu.com/a/288377862 _104421 [retrieved on January 23, 2022].

27. Yang, John Z., "Key Success Factors of Multinational Firms in China," *Thunderbird International Business Review* 40, no. 6 (1998): 633–68.

28. "The Making of the Richest Automaker: Turning a Small Factory That Lost 300,000 U.S. Dollars to Earn 60 Billion U.S. Dollars with *On the Protracted War*," http://www.sino-manager.com/65645.html [retrieved on July 1, 2021].

29. "Rubao Tech: Protracted War in the Mobile Internet Field," http://www.iceo .com.cn/confer2013/2013/0530/267463.shtml [retrieved on July 1, 2021].

30. Thomas, Neil, "When It Comes to Negotiating with China, the Devil Is in the Details," https://www.washingtonpost.com/outlook/2019/03/26/when-it-comes -negotiating-with-china-devil-is-details/ [retrieved on July 1, 2021].

31. Pye, Lucian, *Chinese Commercial Negotiating Style* (Santa Monica, CA: RAND, 1982), xi–xii.

32. "Xi's US Strategy Recalls Mao's 'Protracted War,'" https://asia.nikkei.com /Editor-s-Picks/China-up-close/Xi-s-US-strategy-recalls-Mao-s-protracted-war [retrieved on July 1, 2021].

33. Mao, *Collected Works,* vols. 1–6; Mao, *Selected Works,* vol. 4. See also summaries such as "Mao Zedong Military Thought," http://www.cdsndu.org/html_ch /to_articleContent_article.id=8a28e6d84a9a04ff014a9b359da60228.html   [retrieved on July 24, 2021].

34. See, e.g., Marquis, Christopher, and Kunyuan Qiao, "Communist Ideological Imprinting and Internationalization: A Study of Chinese Entrepreneurs," paper presented at the Academy of Management Proceedings, Atlanta, GA, 2017; and Marquis, Christopher, and Kunyuan Qiao, "Waking from Mao's Dream: Communist Ideological Imprinting and the Internationalization of Entrepreneurial Ventures in China," *Administrative Science Quarterly* 65, no. 3 (2020): 795–830.

35. "Entrepreneurs under the Influence of *Selected Works of Mao Zedong,*" https://zhuanlan.zhihu.com/p/146592060 [retrieved on July 1, 2021]; "Jack Ma: I Went to Yan'an at the Hardest Time and Decided to Establish Taobao There," http://finance.sina.com.cn/chanjing/gsnews/2017-09-06/doc-ifykuffc3980865 .shtml [retrieved on August 15, 2021].

36. "Build a Strong Party to Make the Enterprise Stronger—Cui Genliang, Secretary of the Party Committee and Chairman of Jiangsu Hengtong Group," https://www.ccdi .gov.cn/lswh/renwu/201604/t20160428_120623.html [retrieved on July 1, 2021].

37. See, e.g., Marquis and Qiao, "Communist Ideological Imprinting"; Marquis and Qiao, "Waking from Mao's Dream"; and "An Old Party Member's Family and Country Feelings—Interview with Li Shijiang, Chairman of Do-Fluoride Chemical Co., Ltd.," http://www.dfdchem.com/News/media/12193/View.html [retrieved on July 1, 2021].

38. Mao, Zedong, *Quotations from Chairman Mao Zedong* [in Chinese] (Beijing: People's Liberation Army General Political Department, 1966), 89.

PART III: THE EFFECTS OF MAO'S MASS CAMPAIGNS: THE GREAT LEAP FORWARD, THE CULTURAL REVOLUTION, AND THE THIRD FRONT

Epigraphs: November 13, 1957, *People's Daily,* also documented in "Scholar: The 'Great Leap Forward' Is Mao Zedong's 'Chinese Dream,'" https://www.bbc.com /zhongwen/simp/china/2014/11/141113_great_leap_forward [retrieved on April 24, 2022]; Mao Zedong's letter to Jiang Qing on July 8, 1966. In "Major Events of Chinese Communist Party 1966," http://cpc.people.com.cn/GB/64162/64164 /4416081.html [retrieved on April 24, 2022]; Chen, Donglin, "The Historical Significance and Modern Enlightenment of Mao Zedong's Thought on Three-Front Construction," https://www.dswxyjy.org.cn/n1/2019/0228/c423718-30948363 .html [retrieved on April 24, 2022].

CHAPTER 7: THE GREAT LEAP FORWARD AND RESOURCE USE

Epigraph: "Lu Guanqiu of Wanxiang: Never Fail in Business for Four Decades," http://business.sohu.com/20080925/n259746692.shtml [retrieved on July 5, 2021].

1. "Big Guys with Low Academic Qualifications: 'Superman' Li Ka-shing Only Has a Primary School Degree," http://finance.sina.com.cn/360desktop/leadership/crz /20130609/144915756564.shtml [retrieved on July 5, 2021].

2. "Big Guys."

3. "Starting from 4,000 Yuan/RMB and Reaching 49 Billion Yuan/RMB, with National Leaders Visiting the United States Three Times in Four Years, Lu Guanqiu Spent His Entire Life Telling What the Spirit of Entrepreneurship Is," https://zhuanlan.zhihu.com/p/30495452 [retrieved on July 16, 2021]; "Lu Guanqiu of Wanxiang."

4. "Starting from 4,000 Yuan/RMB."

5. "Starting from 4,000 Yuan/RMB"; "Wanxiang Annual Ring 30 Years," https://business.sohu.com/20080310/n255621457.shtml [retrieved on July 5, 2021].

6. Andriani, Pierpaolo, and Gino Cattani, "Exaptation as Source of Creativity, Innovation, and Diversity: Introduction to the Special Section," *Industrial and Corporate Change* 25, no. 1 (2016): 115–31.

7. Marquis, Christopher, and Zhi Huang, "Acquisitions as Exaptation: The Legacy of Founding Institutions in the US Commercial Banking Industry," *Academy of Management Journal* 53, no. 6 (2010): 1441–73.

8. Ching, Kenny, "Exaptation Dynamics and Entrepreneurial Performance: Evidence from the Internet Video Industry," *Industrial and Corporate Change* 25, no. 1 (2016): 181–98.

9. Kennedy, Mark, "Obama-Backed Documentary on Ohio Factory Wins Academy Award," https://abcnews.go.com/Entertainment/wireStory/obama-backed-documentary-ohio-factory-wins-academy-award-68872312 [retrieved on July 5, 2021].

10. "Cao Dewang's Early Experience and Venture Journey," https://zhuanlan.zhihu.com/p/82258592 [retrieved on April 24, 2022]; "Cao Dewang of Fuyao Glass," https://zhuanlan.zhihu.com/p/83919746 [retrieved on April 24, 2022]; Baidu's elaboration, Cao Dewang, https://baike.baidu.com/item/%E6%9B%B9%E5%BE%B7%E6%97%BA [retrieved on July 5, 2021].

11. Marquis, Christopher, and Kunyuan Qiao, "What Does Not Starve You Makes You More Economical: A Study of Resource Scarcity Imprint of Chinese Entrepreneurs," paper presented at the Academy of Management, Chicago, IL, 2018.

12. "Wang Shi: Hardships and Sufferings Are Wealth," https://finance.sina.cn/chanjing/gsxw/2019-11-02/detail-iicezuev6608505.d.html [retrieved on April 24, 2022]; Towson, Jeffery, "Wang Shi and the Story of Vanke," https://jefftowson.com/2018/12/%E7%8E%8B%E7%9F%B3%E4%B8%8E%E4%B8%AD%E5%9B%BD%E4%B8%87%E7%A7%91%E7%9A%84%E6%95%85%E4%BA%8B%EF%BC%88%E7%AC%AC%E4%B8%80%E9%83%A8%E5%88%86/ [retrieved on July 5, 2021].

13. "Be a Revolutionary Facilitator," https://www.marxists.org/chinese/maozedong/marxist.org-chinese-mao-19571009.htm [retrieved on July 5, 2021].

14. "Mao Had a Lifelong Hatred of Stalin and Claimed Stalin Tortured Us Four Times," http://mil.news.sina.com.cn/2015-11-24/1126844675.html [retrieved on April 24, 2022]; "Mao's Visit to Soviet Union in 1949: Enthusiastic to Go but Dismal to Return," http://news.ifeng.com/special/60nianjiaguo/60biaozhirenwu/renwuziliao/200908/0817_7766_1305972.shtml [retrieved on July 5, 2021].

15. Qi, Weiping, and Jun Wang, "A Historical Investigation on the Evolutionary Stage of Mao Zedong's Thought of 'Catching Up with and Surpassing the U.K. and the U.S.," http://ww2.usc.cuhk.edu.hk/PaperCollection/Details.aspx?id=3683 [retrieved on April 23, 2022]. The slogan is sometimes given as "Catching up with the

United Kingdom and surpassing the United States" or "Catching up with the United States and surpassing the United Kingdom"; however, a literal approach to understanding this phrase is not the best way to understand Mao's intentions—the idea was to catch up and surpass these two most developed countries.

16. Shen, Zhihua [沈志华], 无奈的选择: 冷战与中苏同盟的命运 / *The Cold War and the Fate of Sino-Soviet Alliance, 1945–1959* [in Chinese] (Beijing: Social Science Academic Press [社会科学文献出版社], 2013).

17. Kung, James Kai-sing, and Justin Yifu Lin, "The Causes of China's Great Leap Famine, 1959–1961," *Economic Development and Cultural Change* 52, no. 1 (2003): 51–73; Lin, Justin Yifu, "Collectivization and China's Agricultural Crisis in 1959–1961," *Journal of Political Economy* 98, no. 6 (1990): 1228–52; Lin, Justin Yifu, "Rural Reforms and Agricultural Growth in China," *American Economic Review* 82, no. 1 (1992): 34–51.

18. Cheng, Peng, "With a Yield of Over 3,000 Jin per Mu, Yuan Longping Broke the Record Again!," http://www.nbd.com.cn/articles/2020-11-02/1539174.html [retrieved on July 5, 2021].

19. Fan, Ziying, Wei Xiong, and Li-An Zhou, "Information Distortion in Hierarchical Organizations: A Study of China's Great Famine," working paper, Princeton University, 2016.

20. In 1950 Qian Xuesen was arrested as a communist sympathizer and stripped of his security clearances; in 1955 he was said to have been traded to China for Korean War prisoners. Li, Rui [李锐] 大跃进亲历记 / *The Experience of the Great Leap Forward* [in Chinese] (Shanghai: Shanghai Far East Press, 1996). However, Qian's theory was only applicable to the ideal case with full photosynthesis to grow rice—for instance, in reality, the effectiveness can be less than 1 percent.

21. Data are from Meng, Xin, Nancy Qian, and Pierre Yared, "The Institutional Causes of China's Great Famine, 1959–1961," *Review of Economic Studies* 82, no. 4 (2015): 1568–611. Kung, James Kai-Sing, and Shuo Chen, "The Tragedy of the Nomenklatura: Career Incentives and Political Radicalism during China's Great Leap Famine," *American Political Science Review* 105, no. 1 (2011): 27–45.

22. Sun, Zhonghua, "The Origin of Liu Shaoqi's 'Thirty-Percent Natural Calamity and Seventy-Percent Man-Made Calamities,'" http://cpc.people.com.cn/GB /64162/64172/85037/85039/5898093.html [retrieved on July 5, 2021].

23. Interestingly, the final, posthumous verdict on Mao also held that overall he was 70 percent right and 30 percent wrong.

24. In another work, we show, using a cutting-edge statistical analysis, that it was the Great Leap Forward rather than the general poor living conditions that drove this pattern. See Marquis and Qiao, "What Does Not Starve You."

25. Bianchi, Emily C., and Aharon Mohliver, "Do Good Times Breed Cheats? Prosperous Times Have Immediate and Lasting Implications for CEO Misconduct," *Organization Science* 27, no. 6 (2016): 1488–503.

26. Ardelt, Monika, "Social Crisis and Individual Growth: The Long-Term Effects of the Great Depression," *Journal of Aging Studies* 12, no. 3 (1998): 291–314.

27. "The Way to Happiness of Seventy-Year-Old Female Entrepreneur Chen Ruifeng," http://www.ptsql.org/hxqj/201909/t20190926_1406444.htm [retrieved on July 5, 2021].

28. "The Pre-autobiography of the Richest Man in China: Xu Jiayin," https://business.sohu.com/20130207/n365817055.shtml [retrieved on July 2, 2021].

29. Song, Chengliang, "Unveiling Xu Jiayin: Iron Management and Would Punish for Wasting Even a Bottle of Water," http://sports.ifeng.com/gnzq/detail_2013_11/12/31173351_0.shtml [retrieved on July 2, 2021]; Che, Chang, "The Fall of Evergrande Boss," https://supchina.com/2021/09/21/the-fall-of-the-evergrande-boss/ [retrieved on September 28, 2021]. Although nowadays Xu is a bit less frugal, overall, his spending is relatively low compared to the wealth he has created.

30. "Hot Spot Analysis: How Do China Evergrande's Debt Problems Constitute Systemic Risks?," https://cn.reuters.com/article/china-evergrande-debt-risk-0914-idCNKBS2GA0XQ [retrieved on October 16, 2021].

31. Marquis and Qiao, "What Does Not Starve You." We also consider zero to eight years old as an alternative way to define early life and find similar results.

32. Jing, Jun, "Villages Dammed, Villages Repossessed: A Memorial Movement in Northwest China," *American Ethnologist* 26, no. 2 (1999): 324–43.

33. Liu, Yuan, "Son of Sea from Binzhou: Wang Dianjie—Four-Word Mantra Made Me Invincible," https://www.binzhouw.com/app/detail/184/162383.html [retrieved on July 5, 2021].

34. Marquis and Qiao, "What Does Not Starve You."

35. "Unveiling Reasons Why 95% New Ventures Would Be Dead," https://m.sohu.com/n/521721492/ [retrieved on July 5, 2021].

36. "Enterprising at the Risk of Losing Permanent Employment, Achieving Successes after Hard Experiences," https://kknews.cc/zh-my/news/nb8pao3.html [retrieved on July 5, 2021].

37. "Kaixuan Chen—Chairman of Liby Group—Story Begins from Three Rooms," http://www.acfic.org.cn/fgdt1/qiyejiazhisheng/201808/t20180828_55613.html [retrieved on July 5, 2021].

38. Bernile, Gennaro, Vineet Bhagwat, and P. Raghavendra Rau, "What Doesn't Kill You Will Only Make You More Risk-Loving: Early-Life Disasters and CEO Behavior," *Journal of Finance* 72, no. 1 (2017): 167–206.

39. Chu, Junhong, Ivan P. L. Png, and Junjian Yi, "Entrepreneurship and the School of Hard Knocks: Evidence from China's Great Famine," SSRN, 2016, https://dx.doi.org/10.2139/ssrn.2789174 [retrieved on April 11, 2022].

40. Terry, Mark, "Compare: 1918 Spanish Influenza Pandemic versus COVID-19," https://www.biospace.com/article/compare-1918-spanish-influenza-pandemic-versus-covid-19/ [retrieved on July 5, 2021].

41. Almond, Douglas, "Is the 1918 Influenza Pandemic Over? Long-Term Effects of In Utero Influenza Exposure in the Post-1940 US Population," *Journal of Political Economy* 114, no. 4 (2006): 672–712; Lin, Ming-Jen, and Elaine M. Liu, "Does In Utero Exposure to Illness Matter? The 1918 Influenza Epidemic in Taiwan as a Natural Experiment," *Journal of Health Economics* 37 (2014): 152–63.

42. Giuliano, Paola, and Antonio Spilimbergo, "Growing Up in a Recession," *Review of Economic Studies* 81, no. 2 (2014): 787–817.

43. Gong, Jie, Yi Lu, and Huihua Xie, "The Average and Distributional Effects of Teenage Adversity on Long-Term Health," *Journal of Health Economics* 71 (2020): 102288; Chen, Yuyu, and Li-An Zhou, "The Long-Term Health and Eco-

nomic Consequences of the 1959–1961 Famine in China," *Journal of Health Economics* 26, no. 4 (2007): 659–81.

44. Xu, Yao, Limin Zhang, and Jinsheng Jia, "Lessons from Catastrophic Dam Failures in August 1975 in Zhumadian, China," in *Geocongress 2008: Geosustainability and Geohazard Mitigation,* edited by Krishna R. Reddy, Milind V. Khire, and Akram N. Alshawabkeh, 162–69 (Reston, VA: American Society of Civil Engineers, 2008).

45. Slade, Hollie, "20 Amazing Companies Founded during the Financial Crisis," https://www.forbes.com/sites/hollieslade/2014/01/22/20-amazing-companies-founded-during-the-financial-crisis/#234c7f017377 [retrieved on July 5, 2021].

46. Qin, Xin, Kai Chi Yam, Chen Chen, Wanlu Li, and Xiaowei Dong, "Talking about Covid-19 Is Positively Associated with Team Cultural Tightness: Implications for Team Deviance and Creativity," *Journal of Applied Psychology* 106, no. 4 (2021): 530–41; Yam, Kai Chi, Joshua Conrad Jackson, Christopher M. Barnes, Jenson Lau, Xin Qin, and Hin Yeung Lee, "The Rise of Covid-19 Cases Is Associated with Support for World Leaders," *Proceedings of the National Academy of Sciences* 117, no. 41 (2020): 25429–33.

CHAPTER 8: THE CULTURAL REVOLUTION AND
INSTITUTIONAL CONFIDENCE

Epigraph: "Huang Nubo Responded to Zhongkun Scolding: I Used to Be a Red Guard and Can Have No Ethical Bottom Line," http://finance.ifeng.com/business/renwu/20130116/7562961.shtml [retrieved on July 5, 2021].

1. "Cultural Revolution Demons Haunt Chinese Billionaire Huang Nubo," https://www.straitstimes.com/asia/east-asia/cultural-revolution-demons-haunt-chinese-billionaire-huang-nubo [retrieved on July 5, 2021].

2. "Annual Report of Entrepreneurs' Corruption Crimes: 150 Persons Were Acquitted and Nobody Was Sentenced to Death," https://www.thepaper.cn/newsDetail_forward_2089899 [retrieved on July 5, 2021].

3. "Entrepreneurs: Crimes and Punishments over 30 Years," http://www.iceo.com.cn/zazhi/1999/1130/173865.shtml [retrieved on July 5, 2021].

4. "Defaulter Huang Nubo Sold His Zhongkun Plaza and Claimed That He Took a Mess Over," https://finance.sina.com.cn/roll/2019-02-16/doc-ihrfqzka6312496.shtml [retrieved on July 5, 2021].

5. See studies on entrepreneurs' intentions to leave their home country to escape governmental harassment—e.g., Witt, Michael A., and Arie Y. Lewin, "Outward Foreign Direct Investment as Escape Response to Home Country Institutional Constraints," *Journal of International Business Studies* 38, no. 4 (2007): 579–94.

6. "China Tycoon Huang Nubo Angered by Iceland Land Move," https://www.bbc.com/news/world-asia-15916486 [retrieved on July 5, 2021].

7. "Huang Nubo Responded"; "Cultural Revolution Demons."

8. Yuan, Li, "Chinese Entrepreneurs Lose Their Hope for Future," https://cn.nytimes.com/china/20190224/china-entrepreneurs-confidence/ [retrieved on July 5, 2021].

9. "Losing Confidence in Xi Jinping Administration, Many Chinese Entrepreneurs Choose to Flee from China," https://www.rolia.net/zh/post.php?f=0&p

=11954746 [retrieved on April 24, 2022]; Zhang, Weiguo, "Chinese Entrepreneurs Are Losing Their Confidence Gradually," https://2newcenturynet.blogspot.com /2016/06/blog-post_82.html?m=0 [retrieved on July 5, 2021].

10. Wu, Chao, "Review of Studies on the Origins of the Cultural Revolution," http://cpc.people.com.cn/GB/68742/84762/84763/7366458.html [retrieved on July 5, 2021]; MacFarquhar, Roderick, *The Origins of the Cultural Revolution,* vol. 1 (New York: Columbia University Press, 1974); MacFarquhar, Roderick, *The Origins of the Cultural Revolution,* vol. 2 (Oxford: Oxford University Press, 1983); MacFarquhar, Roderick, *The Origins of the Cultural Revolution,* vol. 3 (New York: Columbia University Press, 1997); Dikötter, Frank, *The Cultural Revolution: A People's History, 1962–1976* (New York: Bloomsbury, 2016).

11. In China and the CCP system, party leader—called chairman in Mao's period—is above the government leader—i.e., president. Hence, President Liu was subordinate to Chairman Mao. This is still true—e.g., after the CCP abolished the position of chairman of the Central Committee, the general secretary became the supreme leader. The CCP's general secretary and the Chinese government's president are typically assumed by the same person since the Jiang Zemin administration (1989–2003), and thus we would assume the Chinese president was the supreme leader of China. See O'Keeffe, Kate, and Katy Stech Ferek, "Stop Calling China's Xi Jinping 'President,' U.S. Panel Says," https://www.wsj.com/articles/stop-calling -chinas-xi-jinping-president-u-s-panel-says-11573740000 [retrieved on July 5, 2021].

12. Li, Qingping, "On Liu Shaoqi and the Party's Theoretical Construction," https://www.dswxyjy.org.cn/n1/2019/0228/c425376-30909338.html [retrieved on April 28, 2022]. "Chairman Mao said, 'I would not be able to catch up with Liu Shaoqi if I do not study for three days.' What did Liu Shaoqi say in response?" https://www.163.com/dy/article/GP0DKBHH0543ONRD.html [retrieved on May 22, 2022].

13. *Encyclopedia Britannica,* s.v. "Wang Guangmei," https://www.britannica .com/biography/Wang-Guangmei [retrieved on July 5, 2021]; "Real and Fake First Lady: Jiang Qing, Wang Guangmei, and (Indonesia's) Sukarno," https://medium.com /birthday-paper/%E7%9C%9F%E5%81%87-%E7%AC%AC%E4%B8%80%E 5%A4%AB%E4%BA%BA-%E7%8E%8B%E5%85%89%E7%BE%8E-%E6% B1%9F%E9%9D%92%E5%92%8C%E5%93%88%E8%92%82%E5%A6% AE%E7%9A%841962-%E9%92%B1%E9%92%A2%E8%80%81%E5%B8% 88%E8%AF%BE%E4%B8%8A%E7%9A%84%E7%94%9F%E6%97%A5% E6%8A%A5%E5%B1%95%E7%A4%BA%E2%91%A9-622bb984d4db [retrieved on July 5, 2021]. Interestingly, under CCP regulations, Jiang could not become "first lady" since Mao married her without formally divorcing his ex-wife, He Zizhen. Many high-ranking officials objected to Mao's marriage with Jiang since he had not divorced and Jiang was a stigmatized actress who was too young for Mao. The compromise was that the marriage was approved on the condition that Jiang would not be involved in CCP affairs for twenty years after their marriage in 1938 and she could not claim to be the "wife of Mao." See "CCP's Central Committee Regulates Jiang Qing, Who Cannot Enter Politics for 20 Years," http://history .people.com.cn/n/2013/0106/c198865-20105238.html [retrieved on July 5, 2021].

14. "Liu Shaoqi Responded to Mao Zedong: Cannibalization Would Make Leaders Stigmatized Forever in History Books," https://web.archive.org/web/20131031131413/http://www.stnn.cc/reveal/200711/t20071116_670118_1.html [retrieved on July 5, 2021].

15. There are many parts of the Cultural Revolution that are beyond the scope of our discussion—e.g., damages to traditional culture. The Cultural Revolution condemned representatives of traditional culture. The mass rallies that characterized the period targeted anything and anybody related to traditional Chinese culture and norms, particularly Confucianism.

16. "Today in History (August 5, 1966): Mao Zedong Posted a Big-Character Poster 'Bombard the Headquarter of the Capitalist Order,'" https://news.china.com/history/today/0805/ [retrieved on July 5, 2021].

17. Xue, Qingchao, "Mao Chose and Changed His Successor Five Times: Much Experience and Great Expenses," http://cpc.people.com.cn/GB/85037/8217222.html [retrieved on July 5, 2021]. Lin was Mao's successor at the beginning of the Cultural Revolution but hoped to replace Mao in a later stage. His plot to usurp power from Mao was leaked and Lin fled to the Soviet Union. His plane, however, was said to have crashed in Mongolia.

18. "The 50th Anniversary of the Cultural Revolution: The Anti-cultural Revolution Must Be Done Again," https://web.archive.org/web/20200625142850/http://www.hybsl.cn/beijingcankao/beijingfenxi/2016-01-08/56368.html [retrieved on October 30, 2021].

19. "One of the Studies on the Cultural Revolution: Rebellion Is Reasonable," https://boxun.com/news/gb/pubvp/2011/12/201112310529.shtml [retrieved on July 5, 2021].

20. The official CCP account suggests that Xi performed well in the countryside.

21. "Female Sent-Down Youths Sold Their Virginity to Return to Cities," https://m.sohu.com/n/556281862/ [retrieved on July 5, 2021].

22. Xue, "Mao Chose and Changed."

23. "Huang Nubo Responded."

24. "The 'Gang of Four' Ordered Repeated Publicity 'Following the Established Guidelines,'" http://phtv.ifeng.com/program/fhdsy/detail_2011_11/18/10746134_0.shtml?_from_ralated [retrieved on July 5, 2021].

25. Krosnick, Jon A., and Duane F. Alwin, "Aging and Susceptibility to Attitude Change," *Journal of Personality and Social Psychology* 57, no. 3 (1989): 416–25.

26. China ranked eightieth in corruption according to Transparency International, https://www.transparency.org/country/CHN [retrieved on April 24, 2022]. E.g., in 2015, "There Are Many Corruption Crime Cases for Private Entrepreneurs, the Main Trigger Is the Low Cost of Bribing," http://politics.people.com.cn/n1/2016/0419/c1001-28286659.html [retrieved on April 24, 2022]; and in 2017, "Annual Report."

27. "Rethinking Tang Wanxin's Delong Case: The Tragedy Began with the Absence of Belief and Responsibility," https://finance.qq.com/a/20101025/005610.htm [retrieved on July 5, 2021].

28. "Delong Case Was Trialed and It Was Hard to Implement the Hundreds of Millions (U.S. Dollars) Fines," http://finance.people.com.cn/GB/8215/65466/65542/4439983.html [retrieved on July 5, 2021].

29. "Mou Qizhong's Life in Prison: Concern about the 18th Congress of CCP and Wanted to Establish an Internet University after Getting Out," http://news.ifeng.com/shendu/nfrwzk/detail_2013_01/09/20997850_3.shtml [retrieved on July 5, 2021].

30. "Small Wizard Mou Qizhong," https://blog.boxun.com/sixiang/000525/7.htm [retrieved on July 5, 2021]. Xu Jiayin, born in 1958, experienced the Cultural Revolution and was once the richest man in China. He has also reportedly been freewheeling, bribing relatives of high-ranking officials such as the former vice president Zeng Qinghong and former prime minister Wen Jiabao. Che, Chang, "The Fall of Evergrande Boss," https://supchina.com/2021/09/21/the-fall-of-the-evergrande-boss/ [retrieved on September 28, 2021].

31. "The Richest Man Fell: From Orphan to Rich, from Poor Student to Meet with Chief Representative of North Korea, and Finally Was Thrown into Prison," http://www.360doc.com/content/20/0710/13/8250148_923357960.shtml [retrieved on July 5, 2021].

32. "The Richest People in China," https://www.hurun.net/zh-CN/Rank/HsRankDetails?num=QWDD234E [retrieved on August 16, 2021].

33. "The 35 Richest Chinese on the Hurun Report in 2017 Were Sentenced! Rich List or Slaughter List?," https://www.sohu.com/a/48957025_121315 [retrieved on August 16, 2021].

34. Data are from "Richest People in China."

35. "Huang Nubo Responded."

36. "The Richest Owner of a Publicly Traded Firm in Sichuan: Became Rich Suddenly and Deceived Dispersed and Institutional Investors," http://finance.sina.com.cn/stock/s/2019-05-28/doc-ihvhiews5204918.shtml [retrieved on April 24, 2022]; "Inside the Fall of 7 Billion U.S. Dollars Yinji Media: The Mysterious Actual Controller and the Loss of 1 Billion U.S. Dollars during Spring Festival," https://money.163.com/19/0917/07/EP8QRB5S00259C76.html [retrieved on July 5, 2021].

37. "Unveiling Success of Jia Yueting: How He Became Chinese Steve Jobs," https://zhuanlan.zhihu.com/p/46061759 [retrieved on July 5, 2021]; "Luo Yonghao Sold 160 Million U.S. Dollars with His Live Chat," https://t.qianzhan.com/daka/detail/200402-5d96ece3.html [retrieved on July 5, 2021].

38. "People Become Beasts—Song Yongyi Talks about the Cannibalism of People in Guangxi during the Cultural Revolution," https://www.rfa.org/mandarin/yataibaodao/zhengzhi/ck-04282016105141.html [retrieved on August 16, 2021].

39. "Cultural Revolution Demons."

40. "Why Are Rich Chinese Entrepreneurs Leaving China?," https://www.asianentrepreneur.org/why-are-rich-chinese-entrepreneurs-leaving-china/ [retrieved on July 5, 2021].

41. "Liu Chuanzhi's Feebleness: Hope to Reform the Current Political Institution but Is Also Dependent upon It," https://finance.sina.cn/chanjing/gl/2015-03-16/detail-iavxeafs1805302.d.html [retrieved on July 5, 2021].

42. Xu, Youyu, "The Complex Influence of the Cultural Revolution on China: Understanding and Reflecting the Cultural Revolution," http://hxzq.net/aspshow/showarticle.asp?id=7666 [retrieved on July 5, 2021].

43. "'Exit of Private Economy': Increasing State Advances and the Private Sector Retreats and Panic Spread among Chinese Private Enterprises," https://www.bbc.com/zhongwen/simp/chinese-news-45522113 [retrieved on July 5, 2021].

44. Ghosh, Shona, "An Arrest, a Debutante Ball, and 2 Marriages: Inside the Lives of the Superrich Huawei Dynasty," https://www.businessinsider.com/insane-life-huawei-founder-ren-zhengfei-ultra-wealthy-family-2018-12 [retrieved on July 5, 2021]. Ren Meng Wanzhou adopted her surname from her mother, Ren's ex-wife.

45. "Tang Wanxin: Last Dream of the Delong Empire," http://news.sina.com.cn/c/2005-01-12/15065519168.shtml [retrieved on July 5, 2021].

46. "Ten Years of the Cultural Revolution," http://www.gov.cn/test/2005-06/24/content_9300.htm [retrieved on July 5, 2021].

47. "Xi Jinping's Anti-corruption Defeated 1.73 Million Party Members and Cadres Last Year," https://www.rfi.fr/cn/%E4%B8%AD%E5%9B%BD/20190109-%E4%B9%A0%E8%BF%91%E5%B9%B3%E5%8F%8D%E8%85%90%E5%8E%BB%E5%B9%B4%E6%89%93%E5%80%92173%E4%B8%87%E4%BA%BA%E6%AC%A1%E5%85%9A%E5%91%98%E5%B9%B2%E9%83%A8-%E8%85%90%E5%8A%BF%E4%BB%8D%E5%A6%82%E9%87%8E%E7%81%AB [retrieved on July 5, 2021].

48. "Zhu Yuanzhang's Anti-corruption Campaign Killed 150,000 People. Why Did Corrupt Officials Continue to Emerge in the Ming Dynasty? Only Because of the Defect," https://k.sina.cn/article_7277845125_1b1cb1a8500101jjlh.html?from=history [retrieved on July 5, 2021].

49. "Comment on China: Xi Jinping, Mao Zedong in Version 2.0?," https://www.bbc.com/zhongwen/simp/focus_on_china/2013/10/131007_cr_xijinping_maozedong [retrieved on July 5, 2021].

50. For example, "Xi Jinping Unifies the Arena, Komsomol Faction and Shanghai Faction Have Become the Past?," https://www.dw.com/zh/%E4%B8%80%E7%BB%9F%E6%B1%9F%E6%B9%96%E4%B9%A0%E8%BF%91%E5%B9%B3-%E5%9B%A2%E6%B4%BE%E6%B5%B7%E6%B4%BE%E6%88%90%E8%BF%87%E5%BE%80/a-41131029 [retrieved on July 5, 2021]; and "The Gangs behind the Falling 'Big Tigers': Secretary Gang, Petroleum Gang, Shanxi Gang," http://yuqing.people.com.cn/n/2015/0104/c391525-26318527.html [retrieved on July 5, 2021].

51. Zhu, Bailiang, and Keith Bradsher, "China's Communists to Private Business: You Heed Us, We'll Help You," https://www.nytimes.com/2020/09/17/business/china-communist-private-business.html [retrieved on July 5, 2021].

52. "Night Talk on Zhongnanhai: Xi Jinping Has Inherited Mao Zedong's Addiction to Struggle 100 Percent," https://www.rfa.org/mandarin/zhuanlan/yehuazhongnanhai/gx-09142020153739.html [retrieved on July 5, 2021].

53. "Xi Jinping: Speech at the Celebration of the Centenary of the Founding of the Chinese Communist Party," http://www.gov.cn/xinwen/2021-07/01/content_5621847.htm [retrieved on July 10, 2021].

54. "Let's Talk about Current Affairs: Re-setting the Cultural Revolution, Xi Jinping Releases Red Flags?," https://www.voachinese.com/a/voaweishi-20210505

-voaio-xi-jinping-redefine-the-cultural-revolution/5879045.html [retrieved on July 5, 2021].

55. Goh, Brenda, and David Stanway, "China Cracks Down on 'Chaotic' Celebrity Fan Culture after Scandals," https://www.reuters.com/world/china/china-crack-down-chaotic-online-fan-culture-2021-08-27/ [retrieved on April 12, 2022]; Li, Guangman, "Everyone Can Feel That a Profound Change Is Underway!," http://politics.people.com.cn/n1/2021/0829/c1001-32211523.html [retrieved on October 5, 2021]; Fan, Wenxin, "Chinese Essayist Revives Worries about a New Cultural Revolution," https://www.wsj.com/articles/chinese-essayist-revives-worries-about-a-new-cultural-revolution-11630670154 [retrieved on October 5, 2021].

56. "Xi Jinping: Speech at the Opening Ceremony of the 11th National Congress of the Chinese Federation of Literary and Art Circles and the Tenth National Congress of the Chinese Writers Association," https://news.sina.com.cn/c/xl/2021-12-15/doc-ikyamrmy9042087.shtml [retrieved on January 1, 2022].

57. Shi, Yangkun, "The Village Where Chairman Mao's Legacy Lives On," http://www.sixthtone.com/news/1007529/the-village-where-chairman-maos-legacy-lives-on [retrieved on July 5, 2021].

58. These include, e.g., "Open Website for the Checking Individuals' Default History," http://zxgk.court.gov.cn/shixin/ [retrieved on April 24, 2022]; "Name Search for Defaulters," https://www.creditchina.gov.cn/gerenxinyong/personsearch/?tablename=credit_zgf_zrr_sxbzxr&gsName=%E5%A4%B1%E4%BF%A1%E8%A2%AB%E6%89%A7%E8%A1%8C%E4%BA%BA%E5%90%8D%E5%8D%95%E6%9F%A5%E8%AF%A2 [retrieved on April 24, 2022].

59. Kozhikode, Rajiv Krishnan, "Dormancy as a Strategic Response to Detrimental Public Policy," *Organization Science* 27, no. 1 (2016): 189–206.

CHAPTER 9: THE THIRD FRONT CONSTRUCTION AND PRIVATE ENTREPRENEURSHIP

Epigraph: "The Big Third Front," documentary, https://www.youtube.com/watch?v=yohNlSEmCH4 [retrieved on July 5, 2021].

1. "What Is the Third Front Construction in the 1960s and What Are Long-Term Consequences of the Campaign?," https://www.zhihu.com/question/20871709 [retrieved on July 5, 2021].

2. "The Big Third Front."

3. Xia, Fei, "Third-Front Construction: An Important Strategic Decision by Mao Zedong," http://cpc.people.com.cn/GB/85037/8627645.html [retrieved on April 24, 2022].

4. "Three-Year Continuous Adjustment of Decision-Making and Third Front Construction Layout," http://www.wenming.cn/hswh/xydll/dsgs/202103/t20210304_5965645.shtml [retrieved on August 11, 2021].

5. "Big Third Front."

6. "Third Front! Third Front! (A Long Essay on the Historical Event That Changed My Parents and Me for the Whole Life)," https://bbs.wenxuecity.com/memory/880875.html [retrieved on April 24, 2022]; Zong, Hairen, "Ten Years since

Hu Jintao Entered Zhongnanhai," http://www.cnd.org/HXWZExpress/02/05/020509-2.gb.html [retrieved on July 5, 2021].

7. "Third Front Construction," https://baike.baidu.com/item/%E4%B8%89%E7%BA%BF%E5%BB%BA%E8%AE%BE [retrieved on July 5, 2021].

8. "Third Front! Third Front!"

9. Naughton, Barry, "The Third Front: Defence Industrialization in the Chinese Interior," *China Quarterly* 115 (1988): 351–86.

10. "The Third-Front/Third-Line," https://www.globalsecurity.org/military/world/china/third-front.htm [retrieved on April 24, 2022].

11. "What Is the Current Status of Plants and Firms in the Third Front Construction?," https://www.zhihu.com/question/37471488 [retrieved on July 5, 2021].

12. "The Third Front Tianxing Meter Plant, Where Is It Now?," http://www.yejienet.com/a3169120140625-1.html [retrieved on July 5, 2021].

13. "Chengdu Tianxing Instrument and Meter Co. Ltd.," https://bkso.baidu.com/item/%E6%88%90%E9%83%BD%E5%A4%A9%E5%85%B4%E4%BB%AA%E8%A1%A8%E8%82%A1%E4%BB%BD%E6%9C%89%E9%99%90%E5%85%AC%E5%8F%B8 [retrieved on April 24, 2022]; Private Equity Daily (PEDaily) website, https://zdb.pedaily.cn/enterprise/show8181/ [retrieved on July 5, 2021].

14. "Plant Manager Laid Off Workers with His Wife as a First Example, the Third Front Construction Firm Succeeded in Transformation and Earned Billions of U.S. Dollars per Year," https://www.bilibili.com/video/av53837897 [retrieved on July 5, 2021].

15. "The Third Front Construction Provided Foundation of Chongqing's Manufacturing Industry," http://news.sohu.com/20051227/n241157087.shtml [retrieved on April 23, 2022]; "The Development of Manufacturing Industry in Western China: From Third Front Construction to Regional Development," http://www.gov.cn/jrzg/2009-09/17/content_1419938.htm [retrieved on July 5, 2021].

16. "Transformation of Motor Producers: Transformation and Upgrading of Private Enterprises," http://m.xinhuanet.com/cq/2018-12/18/c_1123867947.htm [retrieved on April 23, 2022]; "'Chongqing's Richest Man' Yin Mingshan's Curtain Call—Began with Plagiarism, and Finally Returned," https://t.cj.sina.com.cn/articles/view/5108257900/13079d46c01900y7ad [retrieved on July 5, 2021].

17. "Big Third Front."

18. "Third Front! Third Front!"

19. "Industrialization in Sichuan for 70 Years: A Big Jump for a Thousand Years and We Will Create New History," https://www.thepaper.cn/newsDetail_forward_4287887 [retrieved on July 5, 2021].

20. "Jingmen: Getting on the Highland of Industrialization in Hubei Province," https://www.hubei.gov.cn/zwgk/szsmlm/shzqb/201811/t20181129_1372465.shtml [retrieved on April 23, 2022]; "The Top 100 Cities with Highest Entrepreneurship Rate: Beijing, Shanghai, and Shenzhen Rank the Top 3," http://www.drc.sz.gov.cn/csfz/201807/t20180704_13523415.htm [retrieved on July 5, 2021].

21. Gallup, John Luke, Jeffrey D. Sachs, and Andrew D. Mellinger, "Geography and Economic Development," *International Regional Science Review* 22, no. 2 (1999): 179–232.

22. "Enterprise Survey for Innovation and Entrepreneurship in China," https://opendata.pku.edu.cn/dataset.xhtml?persistentId=doi:10.18170/DVN/DLBWAK [retrieved on July 5, 2021].

23. Zhu, Biyao, Heming He, and Maoyu Mao, "The Governance Transformation of My Country's 'Third Front Cities' in the Context of Decentralization: Taking Shiyan, Hubei as an Example" [in Chinese], in *2017 China Urban Planning Annual Conference Proceedings*, vol. 2017, no. 12 (2017), Urban and Rural Governance and Policy Research (Guangdong, China: China Urban Planning Annual Conference, 2017), 1–14.

24. Naughton, "Third Front."

25. "The First in the Country! Sichuan Panzhihua Introduced a New Policy: Families with Two or Three Children Will Receive a Subsidy of 500 Yuan/RMB per Child per Month," https://finance.sina.com.cn/china/dfjj/2021-07-28/doc-ikqcfn ca9525534.shtml [retrieved on April 24, 2022]; "Panzhihua: From an Industrial City to a Cultural City," http://www.ce.cn/culture/gd/202101/04/t20210104_36183745 .shtml [retrieved on August 16, 2021].

26. "Tribute to Those Who Still Stick to the Third Front Construction Enterprise in Hanzhong," https://www.163.com/dy/article/FNEP0GD70517NRUJ.html [retrieved on April 24, 2022]; " 'Five Development Concepts' Implement Industrial Transformation and Upgrading, Leading the High-Quality Development of Hanzhong's Economy," https://www.163.com/dy/article/G9OL7L220534HKUR.html [retrieved on August 16, 2021].

27. "Cases and Examples of Cities in the U.S. Rust Belt," http://us.mofcom.gov .cn/article/ztdy/201612/20161202173241.shtml [retrieved on July 5, 2021]. Overall, high-end technology, diversified investment, attraction of talent, and a focus on environmental protection are important factors for facilitating the transformation of former rust belt cities.

28. "Dare to Use 80% of Fiscal Revenue to Invest in the Future, Hefei 'Deserves' to Make Money," https://tech.sina.com.cn/roll/2020-06-13/doc-iircuyvi8235075 .shtml [retrieved on August 16, 2021].

29. "Who Is the New Energy Capital | Hefei's Strongest VC," https://www.36kr .com/p/1163260041102468 [retrieved on August 16, 2021].

30. Duan, Wen, "The Hard Transformation and Courageous Exploration: Post–Third Front Construction Development of Mianyang in the High-Tech Innovation Era," http://www.scdfz.org.cn/ztzl/scsxjs/rhfz/content_16967 [retrieved on April 24, 2022]; " 'Mianyang Practice' for Stable Industrial Growth and Transformation and Upgrading," http://m.stdaily.com/zhuanti01/znzz/2020-05/18/content_942746 .shtml [retrieved on July 5, 2021].

31. "Liupanshui: A Third Front City's Transformation and Development," http://www.lvcnn.com/cn/mobile/news.php?id=28659 [retrieved on April 24, 2022]; "City Transformation; How Industrial Legacy Can Still Be Alive in the Present Period," http://www.xinhuanet.com/fortune/2020-01/08/c_1125433074.htm [retrieved on July 5, 2021].

32. "First Time in 40 Years! The Permanent Population of Beijing and Shanghai Has Decreased, Where Are All the People Going?," https://www.sohu.com/a /218554989_115362 [retrieved on August 11, 2021].

33. "The Central Ten-Thousand-Word Document Supports the 'Western Development,' Chongqing, Chengdu, and Xi'an Will Build a New Pattern," https://www .sohu.com/a/396014807_116237 [retrieved on August 11, 2021]; Feng, Kui, "Optimizing the Governance of Central Cities and Urban Agglomerations to Promote the Development of the Western Region," http://www.chinado.cn/?p=9544 [retrieved on August 11, 2021].

34. "The Ministry of Science and Technology Deploys Scientific and Technological Innovation in the Western Development: Chongqing, Chengdu, and Xi'an Are Assigned Important Tasks," https://finance.sina.com.cn/tech/2021-03-02/doc -ikftpnnz0495032.shtml [retrieved on August 11, 2021].

PART IV: THE EFFECTS OF MAO'S SOCIALIST INSTITUTIONS: POLITICAL AND ECONOMIC SYSTEMS

Epigraphs: Xie, Chuntao, "Exploring China's Own Construction Path," http:// dangshi.people.com.cn/n/2014/0915/c85037-25664621-2.html [retrieved on April 24, 2022]; Xiao, Shaoliang, "On the State Ownership of the Socialist Means of Production," http://www.wyzxwk.com/Article/lixiang/2021/03/432746.html [retrieved on August 27, 2021]; Han, Qi, "Historical Review and Realistic Reflection of Mao Zedong's Reform of Decentralization," https://www.1xuezhe.exuezhe.com/Qk/art /595014?dbcode=1&flag=2 [retrieved on August 27, 2021]; "Encyclopedia of the CCP: What Is a CCP Branch?," http://www.cac.gov.cn/2021-03/19/c_16177 29402209763.htm [retrieved on August 27, 2021].

CHAPTER 10: THE POLITICAL SYSTEM AND PRIVATE ENTERPRISES IN CHINA

Epigraph: "Changes in the Relationship between Central and Local Governments in the Mao Zedong Era," http://theory.people.com.cn/n/2014/0825/c388253 -25532921.html [retrieved on June 24, 2021].

1. Chen, Ye, Hongbin Li, and Li-An Zhou, "Relative Performance Evaluation and the Turnover of Provincial Leaders in China," *Economics Letters* 88, no. 3 (2005): 421–25; Li, Hongbin, and Li-An Zhou, "Political Turnover and Economic Performance: The Incentive Role of Personnel Control in China," *Journal of Public Economics* 89, no. 9 (2005): 1743–62; Rithmire, Meg, "Land Politics and Local State Capacities: The Political Economy of Urban Change in China," *China Quarterly* 216, no. 4 (2013): 872–95; Saich, Tony, *From Rebel to Ruler: One Hundred Years of the Chinese Communist Party* (Cambridge, MA: Harvard University Press, 2021); "On Ten Major Relationships," April 25, 1956, https://www.marxists.org/chinese /maozedong/marxist.org-chinese-mao-19560425.htm [retrieved on August 7, 2021].

2. Rithmire, Meg, "The 'Chongqing Model' and the Future of China," Harvard Business Case no. 716-004 (2015).

3. "The Other Side of Wang Shi: Used to Be Appreciated by Zhu Rongji and Rejected Bo Xilai's Invitation," http://news.sina.com.cn/c/nd/2016-06-28/doc -ifxtmses1369858.shtml [retrieved on June 24, 2021].

4. Jacob, Andrew, "Anxious Liberals Look to a Provincial Party Chief," https://cn.nytimes.com/china/20121106/c06wang/dual/ [retrieved on August 13, 2021].

5. Jacob, "Anxious Liberals"; Rithmire, "'Chongqing Model.'"

6. Zhao, Dingxin, *Eastern Zhou China Warfare and the Formation of the Confucian-Legalist State* (Shanghai: Sanlian, 2006); Zhao, Dingxin, *The Confucian-Legalist State: A New Theory for Chinese History* (New York: Oxford University Press, 2015).

7. See Hsieh, Chang-tai, "Countering Chinese Industrial Policy Is Counterproductive," https://www.thewirechina.com/2021/09/19/countering-chinese-industrial-policy-is-counterproductive/ [retrieved on September 28, 2021]. See also Walder, Andrew G., "Local Governments as Industrial Firms: An Organizational Analysis of China's Transitional Economy," *American Journal of Sociology* 101, no. 2 (1995): 263–301. The paper compares Chinese cities as local factories.

8. Weber, Isabella M., *How China Escaped Shock Therapy: The Market Reform Debate* (Oxfordshire, UK: Routledge, 2021); Schurmann, Franz, *Ideology and Organization in Communist China* (Berkeley: University of California Press, 1968).

9. Sachs, Jeffrey D., and Wing Thye Woo, "Structural Factors in the Economic Reforms of China, Eastern Europe, and the Former Soviet Union," *Economic Policy* 9, no. 18 (2014): 101–45; Qian, Yingyi, Gérard Roland, and Chenggang Xu, "Why Is China Different from Eastern Europe? Perspectives from Organization Theory," *European Economic Review* 43, no. 4 (1999): 1085–94; Qian, Yingyi, and Chenggang Xu, "The M-Form Hierarchy and China's Economic Reform," *European Economic Review* 37, no. 2 (1993): 541–48.

10. Saich, *From Rebel to Ruler.*

11. Malloy, Allie, "Biden Calls on New York Gov. Andrew Cuomo to Resign after Report Details Sexual Harassment Allegations," https://www.cnn.com/2021/08/03/politics/joe-biden-andrew-cuomo-reaction/index.html [retrieved on August 13, 2021].

12. Myers, Steven Lee, "China Ousts 2 Party Officials amid Outrage about Coronavirus Response," https://www.nytimes.com/2020/02/13/world/asia/china-coronavirus-xi-jinping.html [retrieved on August 13, 2021].

13. Xu, Chenggang, "The Fundamental Institutions of China's Reforms and Development," *Journal of Economic Literature* 49, no. 4 (2011): 1076–151. Some scholars have also called this a Leninist party with micropolitics in localities. Schurmann, *Ideology and Organization in Communist China*; Saich, *From Rebel to Ruler.*

14. Peng, Yusheng, "Chinese Villages and Townships as Industrial Corporations: Ownership, Governance, and Market Discipline," *American Journal of Sociology* 106, no. 5 (2001): 1338–70.

15. "Huaxi Village: Is China's 'No. 1 Village' in Decline?," https://www.163.com/dy/article/FUI970LT0543SZ2V.html [retrieved on July 16, 2021].

16. See, for example, "Changes in the Relationship."

17. Hu, Heng, "On the Origin and Reflections of 'Imperial Power Does Not Reach beyond the County Level,'" http://epaper.gmw.cn/zhdsb/html/2015-11/04/nw.D110000zhdsb_20151104_2-05.htm?div=-1 [retrieved on June 24, 2021].

18. Saich, *From Rebel to Ruler*. See also the interview of the author at Chotiner, Isaac, "Reconsidering the History of the Chinese Communist Party on the Centenary of the C.C.P., a Scholar Examines the Roots of Xi Jinping's Authoritarianism," https://www.newyorker.com/news/q-and-a/reconsidering-the-history-of-the-chinese-communist-party [retrieved on August 26, 2021].

19. Suny, Ronald, *The Revenge of the Past: Nationalism, Revolution, and the Collapse of the Soviet Union* (Palo Alto, CA: Stanford University Press, 1993); Pei, Minxin, *From Reform to Revolution: The Demise of Communism in China and the Soviet Union* (Cambridge, MA: Harvard University Press, 2009); Brower, Daniel, *Turkestan and the Fate of the Russian Empire* (Oxfordshire, UK: Routledge, 2012).

20. Qian, Roland, and Xu, "Why Is China Different?"; Qian and Xu, "M-Form Hierarchy."

21. Huang, Shuozhong, "Xi Zhongxun and Reform and Opening-Up of Guangdong Province," http://dangshi.people.com.cn/n1/2020/0107/c85037-31537492.html [retrieved on August 13, 2020].

22. Efron, Sonni, "Profile: A Reformist Alternative to Yeltsin: Economist Grigory Yavlinsky, the Liberals' Choice, Outpolls the Russian Leader in Popularity," https://www.latimes.com/archives/la-xpm-1993-10-12-wr-45027-story.html [retrieved on June 24, 2021].

23. Qian, Roland, and Xu, "Why Is China Different?"; Qian and Xu, "M-Form Hierarchy"; Marangos, John, "The Political Economy of Shock Therapy," *Journal of Economic Surveys* 16, no. 1 (2002): 41–76.

24. "Deng Xiaoping: Emancipating the Mind, Seeking Truth from Facts, and Uniting as One in Looking to the Future," http://cpc.people.com.cn/n1/2018/0531/c69113-30025177.html [retrieved on June 24, 2021]; "Big Events for Stock Market in China: Deng Xiaoping's Speech Lays the Foundation of Stock Market Development," http://money.163.com/10/1020/16/6JF1GS6N00254JPL.html [retrieved on June 24, 2021].

25. Weber, *How China Escaped*.

26. Wu, Wei, "The Price Reform Was Stopped, and Beijing Intends to Down with Zhao Ziyang," https://cn.nytimes.com/china/20141103/cc03wuwei35/ [retrieved on August 13, 2021].

27. Some scholars have discussed why China escaped shock therapy—for example, Weber, *How China Escaped*. However, we provide explanations rooted in China's institutions as reflections of Maoist imprints.

28. Rithmire, "Land Politics"; Chen, Li, and Zhou, "Relative Performance Evaluation"; Li and Zhou, "Political Turnover."

29. "Xi Jinping: We Should Not Simply Use GDP to Determine Heroes," http://www.xinhuanet.com//world/2013-10/07/c_117609149.htm [retrieved on June 24, 2021].

30. "Wang Qingxian, the New Secretary of the Qingdao Municipal Party Committee, Thoroughly Explained the Methodology of Investment Promotion!," http://tzfz.fznews.com.cn/node/11851/20190130/5c5108ee8a62d.shtml [retrieved on Jun 23, 2021].

31. Hsieh, "Countering Chinese Industrial Policy." See also McGregor, Richard, *The Party: The Secret World of China's Communist Leaders* (New York: HarperCollins,

2010); Bai, Chong-En, Chang-Tai Hsieh, and Zheng Song, "Special Deals with Chinese Characteristics," *NBER Macroeconomics Annual* 34, no. 1 (2020): 341–79.

32. Chen, Li, and Zhou, "Relative Performance Evaluation"; Li and Zhou, "Political Turnover."

33. Marquis, Christopher, and András Tilcsik, "Imprinting: Toward a Multilevel Theory," *Academy of Management Annals* 7, no. 1 (2013): 195–245.

34. Wang, Danqing, Fei Du, and Christopher Marquis, "Defending Mao's Dream: Politicians' Ideological Imprinting and Firms' Political Appointment in China," *Academy of Management Journal* 62, no. 4 (2019): 1111–36.

35. "Governing China: The Guangdong Model," https://www.economist.com /asia/2011/11/26/the-guangdong-model [retrieved on June 24, 2021].

36. Marquis, Christopher, and Kunyuan Qiao, "Waking from Mao's Dream: Communist Ideological Imprinting and the Internationalization of Entrepreneurial Ventures in China," *Administrative Science Quarterly* 65, no. 3 (2020): 795–830; Wang, Du, and Marquis, "Defending Mao's Dream"; Liang, Hao, Rong Wang, and Haikun Zhu, "Growing Up under Mao and Deng: On the Ideological Determinants of Corporate Policies," SSRN, 2019, https://papers.ssrn.com/sol3/papers.cfm ?abstract_id=3494916 [retrieved on April 7, 2022].

37. We used ordinary least squares regression to see the difference between party secretaries who joined the CCP before 1978 and those after regarding their practices related to number of new firms, foreign investments, and venture capital and private equity investments. The regression results show that party secretaries who joined the CCP before 1978 are more antagonistic toward entrepreneurship ($\beta=-6.440, p=.000; -10.36$ percent $= 55.73 / 62.17$), foreign investment ($\beta=-7.530, p=.000; -12.17$ percent $= 54.35 / 61.88$), and venture capital and private equity investments ($\beta=-2.386, p=.000; -4.18$ percent $= 54.74 / 57.13$). The overall index of entrepreneurship and innovation is also smaller ($\beta=-6.197, p=.000; -10.15$ percent $= 54.86 / 61.06$) for party secretaries who joined the CCP before 1978.

We then analyzed the mayors of these Chinese cities regarding their practices related to number of new firms, foreign investments, and venture capital and private equity investments. The regression results show that mayors who joined the CCP before 1978 are more antagonistic toward entrepreneurship ($\beta=-8.360, p=.000; -12.99$ percent $= 56.00 / 64.36$), foreign investment ($\beta=-9.764, p=.000; -15.15$ percent $= 54.67 / 64.43$), and venture capital and private equity investments ($\beta=-5.026, p=.000; -8.46$ percent $= 54.38 / 59.41$). The overall index of entrepreneurship and innovation is also smaller ($\beta=-8.752, p=.000; -13.74$ percent $= 54.95 / 64.30$) for party secretaries who joined the CCP before 1978.

38. "Funing Sanzao Town Tax-Free Zone (Industrial Park) Has Become the New Engine of the Town's Economic Development," https://jsnews.jschina.com.cn/yc/a /202005/t20200508_2546953.shtml [retrieved on October 15, 2021].

39. Lu, Yi, Jin Wang, and Lianming Zhu, "Place-Based Policies, Creation, and Agglomeration Economies: Evidence from China's Economic Zone Program," *American Economic Journal: Economic Policy* 11, no. 3 (2019): 325–60.

40. We use a probit model to investigate the relationship between joining the CCP before 1978 and the likelihood of establishing a special economic zone. The results provide further evidence that party secretaries ($\beta=-0.704, p=.000$) and may-

ors ($\beta = -0.681$, $p = .000$) who joined the CCP in the Maoist period are more antagonistic toward business.

41. Wang, Du, and Marquis, "Defending Mao's Dream"; Zhang, Jianjun, Christopher Marquis, and Kunyuan Qiao, "Do Political Connections Buffer Firms from or Bind Firms to the Government? A Study of Corporate Charitable Donations of Chinese Firms," *Organization Science* 27, no. 5 (2016): 1307–24.

42. "Kunshan Bombing Case Exposes Investment Insider," http://www.china.org .cn/chinese/2014-08/12/content_33215227.htm [retrieved on October 15, 2021].

43. We first coded CEOs' membership in either of the two political councils—the National People's Congress or the Chinese People's Political Consultative Conference—based on their CVs. Then, based on the location of these publicly traded firms, we computed the aggregate number at the city level. After that, we use a negative binomial model to estimate the number of such business-government ties based on whether the focal politician joined the CCP before 1978. The results are consistent with our illustration in fig. 10.6—party secretaries ($\beta = -0.659$, $p = .000$) and mayors ($\beta = -0.402$, $p = .000$) who joined the CCP in the Maoist period appoint fewer businesspeople to political councils. We understand that it may also be possible that the higher-level CCP-government selects people for certain areas, such that more liberal officials are appointed to economically liberal regions where the number of business-government ties is higher and entrepreneurship and foreign investments are more common. We consider these issues in our supplementary statistical tests.

For all these analyses, we consider potential problems of endogeneity. First, CCP-government leaders might not be randomly assigned to different cities. For example, leaders who are more open to business-related ideas and activities might be sent to cities with more vibrant private economies, and thus it is not the politicians' background that affects these business-related actions but rather assignment by the higher level. We utilize the anti-corruption movement in China and keep political leaders whose predecessors are removed from offices suddenly to deal with the endogeneity issue. In this way, their assignment might not be driven by a high-level CCP committee's consideration of matching leaders with cities. Using this sample, we still find that political leaders—both party secretaries and mayors—who joined the CCP before 1978 are more antagonistic toward entrepreneurship, innovation, and foreign investment.

Second, politicians' ages might be a concern and introduce an omitted variable bias. Therefore, we include their ages, and the results are consistent with our main analyses. Furthermore, our results are consistent with studies that use more robust methods and are published in leading academic journals, such as Hu, Helen Wei, and Dean Xu, "Manager or Politician? Effects of CEO Pay on the Performance of State-Controlled Chinese Listed Firms," *Journal of Management,* online ahead of print (2021), https://doi.org/10.1177/01492063211015301 [retrieved on April 12, 2022]; Zhou, William Chongyang, and Sunny Li Sun, "Governors' Pro-market Ideology as Institutional Enablement of Firm Internationalization," *Cross Cultural and Strategic Management* 28, no. 4, online ahead of print (2021), https://doi.org/10 .1108/CCSM-09-2020-0182 [retrieved on April 12, 2022]; Liang, Wang, and Zhu, "Growing Up under Mao"; and Wang, Du, and Marquis, "Defending Mao's Dream."

44. Inoue, Carlos F. K. V., Sergio G. Lazzarini, and Aldo Musacchio, "Leviathan as a Minority Shareholder: Firm-Level Implications of State Equity Purchases," *Academy of Management Journal* 56, no. 6 (2013): 1775–801.

45. Hayek, Friedrich August, "The Use of Knowledge in Society," *American Economic Review* 35, no. 4 (1945): 519–30.

46. Shleifer, Andrei, and Robert W. Vishny, "Politicians and Firms," *Quarterly Journal of Economics* 109, no. 4 (1994): 995–1025.

47. "Jack Ma: 'I Am Busier Than the President, but I Don't Have the Power of the President.' The Masses of the People: 'That's a Blessing,'" https://blog.dwnews.com/post-1400482.html [retrieved on October 5, 2021].

48. "Jack Ma's Latest Voice: The Pawnshop Ideology of China's Banking Industry Has Harmed Many Entrepreneurs," https://finance.sina.com.cn/tech/2020-10-25/doc-iiznctkc7565888.shtml [retrieved on August 13, 2021].

49. Dickson, Bruce J., *Red Capitalists in China: The Party, Private Entrepreneurs, and Prospects for Political Change* (Cambridge: Cambridge University Press, 2003).

50. Madden, Normandy, "Why Google Wasn't Winning in China Anyway," https://www.businessinsider.com/why-google-wasnt-winning-in-china-anyway-2010-1 [retrieved on July 2, 2021].

51. Dai, Sarah, "Tesla's Elon Musk Thanks Chinese Government ahead of Expected Approval for Shanghai Factory," https://www.scmp.com/tech/china-tech/article/2144472/teslas-elon-musk-thanks-chinese-government-ahead-expected-approval [retrieved on July 2, 2021].

52. Kolodny, Lora, "Elon Musk Says 'China Rocks' While the U.S. Is Full of 'Complacency and Entitlement,'" https://www.cnbc.com/2020/07/31/tesla-ceo-elon-musk-china-rocks-us-full-of-entitlement.html [retrieved on July 2, 2021].

53. "Musk Is Moved 'Thanks to the Chinese Government,' and It Will Be Even More Difficult for NIO," https://www.36kr.com/p/1724956672001 [retrieved on July 2, 2021].

54. Kirkpatrick, David, "How Microsoft Conquered China," https://archive.fortune.com/magazines/fortune/fortune_archive/2007/07/23/100134488/index.htm [retrieved on July 2, 2021].

CHAPTER 11: THE SOCIALIST ECONOMY AND PRIVATE FIRMS IN CHINA

Epigraph: Mao, Zedong, "The Purpose of the Socialist Revolution Is to Liberate the Productive Forces," http://www.yhcw.net/famine/Documents/mzdwj/mx07001.htm [retrieved on April 24, 2022]. "The First Implementation of Building the Branch on the Company," https://www.sohu.com/a/458996110_120914498 [retrieved on August 7, 2021].

1. "On September 7, 1953 Mao Zedong Talks about the Policy of Socialist Transformation of Industry and Commerce," http://news.sohu.com/20080907/n259414694.shtml [retrieved on August 7, 2021].

2. "The Treachery of Socialist Transformation: After 1949," https://www.voachinese.com/a/a-21-w2008-02-24-voa3-58628727/1093738.html [retrieved on June 24, 2021].

3. "Rong Yiren Accepted Socialist Transformation Marshall Chen Yi Called Him 'Red Capitalist,'" http://history.sina.com.cn/bk/jgcqs/2014-09-18/1742100452.shtml [retrieved on June 24, 2021].

4. "Our Oath: We Are Obliged to Defend Mao Zedong," http://www.people.com.cn/GB/shizheng/8198/30446/30459/2260723.html [retrieved on June 24, 2021].

5. "Witness the New Birth of Tong Ren Tang," http://www.ceweekly.cn/2009/0927/48282.shtml [retrieved on August 7, 2021]; Sun, Hongqun, and Yongnian Jin, "Beijing Tong Ren Tang before and after the Public-Private Partnership," *Beijing Party History* [in Chinese] 4 (2000): 47–50; Schurmann, Franz, *Ideology and Organization in Communist China* (Berkeley: University of California Press, 1968).

6. "A New Summary of the Basic Socialist Economic System," http://www.xinhuanet.com/politics/2019-12/27/c_1125394868.htm [retrieved on August 7, 2021].

7. Shen, Hongbo, and Shuang Li, "How to Correctly Understand and Grasp the Status and Function of State-Owned Enterprise Party Building," http://theory.people.com.cn/n1/2020/0701/c40531-31766661.html [retrieved on August 7, 2021]; "The CCP Issued a Document to Urge Private Enterprises, Hong Kong and Macao Enterprises to 'Listen to the Party and Follow the Party,'" https://www.rfa.org/mandarin/yataibaodao/zhengzhi/ql1-09162020061254.html [retrieved on August 7, 2021].

8. Brown, Chad, and Jennifer Hillman, "The October Truce on US-China Trade Failed to Address Subsidies," https://voxeu.org/content/october-truce-us-china-trade-failed-address-subsidies [retrieved on July 16, 2021].

9. Badkar, Matma, "This Chart Busts the Myth That China's Economy Is Driven by Gov't-Owned Businesses," https://www.businessinsider.com/chart-debunks-state-owned-enterprises-myth-2012-4 [retrieved on July 16, 2021].

10. Cotton, Tom, "Beat China: Targeted Decoupling and the Economic Long War, " https://www.cotton.senate.gov/imo/media/doc/210216_1700_China%20Report_FINAL.pdf [retrieved on July 16, 2021].

11. "Common Program of the Chinese People's Political Consultative Conference—Has a Temporary Constitutional Role and Laid the Foundation for the Founding of New China," http://www.ccphistory.org.cn/node2/shds/n58/u1ai39502.html [retrieved on July 16, 2021]; "Common Program of the Chinese People's Political Consultative Conference," §4.30, http://fgcx.bjcourt.gov.cn:4601/law?fn=chl521s829.txt [retrieved on July 16, 2021].

12. "Why Does the National Flag Have to Be Five Stars? Uncover the Story behind the Numbers for You," https://m.thepaper.cn/baijiahao_5086990?sdkver=e06426d6&clientprefetch=1 [retrieved on Jun 21, 2021].

13. Private ownership did not totally disappear, as there was an underground, gray economy. For example, some people were selling their own products at the risk of being detained and their properties being confiscated, such as Cao Dewang of Fuyao that we have mentioned in chapter 7.

14. Xu, Dean, Jane W. Lu, and Qian Gu, "Organizational Forms and Multi-population Dynamics: Economic Transition in China," *Administrative Science Quarterly* 59, no. 3 (2014): 517–47.

15. See "Flying for Forty Years: Four Waves of Opportunities for Private Firms to Take Off in China," https://www.3wcoffee.com/qfnews/detail?id=1893 [retrieved on June 21, 2021]; Chen, Guangjin, Jun Li, and Harry Matlay, "Who Are the Chinese Private Entrepreneurs?," *Journal of Small Business and Enterprise Development* 13, no. 2 (2006): 148–60; Dai, Shuanping, Yuanyuan Wang, and Yang Liu, "The Emergence of Chinese Entrepreneurs: Social Connections and Innovation," *Journal of Entrepreneurship in Emerging Economies* 11, no. 3 (2019): 351–68; and Hong, Zhaohui, "Mapping the Evolution and Transformation of the New Private Entrepreneurs in China," *Journal of Chinese Political Science* 9, no. 1 (2004): 23–42.

16. Bruton, Garry D., Hailin Lan, and Yuan Lu, "China's Township and Village Enterprises: Kelon's Competitive Edge," *Academy of Management Executive* 14, no. 1 (2000): 19–27; Fu, Xiaolan, and V. N. Balasubramanyam, "Township and Village Enterprises in China," *Journal of Development Studies* 39, no. 4 (2003): 27–46; Che, Jiahua, and Yingyi Qian, "Institutional Environment, Community Government, and Corporate Governance: Understanding China's Township-Village Enterprises," *Journal of Law, Economics, and Organization* 14, no. 1 (1998): 1–23.

17. Huang, Yasheng, *Capitalism with Chinese Characteristics: Entrepreneurship and the State* (Cambridge: Cambridge University Press, 2008).

18. Hsieh, Chang-Tai, and Zheng Michael Song, "Grasp the Large, Let Go of the Small: The Transformation of the State Sector in China," NBER Working Paper 21006, National Bureau of Economic Research, 2015.

19. Kennedy, Mark, "Obama-Backed Documentary on Ohio Factory Wins Academy Award," https://abcnews.go.com/Entertainment/wireStory/obama-backed-documentary-ohio-factory-wins-academy-award-68872312 [retrieved on July 5, 2021].

20. Yu, Donghui, "Liu Chuanzhi Has Been in the Sea for 30 Years of Entrepreneurship and Sighs: There Are Countless Hurdles to Life and Death," http://finance.sina.com.cn/leadership/crz/20150102/222021214387.shtml [retrieved on July 16, 2021].

21. "Local Governments as a Driving Force of This Round of 'the State Advances and Private Sector Retreats,'" http://news.ifeng.com/opinion/topic/zaiguoyouhuayundong/200907/0727_7531_1271198.shtml [retrieved on June 24, 2021].

22. "Xi Jinping: Make State-Owned Enterprises Stronger, Larger, and Better in a Taken for Granted Fashion," http://www.xinhuanet.com/politics/2016-07/04/c_1119162333.htm [retrieved on June 24, 2021].

23. "'Five in One' Spread the Chapter (Questions and Answers on the Study of Xi Jinping's Thoughts on Socialism with Chinese Characteristics in the New Era (28))—About the Overall Layout of the Cause of Socialism with Chinese Characteristics," http://paper.people.com.cn/rmrb/html/2021-08/25/nw.D110000renmrb_20210825_1-05.htm [retrieved on October 1, 2021], with translation in Kewalramani, Manoj, "Xi's Ethnic Policies—Li on Developing the Northeast—Yang Jiechi at BRICS Security Talks—China-Turkey Partnership—Xi Thought: Public & Private Sector + Core Technology Research—A New Struggle," https://trackingpeoplesdaily.substack.com/p/xis-ethnic-policies-li-on-developing [retrieved on October 1, 2021].

24. Lynch, David J., "Initial U.S.-China Trade Deal Has Major Hole: Beijing's Massive Business Subsidies," https://www.washingtonpost.com/business/economy

/initial-us-china-trade-deal-has-major-hole-beijings-massive-business-subsidies /2019/12/30/f4de4d14-22a3-11ea-86f3-3b5019d451db_story.html [retrieved on June 24, 2021].

25. "Government Motion: Private Firms in Shaoxing Are Facing Governmental Supervision like State-Owned Enterprises," http://news.ifeng.com/opinion/topic /zaiguoyouhuayundong/200907/0727_7531_1271140.shtml [retrieved on June 21, 2021].

26. Du, Jun, Xiaoxuan Liu, and Ying Zhou, "State Advances and Private Retreats? Evidence of Aggregate Productivity Decomposition in China," *China Economic Review* 31 (2014): 459–74; "China's State Capitalism: Not Just Tilting at Windmills," https://www.economist.com/leaders/2012/10/06/not-just-tilting-at -windmills [retrieved June 21, 2021].

27. "Government Motion."

28. "General Secretary Xi Jinping: Constantly Open Up a New Realm of Contemporary Chinese Marxist Political Economy," http://www.moe.gov.cn/s78/A01 /s4561/jgfwzx_xxtd/202008/t20200817_478589.html [retrieved on August 7, 2021].

29. "'Five in One,'" with translation in Kewalramani, "Xi's Ethnic Policies."

30. "Who Made Hualian Sanxin Almost Broke?," http://finance.ifeng.com/news /hgjj/20090602/733595.shtml [retrieved on April 24, 2022]. The government official's words are from "Government Motion."

31. "'Exit of Private Economy': Increasing State Advances and the Private Sector Retreats and Panic Spread among Chinese Private Enterprises," https://www.bbc .com/zhongwen/simp/chinese-news-45522113 [retrieved on June 24, 2021].

32. Around 294,000 people were documented to have suffered from this in some way, including 6 babies who died from kidney stones and 54,000 babies who were hospitalized. The scandal hampered the growth of the dairy industry and many manufacturers, including Mengniu. See Branigan, Tania, "Chinese Figures Show Fivefold Rise in Babies Sick from Contaminated Milk," https://www.theguardian .com/world/2008/dec/02/china [retrieved on July 16, 2021].

33. "Mengniu and Guangming Are in Trouble Again, the Dairy Industry May Be in a Second Wave of Crisis," http://finance.sina.com.cn/chanjing/b/20090213 /09595852096.shtml [retrieved on July 16, 2021].

34. "The 'State Advances and Private Sector Retreats' That Underlies China Oil and Foodstuffs Corporation's Investment in Mengniu," http://news.ifeng.com/opinion /topic/zaiguoyouhuayundong/200907/0727_7531_1271193.shtml [retrieved on June 21, 2021]; "Evolution of Mengniu: Gensheng Niu Needs China Oil and Foodstuffs Corporation More," https://business.sohu.com/20090921/n266871745.shtml [retrieved on June 21, 2021].

35. Data are from "321 A-Share Listed Companies 'Change Ownership' in 2020," https://www.jwview.com/jingwei/html/m/02-01/378688.shtml [retrieved on August 7, 2021]; "Securities Daily: State-Owned Listed Companies Participated in 655 A-Share Mergers and Acquisitions during the Year," http://www.sasac.gov.cn /n2588025/n2588139/c16181884/content.html [retrieved on August 7, 2021]; "41 Private Enterprises Were Nationalized, How Did Those Bosses Eliminate Listed Companies?," https://www.sohu.com/a/363609918_534161 [retrieved on August 7,

2021]; "The State Advances and Private Sector Retreats! 90 A-Share Listed Companies Have Changed from Private Enterprises to State-Owned Enterprises in the Past 3 Years," https://news.creaders.net/china/2021/05/05/2350106.html [retrieved on August 7, 2021]; and "Local State-Owned Assets Take the Initiative to Help Private Enterprises: 29 Firms Have Been Invested This Year, Non-uniform Deployment," https://www.guancha.cn/politics/2018_10_19_476098.shtml [retrieved on August 7, 2021].

36. "Return to the Public-Private Partnership in the 1950s? The Governments of Hangzhou and Other Places Dispatched Personnel to Private Enterprises," https://www.rfa.org/mandarin/yataibaodao/jingmao/ql1-09232019065851.html [retrieved on June 21, 2021].

37. Bradsher, Keith, Stevenson, Alexandra, "Beijing Takes Over Anbang, Insurer That Owns Waldorf Astoria," https://cn.nytimes.com/business/20180223/china-anbang-waldorf-astoria/ [retrieved on June 24, 2021]; Moss, Trefor, Xie, Stella Yifan, "Hainan Airlines Group Has in Fact Been Taken Over by the Government Due to the Impact of COVID-19," https://cn.wsj.com/articles/%E6%B5%B7%E8%88%AA%E4%B8%8D%E5%A0%AA%E7%96%AB%E6%83%85%E5%86%B2%E5%87%BB%EF%BC%8C%E5%B7%B2%E5%AE%9E%E9%99%85%E4%B8%8A%E8%A2%AB%E6%94%BF%E5%BA%9C%E6%8E%A5%E7%AE%A1-11583116792 [retrieved on June 24, 2021].

38. He, Laura, "Xi Jinping Wants China's Private Companies to Fight Alongside the Communist Party," https://www.cnn.com/2020/09/22/business/china-private-sector-intl-hnk/index.html [retrieved on April 7, 2022]; Wei, Lingling, "China's Xi Ramps Up Control of Private Sector. 'We Have No Choice but to Follow the Party,'" https://www.wsj.com/articles/china-xi-clampdown-private-sector-communist-party-11607612531 [retrieved on April 7, 2022]; Nagarajan, Shalini, "China's Xi Jinping Personally Halted Ant's Record-Breaking $37 Billion IPO after Boss Jack Ma Snubbed Government Leaders, Report Says," https://markets.businessinsider.com/news/stocks/ant-group-ipo-personally-halted-china-xi-jinping-jack-wsj-2020-11-1029800224# [retrieved on April 14, 2022]; Yang, Yingzhi, and Brenda Goh, "Beijing Took Stake and Board Seat in Key ByteDance Domestic Entity This Year," https://www.reuters.com/world/china/beijing-owns-stakes-bytedance-weibo-domestic-entities-records-show-2021-08-17/ [retrieved on August 22, 2021].

39. "Ant Financial and Inner Mongolia Junzheng Reconciled and the Holding of Tianhong Fund Was Settled," https://finance.china.com.cn/money/fund/jjyw/20150217/2967523.shtml [retrieved on August 26, 2021]; "Ma Yun's Circle of Friends: Who Are the Shadow Bosses behind the Ants?," https://finance.sina.com.cn/money/bank/bank_hydt/2020-11-09/doc-iiznctkeo482153.shtml [retrieved on August 26, 2021].

40. Qiao, Kunyuan, and Christopher Marquis, "Internal Logics of Control: A Study of the Relationship between Internal and External CSR in China," *Academy of Management Proceedings* 2019, no. 1 (2019): 13421.

41. Qiao and Marquis; Perkins, Dwight, "Completing China's Move to the Market," *Journal of Economic Perspectives* 8, no. 2 (1994): 23–46.

42. "How to Understand Hangzhou Government's Sending 100 Officials to Important Firms Such as Alibab, Geely, and Wahaha?," https://www.zhihu.com/question/347302891 [retrieved on June 24, 2021].

43. "Hangzhou Sent Government Affairs Representatives to Private Firms, and They Are Training Them: What Is Attitude of Private Firms?," http://www.jwview .com/jingwei/html/09-25/261081.shtml [retrieved on June 24, 2021].

44. An item from the Chinese Private Enterprise Survey questionnaire asks entrepreneurs to evaluate their difficulty in financing, with 1 = no difficulty, 2 = some difficulty, and 3 = a lot of difficulty. We used two approaches to test the difference statistically. First, we used a paired t-test for the Chinese Private Enterprise Survey data and found that the average response value of entrepreneurs receiving state investments into their ventures is 1.93, while that for those without state investments is 2.02. The t statistic is 3.994 and significant at the 1 percent level, suggesting that state ownership might help alleviate the financing problems of private entrepreneurs. Second, we used an ordered probit model for an investigation. The results support the paired t-test: other things being equal, entrepreneurs receiving state investments are overall facing less difficulty ($\beta = -0.145, p = .000$).

45. Marquis, Christopher, and Kunyuan Qiao, "Waking from Mao's Dream: Communist Ideological Imprinting and the Internationalization of Entrepreneurial Ventures in China," *Administrative Science Quarterly* 65, no. 3 (2020): 795–830; Zhang, Jianjun, Christopher Marquis, and Kunyuan Qiao, "Do Political Connections Buffer Firms from or Bind Firms to the Government? A Study of Corporate Charitable Donations of Chinese Firms," *Organization Science* 27, no. 5 (2016): 1307–24.

46. Maung, Min, Craig Wilson, and Xiaobo Tang, "Political Connections and Industrial Pollution: Evidence Based on State Ownership and Environmental Levies in China," *Journal of Business Ethics* 138, no. 4 (2016): 649–59; Cheung, Yan-Leung, Lihua Jing, P. Raghavendra Rau, and Aris Stouraitis, "Guanxi, Political Connections, and Expropriation: The Dark Side of State Ownership in Chinese Listed Companies," working paper, City University of Hong Kong, 2005; Marquis and Qiao, "Waking from Mao's Dream."

47. Li, Hongbin, Lingsheng Meng, and Junsen Zhang, "Why Do Entrepreneurs Enter Politics? Evidence from China," *Economic Inquiry* 44, no. 3 (2006): 559–78; Marquis and Qiao, "Waking from Mao's Dream."

48. We used both a paired t-test and ordinary least squares regression to test the relationship between ratio of profits appropriated by the government and state ownership. The results support our findings illustrated in fig. 11.4 ($\beta = -0.011, p = .000$).

49. The decentralized structure provides incentives for local politicians, who are still subject to the tight, centralized political control.

50. "General Secretary Xi Jinping."

51. "'Five in One,'" with translation in Kewalramani, "Xi's Ethnic Policies"; Li, Jie, "The Adherence, Development and Innovation of Mao Zedong Thought by Xi Jinping's Socialism with Chinese Characteristics in the New Era," http://www .qstheory.cn/politics/2019-02/03/c_1124083205.htm [retrieved on August 7, 2021].

52. McNally, David, "From Financial Crisis to World-Slump: Accumulation, Financialisation, and the Global Slowdown," *Historical Materialism* 17, no. 2 (2009): 35–83.

53. "Xi Jinping Talks about Market Economy: The Attribute 'Socialism' Must Not Be Forgotten," http://cpc.people.com.cn/xuexi/n1/2019/0128/c385476-30592929 .html [retrieved on August 7, 2021].

54. "Government Motion."

55. "From Public-Private Cooperative Managing to Nationalization: Private Entrepreneurs Rush to Retire," https://www.rfa.org/mandarin/yataibaodao/jingmao /ql1-12172019063409.html [retrieved on June 24, 2021].

56. Meisner, Maurice, *Mao's China and After: A History of the People's Republic* (New York: Free Press, 1999). See also Wang, Xinzhe, "The Leadership of the Party Is the Fundamental Guarantee for Taking a New Road of Industrialization with Chinese Characteristics," https://www.ccdi.gov.cn/lswh/lilun/202104/t20210421 _240032.html [retrieved on August 7, 2021]; "Four: The Booming Industrial Economy," http://www.stats.gov.cn/ztjc/ztfx/xzg50nxlfxbg/200206/t20020605_35962.html [retrieved on August 7, 2021]; "The 60 Years Report of New China: From the Poor and Nothing to the Modern Industrial System," http://www.gov.cn/gzdt/2009 -09/21/content_1422263.htm [retrieved on August 7, 2021].

57. Wang, Jing, and Yupeng Wang, "Why Should China Nurture Stronger, Better, and Bigger State-Owned Enterprises?," http://politics.people.com.cn/n1/2019 /1027/c429373-31422097.html [retrieved on August 8, 2021].

58. Mitter, Rana, and Elsbeth Johnson, "What the West Gets Wrong about China: Three Fundamental Misconceptions," *Harvard Business Review* 99, no. 3 (2021): 2–8.

59. "Xi Jinping: Speech at the Symposium on Private Enterprises," http://www .xinhuanet.com/politics/2018-11/01/c_1123649488.htm [retrieved on August 8, 2021].

60. "'Five in One,'" with translation in Kewalramani, "Xi's Ethnic Policies."

61. McDonald, Joe, "China Chases 'Rejuvenation' with Control of Tycoons, Society," https://apnews.com/article/technology-lifestyle-asia-beijing-xi-jinping-1a03 a0ad19397face74b2e2dd2130d33 [retrieved on September 28, 2021].

62. Beddor, Christopher, "China's Embrace of Private Investment Is Getting Tighter," https://cn.nytimes.com/business/20171016/china-private-investment/dual/ [retrieved on June 24, 2021]; Ip, Richard, "The Risk of More Communist Party Influence in Chinese Firms," https://www.ejinsight.com/eji/article/id/2019824/20181220 -the-risk-of-more-communist-party-influence-in-chinese-firms [retrieved on June 24, 2021].

63. "A Hundred Years' Dream, the Red Flag of the Party | Zhou Haijiang: Party Building Leads the High-Quality Development of Hongdou," http://www.taweekly .com/zzdd/202105/t20210520_4143325.html [retrieved on July 27, 2021].

64. "Analysis Report on the Current Situation of Party Organization Construction in My Country's Private Enterprises," http://www.acfic.org.cn/fgdt1/zjgd /201905/t20190523_125262.html [retrieved on June 21, 2021]. The naming conventions of such party organizations also vary by size. When its members number over one hundred people, the organization is called a CCP committee.

65. "Ma Yun Listens to the CCP Class in Yan'an: Look at the CCP's Perseverance in the Difficult Environment," http://roll.sohu.com/20150828/n419979097 .shtml [retrieved on August 7, 2021].

66. Laband, Jake, "Fact Sheet: Communist Party Groups in Foreign Companies in China," https://www.chinabusinessreview.com/fact-sheet-communist-party-groups -in-foreign-companies-in-china/ [retrieved on June 24, 2021].

67. "Why Do Private Enterprises Need to Build CCP Branches? The Central Organization Department Gave a Positive Response," https://www.guancha.cn/politics/2017_10_23_431863.shtml [retrieved on August 8, 2021].

68. Blanchette, Jude, "Against Atrophy: Party Organisations in Private Firms," https://perma.cc/3PEX-RGPT [retrieved on November 20, 2021].

69. "Xi Jinping: Speech."

70. Ip, "Risk of More"; Lin, Zhang, "Chinese Communist Party Needs to Curtail Its Presence in Private Businesses," https://www.scmp.com/economy/china-economy/article/2174811/chinese-communist-party-needs-curtail-its-presence-private [retrieved on April 14, 2022]; Tai, Catherine, "China's Private Sector Is under Siege," https://thediplomat.com/2018/12/chinas-private-sector-is-under-siege/ [retrieved on June 24, 2021].

71. Yue, Wenxiao, "China Watch: Huawei America Was 'Criminal' and 'Party Branch'?," https://m.soundofhope.org/post/275480 [retrieved on June 21, 2021].

72. "The Threat Posed by the Chinese Government and the Chinese Communist Party to the Economic and National Security of the United States," https://www.fbi.gov/news/speeches/the-threat-posed-by-the-chinese-government-and-the-chinese-communist-party-to-the-economic-and-national-security-of-the-united-states [retrieved on October 5, 2021].

73. Yan, Xiaojun, and Jie Huang, "Navigating Unknown Waters: The Chinese Communist Party's New Presence in the Private Sector," *China Review* 17, no. 2 (2017): 37–63.

74. "Why Is Jack Ma So Red?," https://posts.careerengine.us/p/5b34d965eaf58f74f6cce9e6 [retrieved on July 1, 2021].

75. "Why Internet Firms All Established a CCP Branch?," https://www.sohu.com/a/153778333_116219 [retrieved on June 24, 2021].

76. "Making a Model of Employees in a Global Firm—Exploration of Modeling Effect of CCP Members in Fuyao's CCP Committee," http://dangjian.people.com.cn/n/2014/1217/c391506-26225524.html [retrieved on June 24, 2021].

77. "CCP Construction Is the Political Guarantee and Powerhouse for Healthy Development of Private Firms," http://dangjian.com/specials/fg/fgdjzy/201602/t20160214_3141438.shtml [retrieved on June 24, 2021].

78. "Let the Communist Party's Flag Fly: A Study of Provincial Model CCP Branch—CCP Committee of Hengtong Group," https://k.sina.com.cn/article_5675440730_15248 5a5a02000iphh.html?from=news&subch=onews [retrieved on June 24, 2021].

79. "What Does a Communist Party Branch Mean to Private Firms?," http://www.fgdjw.com.cn/fgdjw/system/2014/02/20/017702760.shtml [retrieved on April 24, 2022].

80. "Research on the Mechanism of Party Organizations in Private Enterprises," https://zjnews.zjol.com.cn/05zjnews/system/2011/11/21/018013484.shtml [retrieved on June 24, 2021].

81. The Chinese Private Enterprise Survey questionnaire asks how many employees receive insurance for medical care, old age (retirement), unemployment, injury, and birth and fertility. We calculated coverage of these five indicators by scaling them with the total number of employees. We used both a paired *t*-test and ordinary

least squares regression to examine how these indicators differ between private firms with and without a CCP branch. The results show that firms with a CCP branch purchase insurance for medical care for 7.2 percent ($\beta=0.072$, $p=.000$) more employees; retirement care for 9.7 percent ($\beta=0.097$, $p=.000$) more employees; unemployment for 13.1 percent ($\beta=0.131$, $p=.000$) more employees; injury for 9.2 percent ($\beta=0.092$, $p=.000$) more employees; and birth and fertility for 15.5 percent ($\beta=0.155$, $p=.000$) more employees.

82. Ngo, Hang-Yue, Chung-Ming Lau, and Sharon Foley, "Strategic Human Resource Management, Firm Performance, and Employee Relations Climate in China," *Human Resource Management* 47, no. 1 (2008): 73–90.

83. We also used both a paired *t*-test and ordinary least squares regression to examine how return on assets differs between private firms with and without a CCP branch. Our results show that firms with a CCP branch have a 2.1 percent ($\beta=0.021$, $p=.000$) higher profitability.

84. "Why Should Private Firms Strengthen the Communist Party Influence?," http://politics.people.com.cn/n1/2019/1015/c429373-31400444.html [retrieved on June 24, 2021].

85. "Li Shimo: Reading 'Seeking Truth' / Qiushi and Investing-China's Institutional Advantages and Investment Directions in the New World Pattern," https://www.guancha.cn/Shipin/2020_11_14_571405.shtml [retrieved on October 7, 2021].

86. "Tencent: When the 'Penguin' Wears the CCP Emblem," http://news.12371.cn/2018/04/02/ARTI1522647889151198.shtml [retrieved on June 24, 2021].

87. "Why Internet Firms?"

88. Fleisher, Belton, *Policy Reform and Chinese Markets: Progress and Challenges* (Cheltenham, UK: Edward Elgar, 2008).

89. Hogan, Michael J., *The End of the Cold War: Its Meaning and Implications* (Cambridge: Cambridge University Press, 1992).

CONCLUSION

Epigraph: Oxford Essential Quotations, https://www.oxfordreference.com/view/10.1093/acref/9780191843730.001.0001/q-oro-ed5-00002969 [retrieved on February 2, 2022].

1. Bellah, Robert N., *The Broken Covenant: American Civil Religion in Time of Trial* (New York: Seabury, 1975), chap. 5.

2. Mitter, Rana, and Elsbeth Johnson, "What the West Gets Wrong about China: Three Fundamental Misconceptions," *Harvard Business Review* 99, no. 3 (2021): 2–8.

3. Chang, Gordon G., *The Coming Collapse of China* (New York: Random House, 2001).

4. Page 15 of Perry, Elizabeth J., "Is the Chinese Communist Regime Legitimate?," in *The China Questions,* edited by Rudolph Jennifer and Szonyi Michael, 11–17 (Cambridge, MA: Harvard University Press, 2018).

5. Blanchette, Jude, *China's New Red Guards: The Return of Radicalism and the Rebirth of Mao Zedong* (Oxford: Oxford University Press, 2019), 16.

6. "'Straighten Origins, Clear Sources, Clear Reasons to Increase Trustworthiness' Officially Released," https://www.piyao.org.cn/2021-07/15/c_1211241937.htm [retrieved on November 20, 2021].

7. Wu, Kepeng, "Be Wary of the Historical Nihilism in Mao Zedong's Research in Recent Years," http://www.dswxyjy.org.cn/n1/2017/1012/c398751-29583111.html [retrieved on August 8, 2021].

8. Yang, Jisheng, *Tombstone: The Untold Story of Mao's Great Famine,* translated by Stacy Mosher and Jian Guo (London: Allen Lane, 2012).

9. "Remarks by President Biden in Press Conference," March 25, 2021, https://www.whitehouse.gov/briefing-room/speeches-remarks/2021/03/25/remarks-by-president-biden-in-press-conference/ [retrieved on November 3, 2021].

10. Sanger, David E., and Michael D. Shear, "G7 Leaders Offer United Front as Summit Ends, but Cracks Are Clear," https://www.nytimes.com/2021/06/13/us/politics/g7-summit-ends.html [retrieved on June 24, 2021].

11. Reuveny, Rafael, and Aseem Prakash, "The Afghanistan War and the Breakdown of the Soviet Union," *Review of International Studies* 25, no. 4 (1999): 693–708.

12. Ni, Adam, "Dynastic Cycle and Shadows of the Past over Xi's China," https://www.thechinastory.org/dynastic-cycle-and-shadows-of-the-past-over-xis-china/ [retrieved on June 24, 2021].

13. "Remarks as Prepared for Delivery of Ambassador Katherine Tai Outlining the Biden-Harris Administration's 'New Approach to the U.S.-China Trade Relationship,'" https://ustr.gov/about-us/policy-offices/press-office/speeches-and-remarks/2021/october/remarks-prepared-delivery-ambassador-katherine-tai-outlining-biden-harris-administrations-new [retrieved on April 24, 2022].

14. For example, making China great again was mentioned twenty-six times by Xi during his centenary speech: "Xi Jinping: Speech at the Celebration of the Centenary of the Founding of the Chinese Communist Party," http://www.gov.cn/xinwen/2021-07/01/content_5621847.htm [retrieved on July 10, 2021].

15. "D&G Insulted China, Spokesperson Dilraba and Wang Junkai Resisted! This Big Name Must Die!," https://www.sohu.com/a/276958415_755123 [retrieved on July 17, 2021].

16. "Good Days for Foreign Brands Are Over! H&M's Sales in the Chinese Market Plummeted, and Domestic Brands Are Occupying the Market," https://www.163.com/dy/article/GE8MMHUE0550AQCS.html [retrieved on July 17, 2021].

17. McGinnis, Ariel, James Pellegrin, Yin Shum, Jason Teo, and Judy Wu, "The Sichuan Earthquake and the Changing Landscape of CSR in China," *Knowledge@Wharton,* April 20, 2009.

18. Hilgers, Lauren, "'We Are So Divided Now': How China Controls Thought and Speech beyond Its Borders," https://www.theguardian.com/news/2021/oct/26/we-are-so-divided-now-how-china-controls-thought-and-speech-beyond-its-borders [retrieved on November 20, 2021].

19. Porter, Michael E., *Competitive Strategy* (New York: Free Press, 1980/1998).

20. "The Localization of Foreign Brands in China," http://yuqing.people.com.cn/n/2014/0519/c358832-25034088.html [retrieved on August 10, 2021].

21. Jacobs, Harrison, "KFC Is by Far the Most Popular Fast Food Chain in China and It's Nothing like the US Brand—Here's What It's Like," https://www .businessinsider.com/most-popular-fast-food-chain-in-china-kfc-photos-2018-4 [retrieved on July 2, 2021].

22. Mullin, Kyle, "You Want Youtiao with That? McDonald's Tackles the Street Food Favorite," https://www.thebeijinger.com/blog/2018/09/10/you-want-youtiao -with-that-mcdonalds-tackles-the-street-favorite [retrieved on July 2, 2021].

23. "Missing China's E-commerce Market, Where Does Amazon's 'Localization' Lose?," http://www.xinhuanet.com/fortune/2019-04/25/c_1124412269.htm [retrieved on August 10, 2021].

24. Rein, Shaun, "Why Best Buy Failed in China," https://www.cnbc.com/id /41882157 [retrieved on July 2, 2021].

25. Peng, Mike W., "Towards an Institution-Based View of Business Strategy," *Asia Pacific Journal of Management* 19, no. 2 (2002): 251–67; Peng, Mike W., Sunny Li Sun, Brian Pinkham, and Hao Chen, "The Institution-Based View as a Third Leg for a Strategy Tripod," *Academy of Management Perspectives* 23, no. 3 (2009): 63–81; Peng, Mike W., Denis Y. L. Wang, and Yi Jiang, "An Institution-Based View of International Business Strategy: A Focus on Emerging Economies," *Journal of International Business Studies* 39, no. 5 (2008): 920–36.

26. Marquis, Christopher, Qi Li, and Kunyuan Qiao, "The Chinese Collectivist Model of Charity," *Stanford Social Innovation Review* 15, no. 3 (2017): 40–47.

27. Baumol, William J., "Entrepreneurship: Productive, Unproductive, and Destructive," *Journal of Political Economy* 98, no. 5 (1990): 893–921; Chan, Cheris Shun-ching, "Invigorating the Content in Social Embeddedness: An Ethnography of Life Insurance Transactions in China," *American Journal of Sociology* 115, no. 3 (2009): 712–54.

28. James, Steve, Mark Mitten, Julie Goldman, Fenell Doremus, and Nick Verbitsky, "Abacus: Small Enough to Jail," https://www.pbs.org/wgbh/frontline/film /abacus/ [retrieved on July 25, 2021].

29. "Negotiations, Chinese Style," https://www.chinabusinessreview.com /negotiations-chinese-style/ [retrieved on April 15, 2022]; "Negotiating and Dealing with Chinese Business Partners," http://www.iberchina.org/files/china_negotiation _conflicts.pdf [retrieved on July 25, 2021]; Måttgård, David, and John Åström, "Business Negotiations with the Chinese: The Swedish Perspective," MA thesis, Luleå University of Technology, 2005.

30. Pye, Lucian, *Chinese Commercial Negotiating Style* (Santa Monica, CA: RAND, 1982).

31. See, e.g., Pieke, Frank N., *Knowing China* (Cambridge: Cambridge University Press, 2016), 24.

32. Sun, Lei, "Inherit and Promote the Excellent Chinese Traditional Culture," http://theory.people.com.cn/n1/2021/0218/c40531-32030464.html [retrieved on July 25, 2021].

33. "Coronavirus: Trump Feuds with Governors over Authority," https://www .bbc.com/news/world-us-canada-52274969 [retrieved on July 18, 2021].

34. Saich, Tony, *From Rebel to Ruler: One Hundred Years of the Chinese Communist Party* (Cambridge, MA: Harvard University Press, 2021). See also the inter-

view of the author at Chotiner, Isaac, "Reconsidering the History of the Chinese Communist Party," https://www.newyorker.com/news/q-and-a/reconsidering-the -history-of-the-chinese-communist-party [retrieved on August 26, 2021].

35. "National People's Congress Closing: Xi Jinping's Speech Emphasizes 'the Party Leads Everything,'" https://www.bbc.com/zhongwen/simp/chinese-news -43468026 [retrieved on July 26, 2021].

36. Mai, Jun, "Xi Jinping Asks: Why Do Chinese Officials Lack Initiative and Wait for Orders from the Top?," https://www.scmp.com/news/china/politics/article /3140600/why-do-chinese-officials-lack-initiative-and-wait-orders-top [retrieved on July 18, 2021].

37. "Thank You! Xie Gaohua!," https://new.qq.com/omn/20191023/2019 1023A0MFU300.html?pc [retrieved on July 18, 2021].

38. "The Founders of Guangdong's Reform and Opening-Up," http://dangshi .people.com.cn/n/2013/1012/c85037-23179378-3.html [retrieved on July 18, 2021].

39. Mai, "Xi Jinping Asks."

40. Ronkin, Noa, "Coronavirus Crisis Exposes Fundamental Tension in Governing China, Says Stanford Sociologist and China Expert Xueguang Zhou," https:// fsi.stanford.edu/news/coronavirus-crisis-exposes-fundamental-tension-governing -china-says-stanford-sociologist-and [retrieved on August 26, 2021].

41. "The Chinese Communist Party's Military-Civil Fusion Policy," https://2017 -2021.state.gov/military-civil-fusion/index.html [retrieved on October 16, 2021].

42. Qiao, Kunyuan, "Performance and Interim Rank in Dynamic Political Tournament: Evidence from China," discussion paper, Pennsylvania State University, 2014.

43. Jia, Ruixue, "Pollution for Promotion," 21st Century China Center, 2017; Cai, Hongbin, Yuyu Chen, and Qing Gong, "Polluting Thy Neighbor: Unintended Consequences of China's Pollution Reduction Mandates," *Journal of Environmental Economics and Management* 76 (2016): 86–104.

44. Luo, Huiying, Xiaohui Liu, Aiqi Wu, and Xiaotong Zhong, "Is It Possible to Escape? Local Protectionism and Outward Foreign Direct Investment by Chinese Privately-Owned Enterprises," *Asia Pacific Journal of Management,* online ahead of print (2019), https://doi.org/10.1007/s10490-019-09697-7.

45. Chang, Maria Hsia, "The Thought of Deng Xiaoping," *Communist and Post-Communist Studies* 29, no. 4 (1996): 377–94.

46. "Xi Jinping Talks about Market Economy: The Attribute 'Socialism' Must Not Be Forgotten," http://cpc.people.com.cn/xuexi/n1/2019/0128/c385476-3059 2929.html [retrieved on August 7, 2021].

47. Su, Mi, "'Resurrected' in the Land of Nothingness: How Far Can the Chinese Leftist Website Go?," https://www.dwnews.com/%E4%B8%AD%E5%9B%BD /60066100/%E4%B9%8C%E6%9C%89%E4%B9%8B%E4%B9%A1%E8%B5 %B7%E6%AD%BB%E5%9B%9E%E7%94%9F%E4%B8%AD%E5%9B%B D%E5%B7%A6%E6%B4%BE%E7%BD%91%E7%AB%99%E8%B F%98%E8%83%BD%E8%B5%B0%E5%A4%9A%E8%BF%9C [retrieved on October 8, 2021].

48. Carter, James, "The Real Battle at Lake Changjin," https://supchina.com /2021/12/01/the-real-battle-at-lake-changjin/ [retrieved on January 1, 2022].

49. Myers, Steve Lee, and Amy Chang Chien, "For China's Holidays, a Big-Budget Blockbuster Relives an American Defeat," https://www.nytimes.com/2021/10/05/world/asia/battle-lake-changjin.html [retrieved on October 8, 2021].

50. Carter, "Real Battle at Lake Changjin."

51. Gruin, Julian, *Communists Constructing Capitalism: State, Market, and the Party in China's Financial Reform* (Manchester: Manchester University Press, 2019).

52. Lai, Karyn, *An Introduction to Chinese Philosophy* (Cambridge: Cambridge University Press, 2017).

53. "Mao Zedong's Historical Achievements (in Memory of the 120th Anniversary of Comrade Mao Zedong's Birth)," http://politics.people.com.cn/n/2013/1225/c1001-23937154.html [retrieved on July 25, 2021].

54. "Mao Zedong and 'Twenty-Four History,'" http://dangshi.people.com.cn/n1/2019/0807/c85037-31280331.html [retrieved on July 25, 2021].

55. Wang, Jin [王瑾], and Shifang Wen [文世芳], "1948~1989年《人民日报》对历史虚无主义的解析 / An Analysis of Historical Nihilism in 'People's Daily' from 1948 to 1989," *Contemporary Chinese History Studies* [in Chinese], no. 2 (2017): 6–17, 127.

56. "Xi Jinping: Speech."

57. Mai, Jun, "China Deletes 2 Million Online Posts for 'Historical Nihilism' as Communist Party Centenary Nears," https://www.scmp.com/news/china/politics/article/3132957/china-deletes-2-million-online-posts-historical-nihilism [retrieved on July 18, 2021].

58. "Xi Jinping: Explanation of the 'Resolution of the Central Committee of the Chinese Communist Party on Major Achievements and Historical Experience of the Party's Centennial Struggle,'" http://www.gov.cn/xinwen/2021-11/16/content_5651271.htm [retrieved on April 15, 2022]; "Xi Focus: 19th CPC Central Committee to Hold Sixth Plenary Session in November," http://www.news.cn/english/2021-08/31/c_1310160056.htm [retrieved on April 15, 2022]; Buckley, Chris, "China's History Is Revised, to the Glory of Xi Jinping," https://www.nytimes.com/2021/11/16/world/asia/china-history-xi-jinping.html [retrieved on November 20, 2021].

59. Platt, Kevin M. F., "Secret Speech: Wounding, Disavowal, and Social Belonging in the USSR," *Critical Inquiry* 42, no. 3 (2016): 647–76.

60. Gillespie, Michael Allen, *Nihilism before Nietzsche* (Chicago: University of Chicago Press, 1995).

61. Lai, *Introduction to Chinese Philosophy*.

62. Yuan, Li, "'Who Are Our Enemies?' China's Bitter Youths Embrace Mao," https://www.nytimes.com/2021/07/08/business/china-mao.html [retrieved on July 13, 2021].

63. There are many other qualities based on different interpretations such as cautiousness, sincerity, rectitude, propriety, honesty, and objectivity. *Encyclopedia Britannica,* s.v. "Doctrine of Mean" (New York: Rosen, 2008). However, the most commonly accepted meanings are moderation and modesty.

64. Pound, Ezra, *Confucius: The Unwobbling Pivot / The Great Digest / The Analects* (New York: New Directions, 1969). Also see Legg, James, "The Doctrine of the Mean," https://www.sacred-texts.com/cfu/conf3.htm [retrieved on July 25, 2021].

65. "Mao Zedong Once Commented on 'The Doctrine of the Mean': It Has an Element of Eclecticism/Moderatism," http://history.sina.com.cn/bk/ds/2013-12-25/105177980.shtml [retrieved on July 25, 2021]; "Comrade Mao Zedong's Comments on the Doctrine of Mean," http://m.szhgh.com/show.php?classid=81&id=122502 [retrieved on July 25, 2021].

66. "Mao Zedong Once Commented."

67. Zinchenko, Yury P., "Extremism from the Perspective of a System Approach," *Psychology in Russia* 7, no. 1 (2014): 23–33; "Russian National Character: Easy to Go to Extremes and Blindly Xenophobic?," http://culture.ifeng.com/abroad/200808/0812_4088_714775.shtml [retrieved on July 18, 2021].

68. Admittedly, the CCP-government did work to export communism to Southeast Asian and Latin American countries during Mao's period, but Deng ceased this practice and canceled economic and military support to communist guerillas in these countries. "Deng Xiaoping: China Will Not Export Revolution," http://history.sina.com.cn/bk/ds/2014-08-29/105498967.shtml [retrieved on July 18, 2021].

69. "Xi Jinping Said That Cooperation between China and the United States Will Benefit and Confrontation Will Harm Both Sides and Is Willing to Promote Bilateral Relations Based on Cooperation," https://www.reuters.com/article/xi-trump-summit-sinous-relation-0629-idCNKCS1TU06N [retrieved on July 18, 2021].

70. Dahlburg, John-Thor, "Gorbachev: Socialism Must Have a 'Human Face,'" https://apnews.com/4afoc8eb2eebd3c3ceeca9db4ba63b27 [retrieved on June 24, 2021]; Chernyaev, Anatoly Sergeevich, *My Six Years with Gorbachev,* edited by Robert English and Elizabeth Tucker (University Park: Pennsylvania State University Press, 2012); Sheehy, Gail, *The Man Who Changed the World: The Lives of Mikhail S. Gorbachev* (New York: HarperCollins, 1990).

71. Henderson, Jane, "Making a Drama Out of a Crisis: The Russian Constitutional Court and the Case of the Communist Party of the Soviet Union," *King's Law Journal* 19, no. 3 (2008): 489–506; Tumarkin, Nina, *Lenin Lives! The Lenin Cult in Soviet Russia* (Cambridge, MA: Harvard University Press, 1997).

72. "Hu Jintao Accuses Western Culture of Invading China's Space for Speech," https://www.rfi.fr/cn/%E4%B8%AD%E5%9B%BD/20120102-%E8%83%A1%E9%94%A6%E6%B6%9B%E8%B4%A3%E8%A5%BF%E6%96%B9%E6%96%87%E5%8C%96%E4%BE%B5%E7%95%A5%E4%B8%AD%E5%9B%BD%E8%A8%80%E8%AE%BA%E7%A9%BA%E9%97%B4%E5%8A%BF%E7%BC%A9 [retrieved on June 24, 2021].

73. Central Party School Press [中共中央党校出版社], 习近平的七年知青岁月 / *Xi Jinping's Seven Years as a Sent-Down Youth* (Beijing: Central Party School Press, 2017); Page, Jeremy, Bob Davis, and Tom Orlik, "China's New Boss—Xi Jinping Has Charisma, a Common Touch and a Beloved Pop-Star Wife. But Can He Reform a Communist Elite Accustomed to the Fruits of Corruption?," https://www.wsj.com/articles/SB10001424127887324439804578106860600724862 [retrieved on July 25, 2021]; Wang, Min, "An Analysis of the Excellent Quality of College Students Studying Young Xi Jinping," *Chinese Studies* 9, no. 3 (2020): 77–81; McGregor, Richard, "Xi Jinping's Quest to Dominate China," *Foreign Affairs* 98 (2019): 18.

74. Huang, Zheping, "Fighting Corruption, Maintaining Harmony, and Davos: A Resume for China's President Xi Jinping," https://qz.com/1103045/chinas-19th-communist-party-congress-a-resume-for-president-xi-jinping/ [retrieved on June 24, 2021].

75. Page, Jeremy, "How the U.S. Misread China's Xi: Hoping for a Globalist, It Got an Autocrat," https://www.wsj.com/articles/xi-jinping-globalist-autocrat-misread-11608735769 [retrieved on June 24, 2021].

76. "Analysis: How Influential Is Jiang on Earth," https://www.bbc.com/zhongwen/simp/mobile/indepth/2011/07/110707_ana_jiang_influence.shtml [retrieved on June 24, 2021].

77. Because his father fell out of power and he was then labeled as a son of gangsters by the CCP during the famous Cultural Revolution initiated by Mao, Xi suffered from discrimination and had to spend more than seven years in the poor rural area. After his father resumed a national leadership position, Xi realized the importance of becoming a politician and staying in power.

78. "Who Does Not Reform Will Step Down—Ta Kung Pao Celebrates Deng Xiaoping's Reform," http://news.takungpao.com/mainland/focus/2017-02/3422196.html [retrieved on June 24, 2021].

79. "Charting China's 'Great Purge' under Xi," https://www.bbc.com/news/world-asia-china-41670162 [retrieved on June 24, 2021].

80. Blinken, Antony J., "The Administration's Approach to the People's Republic of China," May 26, 2022, https://www.state.gov/the-administrations-approach-to-the-peoples-republic-of-china/ [retrieved on May 27, 2022].

81. Blanchette, *China's New Red Guards*.

82. There are two popular candidates based on various press accounts—Chen Min'er and Hu Chunhua. Both had good economic performance when they were top leaders of their respective provinces. Hu is more liberal than Chen, but we think Chen is more likely to become Xi's successor because he is Xi's longtime subordinate, whereas Hu is more closely connected to the previous president, Hu Jintao. However, recently there have rumors suggesting that Li Keqiang might succeed the criticized Xi.

83. "Who Will Stir Up China's Economic Leaders? Xi Jinping Places His Hopes on Them . . . ," https://m.creader.com/news/page/1091247 [retrieved on August 8, 2021].

84. "'Xi Jinping Talks about Core Values'—the Root and Soul of the Nation," http://cpc.people.com.cn/n/2014/0731/c64387-25373960.html [retrieved on August 13, 2021].

85. Jiang, Yihua, "The Chinese Communist Party and Chinese Excellent Traditional Culture," http://www.qstheory.cn/dukan/hqwg/2021-06/24/c_1127594715.htm [retrieved on August 13, 2021].

86. Graziosi, Graig, "Biden Says Chinese President Xi Jinping 'Doesn't Have a Democratic Bone' in His Body," https://www.independent.co.uk/news/world/americas/us-politics/biden-xi-jinping-china-preisdent-b1822601.html [retrieved on July 25, 2021].

87. Doshi, Rush, *The Long Game: China's Grand Strategy to Displace American Order* (Oxford: Oxford University Press, 2021).

88. Edel, Charles, and David Shullman, "In the Case of Conflict with China, Check Your Cold War Analogies," https://www.washingtonpost.com/outlook/2021

/11/15/case-conflict-with-china-check-your-cold-war-analogies/ [retrieved on November 20, 2021].

89. Kine, Phelim, "Xi Jinping's Global Vision," https://www.politico.com /newsletters/politico-china-watcher/2021/09/23/xi-jinpings-global-vision-494439 [retrieved on September 28, 2021].

90. "'A Coup for China': Analysts React to the World's Largest Trade Deal That Excludes the U.S.," https://www.cnbc.com/2020/11/16/rcep-15-asia-pacific-countries -including-china-sign-worlds-largest-trade-deal.html [retrieved on August 10, 2021].

91. Snidal, Duncan, "The Limits of Hegemonic Stability Theory," *International Organization* 39, no. 4 (1985): 579–614; Grunberg, Isabelle, "Exploring the 'Myth' of Hegemonic Stability," *International Organization* 44, no. 4 (1990): 431–77.

92. Kine, "Xi Jinping's Global Vision."

93. Economy, Elizabeth, "Xi Jinping's New World Order: Can China Remake the International System?," https://www.foreignaffairs.com/articles/china/2021-12 -09/xi-jinpings-new-world-order [retrieved on January 1, 2022].

94. Eisenman, Joshua, and Michael Sobolik, "U.S. Institutions Must Get Smarter about Chinese Communist Party Money," https://foreignpolicy.com/2021/08/31 /chinese-communist-party-money-us-institutions/ [retrieved on September 28, 2021].

95. Doshi, *Long Game;* Kine, "Xi Jinping's Global Vision."

96. We acknowledge that there has been rich scholarship about Mao and the CCP in general; our contribution is to discuss Mao and the CCP in the current, capitalist context in China. We argue that Mao has had an enduring effect on Chinese business and entrepreneurship.

97. Marquis, Christopher, and Kunyuan Qiao, "Waking from Mao's Dream: Communist Ideological Imprinting and the Internationalization of Entrepreneurial Ventures in China," *Administrative Science Quarterly* 65, no. 3 (2020): 795–830.

98. "AmCham Survey Findings Show US Businesses Bullish on China in 2021," https://www.china-briefing.com/news/amcham-survey-findings-show-us -businesses-bullish-on-china-in-2021/ [retrieved on February 1, 2022].

99. Mitter and Johnson, "What the West Gets Wrong."

100. Kristof, Nicholas, "Looking for a Jump-Start in China," https://www.nytimes .com/2013/01/06/opinion/sunday/kristof-looking-for-a-jump-start-in-china.html [retrieved on August 8, 2021].

101. Blanchette, *China's New Red Guards.*

METHODOLOGICAL APPENDIX

1. "Regional Distribution of Best Private Enterprises in China: Jiangsu and Zheji-ang Took the Lead and Chongqing Surpassed Tianjin," https://finance.sina.com.cn /china/2019-08-29/doc-iicezueu2028692.shtml [retrieved on July 1, 2021].

2. The survey continued after 2012, but there were further restrictions on use of the data, so we did not subscribe to later waves of it.

3. Hannigan, Timothy R., Richard F. J. Haans, Keyvan Vakili, Hovig Tchalian, Vern L. Glaser, Milo Shaoqing Wang, Sarah Kaplan, and P. Devereaux Jennings,

"Topic Modeling in Management Research: Rendering New Theory from Textual Data," *Academy of Management Annals* 13, no. 2 (2019): 586–632.

4. Morris, Rebecca, "Computerized Content Analysis in Management Research: A Demonstration of Advantages and Limitations," *Journal of Management* 20, no. 4 (1994): 903–31; Short, Jeremy C., and Timothy B. Palmer, "The Application of Diction to Content Analysis Research in Strategic Management," *Organizational Research Methods* 11, no. 4 (2007): 727–52.

5. Wang, Danqing, Fei Du, and Christopher Marquis, "Defending Mao's Dream: Politicians' Ideological Imprinting and Firms' Political Appointment in China," *Academy of Management Journal* 62, no. 4 (2019): 1111–36.

Acknowledgments

This book is built on decades of research and life in China, and it reflects the deep influence of many on our individual and collective thought. Both of us have published intensively on business and entrepreneurship in China, including numerous academic articles in leading management, sociology, and economics journals, as well as Harvard Business School case studies. These writings cover a broad range of topics, such as business-government relations, corporate governance, corporate social responsibility, finance, human resource management, innovation, internationalization, and sustainability of many types of Chinese enterprises—state-owned firms, privately owned firms, publicly traded firms, and entrepreneurial start-ups. We owe a debt of gratitude to all of the people who collaborated on, edited, and reviewed this work who have shaped our thinking.

Chris has long been interested in East Asian culture. In high school he did an independent research project on the role of Confucianism in contemporary China. He is grateful to his early teachers such as Dr. Diana Wood, who spurred his initial interest in China. He traveled to the region for the first time in 1996, when he was fortunate to have had an opportunity to live and work in Taiwan for a short period and take a six-week backpacking trip around mainland China. At the time, bikes and small cars were the common means of transportation. Chris still remembers standing on the Bund, the Shanghai waterfront, and talking to someone who told him that the poor region across the Huangpu River now known as Pudong would become the financial capital of China. He thought this person was crazy. Even Shanghai natives followed the dictum, "I would rather have a bed in Puxi [on the west bank of the Huangpu River] than a room in Pudong [on the east bank]." Today, three of the tallest buildings in the world are on that relatively undeveloped spot Chris viewed in 1996. In fact, one may drive more than twenty miles into Pudong while only seeing high-rises.

After joining Harvard Business School as a professor in 2005, Chris began to study business in China more formally, working with a large and diverse group of colleagues and students. During his frequent visits to China and times living in Beijing and Shanghai in 2011, 2012, and 2014–2015, he was continually amazed by the pace and intensity of the entrepreneurship and rapid development in China and, at the same time, by the persistence of Maoism. He is grateful to the business schools of Peking University, Fudan University, and Shanghai Jiaotong University for hosting those visits, with a special thanks to Dean Yuan Li, Runtian Jing, and Zucheng Zhou for their close partnership.

One memorable event was when he took a research trip to Changsha in Hunan Province in 2011. For five days he stayed in the corporate dormitory of Broad Air, a leading environmentally focused company with an impressive corporate campus where employees lived, ate, and worked under the guidance of founding chairman Zhang Yue. One day he visited the nearby town of Shaoshan, birthplace of Mao Zedong. The town was flooded with visitors, mostly rural Chinese who came to honor and even worship the chairman. Chris was the only Westerner in sight.

He is grateful for opportunities to visit with and study the leadership of many private Chinese companies in depth, such as Broad Air, Tsing Capital, SMIC, and Continental Hope Group, and state-owned enterprises such as State Grid, COSCO, Jiangsu Broadcasting, and Shenhua Energy. This access to executives, staff, and corporate facilities at many Chinese companies for over a decade has shaped his understanding of business and politics in China. To cite one example of how these many experiences challenged his Western biases, when he entered the office of COSCO shipping CEO Wei Jiafu in 2012, he was shocked to find a life-size statue of Mao next to the flag of the CCP. But over time, he came to a better understanding of how Mao imbues all aspects of life in China.

While the US media tend to discuss China as a communist country, focusing on the downside of the regime, when Chris led groups of Harvard and Cornell students to China to study, those who had never been were consistently shocked by the economic vibrancy they saw. He learned a lot by seeing China through these "newcomers'" eyes. Every year, one or more of them would take him aside and exclaim, "China is not really a communist country!" He encountered the same surprise and confusion when he talked to practitioners who were new to China. At the same time, while serving on admissions panels, he would see that candidates from Chinese universities had taken multiple levels of classes on Mao Zedong Thought / Maoism (毛泽东思想), which interestingly showed up on their translated transcripts as the more neutral "Chinese Philosophy." Chris came to recognize that Western portrayals of China did not capture the system on the ground, and further, that China's deep ties to Mao go a long way toward explaining the coexistence of communist rule and capitalist economy, or simply put, the unique mix of Mao and markets. Such a perspective has become even more salient in recent years, as President Xi Jinping frequently employs Mao's rhetoric in his speeches and tries to imitate him in many other ways.

Overall, Chris is grateful for his almost twelve years at both Harvard Business School and Harvard Kennedy School and to colleagues at those institutions such as Regina Abrami, Bill Kirby, Elizabeth Köll, Warren McFarland, Meg Rithmire, Tony Saich, and especially the late Ezra Vogel, who hosted a monthly dinner and discussion group for social scientists studying China. The highlight of Chris's seven-plus years at Cornell's S. C. Johnson College of Business with respect to his China studies was his work with students—for instance, those in the Doing Business in China class he taught, students on trips to China, and especially doctoral students who were interested in China, with Kunyuan at the top of that list. He also appreciated the engagement of Victor Nee from Cornell's Sociology Department on Chinese management, business, entrepreneurship, and related topics.

Chris's recent move to the University of Cambridge's Judge Business School as the Sinyi Professor of Chinese Management promises to offer a fruitful new path in his research on China, and he looks forward to engaging on the school's China work with the former dean Christophe Loch, current dean Mauro Guillén, and faculty such as Peter Williamson. Finally, over the past five-plus years the biggest influence on his thinking about China has been his wife, Claudine (Ying) Li, and he is grateful for her love, support, and insight into many topics related to Chinese politics, media, and international relations more generally.

Kunyuan was born in China. His grandfather imbued him with a strong interest in history, starting in his early childhood. He taught him to sing songs that extolled Mao, which entertained the whole family, and told him stories about Mao's adventures at bedtime. Meanwhile, Kunyuan and his family experienced major historical events, such as the collapse of communism in Eastern Europe and the Soviet Union in the early 1990s; Deng Xiaoping's 1992 Southern Tour, which expedited reform and opening up; and the drastic market reforms of Chinese enterprises and the resulting layoffs. The country seemed to have lost its communist footing and said farewell to

Mao: corruption was rampant, workers—the class base of communism—lost their jobs (breaking the metaphorical "iron rice bowl," which described the supposed permanence of those jobs), marketization provided critical incentives for people to develop a private economy, and income inequality widened significantly. In his early research, Kunyuan found that many government officials—cadres of the Chinese Communist Party—tried to attract and collaborate with businesspeople to develop their local economies. Capitalist principles still dominate many aspects of Chinese society. But on the other hand, one-party rule is still in place, and the political climate is becoming more conservative; Mao and Maoist principles are more and more frequently evoked.

Kunyuan has been puzzled by these paradoxes. Should we look at China through the lens of other (former) communist countries, such as the Soviet Union, Yugoslavia, and the rest of the former Eastern Bloc, or is China like capitalist countries such as the United States and those in Western Europe? Compared with communist countries, China is too capitalistic, and compared with capitalist countries, China appears avowedly communist. Given his obsession with history, he gradually came to the conclusion that Mao and Maoism provide the key.

Kunyuan is grateful for his training in both economics and sociology, and retains his long-standing interest in history. Cornell—with its founding principle imprinted by Ezra Cornell, "I would found an institution where any person can find instruction in any study"—particularly enables Kunyuan to combine the strengths of all three of these disciplines and develop into a researcher in the field of management and organizations and in social sciences in general. Working on this book has been useful for him to broaden theoretical perspectives, integrate multiple research projects, connect academic theories and ideas to real life, and prepare for teaching in business schools (for example, MBA programs and executive education) as he begins his career as a faculty member at Georgetown University's McDonough School of Business.

A number of friends and colleagues have generously read drafts of the book and provided insightful feedback, including Jason Kelly, Cheng Li, George Shen, Dean Xu, Chenjian Zhang, and Eric Yaofei Zhao. We are grateful to them as well as others who have read or commented on parts of the book, such as Wendy Chen, Bonnie Cao, and Fuyuan Luo. We also want to thank Anla Cheng, Jeremy Goldkorn, Kaiser Kuo, and the team at the China-focused media platform SupChina for providing generous help and guidance as we developed some of the early essays related to this book and helping us think about how to position our ideas for a general audience.

We are grateful to Fei Du, Hao Liang, and Danqing Wang for their help in validating the list of keywords and for our long-term collaboration with them, as well as many others, including Zhi Huang, Susan Jackson, Yuan Li, Xiaowei Rose Luo, Cuili Qian, Dongning Yang, Zoe Yang, Juelin Yin, Hongyu Zhang, Jianjun Zhang, and Yanhua (Zhou) Bird. Peng Lu from the Chinese Academy of Social Sciences also provided valuable access to and assistance with the Chinese Private Enterprise Survey data. Furthermore, we also appreciate guidance from Meg Rithmire and Tony Saich on some important resources for our book.

Faculty and students at both Cornell and the University of Electronic Science and Technology of China have provided enormous help in collecting data and conducting interviews of entrepreneurs. Chris in particular is grateful for the support of UESTC and, since 2019, for being able to closely connect to the business sector in Chengdu, China. We especially would like to thank Dean Yongkai Ma for his support and friendship, Henry Gui for his leadership, Ying Wang for her administrative help, and Xueyun Luo, Qian Wang, Yichen Wang, Sai Xu, and Kai Xie for their research help. We are also indebted to the entrepreneurs we interviewed; their insights were invaluable contributions to our book.

We would also like to thank Jim Levine and his literary agency for their support and guidance, as well as the editorial team at Yale University Press, led by Seth Ditchik, for making this book a reality. In addition, we greatly appreciate Arthur Goldwag's insightful commentary and editorial guidance on an early draft of the book.

Last but not the least, we are grateful for financial support from Cornell's Innovation, Entrepreneurship, and Technology Theme and Center for Social Sciences Research. Conferences at the Academy of Management; seminars held at Harvard University, the University of Cambridge, London Business School, and the University of Texas at Dallas; and events held at China EconTalk and SupChina provided us with opportunities to take feedback from both researchers and general audience members and improve the work.

Index

Figures and tables are indicated by *f* or *t* following the page number. Information found in endnotes is indicated by an "n" and note number following the page number.

Meng Dongbo, 10
Meng Jun, 10
Mengniu, 98, 218, 335n32
Microsoft, 96, 207, 208
military: CCP leadership of, 37–38, 47, 125, 132–134, 245–246 (*see also* Central Military Commission); Kuomintang, 112, 309n7; Mao's Military Thought, 11, 12, 43–44, 123–135, 197, 240–241, 243, 258, 279n41; option to join, 288n41; political system and, 197, 245–246; Third Front Construction for protection of, 45–46, 137, 177, 180
Military Thought, 123–135; "concentrating forces to annihilate the enemy" as, 129; consumer orientation reflecting, 133–134; "engage in protracted war" as, 129–131, 243; motivation of employees by example reflecting, 133; "never fight an unprepared war" as, 126–127, 241; organizational principles based on, 132–134; overview of, 134–135; principles of, 44, 125; private enterprise application of, 11, 12, 123–135, 240–241, 243, 279n41; "a single spark can start a prairie fire" as, 127–128, 243; strategic doctrines of, 125, 126–131, 197; "surround cities from the countryside" as, 12, 123, 128–129, 240–241, 258; team-building reflecting, 132; Theory of the People's Military in, 132–134, 135; writings on, 43–44, 124–125, 130–131
Ming dynasty, 79
Minsheng Group, 16
Mobike, 128, 230
moderatism, 250–251, 344n63
Modern Agricultural Industrial Park of Shuicheng County, 185
Mongolia, 80–81
Montesquieu, 34
motivation of employees by example, 133
Mou Qizhong, 165, 167t, 308n49
Mozi, 99
Mu family, 20
Musk, Elon, 207–208
My Father and Mother (Ren Zhengfei), 9
myths, 21–26

Nan Cunhui, 300n38
Nasser, Gamal Abdel and Nasserism, 64–65
National Artificial Intelligence Innovation Application Pilot Zone, 186

nationalism, 75–96; "China first" spirit of, 94; consumer or market, 93; country-over-capital principle fostering, 237–238; decline of, 89–90; defined, 42–43; economy and, 90–91, 94–95; globalization and, 77, 89–90; indoctrination on, 81–88; internationalization resistance and, 75, 77, 85–86, 88, 88f, 94–95, 301n41; isolationism and, 89, 95–96; as Maoist ideological principle, 42–43, 78–81; media on, 78, 80, 82–85, 83f, 91–92, 95, 247–248; overview of, 95–96; political system shaping, 79–80; private enterprises and, 75–78, 85–90, 87f–88f, 92–96, 237–238, 301n41; revival of, 90–95, 90f; Xi's promotion of, 77, 91, 93–94
National People's Congress, 15, 89, 204, 331n43
NBA, 237
Nehru, Jawaharlal, 78
neo-Maoist movement, 72, 206, 254, 260
New Development Bank, 95, 258
New Hope Group, 98, 103, 154, 240
Newsweek, 140
New Youth (La Jeunesse), 80
Nian Guangjiu, 214t
Nietzsche, Friedrich, 155
Nike, 93, 96, 237
1921, 63
Ningxia Daily, 102
NIO, 92, 185, 208
Niu Gensheng, 98, 218
Nokia, 122
nongovernmental organizations, 117
norms-over-rules principle, 241–243
Nortel Networks, 12
Northern and Southern dynasties, 193
"Notice to the Central Committee of the CCP" ("516 Notice"), 159

oaths, to CCP, 54
Obama, Barack and administration, 1
October Revolution (1917), 24, 36, 44, 143, 288n38
oFo, 108–109, 128, 230
Old Ideas, 62, 321n15
On Contradiction (Mao Zedong), 38–39
"On the Correct Handling of Contradictions among the People" (Mao Zedong), 102, 115
one-party rule, 2, 64, 67, 257